Japanese F
Finance and Markets

Japanese Firms, Finance and Markets

edited by
Paul Sheard

Addison Wesley Longman
in association with
The Australia–Japanese Research Centre
The Australian National University

Addison Wesley Longman Australia Pty Limited
95 Coventry Street
Melbourne 3205 Australia

Offices in Sydney, Brisbane, Perth, and associated companies throughout the world.

Copyright © 1996 Addison Wesley Longman Australia Pty Limited
First published 1996

All rights reserved. Except under the conditions described in the Copyright Act 1968 of Australia and subsequent amendments, no part of this publication may be reproduced, stored in a retrieval system or transmitted in any form or by any means, electronic, mechanical, photocopying, recording or otherwise, without the prior permission of the copyright owner.

Copy edited by Beth Thomson
Index by Angela Grant
Typeset by Minni Reis
Printed in Australia by The Australian Print Group

National Library of Australia
Cataloguing-in-Publication data

   Japanese firms, finance and markets.

   Includes index.
   ISBN 0 582 81108 2.

   I. Corporations - Japan. 2. Japan - Economic policy.
   I. Sheard, P.

338.70952

The publisher's policy is to use **paper manufactured from sustainable forests**

Contents

Tables vii
Figures ix
Acknowledgements xi
Contributors xii

1 Introduction 1
  Paul Sheard

Part I *Keiretsu* and Competition: Vertical Organisation versus Markets

2 *Keiretsu* and market access: an economics of organisation approach 21
  Paul Sheard
3 Price formation and the structure of the distribution system 54
  Kenn Ariga and Yasushi Ohkusa

Part II Corporate Governance Structures

4 Corporate governance and employment incentives: is the Japanese system really different? 91
  Gerald T. Garvey and Peter L. Swan
5 Reciprocal delegated monitoring in the main bank system 124
  Paul Sheard
6 Moral hazard and main bank monitoring 143
  Luke Gower

7   Banks, blockholders and corporate governance: the role of external appointees to the board   166
Paul Sheard

Part III   The Financial System: Present and Future

8   The financial system and corporate competitiveness   191
Masasuke Ide

9   The impact of financial deregulation on corporate financing   222
Takeo Hoshi

10   Financial liberalisation and the safety net   249
Akiyoshi Horiuchi

11   Deregulation and the structure of the money market   274
Gordon de Brouwer

Appendixes

Appendix 3.1	Data selection and classification	79
Appendix 3.2	Model and estimation procedure	81
Appendix 3.3	Estimation method	84
Appendix 6.1	Derivation of the asset equations	160
Appendix 7.1	Variables and data sources	182

Index   301

Tables

Table 3.1	Cost characteristics of four types of distribution channel	63
Table 3.2	Summary statistics of estimation	67
Table 3.3	Wholesale price index versus consumer price index	67
Table 3.4	Type of distribution channel and price responsiveness	73
Table 3.5	Cross-section regressions: price responsiveness	74
Table 3.6	Cross-section regressions: asymmetry in price adjustments	75
Table 3.7	Response of prices, marginal costs and mark-ups to yen appreciation, 1985–88 and 1990–93	78
Table 7.1	Indexes of distribution of board positions by background status	170
Table 7.2	Tobit estimation of proportion of directors entering from other firms for listed Japanese firms, 1991	174
Table 7.3	Tobit estimation of proportion of directors entering from banks for listed Japanese firms, 1991	177
Table 7.4	Logit estimation of likelihood of president having come from outside firm for listed Japanese firms, 1991	178
Table 7.5	Multinomial logit estimation of background of president for listed Japanese firms, 1991	180
Table 8.1	Characteristics of Japan's traditional financial system	192
Table 8.2	Major financial institutions in Japan and the United States	193
Table 8.3	Stock ownership structure in Japan and the United States	195
Table 8.4	Characteristics of major shareholders in Japan and the United States	198
Table 8.5	International comparison of price/earnings ratios, 1980–95	205
Table 8.6	Financial performance of large Japanese and US industrial companies	208

Tables

Table 8.7	Minimum required profitability of large Japanese and US industrial companies in the 1980s	208
Table 8.8	Profitability of cross-country foreign direct investment in the United States and Japan, 1980–88	210
Table 8.9	Trends in the profitability of large Japanese and US companies, 1971–95	212
Table 9.1	Companies eligible to issue unsecured bonds, 1979–88	226
Table 9.2	Bond issue criteria for convertible bonds (domestic secured and foreign unsecured), October 1976 – present	229
Table 9.3	Sources of funds for large corporations, 1966–90	231
Table 10.1	Average annual change in number of branch offices and amount of deposits	254
Table 10.2	Prudential regulations as of January 1962	255
Table 10.3	Japanese government debt, 1965–90	258
Table 10.4	Structure of fundraising by big and small/medium sized business, 1970–89	259
Table 10.5	Bank loans to small and medium sized firms, 1968–89	260
Table 10.6	Major city bank loans to small and medium sized firms, 1975–89	261
Table 10.7	Bank credit to manufacturing, real estate industry and non-bank finance companies, 1951–91	262
Table 10.8	Loans sold to Cooperative Credit Purchasing Corporation, FY 1992–93	264
Table 10.9	Chronology of financial assistance provided by Deposit Insurance Corporation, 1992–96	267
Table 11.1	Structure of the Japanese money market, 1970–94	276
Table 11.2	Summary of money market reform, 1985–90	278
Table 11.3	Correlation coefficients for interbank and open market rates	293
Table 11.4	Augmented Dickey–Fuller test statistics	293
Table 11.5	Summary of multivariate Granger causality: final prediction error criterion	295
Table 11.6	Summary of multivariate Granger causality: Hannon–Quinn information criterion	295

Figures

Figure 2.1	Forms of transactional ties between vertically linked markets	29
Figure 2.2	Intermediate markets as a reflection of firm organisation	31
Figure 3.1	Prototypes of vertical transactions	64
Figure 3.2	Impulse response: aggregate wholesale price index, measured as deviation from base run	68
Figure 3.3	Impulse response: aggregate consumer price index, measured as deviation from base run	68
Figure 3.4	Average elasticity of price responses: type I sector	70
Figure 3.5	Average elasticity of price responses: type II sector	70
Figure 3.6	Average elasticity of price responses: type III sector	71
Figure 3.7	Average elasticity of price responses: type IV sector	71
Figure 3.8	Average elasticity of price responses: miscellaneous	72
Figure 6.1	Estimates of compensating balances as a proportion of total loans, May 1973 – May 1988	147
Figure 6.2	Estimates of compensating balances, May 1973 – May 1988	148
Figure 6.3	Average contracted loan rates of city banks, 1973–88	148
Figure 8.1	Distribution of stock market returns for different holding periods, January 1974 – December 1989	203
Figure 9.1	Proportion of bond issues in foreign markets, 1975–93	227
Figure 9.2	Firms eligible to issue convertible bonds, 1977–89	230
Figure 9.3	Bond issues by Japanese companies, 1975–93	232
Figure 9.4	Proportion of bond issues by type of bond, 1975–93	233
Figure 9.5	Straight bond issues by NTT, electricity and other companies, 1975–93	234

Figure 9.6	Bank debt ratio, 1966–93	235
Figure 9.7	Bank debt ratio for firms eligible to issue convertible bonds, 1975–93	235
Figure 9.8	Coefficient of variation of bank debt ratio, 1975–93	236
Figure 9.9	Distribution of corporate bond ownership, 1954–94	239
Figure 9.10	Convertible bond subscriptions by banks and households, 1969–85	239
Figure 9.11	Proportion of bank loans to manufacturing firms, 1974–93	242
Figure 9.12	Proportion of bank loans to small and medium sized firms, 1978–93	242
Figure 9.13	Proportion of bank loans to real estate industry, 1977–93	243
Figure 9.14	Proportion of bank loans to non-banks, 1974–93	243
Figure 10.1	Average profit rates in banking industry, 1955–93	253
Figure 10.2	Ratio of equity capital to total deposits, FY 1960–85	256
Figure 11.1	Instruments and objectives of monetary policy in Japan	287
Figure 11.2	Principal money market operations of Bank of Japan	289
Figure 11.3	Multivariate Granger causality	294

Acknowledgements

This book arises from an ongoing program of research on Japan's corporate organisation and financial system conducted with the support of the Australia–Japan Research Centre at the Australian National University. Several of the chapters were presented at a conference on Japanese Corporate Organisation and Finance held at the Australian National University (ANU) in February 1993. Several others were contributed by researchers affiliated with, or visiting, the Australia–Japan Research Centre at the ANU. I commenced editing the volume while Lecturer in the Department of Economics at the Australian National University and International Cooperation (Osaka Gas) Associate Professor in the Faculty of Economics at Osaka University. Support from the International Cooperation (Osaka Gas) research fund at Osaka University is gratefully acknowledged. My current employer, Baring Asset Management (Japan) Limited, provided valuable support in the latter stages.

Academic Press kindly provided permission to reproduce 'Reciprocal Delegated Monitoring in the Japanese Main Bank System' from the *Journal of the Japanese and International Economies* as Chapter 5 in this volume, as did Elsevier Science B.V. to incorporate much of 'The Economics of Corporate Governance: Beyond the Marshallian Firm' from the *Journal of Corporate Finance* into Chapter 4.

Many individuals provided valuable inputs. I am grateful to the authors for providing contributions and for their cooperation. I would like to thank the participants in the conference, particularly Gordon de Brouwer, Kevin Davis, Steve Dowrick, Mitsuaki Okabe, Ben Smith and Peter Swan, who kindly acted as discussants, and Luke Gower, who drew up a record of discussion. Jenny Corbett provided excellent editorial suggestions and comments on individual chapters. Michael Banton, Kimisato Nagamine, Yutaka Uda and other colleagues at Barings were very supportive and helped to broaden my perspective on the subject matter. Staff at the Australia–Japan Research Centre provided key backup: Beth Thomson copy edited the papers, Minni Reis formatted them and Denise Ryan coordinated the process. Their professionalism and efforts greatly improved the final product. Special thanks go to Peter Drysdale, Executive Director of the Australia–Japan Research Centre, for encouragement and assistance in organising the project and seeing it through to completion.

Paul Sheard
February 1996

Contributors

Kenn Ariga
Institute of Economic Research, Kyoto University, Kyoto, Japan

Gordon de Brouwer
Reserve Bank of Australia, Sydney, Australia

Gerald T. Garvey
Department of Finance, University of Sydney, Sydney, Australia

Luke Gower
Australia–Japan Research Centre, Australian National University, Canberra, Australia

Akiyoshi Horiuchi
Faculty of Economics, University of Tokyo, Tokyo, Japan

Takeo Hoshi
Graduate School of International Relations and Pacific Studies, University of California, San Diego, La Jolla, United States

Masasuke Ide
Nomura School of Advanced Management, Tokyo, Japan

Yasushi Ohkusa
Department of Economics, Osaka City University, Osaka, Japan

Paul Sheard
Strategist, Baring Asset Management (Japan) Limited, Tokyo, Japan

Peter L. Swan
Department of Finance, University of Sydney, Sydney, Australia

1 Introduction

Paul Sheard

This book adds to the growing literature on the Japanese system of corporate organisation and finance. It seeks to inform the ongoing debate over the nature of firms and markets in Japan; the implications that these corporate systems have for Japan's economic performance and for its interactions with the rest of the world; and how the system itself is changing in response to internal and external factors.

Japan's distinctive system of industrial organisation and corporate governance, popularly known as the *keiretsu* system, has been the focus of much academic and policy attention. *Keiretsu* is a loose term, used to refer to various forms of interfirm relations or sets of closely affiliated firms. Commonly the term describes the tightly knit supply relations that exist between large parent firms and their affiliated input suppliers. More generally, it refers to the system whereby cross-shareholdings exist between firms and their main business partners — not just input suppliers and customers but, importantly, 'main banks' and other key financiers.

Competing views exist on the nature and implications of *keiretsu*. A view dominant in the trade debate is that *keiretsu* relations in intermediate supply and distribution networks impede foreign access to the Japanese market (Lawrence 1993). Scholars of Japanese industrial organisation, on the other hand, have pointed to the efficiencies and competitive advantages afforded by quasi-integrated supply networks (Nishiguchi 1994; Sako 1992; Smitka 1991).

Another strand of literature focuses on the financial organisation of Japanese firms, notably the main bank system and the cross-holdings system, and identifies these as the cornerstones of the Japanese system of corporate governance (Aoki and Patrick 1994; Sheard 1994). A key feature of corporate ownership in Japan is the coupling of ownership and business ties. A typical large firm in Japan has extensive interlocking shareholding relations with its business partners: its banks and other financiers, its input suppliers, its customer firms and its trading companies. Large banks, in their role as main banks, play a pivotal role in this system. They not only provide substantial amounts of capital in the form of debt and equity, but fulfil a key role in monitoring, and at times actively intervening in, the affairs of corporate management.

Here again there are divergent views. Many writers evaluate the main bank system positively, arguing that it is an example of a bank oriented rather than stock market based system of corporate monitoring and control (Aoki, Patrick and Sheard 1994). Cross-shareholdings and concentration of corporate governance functions in the hands of delegated monitors (main banks and large parent companies) are complementary to the operation of internalised labour markets and help to lower capital market monitoring costs without inviting undue managerial slack. Another widely held view is that the cross-holdings system confers too much power on incumbent management and is deficient from the viewpoint of transparency, accountability and the provision of high-powered incentives.

Sorting out these arguments and controversies is complicated by the fact that corporate finance patterns and business practices have changed markedly in the past decade as financial markets have been deregulated and the business environment facing major corporations has changed. How important have these changes been and how should they be interpreted? Do they signify the breakdown of the *keiretsu* system, or merely a realignment in the Japanese system of capitalism in response to changes in key parameters? What aspects of financial system design and regulation support the bank centred system of corporate governance, and how are these systems evolving? The contributions to this volume address these and related issues.

Part I *Keiretsu* and competition: vertical organisation versus markets

The two chapters in Part I address some key issues in the *keiretsu* and market access debate. In Chapter 2, '*Keiretsu* and market access: an economics of organisation approach', **Paul Sheard** takes a critical look at the arguments surrounding *keiretsu* and foreign access to the Japanese market. The notion that *keiretsu* forms of business organisation result in the market being closed has become an almost paradigmatic way of thinking about trade issues for policy makers concerned with Japan and in much related academic writing on Japan. Sheard argues that much of this policy debate is misguided and rests on factual and conceptual confusions. He argues strongly for an economics of organisation approach to be applied to the *keiretsu*/market access issue.

The key insight of the economics of organisation approach is that the kinds of (intermediate) markets that exist in an economy, and the forms that they assume, depend critically on how firms have chosen to organise their input and output relations with other firms. Markets do not exist independently of the way in which firms are organised. Trade policy is concerned with securing fair access for (domestic) *firms* to (foreign) *markets*. The organisational forms known as *keiretsu* reflect decisions made by firms about the optimal design of vertical supply chains. They are an aspect of firm and market organisation, and not a barrier to markets of the kind that comes within the legitimate purview of trade policy. Sheard argues that it is wrong to treat upstream–downstream supply ties within a country as analogous to (government induced) non-tariff trade barriers. A better analogy would be with loosely structured vertical integration. The market access problem in the case of *keiretsu* raises issues of business strategy more than of trade policy.

Sheard points to the need to distinguish intermediate from final product markets carefully in the *keiretsu* debate. The set of final product markets is given by technology and consumer preferences, and the presumption is that, barring special cases, these markets should be open. Intermediate product markets are quite different: whether or not a market for an intermediate good exists depends on where firms have located their boundaries. Intermediate product markets may appear 'closed' because they have been internalised or, in the case of *keiretsu* ties, turned into markets in long-term or regularly renegotiated contracts.

To illustrate the point, Sheard contrasts two systems. He provides the example of a three-stage vertical production chain, culminating in the final product. In one system, the upstream firm is integrated over parts and subassemblies; in the other, the upstream firm produces only parts, while the downstream firm produces both subassemblies and the final product in-house. Although the final product market is the same, in one system subassemblies constitute the intermediate product while in the other parts do so. It is possible to say that the intermediate product market (for parts in the former case, for subassemblies in the latter) is 'closed', but conceptually this is quite different from the case in which a market is closed because the government (or some other third party) has introduced an artificial barrier. *Keiretsu* ties are not barriers in that sense, but rather a manifestation of how upstream and downstream firms have voluntarily chosen to structure their transactions.

Sheard argues that antitrust concerns about *keiretsu* are also largely misguided. A problem in the debate is that horizontal and vertical issues in industrial organisation have not been distinguished adequately. Despite frequently being labelled as cartels, *keiretsu* involve ties between firms located at adjacent stages in vertically related markets, not firms operating in the same horizontal market — this notwithstanding the confusing terminology in the literature on 'horizontal groupings'. In general, these firms are not in a position to form cartels or exercise monopoly power (unless one of the firms already has monopoly power, in which case the problem lies there).

In Chapter 3, 'Price formation and the structure of the distribution system', **Kenn Ariga** and **Yasushi Ohkusa** carry out a comprehensive investigation of the Japanese distribution system, with a particular focus on performance as measured by price responsiveness to exogenous shocks. Japan's distribution system is widely regarded as being inefficient, distorted by regulation and, in the context of the *keiretsu* debate, as constituting a prime non-tariff barrier to foreign market access. Ariga and Ohkusa point out that the distribution system is highly complex and diverse, and performs multifarious functions. While it is tempting to view distribution in terms of a monolithic 'system', the Japanese distribution system is nothing more than the sum of all the distribution channels that individual firms in the economy have set up. These are highly diverse and reflect the (constrained) optimal decisions of the parties to the transactions. The authors point out that the nature of distribution channels varies markedly depending on the characteristics of the product and the market. They propose a four-fold typology of distribution systems, according to the nature of agency costs, how information is distributed and what kind of agent plays the key organising role: a trading company, wholesaler, manufacturer or chain store retailer.

In order to get closer to the issue of distribution system performance, Ariga and Ohkusa conduct an econometric analysis of price responsiveness, based on the idea that firms pursue an optimal pricing policy which takes account of both the direct costs of price changes and the opportunity cost of being away from target prices. They construct a data set of upstream and downstream price pairs for 347 commodities and estimate price responsiveness to the deviations of actual prices from their (estimated) target levels.

The authors report a number of interesting findings. One is that prices are far more responsive upward than downward — seven times more so, in fact — due more to the size than the probability of a price change. A second finding is that the asymmetry just noted is far more pronounced at the retail than the wholesale price level. Prices were more flexible downward at the wholesale level, but more flexible upward at the retail level. A third finding is that, when the yen appreciates, retail rather than wholesale prices tend to exhibit sluggishness.

Ariga and Ohkusa also examine price responsiveness in the four types of distribution channel. They conclude that differences in the structure of distribution channels influence performance in terms of price adjustments, particularly at the retail level. One notable result is that *keiretsu* distribution channels, in which resale price maintenance is commonly practised, stand out as having the least responsive retail prices. The authors conclude that geographical segmentation of local retail markets, aided by regulations, *keiretsu* marketing policies and sociocultural factors, has allowed more small-scale retailers to survive than would otherwise be the case. This, they say, has exerted an important influence on price performance in distribution channels.

Part II   Corporate governance structures

The four chapters comprising Part II examine the Japanese system of corporate governance, focusing on the logic of the system and the role of firms.

One of the key ideas to emerge from the recent literature is that the various aspects of Japanese firms, which have been analysed in isolation, can be viewed as being mutually complementary attributes of a more coherent system (Aoki 1994). This insight provides a general organising theme for thinking, not only about the Japanese firm, but also about the broader socioeconomic system of which corporate organisation is but one key element. The area that has received most attention is the connection between a firm's financial organisation and its employment system (Aoki 1989). This theme is explored by **Gerald Garvey** and **Peter Swan** in a general context in Chapter 4, 'Corporate governance and employment incentives: Is the Japanese system really different?'

'Corporate governance' refers to the process by which the capital market monitors the actions of corporate management and holds management accountable for its decisions. Garvey and Swan survey the vast literature in economics on this topic — both theoretical and empirical — and relate it to the Japanese case. The literature on the Japanese system of corporate governance, implicitly or explicitly, often portrays it as being a peculiar, qualitatively different case. The valuable contribution of Garvey and Swan's essay is to place this analysis in the context of a general theory of, and body of empirical work on, corporate governance. In their analysis, rather than being unique, the Japanese system exemplifies in a nice way some general principles of corporate governance.

Garvey and Swan's basic contention is that large firms are managerial, in the sense that decisions are not — and should not be — made solely in the interest of shareholders and that some measure of managerial entrenchment is likely to be efficient. These attributes have often been associated with the Japanese firm, marking ways in which it departs from Western norms, but to the authors they are generic features of corporate governance. In the real world of incomplete contracts and positive transaction (governance) costs, shareholders are no longer pure residual claimants, but must share that status with other contractual parties to the firm. This is a powerful insight: it means that practices that appear on a narrow reckoning to be inefficient or inimical to shareholder interests may not be so when the interests of all relevant parties (suppliers, employees, managers and anyone else with an incomplete contractual claim on the firm's quasi-rents) and dynamic incentive effects are taken into account. This is not to say that, when it comes to assessing issues of corporate governance, 'anything goes'. It does recommend, however, careful analysis of competing hypotheses before seemingly deviant institutional arrangements or behaviour are taken at face value as evidence of managerial rent-seeking and appropriation of shareholder wealth.

These ideas can be applied fruitfully to the link between corporate governance and the employment system operating in Japanese firms. Cross-holdings may seem to give Japanese managers considerable leeway to pursue their own goals, and pure arm's-length shareholders, in a minority as a result of extensive cross-holdings, may appear to be disenfranchised and disadvantaged. But this might be a superficial reading of the situation. Suppose, as considerable evidence seems to suggest, that the autonomy that top management enjoys enables them to credibly commit to providing contracts to their direct employees and, indirectly, to the employees of their suppliers, eliciting in return considerable efforts, firm-specific investments and loyalty to the firm from those employees. If such contracts are efficiency enhancing but infeasible for arm's-length shareholders to agree upon and implement, paradoxically these shareholders may benefit from having the corporate governance playing field seemingly tilted against them in this way.

In Chapter 5, 'Reciprocal delegated monitoring in the main bank system', **Paul Sheard** explores some theoretical underpinnings of the Japanese main bank system. As is well known, banks play an important role in corporate finance and governance in Japan. For most listed firms, one bank, regarded as the 'main bank', is seen as having the most important and closest relationship with the firm. As a key financier, shareholder and business partner, the main bank is thought to play a crucial role in monitoring the activities of the firm, certifying its creditworthiness to the broader capital market and implementing remedial action in the event of managerial failures. (Where there is a large parent firm, the main bank's role becomes secondary.)

The main bank has by no means a dominant position in the firm's finances or management, however — except when the firm is in severe financial distress. Indeed, Sheard notes three features of main bank ties which on the surface seem rather puzzling. First, although the main bank looms large in terms of corporate governance activities, the firm usually deals with many banks, and the main bank, while ranking above other banks, does not have an inordinately large loan or equity share. (Shareholdings are capped at 5 per cent by law.) Second, while the major banks tend to lend to roughly the same set of firms, each does so as main bank to some firms and as non-main bank to others. Third, the main bank is often called upon to take a disproportionately large share of any assistance burden or bank losses that are suffered when the firm fails.

Sheard develops a simple model to help explain these stylised facts. Two ideas are key. One is that monitoring and corporate governance activities (overhauling management, for example, or firm restructuring) are indivisible activities with a strong local public good aspect to them — actions by one creditor or shareholder to improve management are apt to benefit all others. Sheard characterises the main bank system as allowing reciprocal delegation of monitoring among a set of banks. He argues that this provides an arrangement for ensuring that monitoring takes places while avoiding costly duplication. The second key idea is that the convention of imposing a heavy burden on the main bank when there are *ex post* failures can be viewed as part of an incentive arrangement to guard against shirking by the main bank, given that its monitoring efforts are unobservable to the other (delegating) banks.

Although Sheard's model is a highly stylised one, it captures some essential features of real world institutional arrangements and may offer some insights into contentious policy issues in Japanese finance. One such insight is that, in a bank based system such as has existed in Japan, efficient monitoring may involve concentration of information and discretion in the hands of a small number of entities (main banks). Public disclosure may also be rather poor compared with a system that relies on a diverse, decentralised set of monitors, with free entry and exit. These attributes may not constitute a problem if the system is small or in an early stage of development, or if, being mature, it is able to preserve its own set of internal checks and balances. It may lead to acute problems, however, if there is systemic failure (the bubble period in Japan?) or if demand grows for open access, transparency and accountability — either from within the system, as the weight of market transactions increases (financial deregulation), or from without, as the system interacts with the financial systems of other major economies (internationalisation).

A second implication, implicit in the model, concerns the role of regulation. With the deepening of interest in institutions in recent years, some economists have started to develop a more sophisticated (albeit controversial) view of regulation. Rather than viewing it in simple terms as being either distortionary or as a tool for correcting market failures, economists now recognise the important role of government as an institution builder and in influencing the rules of the game through which private sector agents interact (Aoki 1994, pp. 30–1). Firms and markets do not exist in an institutional or historical vacuum, and the private and public sectors are often jointly engaged in a kind of 'team production' of institutions, conventions and rules.

The main bank system is a case in point. Careful inspection suggests that it is as much a regulatory system as a private banking one; indeed the line between the two is blurred. Not only does regulation shape the rules of the main bank system game, it also helps to enforce them. Sheard's model suggests that harsh *ex post* penalties serve to sharpen *ex ante* main bank incentives, but faced with these *ex post* realities banks also have powerful incentives to escape from their implicit obligations. Reciprocal delegated monitoring serves as one mutual enforcement device, but it has limits. When these are exceeded, and bank disputes ensue, the supervisory authorities frequently step in to mediate a solution, often to the apparent detriment of the main banks. The recent housing finance company (*jūsen*) saga in Japan, involving disputes over the split-up of huge bad debt losses among 'founder' banks, other banks and agricultural financing institutions, offers a poignant, if somewhat larger than life, case study example.

In Chapter 6, 'Moral hazard and main bank monitoring', **Luke Gower** pursues further the issue of incentives to monitor and raises doubts about the viability of the main bank system in a substantially deregulated financial system. Gower contrasts the performance of the main bank system in the bubble period of the late 1980s, as reflected in the accumulation of a ¥40 trillion mountain of real estate related bad debts in the first half of the 1990s (Ministry of Finance figures), with the widespread academic assessment of the main bank system as an efficient system of corporate governance. If main banks are such good monitors, how is their poor score card in the bubble period to be explained?

One school of thought is that the asset and real estate bubble was, first and foremost, a macroeconomic phenomenon induced by overly loose monetary policy and misplaced expectations: asset values became detached from underlying fundamentals because of unrealistic expectations; these became self-fulfilling, and therefore seemingly justified, in the short run; and rising liquidity flows — which had fewer productive investment opportunities to chase — fuelled the fire. From this viewpoint, the question of how well main banks monitored may be of second-order significance: conditional on macroeconomic assumptions, at the micro level their monitoring may have been quite normal. The problem was that, like everyone else, the banks were wrong about key economic parameters.

This interpretation may be too kind to the banks, however. Banks are important conduits in the process of credit creation and transmission linking the monetary and real economies. They were key players, not innocent bystanders, in the bubble economy, and part of their job was to form correct expectations about the future path of the economy and key variables. In any case, the argument above rests on a point of logic; on a factual level, there is abundant evidence, at least of an anecdotal kind, to suggest that in the bubble period banks did not screen borrowers adequately and, after the bursting of the bubble, did not intervene aggressively enough to take remedial action. Thus even at the micro level there is reason to believe that the quality of *ex ante*, interim and *ex post* monitoring by main banks has deteriorated.

Gower raises the possibility that the incentives of main banks to undertake adequate monitoring may have been reduced by the increased competition arising from financial deregulation during the 1980s. In particular, he focuses on the possibility that deregulation may have raised the scope for non-main banks to free-ride on main bank monitoring, thus preventing the main bank from being able to appropriate a sufficient share of banking system rents. Gower pursues this hypothesis by setting up a formal model of main bank monitoring. This allows him to investigate the effect of a number of key parameters on main bank incentives.

Gower uses the model to help explain the apparent breakdown in monitoring arrangements in the late 1980s, relative to the earlier period. With financial deregulation and monetary policy changes, implicit changes occurred in the terms of the franchise agreements prevailing between intermediaries and the monetary authorities. In particular, he notes that low deposit costs and the senior priority accorded to non-main banks made them prone to price bank financing too cheaply (to allow main banks to earn sufficient returns on costly monitoring), thus exacerbating main bank incentives to shirk on monitoring responsibilities. He concludes that the traditional system of main bank monitoring is fragile in the face of increasing contestability in financial markets.

Gower's model formalises in a nice way an important theme of the book, that regulatory rules interact with private sector institutions to influence incentives and equilibrium outcomes. It underscores the insight that deregulation is not just a process of removing regulations and allowing freer competition; it also entails changing the rules of the game and altering the incentives of financial intermediaries to provide various systemic public goods, in ways that are not always easy to anticipate.

Chapter 7 by **Paul Sheard**, entitled 'Banks, blockholders and corporate governance: the role of external appointees to the board', analyses empirically the role of banks in corporate governance. In most legal and economic thinking about the publicly incorporated firm, the board of directors is seen as the institutional linchpin of corporate governance (see Chapter 4). In the Anglo-American system, ostensibly at least — and in a latent sense probably in practice — the locus of corporate control resides with the board of directors, and takeover and proxy battles are typically played out as tussles to wrest control of the board from incumbent directors and top management.

Although in Japan as well the board of directors is at the hub of corporate governance, it takes on a somewhat different character from its Anglo-American counterpart. In the Japanese system, the board is really the top layer of management and the highest rank on the internal promotion ladder for 'lifetime' executive employees. Because of the virtual absence of hostile proxy battles and takeovers through the stock market, the board of directors is not usually seen as being an active arena of corporate governance in Japan, as it is in Anglo-American economies with open markets for corporate control. Appearances may be deceptive, however.

Sheard points out that, while the majority of directors in listed Japanese firms have risen up through the internal ranks, a substantial minority enter in mid to late career from outside the firm, notably from banks and large parent companies. In the Anglo-American system, ownership is dispersed and entry to the market for corporate control open; almost by definition attempts by outside third parties to wrest control from incumbent management are public and highly visible. In the Japanese system, a majority corporate control coalition is formed around the key business partners of the firm: banks, parent firms, suppliers and customers (Sheard 1994). In this system, the very (interlocked) actors that have the power to block unwanted hostile intrusions into the affairs of the firm by the broader capital market have the collective latent power to exercise control themselves. However, in contrast to open bidding systems, in an insider oriented system like Japan's, flows of information about top management can be obtained, and subtle — and in some cases more proactive — influence exerted in a low-key, unobtrusive way. Although Japan lacks an active corporate control 'market', one in four directors has entered the firm from outside (usually to become a full-time executive of the new firm), as has one in three chief executive officers (CEOs) — this despite the image of lifetime employment and managerial autonomy.

Sheard explores the role of external appointees to the board by estimating a statistical model of the possible explanatory variables. He finds that the flow of executives onto the board from outside can in part be explained by financial, ownership and other factors related to corporate governance. Outside presence on the board is more pronounced the more highly levered the firm and the more concentrated the main shareholding positions, particularly the top one; it is less pronounced the greater the extent of financial institution shareholding, the larger and older the firm and when there is evidence of residual founding family presence. Firms are more likely to have taken their CEO from outside the firm the larger the top shareholding, the more highly they are levered and the less profitable they are; they are less likely to have an outside CEO the greater the extent of financial institution shareholding, the larger they are and when there is residual family presence.

Sheard's analysis lends support to the emerging view in the literature that the Japanese system of corporate governance differs from its Western counterparts more in its institutional form and processes than in the reduced-form results that it produces. (See Kaplan 1994, Kaplan and Minton 1994, and Morck and Nakamura 1992 for interesting empirical evidence.) This is not to say that the Japanese system is 'perfect'; no system is, and a system that works well in one period or set of circumstances may fail in another.

Three implications of this line of thinking can be noted. One is that, having its own internal logic and functionality, the Japanese system is likely to be more robust in the face of altered circumstances and pressure to change than an assessment taking the Anglo-American system as its benchmark would lead one to believe.

A second point relates to the system view and the law of unintended consequences. Corporate governance systems, like other aspects of the economic system, are not static, centrally planned or entirely controllable and predictable. Nevertheless, key institutional parameters and rules of the game can be changed by legal and regulatory fiat or by the collective agreement of key players. Recent changes in the corporate governance rules in Japan include changes to the commercial and tax codes to allow firms to buy back their own shares, to make it possible for firms to offer stock options (under limited conditions) to their top executives, and to pave the way for representative shareholder suits against directors. Removal of the half-century ban on holding companies — a potentially momentous institutional change — is being debated actively and appears imminent as of the time of writing (early 1996). Somewhat further afield, developments in the asset management and pension industries are intensifying pressure on life insurance companies and trust banks to improve the returns they extract from their corporate equity investments; the banking authorities are under growing pressure to overhaul and redefine the way they manage the safety net (see also Chapter 10). All of these developments have the potential to change the nature of corporate governance in Japan, but given the interlocked nature of the system and the relatively low level of transparency to outsiders, accurately predicting how is no straightforward matter.

Third, a distinction needs to be made between changes that signify a breakdown in the system, changes that signify an evolution and adaptation of the system, and changes that signify realignment within the confines of the current system. Turning that point into a policy issue, the question becomes: does the system need to be replaced, repaired or just fine-tuned? A necessary starting point for addressing this issue is, of course, a well-grounded understanding of how the system currently works, what tradeoffs (costs and benefits) it entails, and how these tradeoffs are changing, and are likely to change, over time. The literature that has developed on this topic, and which is surveyed in Chapters 4 and 7, is useful on that count.

Part III   The financial system: present and future

The four chapters in Part III focus on the financial system: how it has supported the system of corporate finance and governance and how changes in the regulatory environment and economy are influencing that interconnection.

Masasuke Ide's thought provoking essay in Chapter 8, 'The financial system and corporate competitiveness', takes up the issue of how the corporate governance system — and the regulatory system that underpins it — has influenced the behaviour and competitiveness of Japanese firms. This has been a topical issue in the literature. In the late 1980s and early 1990s, before the impact of the bursting of the speculative bubble became obvious, there was a widespread view that, despite its unconventional features, the Japanese corporate governance system, supported by the regulatory framework, was an important factor in explaining the success of Japanese firms.

Some writers took the argument further, claiming that the system lowered the cost of capital for Japanese firms, giving them an unfair advantage in international competition. In this view, the whole *keiretsu* system served as a vehicle for sustaining systemic international predatory pricing by Japan Inc.: financial ties in the domestic system lowered the cost of capital for Japanese exporters and gave them 'deep pockets' to sustain price cutting and expand market share in international markets, while intercorporate ties in domestic distribution markets allowed segmentation of domestic from international markets. In the aftermath of the bubble the focus of this debate has changed somewhat. The problems in the banking system have become apparent and corporate Japan has had to struggle with its own competitiveness problem. It is now possible to give a more balanced assessment of the comparative merits and effects of the Japanese system versus its counterpart in the United States — the country typically taken as the benchmark of comparison. Ide's historical overview and contemporary reassessment of the Japanese system is a timely contribution in this direction.

Ide argues that the major characteristic of the postwar system of Japanese capitalism has been the use of the financial system to achieve strategic resource allocation. The author notes a number of key differences between the diversified and open US system and the elaborately constructed Japanese one. In particular, he focuses on the prevalence in Japan of relationship investors — investors who hold stocks in the context of maintaining a key business relationship — and of certain rules and conventions that resulted in a lowering of the cost of capital for key Japanese firms. Ide makes the interesting observation that in the first half of the postwar period common stocks behaved as if they were quasi-fixed income securities with warrants attached and in the second half as if they were call options on common stocks.

Ide goes on to argue that the relationship investor based system, involving cross-holdings and delegated monitoring by main banks, gave Japanese companies a strong competitive advantage in the international market at least until the end of the 1980s, by virtue of a lower cost of capital or increased tolerance of sustained lower returns. He also notes the limitations to such a system, and the pressure for change that has arisen with the exacerbation of trade frictions from accumulating external imbalances, the bursting of the bubble, financial deregulation, globalisation, societal ageing and pressures to restructure the entire economic system. Ultimately, Ide believes that a transition to a more open market system is inevitable: the cost of capital advantage is evaporating with regulatory and institutional change, and Japanese corporations are being forced to focus more on improving the returns on capital investment.

An issue that has been debated actively in recent years and that continues to invite interest concerns the impact of changes in the financial system on traditional bank–firm ties. Does deregulation and internationalisation of financial markets undermine the traditional main bank system? Do the dramatic changes that have occurred in corporate financing patterns in the past decade or more signify a fundamental shift from a bank to an open market based system? In Chapter 9, 'The impact of financial deregulation on corporate financing', **Takeo Hoshi** attempts to cast light on this set of questions.

Hoshi begins by pointing out that for much of the postwar period the corporate bond market in Japan was heavily regulated and access to foreign markets severely limited, leaving cash hungry firms with little choice but to rely heavily on bank borrowings. Notable changes in corporate financing took place in the 1980s as deregulation and internationalisation opened up new financing opportunities: firms reduced their reliance on bank borrowings and turned to equity and bond markets on a large scale.

Hoshi notes an interesting fact, namely that there was an increase in the heterogeneity of financing during this period. Some firms reduced their reliance on bank borrowings only slightly, while others took full advantage of the opportunities afforded by deregulation to move aggressively away from banks. Citing his earlier joint empirical work, Hoshi argues that these varying responses to deregulation are explained by the differing extent of agency problems among firms — those with a low degree of agency problems being more likely to use bond financing.

It is possible, as Ide argues in Chapter 8, that the changes in financing instruments represent more a diversification of the forms of financing than of the relationships with financiers or the identity of the suppliers of funds. Firms may have moved away from bank borrowings, but will not necessarily have moved away from banks if banks have taken up the bond and equity issues in substantial amounts. Hoshi presents evidence on this point to suggest that the share of banks in bond financing has become relatively minor, while that of households has risen.

Even if there is a relative decline in the share of funds supplied by main banks when the firm increases its reliance on market finance, this does not necessarily imply that the firm has moved out of the orbit of the main bank system (Aoki, Patrick and Sheard 1994). As Hoshi notes, banks still figure prominently as shareholders, and there is little evidence yet in the aggregate data of a weakening in bank–firm ties. It is misleading — although common in popular discussion — to infer that firms have moved away from banks, or abandoned traditional relationships, just because they have reduced their bank borrowings in favour of bond market financing if, as is almost always the case, banks and firms continue to maintain strong ownership ties through cross-holding arrangements.

Toyota, for example, has no bank borrowings (and has not had for many years), but it would be fallacious to infer from this that it has 'moved away from banks'. As of the end of the 1990 financial year (following the peak of the bubble), Sanwa, Sakura and Tōkai Banks were Toyota's three top shareholders, each with a 5 per cent share. Toyota had cross-holding relations with the banks, holding a 2.2 per cent share in Sanwa (making it the bank's number five shareholder), a 5.0 per cent holding in Tokai (making it the top shareholder) and a 2.5 per cent interest in Sakura (making it the number five shareholder). The banks might like Toyota to borrow from them, but the quantitative importance of the banks' shareholdings should not be underestimated.

The market value of Sanwa's holding in Toyota was 90.6 per cent of the value of its largest outstanding loan to any firm as of March 1991; Sakura's was also 90.6 per cent; while the value of Tōkai Bank's holding in Toyota exceeded its largest loan exposure by 43.7 percent (Tōyō Keizai Shinpōsha 1991, p. 405, p. 592, p. 594).

Matsushita is another example of a firm with no bank borrowings, but this does not mean that it has dissolved its relations with its main bank, Sumitomo. At the end of the 1990 financial year Sumitomo Bank was Matsushita's top shareholder with holdings of 4.7 per cent, while Matsushita was number three shareholder in Sumitomo with holdings of 3.5 per cent. The market value of Sumitomo Bank's shareholding in Matsushita was 71 per cent of the size of its largest single loan (Tōyō Keizai Shinpōsha 1991, p. 367, p. 593).

In Chapter 10, 'Financial liberalisation and the safety net', **Akiyoshi Horiuchi** undertakes a critical review of the past and present regulatory underpinnings of the banking system and outlines some suggestions for how the safety net should be managed in the future. A feature of banking policy in the postwar period is that the authorities (the Ministry of Finance and the Bank of Japan) have underwritten a guarantee of the total deposit base. They have done so, not so much by relying on deposit insurance (although such a system was set up in 1971 and first used in 1992), as by their policy towards banks: a combination of conservative management of the financial system to avoid financial failures and active policies aimed at rescuing and reorganising failed institutions. Banks were not allowed to fail, and so deposits were secured in the process. With the rapid accumulation of bad debts in the banking system in the first half of the 1990s, this system has been put to the test. Many observers would claim that it has been found to be inadequate (if not part of the problem to begin with) and in serious need of overhaul.

Horiuchi describes how this system evolved and was managed in the postwar period. He focuses on the role of what he calls 'competition restricting regulations' — interest rate controls, and restrictions on new entry and on the introduction of new products. These protected weaker institutions and allowed banks to accumulate rents. Because the authorities largely controlled the distribution of these rents, at least at the margin, they could use them as an incentive device to enforce compliance with regulatory policy. The existence of an artificial pool of rents in the system in a sense represented a systemic, implicit form of deposit insurance, in that financial failures could be avoided by arranging for strong banks to merge with failing ones. It did not matter if the coffers of the Deposit Insurance Corporation were low, as long as sufficient reserves existed on the balance sheets of the major banks.

Horiuchi documents how structural changes in financial markets have undermined this traditional system, culminating in the excesses of the bubble period and the banking crisis of the mid 1990s. He argues that, as financial liberalisation proceeded, rents were squeezed but that banks responded to a decline in profitability by taking more risk. When the bubble burst, not only was the scale of the bad debts problem unprecedented, the ability of the system to take ad hoc *ex post* remedial action to protect failing institutions and to make good their obligations to depositors was severely stretched. This in turn has precipitated a major re-examination and overhaul of policy on the banking system and the safety net, amidst a series of large-scale bank failures, successive downgradings of bank credit ratings by respected international rating agencies and the emergence of a 'Japan premium' differential between the international funding costs of Japanese banks and their overseas rivals.

Such recent developments in Japanese financial markets invite an interesting analogy to the concepts of a 'pooling equilibrium' and a 'separating equilibrium' in game theory (Kreps 1990, Ch. 17). The famous 'escorted convoy system' (*gosōsendan hōshiki*) can be given an analytical interpretation in terms of the Ministry of Finance (MOF) trying to implement a form of pooling equilibrium in domestic financial markets. (In equilibrium all agents are made to cluster at the same point and appear as similar as possible.) In contrast, competitive markets with diverse information and free entry and exit allow separating equilibria to flourish — differences in asset qualities being reflected in differential credit ratings and funding costs, and high-cost firms being driven from the market.

Using this analogy, the current Japanese financial system can be viewed as being in transition from a pooling equilibrium to a separating equilibrium. One example is the bank debenture market. Until December 1995, the three long-term credit banks, as a matter of convention and helped by the MOF's administrative guidance, had issued bank debentures in the primary market on precisely the same funding terms. This was a classic example of a MOF enforced pooling equilibrium (cartel by another name). On the other hand, international rating agencies have given each of the three long-term credit banks different ratings, reflecting their assessments of asset quality and credit risks. Moreover, and more surprising, within the domestic market, yield differentials for the same issues opened up in the secondary market, as the market expressed its view on asset quality. This is the separating equilibrium in action.

There may be good reasons for wanting to enforce a pooling equilibrium. The interesting point here, though, is that the two ways of running the market are not compatible; in this case, the separating equilibrium was transported into the Japanese market and prevailed over the indigenous pooling equilibrium. Suffice it to note that the Japan premium, and the suppression of information about underlying bank asset quality that underlies it, can be given a similar interpretation.

Horiuchi argues for the authorities to place greater weight in future on disclosure and prudential regulations, such as capital adequacy requirements, and to move away from their current discretionary, interventionist approach. Like many commentators, he favours a more transparent, rules based system in which the MOF adopts a neutral arm's-length stance and concentrates on providing, and maintaining the integrity of, a sophisticated financial market infrastructure.

One implication of a move in such a direction that has not been much debated concerns the corporate governance of Japanese banks. Banks are the most extensively interlocked segment of the cross-holdings structure. On average, about 90 per cent of their shares are held by corporations and financial institutions, most of whom are interlocked business partners (client firms and insurance companies that have close business and co-financing ties) (Sheard 1994). Unlike other corporations, however, banks do not appear to be subject to active corporate governance influences from this potential corporate control coalition. While arguably enjoying a higher degree of managerial autonomy than other firms, residual corporate governance functions are concentrated in the hands of the authorities and discharged in the context of their supervision of the banking system and management of the safety net (Aoki, Patrick and Sheard 1994).

This raises some interesting questions. In recent public announcements and policy documents, the MOF has indicated that it will abandon the escorted convoy system and set the groundwork for a more transparent system with improved disclosure and a high weight given to individual investor responsibility; it intends to establish the preconditions for invoking the payoff mechanism of the deposit insurance system (paying off depositors in failed institutions up to the insured limit, currently ¥10 million per depositor) (Kin'yū Seido Chōsakai 1995; Ōkurashō 1995). In such a scenario, where will the locus of corporate governance over the banks lie, and what will the ground rules be? If the locus of corporate governance devolves to the equity market, how will the shareholding structure of banks change — and how in turn might this impinge upon the role of the banks as main banks to client firms? What part might the introduction of financial holding companies play in this process? Might the reluctance of the banks to assert themselves vis-à-vis the MOF — despite appearing to have increased leeway to do so — reflect not so much the power of the ministry, which on any objective scale must be declining, as a realisation that too bold and sudden a move would only lead to the creation of a vacuum in their own corporate governance structure, which might not be filled in a way entirely to incumbent top management's liking? These are merely interesting speculative questions at this stage but they may emerge in coming years as key issues for corporate Japan.

In the final chapter, 'Deregulation and the structure of the money market', by **Gordon de Brouwer**, the focus switches to the macroeconomic level. Japan's money market underwent substantial reform and liberalisation in the late 1980s. De Brouwer is interested in the impact of these changes on the structure of interest rate linkage between the subsectors of the market, as well as between the Japanese and overseas money markets. This is an important issue from the viewpoint of gauging the effect of financial deregulation on the level of integration both between the international and Japanese markets and within Japan, and for understanding the transmission mechanisms of monetary policy in Japan.

De Brouwer carries out a statistical study of the relationship between four key money market rates for the period 1988–90, using Granger causality tests. The rates used are two interbank rates (the unsecured overnight call rate and the two-week discount bill rate) and two open market rates (the three-month certificate of deposit (CD) rate and the three-month Euroyen deposit rate). Because this period corresponds roughly to the bubble period in Japanese asset markets, the chapter's survey of developments and statistical analysis are useful in understanding how money markets were developing and what role monetary policy played in those eventful years.

The author finds that the Euroyen rate appears to drive the interest rate linkage system, directly 'causing' (in a Granger causality statistical sense) the unsecured call and CD rates and indirectly causing the bill rate. This leads him to conclude that it is the market rather than the monetary authorities that determines interest rates over time. Open market rates predict interbank rates, which themselves are jointly determined. De Brouwer argues from the statistical analysis that between November 1988 and December 1990 the Bank of Japan was either unable or unwilling to influence the formation of open money market interest rates. He notes, however, that the results do not necessarily mean that the Bank's policy was ineffective as they are consistent with it having adopted an accommodative policy stance in this period.

Taken together, the contributions to this volume suggest at least three things: that the financial and industrial organisation of Japanese firms and markets is both distinctive and important for understanding the workings and performance of the economy; that these systems have been subject to considerable forces for change in the past decade or more, but remain largely intact; and that how they adapt and evolve in the coming years will be critical in shaping Japan's socioeconomic landscape into the 21st century. This book will have served its purpose if it contributes in even a small way to a sounder understanding of that process and of the challenges that it involves.

References

Aoki, Masahiko (1989), 'The Nature of the Japanese Firm as a Nexus of Employment and Financial Contracts: An Overview', *Journal of the Japanese and International Economies*, 3 (4), pp. 323–50.

—— (1994), 'The Japanese Firm as a System of Attributes: A Survey and Research Agenda', in Masahiko Aoki and Ronald Dore (eds), *The Japanese Firm: The Sources of Competitive Strength*, Oxford: Oxford University Press, pp. 11–40.

Aoki, Masahiko and Hugh Patrick (eds) (1994), *The Japanese Main Bank System: Its Relevancy for Developing and Transforming Economies*, Oxford: Oxford University Press.

Aoki, Masahiko, Hugh Patrick and Paul Sheard (1994), 'The Japanese Main Bank System: An Introductory Overview', in Masahiko Aoki and Hugh Patrick (eds), *The Japanese Main Bank System: Its Relevancy for Developing and Transforming Economies*, Oxford: Oxford University Press, pp. 3–50.

Kaplan, Steven N. (1994), 'Top Executive Rewards and Firm Performance: A Comparison of Japan and the U.S.', *Journal of Political Economy*, 102 (3), pp. 510–46.

Kaplan, Steven N. and Bernadette Alcamo Minton (1994), 'Appointment of Outsiders to Japanese Boards: Determinants and Implications for Managers', *Journal of Financial Economics*, 36, pp. 225–58.

Kin'yū Seido Chōsakai (1995), *Kin'yū Shisutemu Anteika no tame no Shoshisaku: Shijō Kiritsu ni Motozuku Atarashii Kin'yū Shisutemu no Kōchiku* [Various Measures for the Stabilisation of the Financial System: Building a New Financial System Based on

Market Discipline], Report of the Financial System Research Council, Tokyo, 22 December.

Kreps, David M. (1990), *A Course in Microeconomic Theory*, Princeton, NJ: Princeton University Press.

Lawrence, Robert Z. (1993), 'Japan's Different Trade Regime: An Analysis with Reference to *Keiretsu*', *Journal of Economic Perspectives*, 7 (3), pp. 3–19.

Morck, Randall and Masao Nakamura (1992), Banks and Corporate Control in Japan, University of Alberta, Alberta (mimeo).

Nishiguchi, Toshihiro (1994), *Strategic Industrial Sourcing: The Japanese Advantage*, Oxford: Oxford University Press.

Ōkurashō (Ministry of Finance) (1995), Kin'yū Shisutemu no Kinō Kaifuku ni tsuite [Regarding the Recovery of the Function of the Financial System], Ministry of Finance, Tokyo (mimeo).

Sako, Mari (1992), *Prices, Quality and Trust: Inter-Firm Relations in Britain and Japan*, Cambridge, MA: Cambridge University Press.

Sheard, Paul (1994), 'Interlocking shareholdings and corporate governance', in Masahiko Aoki and Ronald Dore (eds), *The Japanese Firm: The Sources of Competitive Strength*, Oxford: Oxford University Press, pp. 310–49.

Smitka, Michael J. (1991), *Competitive Ties: Subcontracting in the Japanese Automotive Industry*, New York, NY: Columbia University Press.

Tōyō Keizai Shinpōsha (1991), *Kigyō Keiretsu Sōran 1992 Nenban* [Directory of Corporate Affiliations, 1992 Edition], Tokyo: Tōyō Keizai Shinpōsha.

Part I

Keiretsu and Competition: Vertical Organisation versus Markets

Part I

Agenda and Competition, Central Organization versus Markets

2 *Keiretsu* and market access: an economics of organisation approach

*Paul Sheard**

Recent arguments about the alleged closedness of the Japanese market have focused increasingly on the organisation and behaviour of Japanese firms. They have concentrated in particular on various forms of interfirm relationships, captured conveniently, if somewhat ambiguously, in the Japanese term *keiretsu* (affiliated group of businesses). Although the Japanese market is relatively open when judged in terms of traditional measures such as trade barriers, it is commonly believed that the various non-tariff barriers associated with the very way that Japanese firms are organised and behave greatly inhibit the access of foreign firms and products to the Japanese market. Related to this, some argue that corporate organisation not only restricts foreign access to the Japanese market, it also enables Japanese firms to behave in a predatory fashion, yielding them an unfair advantage in international markets. Others go further, saying that the Japanese capitalist system itself operates under its own distinctive logic and is inherently incompatible with the open GATT based international trading system. Systemic free-riding was possible while Japan was a small player in the world economy, but with its emergence as a dominant economy such predatory economic interaction is seen as being unsustainable.[1]

Noted economist Paul Krugman summarises the conventional wisdom about the Japanese market as follows:

---

* An earlier version of this chapter, entitled '*Keiretsu* and Closedness of the Japanese Market: An Economic Appraisal', was circulated in 1992 as Discussion Paper No. 273, Institute of Social and Economic Research, Osaka University. I wrote the paper while visiting the Institute, and the research was supported also by a grant from the Daiwa Bank Foundation for Asia and Oceania. I would like to thank Kōzō Yamamura for encouraging me to write the paper and Charles Horioka, Colin McKenzie, Hajime Miyazaki, Hiroyuki Odagiri, Mark Ramseyer and David Weinstein for their helpful comments. The usual disclaimer applies.

... despite its relative absence of legal barriers to trade, the Japanese market is de facto protected because it is not competitive in the same way as those of other countries. Collusive behavior involving both firms and a highly cartelized distribution sector effectively shut out many foreign products, even when the imports would be cheaper and/or of higher quality than the Japanese version. Foreign direct investment is similarly choked off by an inability to get local business cooperation, and the inability to establish local subsidiaries inhibits exports to Japan. And this more or less conspiratorial system tends particularly to close ranks when a new key technology is at stake, assuring Japanese firms of a chance to capture new markets even when foreign firms have an initial lead (Krugman 1991, pp. 2–3).

As is clear from this quote, there are several different dimensions to the claim that *keiretsu* relations lead to a closed market. At least four distinct views can be identified.[2] One is that *keiretsu* ties lead to cartelisation in the economy, by which is meant the exercise of monopoly or monopsony power by a group of sellers or buyers in a given market (that is, a number of sellers or buyers formally or tacitly coordinating their output or input decisions as if they were a single firm). A second view is that Japanese firms, through their distribution networks, are able to hinder the access of foreign goods, or more generally that the distribution system operates as a non-tariff barrier to trade (Johnson 1990a, p. 122; Lawrence 1991a, p. 330). A third view focuses on the tendency of Japanese firms to maintain long-term transactional relations and preferential trading arrangements with affiliated firms. In this view, the markets foreign goods should be able to penetrate just don't exist to the extent that they do in other economies (Dore 1986, p. 248; Gerlach 1989; Tyson and Zysman 1989b, p. xix). A fourth view argues that Japanese firms are able to gain an unfair advantage in international competition because of their financial organisation, centring on close links with main banks and extensive intercorporate shareholdings.[3]

The purpose of this chapter is to provide a critical economic analysis of the arguments surrounding the *keiretsu* and market closure issue.[4] Many of these rest implicitly or explicitly on economic reasoning or relate to economic models or bodies of literature. This is not to suggest that economists have a monopoly on the analysis of the *keiretsu* question. But the subject matter falls squarely in the purview of economic analysis — and recent developments in industrial organisation and the economics of organisation, not to mention those relating directly to the Japanese firm, have been startling.[5] An important motivation for the chapter is to bring these economic insights and arguments into the mainstream of the debate over *keiretsu*.[6] A theme is that much of the popular discussion associating *keiretsu* with anticompetitive behaviour lacks a solid foundation in economic analysis.

Not all observers view Japanese corporate organisation in a negative light. In recent years increasing attention has been focused on Japanese firms and patterns of economic organisation as providing one important set of factors helping to explain Japan's favourable economic performance, which is seen as stemming in large part from the superior competitive performance of Japanese firms.[7] Viewed in this light,

Japanese practices become, not a target of international censure, but a subject worthy of serious study, one which may conceivably yield lessons for firms, policy makers and governments in both developing and industrialised economies.

Are these two sets of views of Japanese corporate organisation competing hypotheses or, at some level, mutually reconcilable ones? The chapter aims to shed some light on this as well.

Keiretsu: a problematic category

To discuss sensibly what effects *keiretsu* have, we need to be clear about what the term means. Its use as a loan word in English tends to mask the fact that it is used in Japanese in a very broad and loose way to refer to a wide range of interfirm affiliations or sets of companies affiliated in some way. Reflecting the many different forms of intercorporate affiliation in Japan, there are correspondingly many ways of using the term. It is also used somewhat interchangeably with *kigyō shūdan*, meaning 'firm group' but more commonly translated as 'enterprise group'.

At least five common usages or senses of the term *keiretsu* can be identified. First, it is used to refer to the six well-known enterprise groups. Each of these groups comprises firms operating generally in different markets but loosely connected through a common financial ('main bank') affiliation, dispersed interlocking shareholdings, director ties (centring on managers supplied by the core city bank), supplier–purchaser ties (often mediated by one general trading company), a common corporate name and/or logo, and participation in group consultative forums such as the well-known 'presidents' clubs' (*shachōkai*). Four of these groups have antecedents in the four major prewar *zaibatsu* (Mitsui, Mitsubishi, Sumitomo and Fuji), while two (Sanwa and Daiichi Kangyō) owe much of their formation to the postwar period.

A second category comprises sets of firms that have common financial links to a major bank. They are sometimes called 'financial *keiretsu*'. This category subsumes the first, but is used in a broader sense to focus particularly on main bank ties. Thus a firm closely identified with one of the six enterprise groups as a rule has that group's city bank as its main bank. The bank, of course, has main bank financing relations with a much larger set of firms, many of which would not be considered part of the enterprise group.[8] For instance, Mazda is not a member of the Sumitomo presidents' club, but it has a main bank relationship with Sumitomo Bank and is regarded as being affiliated with the Sumitomo group (financial *keiretsu*).

A third category is a group of firms comprising a large parent company and its subsidiaries and affiliates. Although the internal organisation of Japanese firms differs somewhat from the typical Western pattern, this form of *keiretsu* comes closest to the notion of a group of related companies as used in Western business parlance. For example, it is possible to talk of the 'X group of companies' interchangeably with the 'X *keiretsu*', where X could be almost any large listed industrial or commercial firm in Japan, such as Toyota, Matsushita, Toshiba or Nippon Steel.

A fourth sense of the term *keiretsu* is to refer to a group of firms comprising a parent company and its network of suppliers and subcontractors, a so-called 'supplier *keiretsu*'. Again, there is a strong overlap with the former category in that many subsidiaries and affiliates are suppliers or subcontractors to a parent firm. However, a supplier *keiretsu* consists of a greater number of firms than those in which the parent company has substantial equity capital involvement, and connotes a set of firms engaged in long-term transactions in a coordinated production process. Notable examples are found in the assembly industries, such as automobiles and electronics.

A fifth category is a group of firms comprising a large manufacturer and its affiliated wholesalers and distributors, a 'distribution *keiretsu*'.

A number of points can be made in light of the above. First, *keiretsu* can take several different forms involving quite different structures, purposes and intensities of interaction and control. The interactions — and the analytical issues involved — are likely to be different between a distribution network and a supplier network, for instance, or between a bank and a corporate borrower, or between two industrial firms that are members of the same presidents' club. Without carefully specifying what they mean by *keiretsu*, it is unlikely that any two observers who use the term would have exactly the same phenomenon in mind. Second, it should be noted that the categories of *keiretsu* identified above are not mutually exclusive in that a given firm can belong to more than one at the same time. For example, a typical manufacturing firm that is a member of one of the six presidents' clubs would have all five of the *keiretsu* aspects. A third point concerns the issue of uniqueness. The term *keiretsu* tends to conjure up the impression of uniqueness to Japan, but a distinction needs to be made between uniqueness in terms of the kinds of relationships that characterise *keiretsu* and uniqueness in terms of how and to what extent these are manifest in Japan. *Keiretsu* as a particular form of organisation may indeed be unique in some sense to Japan, but the kinds of relationships involved — close bank–firm ties, subcontracting relations, long-term trading ties and interlocking shareholdings — are not.

Notions of market closure

To assess whether firm organisation is a factor leading to closedness of the Japanese market, we need to be precise about what is meant by a closed market. This section tries to give some analytical content to the notion of a closed or open market.

Closure at international borders

Economists usually talk about 'closedness' or 'openness' of markets at the level of national economies in relation to international trade policy and trading regimes, such as the GATT based trading system. This is the context in which the debate about *keiretsu* has arisen, and the language of closed or open markets as applied to international borders has been carried over to the discussion of firm organisation. As a number of observers have noted, it is neither analytically sound nor helpful to an understanding of the issues to analyse *keiretsu* issues in this framework (Komiya and Irie 1990).

The border between two countries, in theory and in practice, represents a natural discontinuity between separate country markets — in terms of geography, language and so on. Because those markets are governed by different sovereign governments, they can be closed, in the sense of restricting the flow of goods and services by various policy actions.

Economists make a number of important distinctions about the barriers to trade at borders. One is between artificial and natural barriers to trade (Leamer 1988, p. 147). The effects of these two kinds of barriers or sources of closedness on economic agents may be the same: artificial barriers to trade, such as government tariffs or quotas, and natural barriers to trade, such as distance or language, may make it equally difficult for a firm to export from one country to another. To economists, however, the two are quite distinct because the removal of one is a feasible policy option while the removal of the other is not. One is a real cost of trade that should be taken into account in arriving at efficient allocations, the other an artificial cost that distorts behaviour away from what it would otherwise be. (Of course, there are numerous policy rationales, such as trade or industrial policy, for distorting behaviour in this way.) In order to overcome natural barriers, a real process of economic transformation is required: transportation to overcome the barrier of distance, or training to overcome the barrier of language, for example. No such real economic process underlies an artificial trade barrier.

In the international trade setting, artificial barriers are normally thought of as being associated with government actions, either directly (as in the case of tariffs, quotas and standards) or indirectly (as in the case of preferential government treatment of domestic firms). A second distinction arises in this context, that between tariff and non-tariff barriers. Traditionally this is a distinction between the kind of instrument that the government uses to discriminate against imports. The identity of the agent responsible for erecting the barrier is the same in both cases, namely the government (Dam 1970).

A feature of the market closure debate as it relates to Japan, and to US–Japan trade in particular, is that corporate organisation and behaviour has been identified as constituting an artificial non-tariff barrier to trade. This blurs the analytical distinction between different sources of closedness and causes considerable confusion in the debate. The reasoning behind such arguments is either that *keiretsu* facilitate or are manifestations of anticompetitive (monopolistic or predatory) behaviour by Japanese firms, or that they reflect a particular pattern of economic (that is, market and firm) organisation not, perhaps, found in other countries, particularly the United States. The arguments need to be examined with reference to the appropriate literature and analytical frameworks available — and still developing — in economics for dealing with these questions.

Anticompetitive firm behaviour

A long tradition in legal and economic policy and analysis considers the possibility that firms collectively or individually can behave in anticompetitive ways. These include colluding to monopolise markets or behaving in a predatory fashion aimed at inhibiting rivals from competing effectively with them, typically by erecting barriers to entry or by driving competitors from the market through what would be considered illegitimate means (Ordover and Saloner 1989; Jacquemin and Slade 1989; *Journal of Economic Perspectives* 1987). Many claim that *keiretsu* relations are anticompetitive, monopolistic or predatory in this antitrust sense.[9] 'Closing the market' in this setting would mean that firms erect barriers to entry to prevent competitors coming into their markets, or that they drive their competitors to the periphery or out of the market through predatory means.

Considerable care must be exercised in the application of antitrust arguments to the analysis of *keiretsu*. The idea that firms can monopolise or close a market to competitors by erecting barriers to entry or engaging in predatory behaviour seems straightforward. However, the issue of what constitutes a barrier to entry or predatory behaviour, even whether these can meaningfully be said to exist, has been contentious in the industrial organisation literature (Gilbert 1989a, 1989b; Ordover and Saloner 1989). Two forms of barrier to entry can be distinguished. One is government imposed or induced barriers. Many economists believe that most, if not all, barriers are of this kind (Demsetz 1982). While no doubt existing in Japan as elsewhere, this form of barrier is not directly relevant to the analysis of *keiretsu*.

The second form of barrier arises from the differences in cost conditions between incumbent firms and potential entrants. A basic notion in economic analysis is that economic actors should ignore costs which are already sunk on the premise that 'it's no good crying over spilt milk'. If entry to a market involves the sinking of substantial costs, then a barrier to entry may exist in that entrants face a class of costs not borne by incumbents. Such barriers to entry may, of course, exist as a natural consequence of technologies and market environments. But firms may also strategically erect such barriers. This is the form of behaviour that would be relevant to the *keiretsu* issue from an antitrust perspective.

Predatory pricing behaviour has been an even more controversial question. Until recently, there was no convincing theoretical explanation for how predatory pricing could possibly work, in the sense of being both feasible and profitable.[10] For predatory pricing to be practicable, the predatory firm has to make sufficiently high (monopoly) profits in a post-predation stage to cover the losses of the predatory, low-pricing stage. It is not clear, though, what would prevent previous or new competitors from entering in the high-pricing stage, given that entry was feasible earlier.

A difficult issue of interpretation, and one that partly accounts for the controversy surrounding antitrust policy, concerns how to define anticompetitive behaviour.[11] If we adopt the traditional economic viewpoint of firms competing with one another in markets, then the successful firms are those that expand market share at the expense of their competitors. It could be said that less successful firms will find those markets 'closed to them'. Normally such terminology would not be employed, however, as it simply describes the dynamic competitive process considered intrinsic to and desirable in a market economy. Firms that engage in anticompetitive behaviour in the antitrust sense seek to both expand market share and disadvantage competitors. In terms of the outcome, legitimate competitive business strategies and illegitimate anticompetitive ones are equivalent. A firm that is observed to have expanded market share, and perhaps to have driven competing firms from the market, may have done so by having fairly won a competitive race or by having engaged in anticompetitive conduct.

One implication of this goes to the heart of the *keiretsu*/market closure issue. Faced with the observation that Japanese firms are successful in obtaining market share in domestic or international markets, and confronted with organisational factor X said to be characteristic of Japanese firms, it is not clear *a priori* whether we have identified: (i) a factor that is irrelevant to explaining the level of market share; (ii) a source of Japanese firms' superiority or competitive advantage; or (iii) an element in the anticompetitive arsenal of Japanese firms.[12] Economic analysis, based on an understanding of the institutional environment, can help to illuminate the issue.

An economics of organisation perspective

The national boundary and antitrust views reflect a traditional strand of economic thinking: namely that markets exist independently of the firms that operate in them. From this point of view, *keiretsu* represent a barrier to the access that third parties, such as foreign firms, can gain to those markets. The modern field of the economics of organisation suggests another perspective: the organisational forms and relationships referred to as *keiretsu* are themselves an integral aspect of the way that markets, as arenas for executing economic transactions, are organised.

The traditional approach in economics was to see firms as a category of economic actor — like households — and markets as the arena in which firms and other economic agents interacted. This is the view that is adopted in the standard economic analysis of markets (supply and demand analysis) and also in the industrial organisation literature surveyed above, although in the latter case firms are held to have some market power rather than being atomistic price takers. The new literature, which dates back to Coase's famous 1937 paper, recognises that the firm is not a given technological entity but a complex contractual network of interacting agents consisting of the suppliers of various forms of factors together with parties that contract for the output so generated.[13] There can be no presumption that the firm embodies only transactions executed in anonymous competitive markets; indeed, such a notion is inconsistent with the reality of the firm as an organisation which embodies production and technological knowhow, transforms these via ongoing intertemporal investment decisions, coordinates the flow of resources, and has at least the expectation of an enduring existence through time.

In this new view, firms or sets of related firms arise as a means of governing transactions. A critical issue in this context concerns how internally and market mediated transactions differ from one another and what determines the location and the nature of the boundary between internal organisation in firms and transacting through a market (Kreps 1990, Ch. 20). A common view is that firms and markets differ as a means of coordinating and motivating (providing incentives for) the deployment of resources (Milgrom and Roberts 1992): whereas firms involve centralised decision making, quantity based information and order flows, and face-to-face interaction among participating agents (managers, suppliers of inputs and consumers of outputs), in markets information and decision making are dispersed or decentralised, decisions are coordinated and made consistent through price adjustments, and interactions are largely anonymous, the identity of the transacting parties being irrelevant.

The economics of organisation approach suggests another perspective on the *keiretsu*/market closure issue. The kinds of markets that exist in an economy, and the form that they take, reflect in part how firms are organised and how interactions among agents in and between firms are structured. Choices by firms about where to locate their organisational boundaries and how to govern transactions across those boundaries, while constrained by available market structures, also, in aggregate, influence the extent and shape of markets.

To see this, consider for simplicity a final good whose production requires two stages of production, processing and assembly, which we can refer to respectively as upstream and downstream stages. The output of the processing stage, an intermediate good, becomes the input of the assembly stage. Three cases can be identified, as depicted in Figure 2.1. In the first, firms are vertically integrated and production of the intermediate good takes place in-house; there is no market for the intermediate good or, as some would put it, the market has been 'internalised' within the firm. At the other extreme, separate firms operate in each of the stages and there is a market (perhaps competitive, perhaps otherwise) in the intermediate good. The middle case in which upstream and downstream firms maintain close or long-term ties (for example, through partial equity, other financing links or long-term trading) can be thought of as being a characterisation of the *keiretsu*. Thus whether a market, as conventionally conceived, exists or not depends on how firms are organised. Moreover, whether a firm is specialised or integrated can itself be viewed as a choice of the firm.

The situation depicted in Figure 2.1 can be used to make several relevant points. One is that, for a given competitive final market structure, there are many ways that firms can be organised vertically. A second is that, in discussing the *keiretsu* case, it is important to clarify the benchmark of comparison. The prevalence of long-term ties, such as appear to characterise interfirm organisation in Japan, is frequently contrasted, explicitly or implicitly, with the case of external market transactions. On such a yardstick, the Japanese case seems to be less infused with market elements. On the other hand, compared with the vertical integration case, it appears to be more market oriented: while the transactions involved are not completely arm's-length, they do take place across firm boundaries in a market setting rather than within an integrated firm. The situation is not as simple, though, as depicted in the figure.

There are in fact two dimensions to what one might think of as vertical integration: how integrated the firm is internally (what functions and production processes are

Figure 2.1   Forms of transactional ties between vertically linked markets

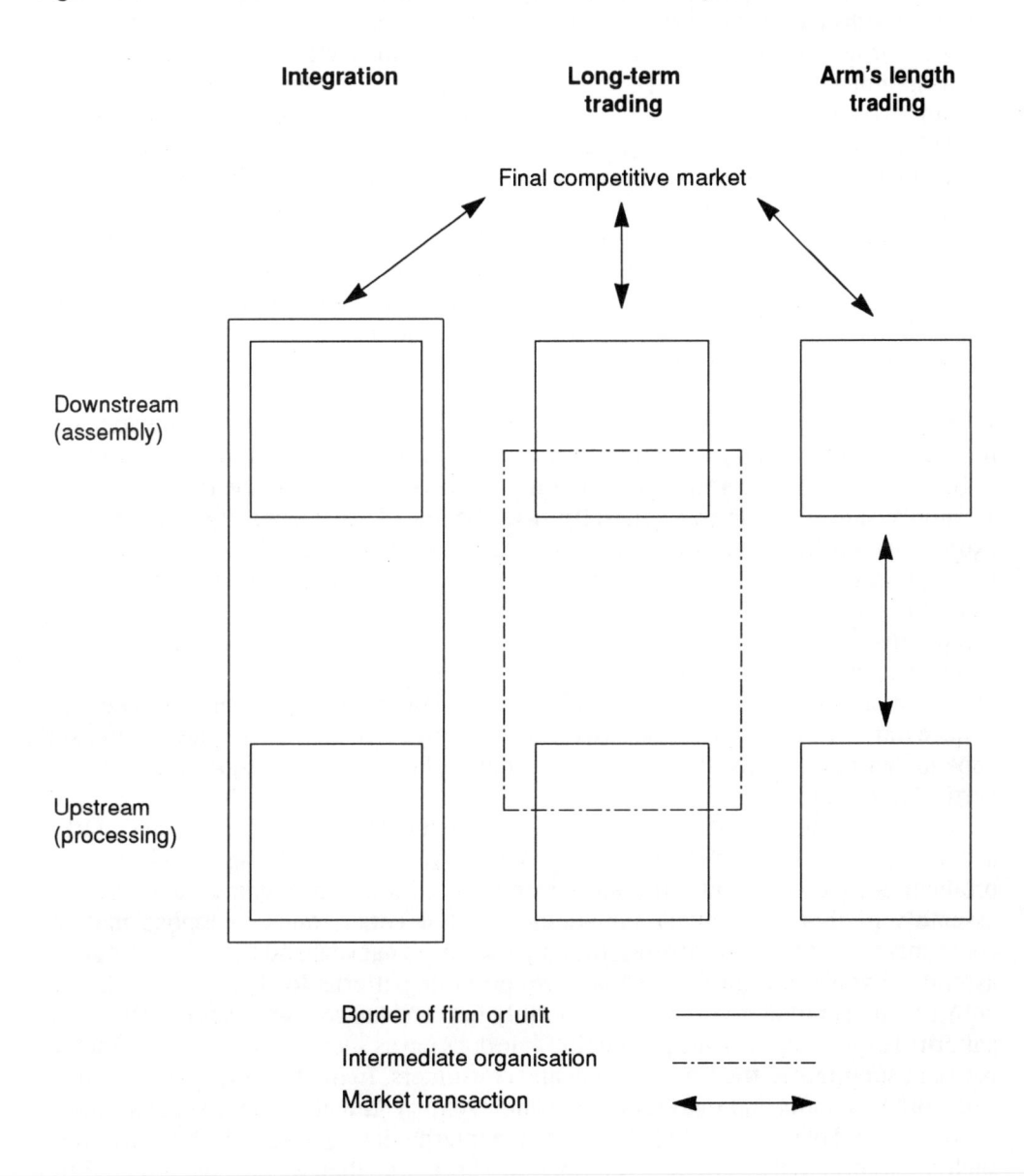

	Integration	Long-term trading	Arm's length trading

Final competitive market

Downstream (assembly)

Upstream (processing)

Border of firm or unit ―――――

Intermediate organisation —·—·—·—

Market transaction ⟷

located in-house or where the boundary of the firm is located), and what *form* interfirm transactions take (whether they are long term or continuous in nature, and therefore resemble internal organisation, or whether they are more like low-commitment, spot market transactions). Viewed in this way, it becomes a subtle question to determine which of two economic systems is more market oriented. Take, for example, the US–Japan auto industry comparison. If we focus on what is happening at the border of the firm, the US case seems the more market oriented. But if we look at where the border is located (the extent of in-house production), the Japanese case appears to be more market oriented in that transactions that are carried out inside the firm in the United States take place between firms in Japan. It is not clear *a priori* which country is more market oriented because what is at issue is not just the nature of interfirm transactions — the focus of attention in discussions of *keiretsu* — but the extent to which firms are vertically (and horizontally) integrated. (A similar point is made by Kawasaki and McMillan 1987, p. 336.)

A third point concerns the important distinction between intermediate and final product markets. Final product markets involve households or individual consumers as buyers, whereas in intermediate product markets firms are on the demand as well as supply side. Economists generally take the set of final consumption goods as exogenous, given the nature of consumer tastes and feasible technologies. There is a presumption that final goods markets should be open (if not there is a role for antitrust and trade policy), and in general these markets, having many buyers and sellers, are competitive.[14]

On the other hand, from an economics of organisation perspective, there can be no presumption that a complete set of well-developed intermediate product markets will, or necessarily should, exist. The existence of a market for an intermediate good itself depends on the organisation of firms, in particular the degree and nature of their vertical integration.[15]

Figure 2.2 illustrates the implications of these insights for the *keiretsu* and market access debate. Extend the example to a production process involving three stages: the production of components; the subassembly of those components; and the final assembly of this (and other) subassemblies. For concreteness, suppose that the components are vinyl and springs, the subassembly a car seat and the final product an assembled vehicle. Figure 2.2 shows two possible patterns for firm and market. In both, the final market involving the assembly firm and the consumers is the same. The pattern of organisation on the production side does not as such influence the interaction between suppliers of the final product and consumers. In the first type, subassembly firms produce parts and put them into a subassembly; the parts are not transacted in the market and the subassembly becomes the intermediate product. If there are many such firms and supply–purchase relations are short term, then we may have something that resembles a competitive market for subassemblies. In the second type, the assembly firm buys the parts and assembles them into a subassembly itself; in this case the market for the intermediate product is parts rather than subassemblies.

Figure 2.2 **Intermediate markets as a reflection of firm organisation**

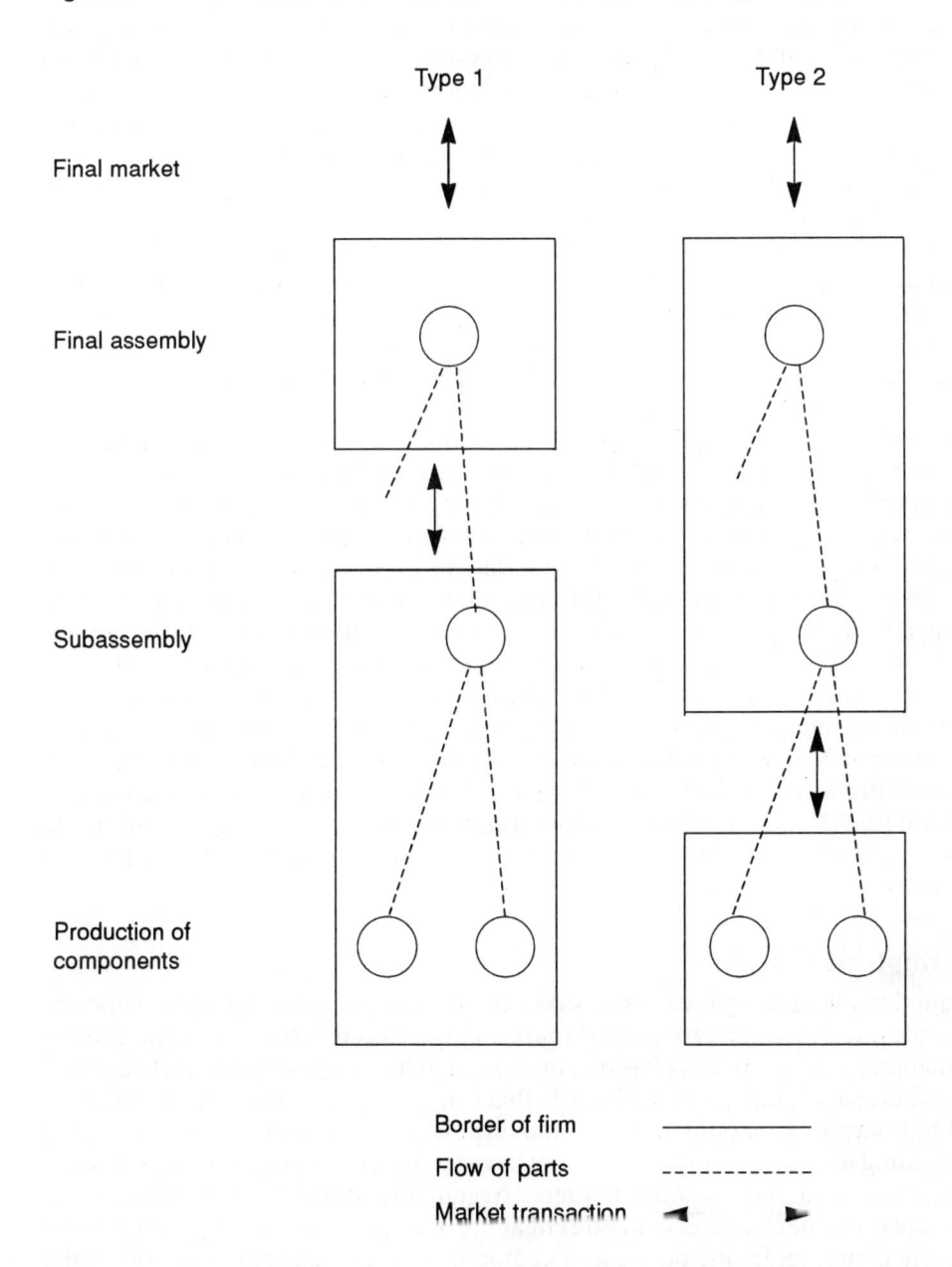

The key point concerns the endogeneity of intermediate product markets; whether and in what form they exist depends on decisions by firms about how to arrange the contractual organisation of their production systems. *A priori* there is no basis for saying that one or other of the modes is better or more logical. Conventional economic analysis gets around this indeterminacy by assuming either that there are no intermediate product markets or, at the other extreme, that there is a market for every possible good — in Williamson's terms, that a market exists at every 'technologically separable interface' (Williamson 1981, p. 1,544).

Ultimately all goods and services are consumed by individuals purchasing in final goods markets. Intermediate goods differ conceptually from consumer goods in that they are valued only in as much as they can be transformed into consumer goods; they are not valued for their own sake, so to speak. This is one reason why economists, in much of their modelling, abstract completely from the existence of intermediate goods and product markets.

It is noteworthy that much of the concern about *keiretsu* focuses on relations in intermediate product markets. Intermediate product markets are held to be closed to foreign suppliers because of *keiretsu* ties between firms that are thought to be preferential towards insiders and exclusionary towards outsiders. The insight of the economics of organisation approach here is that the lack of a market may in this case simply reflect the fact, in a Coase–Williamsonian sense, of the market having been supplanted by a different set of transaction governance mechanisms. These may be internal to the firm, or they may contain contractual attributes suggestive more of a firm-like coordination mechanism than of an arm's-length, anonymous market one.[16] Suppose for argument's sake that the two systems in Figure 2.2 correspond to an auto production system in Japan and the United States respectively.[17] It would then appear, should parts producers in the United States wish to supply to the Japanese market, that they would find the market closed to them. Likewise, producers of subassemblies in Japan who wished to export to the United States would find that the market in question did not exist.

Policy implications

The main threads of the above discussion can be summarised as follows. Although much of the interest in *keiretsu* and the market closure issue has arisen in the context of international trade, where a closed or open market has a well-defined and accepted meaning and usage, analysis of the issue in that framework is inappropriate and prone to lead to unnecessary confusion and counterproductive tensions. Firms, even the largest leading industrial companies, do not have the sovereign power of governments to close markets at international borders. Arguments about *keiretsu* and market closure concern either whether firms are engaging in anticompetitive behaviour, of the variety that comes under the purview of competition policy and antitrust law, or the particular pattern of economic organisation that characterises intermediate product markets, that is, the mix of markets and firms (hierarchies) on the production side of the economy. To make headway, the issues should be analysed with reference to those analytical frameworks.

An important reason for being specific about the analytical framework is that the welfare or policy implications may differ markedly. If *keiretsu* or aspects of *keiretsu* are best explained in the antitrust framework, then criticism that they close off markets or are anticompetitive would be warranted and application of appropriate antitrust measures justified. If *keiretsu* are largely to be explained as a manifestation in the Japanese case of the issues dealt with in the economics of organisation literature, then the policy implications, to the extent that there are any, are more likely to be ones of appropriate corporate strategy in the case of foreign firms, or industrial policy in the case of foreign governments.[18] In the context of US–Japan trade friction, and at the risk of being overly simplistic, the question reduces to whether it is Japan that needs to take remedial action, or the United States.

Evaluating the arguments

There are basically two complementary approaches in economics for evaluating the validity of the arguments surrounding *keiretsu* and market closure. One is to conduct statistical tests of relevant data so as to uncover evidence that might help to discriminate between the competing hypotheses (econometric analysis). The second is to examine the logic and plausibility of the arguments in light of relevant economic theories.[19] Most of the economic contributions to the *keiretsu* debate have been of the former type. They include studies of Japanese trade structure and of import, export and pricing behaviour (Lawrence 1987, 1991a; Lincoln 1990, Ch. 2; Marston 1991; Ohno 1989; Saxonhouse 1986, 1989); research on the efficiency of the distribution system (Ariga, Ohkusa and Namikawa 1991; Ito and Maruyama 1991; Nishimura 1991); and analysis of the cost of capital in Japan and compared with the United States (Ando and Auerbach 1988, 1990; Hodder 1991a, 1991b). A systematic review of these studies and their findings is not attempted here.[20] This chapter is in the spirit of the second approach, although some comments are made on the quantitative approach.

Quantitative studies

Quantitative studies play a central role in the testing of economic theory or investigation of economic policy issues, and it should come as no surprise that the principal contribution of economists to the *keiretsu* debate has been at this level. Some problems or limitations of this approach should, however, be noted.[21] One is that the results of the quantitative studies have tended to be inconclusive. This has generated a series of debates, with researchers on opposite sides either producing different results or adopting contrary interpretations of the results. Although in part this just reflects the hard grind of empirical research, it also reveals deeper structural problems with the approach as applied to the analysis of *keiretsu* issues.

Another problem is that frequently it is not clear which part of the conventional wisdom is being tested or confirmed; hence it is difficult to make clear-cut inferences, no matter what the results. An important case in point concerns a line of studies, adding to the now prolific literature on Japanese trade structure, that incorporates measures of *keiretsu* relations into regression models seeking to explain Japanese imports and exports (Fung 1991; Lawrence 1991a; Noland 1991a). The idea is to test whether *keiretsu* make a difference to imports or exports, within the context of a particular trade model, and to use the results to say something about the alleged exclusionary or anticompetitive nature of *keiretsu*. These studies distinguish 'horizontal' *keiretsu* (essentially the first and second categories described earlier in the chapter) from 'vertical' *keiretsu* (categories 3 and 4). They find that vertical *keiretsu* tend to increase exports and horizontal *keiretsu* to decrease imports, leading to the policy conclusion that vertical *keiretsu* are efficiency enhancing and horizontal *keiretsu* exclusionary or anti-competitive (Lawrence 1991a).

It is far from clear, however, what these studies have actually found, let alone whether inferences such as the above can be drawn. One major problem is that, to the extent that the kinds of measures included in such regression models can be said to capture *keiretsu* relations (a serious concern in light of earlier discussion), they are capturing either: (i) ties which are vertical in the industrial organisation sense (input–output relations, on the supply or the distribution side); or (ii) intermarket connections, such as cross-shareholding, common main bank or trading company affiliation, or information flows between firms operating in separate markets. These are not horizontal connections in the sense used in industrial organisation, namely ties between firms in the same market, and so it is quite misleading to term the first two categories of *keiretsu* 'horizontal' (see also Gerlach 1991, p. 83, on this point).

Given the diversity in both the range and intensity of relations associated with *keiretsu* patterns of organisation, as well as their overlapping, interconnected nature, it is not at all clear what the *keiretsu* variable in such regression models is meant to capture — long-term trading ties, information flows, financial connections, organisation of the production or distribution system, or some historical factor no longer, perhaps, of any direct causal relevance. The approach of throwing in a crude measure of *keiretsu*-ness, such as the proportion of industry sales accounted for by firms identified as being 'in' or a 'member of' a *keiretsu* — suspect concepts in themselves — is not likely to be very informative.

A related point concerns the drawing of inferences. Suppose, as Lawrence (1991a, p. 319) finds, that a proxy for *keiretsu* significantly reduces imports in an import regression equation. Essentially this says that the prevalence of *keiretsu* is associated with a lower than otherwise level of imports, controlling for the effects of other relevant variables. Putting aside a number of important criticisms that could be made about the soundness of the methodology and reliability of the results, we do not know what aspect of *keiretsu* is causing this outcome. This in turn confounds inference making. The result could be due to the exclusionary nature of *keiretsu*, as frequently alleged, but it could also be because *keiretsu* relations contribute to the competitive position of firms; that is, the *keiretsu* variable is picking up some unmodelled source of competitive corporate (comparative) advantage, due to or perhaps correlated with *keiretsu* ties or the *keiretsu* measure. Even if it is found that *keiretsu* ties are associated with a lower level of imports, we do not know whether this is because they unfairly restrict import access or because they contribute to, or in some way reflect, the competitive strength of Japanese firms.[22] In short, these studies treat *keiretsu* as a 'black box' and do not allow the important competing hypotheses — anticompetitive behaviour versus unmodelled source of competitive advantage — to be readily discriminated.

The above discussion begs the important question of whether the arguments alleging *keiretsu* to be exclusionary or anticompetitive themselves make sense. A weakness in the wider debate reflected in these quantitative studies is that the mechanisms by which *keiretsu* are supposed to reduce competition or impede entry are not spelled out. It is important to be specific about this because it allows their plausibility in terms of economic logic to be checked. What is the logic that lies behind the various claims about *keiretsu*, and does it stand up to the scrutiny of economic analysis? The remainder of the section examines this issue.

Distinguishing horizontal from vertical issues

An important insight from industrial organisation antitrust economics of keen relevance to the evaluation of the *keiretsu* debate is that vertical issues must be distinguished clearly from horizontal ones. 'Vertical' refers to activities or practices involving successive stages of production, such as the nature of ties between firms in an upstream industry and those in a downstream industry. 'Horizontal' refers to activities or practices between firms in the same market.

Market power is a horizontal issue. The classic concern in antitrust policy is that firms in a market will jointly collude to restrict output, raise prices and earn supernormal monopoly profits — at the expense of consumers directly, due to the higher prices that must be paid, and at society's expense indirectly, due to the lower level of consumption and attendant foregone gains. Anticompetitive, strategic or predatory behaviour aimed at restricting new entry to the market is not taken for its own sake but for the purpose of being able to monopolise the market.

A key point in this context is that *keiretsu* forms of organisation have nothing directly to do with this classic concern of antitrust since they do not involve horizontal relations, that is, relations between firms *in the same market*. Put even more simply, the firms that are related through *keiretsu* ties could not possibly collude to exercise monopoly power in a market since they do not operate in the same market. All firms in a given industrial market in Japan may hold various forms of *keiretsu* affiliation, but it is a mistake to link the prevalence of *keiretsu* with the principal antitrust concern, exercise of market power. That is not to say that the firms in the market may not be behaving in a joint profit maximising way, for example, by engaging in secret price fixing or tacitly colluding to do so. But this has nothing to do with *keiretsu* per se. No convincing argument has been put forward in the literature to suggest why relationships of the *keiretsu* type would lead a given set of firms in a market to be more collusive or more successful at acting as a joint monopolist.[23]

Keiretsu ties fall into the category of vertical relationships in the above sense, despite the common use of the term 'horizontal' to describe them (see also Saxonhouse 1991a, p. 336, on this point). That is, *keiretsu* relationships involve either various direct or indirect ties between firms in different markets (such as the fractional shareholdings between, say, Sumitomo Metal, a steel producer, and Sumitomo Chemical, a chemicals producer, in the Sumitomo group) or ties between firms that transfer inputs to a product across successive stages of production (such as a parts supplier to an auto assembler; a producer of a raw material to a fabricator or processor; or a manufacturer to a distributor in its sales network).

Vertical ties, such as those that form the basis of *keiretsu*, *in and of themselves* are of no consequence for antitrust issues; they are of concern only in as much as they impinge on the competitive conditions in a horizontal market. As long as the final goods market is competitive, forms of vertical relations can have no anticompetitive implications. This point can be understood by reference to the simple example presented in Figure 2.1. Which of the three ways of organising itself vertically the firm selects is really a choice about how to contract for the supply of inputs, and of itself has no effect on whether the firm possesses any monopoly power in the final market. This is easy to see from the following simple thought experiment. Suppose two firms in vertically related markets, neither of whom possesses any market power in their respective markets to start with, join forces to exert market power. Together they can exert no more market power than they have to begin with, which is zero by assumption.

Or suppose that a downstream monopolist merged with its competitive upstream suppliers. Because the monopolist is already obtaining its inputs at the lowest cost and selling its output at the profit maximising monopoly price, output and profit remain unchanged. The market is monopolised, but this has nothing to do with the vertical organisation. Intuitively, monopoly profits can only be extracted, directly or indirectly, from final consumers — there is only one set of monopoly rents and these cannot be captured more than once, that is, at different stages of production.[24] Of course, as in the latter example there may be vertically related firms that do exercise monopoly power, but the analytical point is that this monopoly power derives from something other than the vertical relationship.

To summarise, vertical ties involve relations across markets; for them to have an anticompetitive effect they must influence competitive conditions *in* a market, for example, by restricting new entry to the market, by impeding the ability of existing firms to compete, or by facilitating collusive practices in the market. It is not obvious, given the institutional structure of *keiretsu* and relevant industrial organisation theory, that *keiretsu* represent an antitrust concern. If it is claimed that they do, the precise arguments need to be spelled out and examined carefully.

The firm's decision on how to contract for the supply of its inputs should be seen as an aspect of its normal market or competitive strategy, analogous to decisions about such things as the extent and nature of the product line, resources devoted to R&D, employment and human resources policy, advertising campaign and so on. Viewed in this light, much of the debate about *keiretsu* concerns the theory of the firm rather than antitrust economics. Each of the above decisions may have a critical impact on the long-term success of the firm — whether it attracts custom and expands its market share — but none would be seen as being anticompetitive or coming under the purview of traditional antitrust policy.

Long-term transactions

A frequently encountered argument, and one which perhaps represents the crux of the debate, is that *keiretsu* ties are exclusionary because they are based on long-term, preferential trading ties. It is commonly argued that access of foreign manufactured goods to the Japanese market is impeded because of the close trading ties that exist between firms.

At a casual level it is hard to disagree with this. If downstream firms have a policy of purchasing a certain input on a long-term basis from designated upstream suppliers, it will be difficult or perhaps impossible for outside suppliers to gain access to the market comprised of the potential purchases of those upstream firms. Upstream firms will appear to be favouring or giving preferential treatment to their traditional suppliers, leading to other suppliers being shut out of the market. As it stands, however, this kind of characterisation of the situation is not very informative as it begs important issues relating to the motivation for and true effects of such transactional ties. The purpose of this section is to examine critically the economic validity of the arguments about the prevalence of long-term transactional ties and market exclusion.

An important distinction needs to be drawn between whether *keiretsu* are exclusionary in a traditional antitrust sense (as part of a strategy to exercise market power) or in an economics of organisation sense (reflecting the contractual make-up of the firm). The relevant question is not 'are long-term trading ties exclusionary' but rather whether and in what ways the exclusion matters. Antitrust economics asks: does the exclusion associated with long-term contracting dampen competition and lead to the exercise or maintenance of monopoly power? The economics of organisation approach notes that long-term transactions reflect decisions by firms about how to contract for the supply of inputs or the disposal of output; it seeks to understand why transactions are organised as they are, giving rise to a particular mix of markets and hierarchies. It does not exclude from consideration the possibility of anticompetitive motivations for contractual arrangements or their anticompetitive effects, but it does not rely on these to explain the observed pattern of economic organisation.

It is instructive to consider the logic of the anticompetitive view of long-term transactions in the stylised setting of Figure 2.1, where the long-term and arm's-length trading examples can be thought of as characterising the situation prevailing in two countries. These countries, referred to as country J and country A, can be thought of respectively as Japan and the United States. A number of pertinent points can be made.

First, as noted earlier, as long as access to the final goods market remains open, the choice of vertical contracting arrangement — long-term contracts or reliance on the spot market — has no consequences for access to the final market. Firms' choices about how to organise their production or distribution systems do not alter the number of firms competing in the market and are not directly relevant to the demand side of the market. The issue is one of choice of organisational arrangement for procuring inputs.

Suppose that, as a result of contracting for inputs in a certain way, a downstream firm finds that it can obtain its inputs at lower cost than can its direct competitors — indeed, a working hypothesis in the economics of organisation is that firms always strive to organise themselves in a cost minimising fashion. Then, under the assumption that the final market is competitive, the firm's cost advantage will be translated into an expanded market share as it uses its cost advantage to cut prices and attract custom away from its competitors. It is quite possible that, indirectly, the firm's choice of contractual arrangement will have consequences for the outcome of competition in the final market. However, from an economics of organisation perspective, this occurs as part of a higher level competitive process which determines not just the equilibrium in final product markets, but also the mix of markets and hierarchies (or organisational configuration) in intermediate product markets.

The distinction between final and intermediate product markets is important. It might appear that, by their choice of organisational or contractual arrangement, downstream firms in country J have excluded upstream firms in country A from access to the parts supply market in their country. It might be felt that closing the market in this way is surely anticompetitive or in some sense unfair to suppliers in country A. This is precisely the form of argument that is prevalent in the debate over the degree of openness of the Japanese market.

A number of considerations suggest that the issue is more complex and subtle than this simple logic would imply. The first point is that a vertical tie between an upstream and a downstream firm does not in itself represent any exclusionary restriction on access of other parts suppliers to the relevant market, namely the final goods market. The procurement decision of the downstream firm in country J does not have a direct impact on the ability of upstream firms in country A to supply their product to the final market as an assembled part. To take an extreme example, if all downstream firms in all countries entered into long-term transactional ties with upstream firms, the intermediate market, represented by the parts purchases of all downstream firms (apart from the particular segment served under the long-term supply contract) would be closed to downstream firms. But the upstream firms would still have access to the final market through their supply relationships with their downstream parent companies and would be competing with one another via these relationships. Put in a slightly different way, if a downstream firm wanted to deny market access to downstream suppliers in country A, it could do so only to the market represented by its own purchasing decisions; it cannot influence the purchasing decisions of other downstream firms, in either country. The insight provided here by the economics of organisation is that there need be no presumption that a market for the upstream output exists in the way that a market for the downstream output does. Failure of the upstream output market to exist — reflecting decisions by firms about how to structure the supply of their inputs — does not imply a lack of competition or exclusion.

It is worth pursuing the alternative hypothesis suggested by an antitrust perspective on vertical *keiretsu* ties. When would the antitrust explanation have force? As noted earlier, for vertical arrangements of any kind to have anticompetitive consequences it must be that they lead to the exercise of market power, in this case, in either the downstream or the upstream output market. There are three possibilities in theory: monopsonisation of their input markets by downstream firms; monopolisation of their output market by upstream firms; and monopolisation of their output market by downstream firms.

Let us look at these three cases in turn. We put aside the contentious issue of *how* the vertical contract has the monopolising effect and simply assume that it does, in order to focus on the possible motivation and effect. A key point in the first two cases is that the interests of the upstream and downstream firms that enter into the long-term transactional relationship are diametrically opposed. In the first case, the aim of the downstream firm is to obtain monopsony power in the market for its inputs, which comes at the suppliers' (and also society's) expense. In the second case, the aim of the upstream firm is to gain monopoly power in the market for its output, with the result that the downstream firm suffers by paying a higher price for its inputs.

Notice that this antitrust analysis does not provide a convincing explanation. Consider the first case of a downstream monopsonist. For this strategy to work, the long-term transactional tie must be able to prevent the upstream firms from transacting with downstream firms other than the one to which it is tied, including firms in country A. This is because, if downstream firms gain monopsony power, upstream firms will be receiving a lower price for their output than at the competitive equilibrium; put simply, upstream firms would benefit by abandoning their long-term ties and supplying at a higher price to outside firms. The threat that they might do so would in turn presumably undermine the ability of the downstream firms to extract monopsony rents. Thus, on the grounds of pure economic logic, this particular antitrust explanation does not appear plausible.

In the second case of the upstream firms gaining monopoly power, the downstream firms in country J would be forced to pay a higher price for their inputs. Again we might ask why they would voluntarily give up the chance to procure inputs from outside firms when by doing so they subject themselves to the exercise of monopoly power. There is a further consideration in this case. When upstream firms behave as a monopolist, downstream firms pay more for their inputs. If the final market is competitive, and downstream firms in country A can obtain a competitive supply of inputs, then upstream firms in country J will be unable to compete in the final market and will lose market share. The attempt by upstream firms to extract monopoly rents in the supply of inputs to downstream firms will fail because, even if they obtain monopoly power in the intermediate market, they have no such monopoly power in the final market; in other words, these firms will suffer the same fate as a firm in a competitive market that tries to raise its price above the prevailing competitive level. Again the antitrust interpretation lacks plausibility.

Finally, consider the third case of an attempt by downstream firms to monopolise the final market through their input supply contracts. This corresponds to the case of vertical foreclosure analysed in the industrial organisation literature (see, for instance, Ordover, Saloner and Salop 1990; Salinger 1988; Spencer and Jones 1991). As argued earlier, vertical contracts cannot directly increase market power in a horizontal market; they can only do so indirectly, that is, by influencing some aspect of the competition in the market. 'Vertical foreclosure' refers to such a situation and works as follows. By entering into long-term supply contracts with upstream firms, downstream firms may be able to foreclose the final market to rival firms by denying them access to, or raising the costs of acquiring, needed inputs. For simplicity, consider the case of a downstream and an upstream firm in country J and in country A. Vertical foreclosure would involve the downstream firm in country J entering into a long-term contract with *both* upstream firms and using the control thus gained to deny the rival downstream firm access to the supply of the input. The rival's ability to compete in the final market would then be impeded; in other words, control of vertical supply becomes an (anti)competitive weapon in the final product market.

Notice that this explanation, while a theoretical possibility, does not fit well with the kinds of exclusionary argument raised in the US–Japan trade context. Japanese manufacturers are usually accused of restricting the access of foreign suppliers to their intermediate production systems, not of trying to take over rival makers' supply networks, which is what would be required for this antitrust explanation to have force. A commonly suggested solution to the perceived problems of access to the Japanese market is for Japanese firms to bring foreign suppliers into their supply networks. It is ironic that such behaviour would be more consistent with an antitrust view than the current alleged exclusionary policies.

The above discussion has proceeded on the premise that long-term contracts can be considered exclusionary, exploring the possible antitrust motivations and implications. This view needs to be examined carefully, however. In order to conceptualise long-term contracting, it is clear that a multiperiod model is required. For expository purposes, all that is required is a two-period model comprising, say, date 0, which can be termed the contracting period, and date 1, the implementation period. Within such a model, it is possible to talk meaningfully about long-term contracts or transactional ties, and to contrast them with a sequence of one-period spot market contracts. Suppose that the setting is one of contracting for input supply. A long-term contract would be one that involved firms making agreements covering date 1 supply at date 0; under period-by-period contracting, date 1 supply decisions would be made at date 1.

The analysis of long-term contracting is still in its relative infancy in economics, although it has been a rapidly developing area of microeconomic theory in recent years.[25] Nevertheless, a number of relevant observations can be made. First, for a long-term contract to be non-trivial it must differ in some way from a series of spot market contracts. It must be possible for the parties to a long-term contract to achieve an outcome that differs from what would be achievable under spot market conditions. Second, when two parties engage in a long-term contract — which by definition is an agreement to restrict their behaviour in some non-trivial way — they must do so because they expect to be better off. Thus explanations of vertical contracts as mechanisms through which one party exploits another — as in the first two cases examined above — lack a convincing basis in economic theory. The antitrust concern about vertical contracts is that the contract will be detrimental to third parties, such as in the third case discussed above. The general lesson, then, is that vertical (or any) contracts will improve the welfare of the contracting parties relative to their reservation utilities at the contracting date, but may have detrimental effects on other parties. If antitrust policy has a role it is because of this last possibility.

This way of looking at long-term contracting provides an insight into the exclusion issue. Suppose that the long-term contract involves an agreement for an upstream firm to supply its output to a downstream firm, and correspondingly for the downstream firm to buy its input from the upstream firm. Viewed at the implementation period, the long-term contract is indeed exclusionary in the sense that, if the contract is enforceable, the two parties cannot trade with parties outside the relationship. But this sense of 'exclusionary' is almost the definition of a long-term contract, in involving the ability to commit in advance to behave in certain ways in the future.

The key issue economically is whether the arrangement is exclusionary at date 0, the contracting stage. Where long-term supply relations prevail, as they do in Japan, foreign firms wishing to supply to intermediate product markets should not expect to have instant access; they are likely to find themselves excluded from immediate entry because of past supply commitments. The market access issue turns on whether foreign suppliers are able to compete on an equal footing with Japanese suppliers when it comes to the renewal of long-term contracts or entering into of new ones. We might term exclusion because of the effects of previous long-term contracts 'second-order exclusion' and exclusion from being able even to compete to supply under long-term contracting 'first-order exclusion'. The distinction, often glossed over in popular discussions, is a critical one analytically.

Are Japanese supply networks exclusionary in a first-order sense? This is a difficult issue on which to garner empirical evidence. For instance, if foreign suppliers fail to gain access over time this could be evidence of first-order exclusion, but it might also indicate that foreign suppliers are unwilling or unable to compete with local Japanese suppliers. Economic theory offers some guidance on this question.

First, note that downstream firms in country J are not in competition with upstream firms in country A; rather, the latter are in competition with upstream firms in country J. First-order exclusion by downstream firms in country J would be tantamount to shielding upstream firms permanently from competition. This is hardly likely to be in the downstream firm's interests as it will wish to subject its suppliers, periodically at least, to the severest possible potential competitive pressure. Suppose that the downstream firm permanently shielded upstream suppliers from the threat of external competitive pressure. It would then in effect be giving up most, if not all, of its bargaining power over its suppliers, as it would not have a credible threat of contract termination.

It is important to realise that fierce competition and second-order exclusion are quite consistent with one another in the two-period characterisation of long-term transacting. Competition (and potential access) occurs in the first period; in the second period, other firms' access is limited precisely because there is a long-term contract. The issue is not whether competition exists, but rather the stage at which competition is injected into the relationship: period by period, as in a spot market world, or at the beginning of a multiperiod interaction, as in the long-term contracting world.

What is the reason for the prevalence of long-term ties among Japanese firms and how are their apparently exclusionary aspects to be understood, if antitrust theories do not seem to provide adequate explanations? Recent literature on the Japanese firm, and in economics more generally, suggests a number of motivations, centring on the role that repeated dealing and long-term contracts play in facilitating efficiency enhancing transactions in a world of non-trivial transaction costs (see, for example, Aoki 1988; Asanuma 1989; Flath 1995; Itoh 1992; Sheard 1989, 1991b). Without attempting an exhaustive survey, some key ideas can be noted. One is that, because long-term contracts reduce information differences among contracting parties and enhance the credibility of promises to make future contingent payments, they facilitate the sharing of risks. A second is that, by facilitating the making of credible commitments that curb opportunistic behaviour, long-term contracts can provide incentives for transacting parties to make valuable specific investments. Many long-term transactional relations in Japan can be viewed in this way: workers making firm-specific investments in human capital in the context of lifetime employment guarantees; suppliers making specific investments in physical or organisational capital in order to supply inputs to particular purchasers; main banks expending resources to accumulate customer-specific information and information processing capacity.

Commitment is the essential ingredient in long-term contracting. As noted earlier, a long-term contract deserves to be identified as such because it allows the transacting parties to limit the realm of their future possible actions in a way that is mutually beneficial. To use an example based on the lifetime employment system, in a world where accumulation of specific or idiosyncratic skills has value, an employee and a firm may both benefit if the employee commits to staying with the firm and the firm commits to not discharging the employee prematurely. The firm will then find it profitable to make costly investments in firm-specific training or to limit the amount of monitoring that it does, while sufficient future income will be assured for the worker to limit his/her mobility, bear part of the cost of investing in human capital, and work hard despite not being monitored as intensely.

What constitutes a commitment, and therefore what allows long-term contracting to take place in a Williamsonian world of costly transacting, imperfect information, bounded rationality and opportunistic behaviour, is a subtle and complex issue. A key point, though, is that commitment and exclusion are two sides of the same coin in this context. A commitment to honour a long-term contract is a promise to exclude certain actions as possibilities, for example, not to abandon the transacting party for another or to use the threat of doing so to extract a better bargain. Thus exclusion goes hand in hand with commitment in long-term contracting and enhances the efficiency of organising economic transactions. In short, the kind of exclusionary behaviour associated with Japanese *keiretsu* ties may be of quite a different kind from that connoted by the language and logic of antitrust.

Conclusion

This chapter has examined the various arguments associating *keiretsu* business structures with anticompetitive and exclusionary behaviour in light of the relevant conceptual frameworks in industrial organisation. It has argued that the antitrust focus is misplaced and that an economics of organisation perspective — viewing *keiretsu* as reflecting the endogenous aspects of firm and market organisation — is more informative. *Keiretsu* are frequently described as being cartel-like, but in fact they have nothing to do with cartels as that term is usually used in antitrust economics. Cartels involve agreements among rival firms operating in the same market, whereas *keiretsu* involve vertical ties between firms in input–output relations. A downstream firm (such as Toyota) may purchase its inputs from an upstream firm (such as Nippon Densō) on a long-term or what appears to be a preferential basis. But this reflects a business decision between two firms about the sourcing of inputs and the dedication of production facilities, and is no more cartel-like than are the transactions between the upstream and downstream units of a vertically integrated firm.

Keiretsu are better understood from the business strategy than from the antitrust or trade policy perspective (Spulber 1992). If *keiretsu* are exclusionary it is because they offer benefits to the transacting partners, and in vertical production chains these can only come from lowered costs — it is the logic of repeated transactions and long-term contracting, not antitrust, that applies. If *keiretsu* present a problem for market access, it is in the sense that intermediate product markets, including markets for distribution inputs, do not exist independently of the way in which firms have decided to locate their boundaries and organise their transactions. The barriers that arise when upstream and downstream firms engage in long-term transactions are analogous to (although arguably much weaker than) the ones that exist when firms are vertically integrated; they bear only a superficial resemblance to the barriers to trade that are erected or induced by government fiat and regulation. They do not keep potential transaction partners from realising mutually beneficial gains from trade, as do government erected tariff and non-tariff barriers, but rather reflect the bargains that private sector agents have struck in striving to capture such gains.

Several recent contributors to the debate have argued that more microlevel investigations of *keiretsu* organisational forms and transactions are needed, and

Japanese agencies, responding to US pressure, have begun such field studies of their own (Noland 1991b, p. 47; Srinivasan 1991, p. 95). A message of this chapter is that this kind of case study work, while having the potential to supply much of what is missing from aggregate quantitative work, should be carefully guided by the insights that economic theories of industrial and business organisation have to offer.

Notes

1. The literature on *keiretsu* and market closure spans several disciplines, notably economics and political science, and is located in the wider debate about Japanese trade and economic structure. A selective list of important contributions includes the collections of papers in Krugman (1991), Yamamura (1990a) and particularly Yamamura (1990b), as well as Gerlach (1989), Johnson (1987), Lawrence (1991a) and Sheard (1991a).
2. There is a fifth view that sees the existence of a quasi-conspiratorial alliance between business and government aimed at discriminating against foreign market access, but since the focus here is on business organisation, extensive discussion of the government's role is not attempted. See Johnson (1990a, 1990b) and Tyson and Zysman (1989a).
3. For a discussion of these views see, for instance, Johnson (1990a, pp. 119–20), Friedman and Lebard (1991, pp. 379–80) and Nakatani (1991).
4. The chapter focuses on product market links. For analyses that overlap somewhat with the perspective developed here, see Asanuma (1991), Haley (1990), Imai (1990), Miwa (1991), Sheard (1991a, 1996) and Yoshitomi (1991). The issue of financial organisation and predatory behaviour raises a somewhat different set of issues and requires separate treatment. See Sheard (1992, 1996) for a discussion of this question.
5. Recent developments in industrial organisation are surveyed in Schmalensee and Willig (1989) and Tirole (1988). Key surveys of the modern theory of the firm and economics of organisation include Holmstrom and Tirole (1989), Milgrom and Roberts (1990a, 1992) and Williamson (1985). Relevant works on the Japanese firm include Aoki (1988, 1989), Aoki and Dore (1994), Imai and Komiya (1994) and Imai and Itami (1985).
6. For valuable contributions by non-economists, see Gerlach (1991) and Okimoto (1987).
7. Among the researchers who take this view are Abegglen and Stalk (1985).
8. Excluding financial institutions, the number of member firms of the six presidents' clubs as of 1991 were as follows: Mitsui, 22; Mitsubishi, 25; Sumitomo, 16; Fuji (Fuyō), 25; Sanwa, 41; Daiichi Kangyō, 42 (unadjusted total, 171) (Tōyō Keizai Shinpōsha 1991, p. 50). The corresponding number of listed firms classified as affiliated with the same six groups as of 1989 was: Mitsui, 106; Mitsubishi, 124; Sumitomo, 107; Fuji, 111; Sanwa, 58; Daiichi Kangyō, 81 (total, 587) (Keizai

Chōsa Kyōkai 1990, p. i). These two classifications correspond roughly to categories 1 and 2 in the text.

9 As Lincoln (1990, pp. 5–6) put it: 'The American criticism of Japan is basically an antitrust view ... The problems, then, stem from the conviction that in many cases market outcomes are shaped by Japanese business practices considered unfair — predatory pricing, patent infringement, industrial espionage, and explicit or implicit protection of Japanese markets from import competition'.

10 Technically, it was not possible to derive a result that corresponded to predatory pricing as an equilibrium in a well-specified game theory model. For recent developments, see Milgrom and Roberts (1990b), Tirole (1988, Ch. 9) and Ordover and Saloner (1989, pp. 545–62).

11 The economic foundations of antitrust law and policy have come under heavy attack in the past decade and a half from both legal scholars and economists, particularly those associated with the school of thought popularly known as the 'Chicago school'. See Armentano (1982), Brozen (1982), Demsetz (1989), Kwoka and White (1989), Mathewson and Winter (1985), Posner (1976) and, for a recent accessible critical survey, Demsetz (1992).

12 The first and third correspond roughly to Lawrence's (1991a, p. 314) 'benign neglect' and 'trust busting' positions; the second is closer to his 'dilemma' position.

13 For a precise statement, see in particular Jensen and Meckling (1976, p. 311) and Fama (1980, p. 290).

14 The number of sellers (being firms) is usually an order of magnitude less than the number of buyers, and if small enough the market may not be competitive. The exercise of market power by sellers in such a case, however, tends to invite new entry or chiselling on collusive agreements by existing firms. For a review of the literature on the relationship between market structure, form of competition and collusion, see Tirole (1988, Chs 5–6) and Shapiro (1989).

15 A point not clarified in the literature is that the principal focus of attention in the Coase–Williamson paradigm is how *intermediate* transactions are organised. The issue is how economic agents cooperating in the production process structure their transactions, rather than whether transactions between firms that produce final consumption goods and the individual consumers of those goods are organised in markets or hierarchies; in a market economy the final transaction governance structure is in general a market. Use of the term 'markets and hierarchies' tends to cloud the fact that it is intermediate product markets, not the final consumption goods, whose organisation is taken as being endogenous, that is, to be explained within the context of the research agenda.

16 For an application of this kind of approach to the analysis of supplier systems in the Japanese automobile industry, see Asanuma (1985a, 1985b).

17 The case of supplier systems, particularly in the automobile industry, has been a focus of US–Japan comparisons in academic studies and a key market access issue in the context of US–Japan trade negotiations. This has motivated its extensive use in this chapter as an illustrative example. See Asanuma (1992), Dyer (1993), McMillan (1990), Minato (1989) and Roehl (1989).

18 There is a further position, not explored explicitly in this chapter, relating to the implications of *keiretsu* for the compatibility of interacting economic systems. This goes somewhat beyond questions of whether *keiretsu* ties are anticompetitive or contribute to the competitive strength of Japanese firms. For a discussion see Aoki (1994); for a theoretical analysis refer to Aoki (1993).

19 A third possibility is to examine real world transactions at a case study level. This can be instructive, but economists are generally sceptical of evidence uncovered in this way. Problems include bias in sample selection and interpretation, and the difficulty of generalising from small samples and of second guessing the motives behind business people's decisions.

20 But see the reviews by Bergsten and Noland (1993), Lawrence (1991b, 1993), Frankel (1991), Gotō (1991), Saxonhouse (1993) and Takeuchi (1989), and comments by Saxonhouse (1991a, 1991b).

21 For a more technical critique of trade related studies, see Srinivasan and Hamada (1991).

22 Weinstein and Yafeh (1993) present some interesting evidence consistent with the latter view.

23 Models of tacit collusion under multimarket contact, developed for the case of multiproduct oligopolists, come closest to being applicable to the intermarket structure of (categories 1 and 2) *keiretsu* (Tirole 1988, p. 251). Lawrence (1993, p. 15) raises the possibility that *keiretsu* facilitate collusion because of multimarket effects. But these models presume that firms in different markets function as a single decision making unit, whereas in reality firms affiliated with *keiretsu* are separate, independent corporations often having only quite loose connections with other firms. For the multimarket collusion story to hold, there would need to be a centralised decision making locus that coordinated and enforced the threat of retaliation towards individual firms deviating from monopoly pricing. A *theoretical* possibility is that the common main bank could perform this role; but this is tantamount to assuming that the banks control borrowing firms' decisions on the product market (pricing and output), which strains the limits of credulity. See Sheard (1996) for further discussion on this point.

24 This insight is a critical one and plays a central role in the literature on vertical restraints. Monopoly pricing at successive stages of production of a good, that is, in a series of vertically related markets, causes the final market price to be too high compared with the price that a monopolist receiving its inputs at undistorted prices would charge. The vertically linked firms could do better collectively by charging a lower final market price (the increased sales would more than compensate for the lower margin) and using lump sum transfers (franchises, licences or other entry fees) to induce participation. Vertical restraints, in the presence of such a chain of monopolies, can achieve this end by eliminating this so-called 'double marginalisation' problem and the distortion in production efficiency associated with substitution away from the optimal input mix when monopoly pricing falls on intermediate inputs rather than the final good. For a review and references to the literature, see Tirole (1988, Ch. 4).

25 For a survey, see Hart and Holmstrom (1987); for a theoretical investigation of the conditions necessary for a long-term contract to differ from a series of short-term contracts, see Fudenberg, Holmstrom and Milgrom (1990). Much of the recent work attempts to develop theoretical underpinnings for Williamson's (1985, Chs 7–8, for example) analysis of hold-up problems associated with specific investments; see, for example, Chung (1991).

References

Abegglen, James C. and George Stalk, Jr. (1985), *Kaisha, The Japanese Corporation*, Tokyo: Charles E. Tuttle.

Ando, Albert and Alan Auerbach (1988), 'The Cost of Capital in the U.S. and Japan: A Comparison', *Journal of the Japanese and International Economies*, 2, pp. 134–58.

—— (1990), 'The Cost of Capital in Japan: Recent Evidence and Further Results', *Journal of the Japanese and International Economies*, 4 (4), pp. 323–50.

Aoki, Masahiko (1988), *Incentives, Information, and Bargaining in the Japanese Economy*, Cambridge, MA: Cambridge University Press.

—— (1989), 'The Nature of the Japanese Firm as a Nexus of Employment and Financial Contracts: An Overview', *Journal of the Japanese and International Economies*, 3, pp. 345–66.

—— (1993), Comparative Advantage of Organizational Conventions and Gains from Diversity: Evolutionary Game Approach, Unpublished paper, Stanford University, Palo Alto.

—— (1994), 'The Japanese Firm as a System of Attributes: A Survey and Research Agenda', in Masahiko Aoki and Ronald Dore (eds), *The Japanese Firm: The Sources of Competitive Strength*, Oxford: Clarendon Press, pp. 11–40.

Aoki, Masahiko and Ronald Dore (eds) (1994), *The Japanese Firm: The Sources of Competitive Strength*, Oxford: Clarendon Press.

Ariga, Kenn, Yasushi Ohkusa and Hisashi Namikawa (1991), 'The Japanese Distribution System', *Ricerche Economiche*, 45 (2–3), pp. 185–230.

Armentano, D.T. (1982), *Antitrust and Monopoly: Anatomy of a Policy Failure*, New York, NY: Basic Books.

Asanuma, Banri (1985a), 'The Organization of Parts Purchases in the Japanese Automotive Industry', *Japanese Economic Studies*, 13 (4), pp. 32–53.

—— (1985b), 'The Contractual Framework for Parts Supply in the Japanese Automotive Industry', *Japanese Economic Studies*, 13 (4), pp. 54–78.

—— (1989), 'Manufacturer–Supplier Relationships in Japan and the Concept of Relation-Specific Skill', *Journal of the Japanese and International Economies*, 3, pp. 1–30.

—— (1991), Interfirm Relationships in Japanese Manufacturing Industry, Unpublished paper, Kyoto University, Kyoto.

—— (1992), 'Japanese Manufacturer–Supplier Relationships in International Perspective: The Automobile Case', in Paul Sheard (ed.), *International Adjustment and the Japanese Firm*, Sydney: Allen and Unwin, pp. 99–124.

Bergsten, C. Fred and Marcus Noland (1993), *Reconcilable Differences? United States–Japan Economic Conflict*, Washington DC: Institute for International Economics.

Brozen, Y. (1982), *Concentration, Mergers, and Public Policy*, New York, NY: Macmillan.

Chung, Tai-Yeong (1991), 'Incomplete Contracts, Specific Investments, and Risk Sharing', *Review of Economic Studies*, 58, pp. 1,031–42.

Coase, Ronald H. (1937), 'The Nature of the Firm', *Economica*, 4, pp. 386–405.

Dam, Kenneth W. (1970), *The GATT: Law and International Organization*, Chicago, IL: University of Chicago Press.

Demsetz, Harold (1982), 'Barriers to Entry', *American Economic Review*, 72, pp. 47–57.

—— (1989), *Efficiency, Competition, and Policy: The Organization of Economic Activity, Volume II*, Oxford: Basil Blackwell.

—— (1992), 'How Many Cheers for Antitrust's 100 Years?', *Economic Inquiry*, 30, pp. 207–17.

Dore, Ronald (1986), *Flexible Rigidities: Industrial Policy and Structural Adjustment in the Japanese Economy 1970–80*, Stanford, CA: Stanford University Press.

Dyer, Jeffrey H. (1993), The Japanese Vertical *Keiretsu* as a Source of Competitive Advantage, University of Pennsylvania, Philadelphia (mimeo).

Fama, Eugene F. (1980), 'Agency Problems and the Theory of the Firm', *Journal of Political Economy*, 88 (2), pp. 288–307.

Flath, David (1995), 'The *Keiretsu* Puzzle', *Journal of the Japanese and International Economies* (in press).

Frankel, Jeffrey A. (1991), 'Japanese Finance in the 1980s: A Survey', in Paul Krugman (ed.), *Trade with Japan: Has the Door Opened Wider?*, Chicago, IL: University of Chicago Press, pp. 225–68.

Friedman, George and Meredith Lebard (1991), *The Coming War with Japan*, New York, NY: St. Martin's Press.

Fudenberg, Drew, Bengt Holmstrom and Paul Milgrom (1990), 'Short-Term Contracts and Long-Term Agency Relationships', *Journal of Economic Theory*, 51, pp. 1–31.

Fung, K.C. (1991), 'Characteristics of Japanese Industrial Groups and Their Potential Impact on U.S.–Japan Trade', in Robert Baldwin (ed.), *Empirical Studies of Commercial Policy*, Chicago, IL: University of Chicago Press, pp. 137–68.

Gerlach, Michael L. (1989), '*Keiretsu* Organization in the Japanese Economy: Analysis and Trade Implications', in Chalmers Johnson, Laura D'Andrea Tyson and John Zysman (eds), *Politics and Productivity: The Real Story of Why Japan Works*, Cambridge, MA: Ballinger Publishing Company, pp. 141–74.

—— (1991), 'Twilight of the *Keiretsu*? A Critical Assessment', *Journal of Japanese Studies*, 18 (1), pp. 79–118.

Gilbert, Richard J. (1989a), 'Mobility Barriers and the Value of Incumbency', in Richard Schmalensee and Robert D. Willig (eds), *Handbook of Industrial Organization, Volume I*, Amsterdam: North-Holland, pp. 475–535.

—— (1989b), 'The Role of Potential Competition in Industrial Organization', *Journal of Economic Perspectives*, 3 (3), pp. 107–27.

Gotō, Fumihiro (1991), 'Is the Japanese Market Really Closed? A Critical Review of the Economic Studies', *Studies in International Trade and Industry*, 8, Ministry of International Trade and Industry Research Institute, Tokyo.

Haley, John O. (1990), 'Weak Law, Strong Competition, and Trade Barriers: Competitiveness as a Disincentive to Foreign Entry into Japanese Markets', in Kōzō Yamamura (ed.), *Japan's Economic Structure: Should It Change?*, Seattle, WA: Society for Japanese Studies, pp. 203–35.

Hart, Oliver and Bengt Holmstrom (1987), 'The Theory of Contracts', in Truman F. Bewley (ed.), *Advances in Economic Theory: Fifth World Congress*, Cambridge, MA: Cambridge University Press, pp. 71–155.

Hodder, James (1991a), 'Is the Cost of Capital Lower in Japan?', *Journal of the Japanese and International Economies*, 5 (1), pp. 86–100.

—— (1991b), 'The Cost of Capital for Industrial Firms in the U.S. and Japan', in William T. Ziemba, Warren Bailey and Yasushi Hamao (eds), *Japanese Financial Market Research*, Amsterdam: North-Holland, pp. 571–93.

Holmstrom, Bengt and Jean Tirole (1989), 'The Theory of the Firm', in Richard Schmalensee and Robert D. Willig (eds), *Handbook of Industrial Organization, Volume I*, Amsterdam: North-Holland, pp. 61–133.

Imai, Ken'ichi (1990), 'Japanese Business Groups and the Structural Impediments Initiative', in Kōzō Yamamura (ed.), *Japan's Economic Structure: Should It Change?*, Seattle, WA: Society for Japanese Studies, pp. 167–202.

Imai, Ken'ichi and Hiroyuki Itami (1985), 'Interpenetration of Organization and Market: Japan's Firm and Market in Comparison with the U.S.', *International Journal of Industrial Organization*, 2, pp. 285–310.

Imai, Ken'ichi and Ryūtarō Komiya (eds) (1994), *Business Enterprise in Japan: Views of Leading Japanese Economists*, Cambridge, MA: MIT Press (translation of *Nihon no Kigyō*, Tokyo: University of Tokyo Press, 1989).

Ito, Takatoshi and Masayoshi Maruyama (1991), 'Is the Japanese Distribution System Really Inefficient?', in Paul Krugman (ed.), *Trade with Japan: Has the Door Opened Wider?*, Chicago, IL: University of Chicago Press, pp. 149–73.

Itoh, Motoshige (1992), 'Organisational Transactions and Access to the Japanese Import Market', in Paul Sheard (ed.), *International Adjustment and the Japanese Firm*, Sydney: Allen and Unwin, pp. 50–71.

Jacquemin, Alexis and Margaret E. Slade (1989), 'Cartels, Collusion, and Horizontal Merger', in Richard Schmalensee and Robert D. Willig (eds), *Handbook of Industrial Organization, Volume I*, Amsterdam: North-Holland, pp. 415–73.

Jensen, Michael C. and William H. Meckling, (1976), 'Theory of the Firm: Managerial Behavior, Agency Costs and Ownership Structure', *Journal of Financial Economics*, 3, pp. 305–60.

Johnson, Chalmers (1987), 'How to Think about Economic Competition from Japan', in Kenneth B. Pyle (ed.), *The Trade Crisis: How Will Japan Respond?*, Seattle, WA: Society for Japanese Studies, pp. 71–83.

—— (1990a), 'Trade, Revisionism, and the Future of Japanese–American Relations', in Kōzō Yamamura (ed.), *Japan's Economic Structure: Should It Change?*, Seattle, WA: Society for Japanese Studies, pp. 105–36.

—— (1990b), '*Keiretsu*: An Outsider's View', *International Economic Insights*, 1 (2), pp. 15–17.

Journal of Economic Perspectives (1987), 'Symposium on Mergers and Antitrust', 1 (2), pp. 3–54.

Kawasaki, Seiichi and John McMillan (1987), 'The Design of Contracts: Evidence from Japanese Subcontracting', *Journal of the Japanese and International Economies*, 1, pp. 327–49.

Keizai Chōsa Kyōkai (1990), *Nenpō 'Keiretsu no Kenkyū' Daisanjūichishū (1991 Nen): Daiichibu Jōjō Kigyōhen* [Corporate Affiliation Research Annual, Number 31 (1991): First-Section Listed Firm Edition], Tokyo: Keizai Chōsa Kyōkai.

Komiya, Ryūtarō and Kazutomo Irie (1990), 'The U.S.–Japan Trade Problem: An Economic Analysis from a Japanese Viewpoint', in Kōzō Yamamura (ed.), *Japan's Economic Structure: Should It Change?*, Seattle, WA: Society for Japanese Studies, pp. 65–104.

Kreps, David M. (1990), *A Course in Microeconomic Theory*, Princeton, NJ: Princeton University Press.

Krugman, Paul (ed.) (1991), *Trade with Japan: Has the Door Opened Wider?*, Chicago, IL: University of Chicago Press.

Kwoka, J.E. and L.J. White (eds) (1989), *The Antitrust Revolution*, Glenview, IL: Scott, Foresman.

Lawrence, Robert Z. (1987), 'Imports in Japan: Closed Markets or Minds?', *Brookings Papers on Economic Activity*, 2, pp. 517–52.

—— (1991a), 'Efficient or Exclusionist? The Import Behavior of Japanese Corporate Groups', *Brookings Papers on Economic Activity*, 1, pp. 311–41.

—— (1991b), 'How Open Is Japan?', in Paul Krugman (ed.), *Trade with Japan: Has the Door Opened Wider?*, Chicago, IL: University of Chicago Press, pp. 9–37.

—— (1993), 'Japan's Different Trade Regime: An Analysis with Reference to *Keiretsu*', *Journal of Economic Perspectives*, 7 (3), pp. 3–19.

Leamer, Edward E. (1988), 'Measures of Openness', in Robert E. Baldwin (ed.), *Trade Policy Issues and Empirical Analysis*, Chicago, IL: University of Chicago Press, pp. 147–200.

Lincoln, Edward J. (1990), *Japan's Unequal Trade*, Washington DC: The Brookings Institution.

Marston, Richard C. (1991), 'Price Behavior in Japanese and U.S. Manufacturing', in Paul Krugman (ed.), *Trade with Japan: Has the Door Opened Wider?*, Chicago, IL: University of Chicago Press, pp. 121–41.

Mathewson, G.F. and R. Winter (1985), *Competition Policy and Vertical Exchange*, Toronto: University of Toronto Press.

McMillan, John (1990), 'Managing Suppliers: Incentive Systems in Japan and the U.S.', *California Management Review*, 32 (4), pp. 38–55.

Milgrom, Paul and John Roberts (1990a), 'Bargaining Costs, Influence Costs, and the Organization of Economic Activity', in James E. Alt and Kenneth A. Shepsle (eds), *Perspectives on Positive Political Economy*, Cambridge, MA: Cambridge University Press, pp. 57–89.

—— (1990b), 'New Theories of Predatory Pricing', in Giacomo Bonanno and Dario Brandolini (eds), *Industrial Structure in the New Industrial Economics*, Oxford: Clarendon Press, pp. 112–37.

—— (1992), *Economics, Organization and Management*, Englewood Cliffs, NJ: Prentice Hall.

Minato, Tetsuo (1989), 'A Comparison of Japanese and American Interfirm Production Systems', in Kichiro Hayashi (ed.), *The U.S.–Japanese Economic Relationship: Can It Be Improved?*, New York, NY: New York University Press, pp. 87–122.

Miwa, Yoshiro (1991), '*Keiretsu* Trades and Product Imports', Discussion Paper 91-F-2, Faculty of Economics, University of Tokyo, Tokyo.

Nakatani, Iwao (1991), 'The Nature of "Imbalance" between the US and Japan', *Proceedings of Seventh Biennial Conference of Japanese Association of Australia, Volume 1, Japan and the World*, Canberra: Australia–Japan Research Centre, Australian National University, pp. 1–7.

Nishimura, Kiyohiko G. (1991), 'The Distribution System of Japan and the United States: A Comparative Study from the Viewpoint of Consumers', Discussion Paper 91-F-10, Faculty of Economics, University of Tokyo, Tokyo.

Noland, Marcus (1991a), Public Policy, Private Preferences, and the Japanese Trade Pattern, Unpublished paper, Johns Hopkins University, Washington DC.

—— (1991b), 'Comment', in Paul Krugman (ed.), *Trade with Japan: Has the Door Opened Wider?*, Chicago, IL: University of Chicago Press, pp. 46–9.

Ohno, Ken'ichi (1989), 'Export Pricing Behavior of Manufacturing: A U.S.–Japan Comparison', *IMF Staff Papers*, 36 (3), pp. 550–79.

Okimoto, Daniel I. (1987), 'Outsider Trading: Coping with Japanese Industrial Organization', in Kenneth B. Pyle (ed.), *The Trade Crisis: How Will Japan Respond?*, Seattle, WA: Society for Japanese Studies, pp. 85–116.

Ordover, Janusz A. and Garth Saloner (1989), 'Predation, Monopolization, and Antitrust', in Richard Schmalensee and Robert D. Willig (eds), *Handbook of Industrial Organization, Volume I*, Amsterdam: North-Holland, pp. 537–96.

Ordover, Janusz A., Garth Saloner and Steven C. Salop (1990), 'Equilibrium Vertical Foreclosure', *American Economic Review*, 80 (1), pp. 127–42.

Posner, Richard (1976), *Antitrust Law: An Economic Perspective*, Chicago, IL: University of Chicago Press.

Roehl, Thomas (1989), 'A Comparison of U.S.–Japanese Firms' Parts-Supply Systems: What besides Nationality Matters?', in Kichiro Hayashi (ed.), *The U.S.–Japanese Economic Relationship: Can It Be Improved?*, New York, NY: New York University Press, pp. 127–54.

Salinger, Michael A. (1988), 'Vertical Mergers and Market Foreclosure', *Quarterly Journal of Economics*, 103, pp. 345–56.

Saxonhouse, Gary (1986), 'What's Wrong with Japanese Trade Structure?', *Pacific Economic Papers*, 137, Australia–Japan Research Centre, Australian National University, Canberra, pp. 1–36.

—— (1989), 'Differentiated Products, Economies of Scale, and Access to the Japanese Market', in Robert C. Feenstra (ed.), *Trade Policies for International Competitiveness*, Cambridge, MA: National Bureau of Economic Research, pp. 145–74.

—— (1991a), 'Comments and Discussion', *Brookings Papers on Economic Activity*, 1, pp. 331–6.

—— (1991b), 'Comment', in Paul Krugman (ed.), *Trade with Japan: Has the Door Opened Wider?*, Chicago, IL: University of Chicago Press, pp. 38–46.

—— (1993), 'What Does Japanese Trade Structure Tell Us about Japanese Trade Policy?', *Journal of Economic Perspectives*, 7 (3), pp. 21–43.

Schmalensee, Richard and Robert D. Willig (eds) (1989), *Handbook of Industrial Organization, Volumes I and II*, Amsterdam: North-Holland.

Shapiro, Carl (1989), 'Theories of Oligopoly Behavior', in Richard Schmalensee and Robert D. Willig (eds), *Handbook of Industrial Organization, Volume I*, Amsterdam: North-Holland, pp. 329–414.

Sheard, Paul (1989), 'The Japanese General Trading Company as an Aspect of Interfirm Risk-Sharing', *Journal of the Japanese and International Economies*, 3 (3), pp. 308–22.

—— (1991a), 'The Economics of Japanese Corporate Organization and the "Structural Impediments" Debate: A Critical Review', *Japanese Economic Studies*, 19 (4), pp. 30–78.

—— (1991b), 'The Economics of Interlocking Shareholding in Japan', *Ricerche Economiche*, 45 (2–3), pp. 421–48.

—— (1992), '*Keiretsu* and Closedness of the Japanese Market: An Economic Appraisal', Discussion Paper No. 273, Institute of Social and Economic Research, Osaka University, Osaka.

—— (1996), '*Keiretsu*, Competition, and Market Access', in Edward M. Graham and J. David Richardson (eds), *Global Competition Policies*, Washington DC: Institute for International Economics (forthcoming).

Spencer, Barbara J. and Ronald W. Jones (1991), 'Vertical Foreclosure and International Trade Policy', *Review of Economic Studies*, 58 (1), pp. 153–70.

Spulber, Daniel F. (1992), 'Economic Analysis and Management Strategy: A Survey', *Journal of Economics & Management Strategy*, 1 (3), pp. 535–74.

Srinivasan, T.N. (1991), 'Comment', *Proceedings of the Eighth ERI International Symposium, External Imbalance, Intra-Industry Trade, and Keiretsu, Part 2: Discussions*, Tokyo: Economic Planning Agency, pp. 92–7.

Srinivasan, T.N. and Koichi Hamada (1991), The U.S.–Japan Trade Problem, Unpublished paper, Yale University, New Haven.

Takeuchi, Kenji (1989), 'Does Japan Import Less than It Should? A Review of the Econometric Literature', *Asian Economic Journal*, September, pp. 138–70.

Tirole, Jean (1988), *The Theory of Industrial Organization*, Cambridge, MA: MIT Press.

Tōyō Keizai Shinpōsha (1991), *Kigyō Keiretsu Sōran 1992 Nenban* [Directory of Corporate Affiliations, 1992 Edition], Tokyo: Tōyō Keizai Shinpōsha.

Tyson, Laura D'Andrea and John Zysman (1989a), 'Development Strategy and Production Innovation in Japan', in Chalmers Johnson, Laura D'Andrea Tyson and John Zysman (eds), *Politics and Productivity: The Real Story of Why Japan Works*, Cambridge, MA: Ballinger Publishing Company, pp. 59–140.

—— (1989b), 'Preface: The Argument Outlined', in Chalmers Johnson, Laura D'Andrea Tyson and John Zysman (eds), *Politics and Productivity: The Real Story of Why Japan Works*, Cambridge, MA: Ballinger Publishing Company, pp. xiii-xxi.

Weinstein, David and Yishay Yafeh (1993), 'Japan's Corporate Groups: Collusive or Competitive? An Empirical Investigation of *Keiretsu* Behavior', Harvard Institute of Economic Research Discussion Paper No. 1623, Harvard University, Boston.

Williamson, Oliver E. (1981), 'The Modern Corporation: Origins, Evolution, Attributes', *Journal of Economic Literature*, 19 (4), pp. 1,537–68.

—— (1985), *The Economic Institutions of Capitalism*, New York, NY: The Free Press.

Yamamura, Kōzō (ed.) (1990a), *Japan's Economic Structure: Should It Change?*, Seattle, WA: Society for Japanese Studies.

—— (1990b), 'Will Japan's Economic Structure Change? Confessions of a Former Optimist', in Kōzō Yamamura (ed.), *Japan's Economic Structure: Should It Change?*, Seattle, WA: Society for Japanese Studies, pp. 13–64.

Yoshitomi, Masaru (1991), Economic Functions of *Keiretsu* (Business Groups) in Japan, Unpublished paper, Economic Planning Agency, Tokyo.

3 Price formation and the structure of the distribution system

Kenn Ariga and Yasushi Ohkusa*

To many observers, the mosaic of small firms comprising the Japanese distribution system resembles an impenetrable mass. Inefficiencies, irrational behaviour and rent seeking activities seem to abound. Even now, retailers with only one or two full-time workers (shopkeepers) comprise more than 50 per cent of all retail shops in Japan, 21 per cent of employment and 11 per cent of gross sales. In the narrow streets of Tokyo, or any other large city, small retail shops are densely distributed. Such shops on average register sales of only about ¥20 million (US$230,000) per year, receiving roughly ¥7 million (US$80,000) as the gross margin. It is quite puzzling to find such shops sitting on pieces of land which often cost more than ¥10 million (US$120,000) per *tsubo* (3.3m^2).

There is no doubt that the socioeconomic environment partially accounts for the predominance of small shops in Japan. The majority of these are food stores: Japanese consumers have a strong preference for fresh foods and this clearly favours small shops catering to housewives who prefer to shop every day.[1] It also goes without saying that regulations restricting the entry of large chain stores have had a significant effect on the current state of the distribution system. Historical factors are also important in the case of distribution.

To the naked eye, one of the major problems with the Japanese distribution system seems to be its extreme decentralisation. This is hardly the whole story, however. The predominance of smaller firms is not limited to the distribution system; it is a feature

---

* Earlier versions of this chapter were presented at the Conference of the Japan Association of Economics and Econometrics, held at Kyushu University in October 1992, and the Japanese Corporate Organisation and Finance Conference, held at the Australian National University in February 1993. We wish to thank Toshiyuki Toyoda, Takeo Hoshi, Ben Smith and Peter Swan for their helpful comments. Special thanks are due to Paul Sheard for his extremely detailed comments and editorial suggestions. Any remaining errors are our own. This research was partially funded by a grant from Nihon Keizai Kenkyū Shōrei Zaidan.

of Japanese industry more generally. Is there any reason to believe that the predominance of small firms[2] in the distribution system per se is a symptom of problems in this sector? Smaller firms in manufacturing, for example, pay less to employees, produce less per employee and have a smaller capital stock per capita than larger firms, features that are all shared with smaller retail shops. In spite of the similarity, we nevertheless believe that the predominance of small retail shops does pose distinct problems for the functioning of the distribution system in Japan, as the subsequent analysis will show.

The distribution system is also characterised as being closed and inaccessible to new entrants, which hinders the entry of foreign producers into the Japanese market. In this sense, the problem in the system seems to be extreme centralisation or vertical integration. How can it be true that the system is too decentralised and, at the same time, too closed? We believe that the Japanese distribution system is a very complex organisation whose development has been heavily shaped by historical forces (in particular, rapid postwar economic growth and accompanying population movement) and by changes to the industrial structure.

Given the complexity and diversity of the Japanese distribution system, our first objective in this chapter is to provide a relatively simple and clear typology of distribution channels to clarify the major characteristics of the governance structures and incentive mechanisms that are in place. Unlike the manufacturing sector, there is no clear-cut measure for the performance of the distribution system. We will concentrate on one key function: price formation. Even in the narrow realm of neoclassical analysis, prices perform a multitude of functions: they guide the allocation of resources across sectors, firms and individuals; they provide essential information, used for deciphering supply and demand changes in the market; and they also work as an important incentive device.

In this regard, too, the Japanese distribution system has often been criticised and many questions raised about its performance. An extreme example is that, despite the substantial appreciation of the yen, domestic prices of some imported consumer goods have actually risen. The apparent insensitivity of domestic prices to changes in exchange rates is alarming.

Our second objective in this chapter is to conduct a formal analysis of the performance of the distribution system in terms of price behaviour. We do this by setting up and estimating a model of price formation, incorporating parameters that account for the responsiveness of individual commodity prices to shocks which alter the target level of these prices. We then relate our findings on this performance measure to the typology of distribution channels.

Extreme decentralisation and market segmentation

Traditional distribution channels

The high ratio of wholesale to retail transaction volumes in the Japanese distribution system is often mentioned by researchers. In other words, merchandise goes through a relatively long chain of distributors before it finally reaches the consumer.[3] Lengthy distribution channels have a clear historical origin. In the Edo era (1603–1867), commercial networks were centred upon two key geographical points: Osaka and Edo (Tokyo). Staples produced in each region were gathered by regional wholesalers, called *seisanchi tonya* (production site wholesalers). These wholesalers then sent the produce to Osaka, the centre of the nationwide merchandise network (*shūsanchi tonya*, or network merchants). A substantial proportion of the merchandise brought into Osaka was distributed to nearby urban population centres, with the remainder being sent to Edo, the largest consumption centre. Distribution in Edo was coordinated by other regional wholesalers (*shōhichi tonya*, or consumption site wholesalers).

It is clear that the prototype of such a network was designed for the smooth aggregation, transportation and distribution of merchandise whose production and consumption sites were geographically separated. Also, regional wholesalers were needed at both ends of the network because of the large number of small-scale producers at one end and of small retail shops at the other. For purely logistical reasons, the distribution network must be lengthy and roundabout to encompass both consumption and production in a distribution system conducted in small units. Small-scale producers require more than just efficient transportation. They often lack the financial ability to absorb risks caused by changes in demand or production technology. Distributors absorb such risks by shifting inventories among many merchants. Since these manufactures are often highly specialised, large wholesalers play a key role by organising the entire production and distribution process involving a large number of small specialised manufacturers.

Taken as a whole traditional distribution networks involve a range of activities, and these are considerably more complex than a narrow definition of distribution functions would suggest. As an example, we will consider the case of the textile distribution channel, which has at least two functions in addition to the usual ones: trade finance, and production–sales coordination.

An example of a traditional distribution channel

As argued above, a lengthy distribution channel is primarily a product of an extremely sophisticated system of specialisation. The textile production process can be broken down into three major steps: spinning thread; weaving fabric; and manufacturing the final product, which involves bleaching, printing, dyeing, design and sewing. At each of these principal stages, wholesalers are the main organisers of the manufacturers. At the upstream level, the (intermediate) products are fairly homogeneous, so wholesalers form markets in which prices are determined fairly competitively. These wholesalers hold inventories which act as an important buffer for smoothing out demand and supply shocks.

In the next stage, fabrics are traded by another set of wholesalers whose principal function is to aggregate the demand for fabrics from downstream, especially apparel makers. Apparel makers are themselves wholesalers in the sense that their principal function is to coordinate a large number of subprocesses and assign them to a multitude of subcontractors. They carry out design and advertising functions and form production and marketing plans. Aside from the benefit of specialisation, lengthy distribution channels help to spread risks over many agents in the industry. For example, sales risks are mainly absorbed by wholesalers at each stage, with a substantial proportion of subcontractors simply receiving a fee for their part in the process, and thus being freed from the sales risk of the product.

Contracts often involve some form of trade finance, especially when products are highly seasonal either on the supply or demand side. For example, wholesalers often make advance payments to finance manufacturers' purchases of new material.[4] Finally, information gathering and processing activities are also important. In the textile industry, a clear division of labour exists in the sense that the principal information activities are performed by wholesalers, whereas manufacturers rarely have such a capability. This is a simple but effective way of avoiding agency problems (problems that arise when one economic agent acts for another): by taking risks and being responsible for the sale of the product, wholesalers are given a natural incentive to collect and process information, and they can exploit economies of scale and scope in doing so. In addition, the kind of information collected and processed at each stage differs substantially. Wholesalers at the upstream level concentrate on inventory adjustment and the processing of current market information. On the other hand, the principal information gathered by apparel makers relates to product development, design and marketing. Hence most of their information is gathered from retail markets.

All in all, the case of the textile industry shows that distributors, especially wholesalers, perform a multitude of functions far beyond the simple physical distribution of merchandise. It also provides an insight into why such intricate and complex organisations emerge.

Problems of extreme decentralisation

It is fair to say that distribution channels in Japan at the onset of the high growth era were mainly organised by networks of nationwide wholesalers. The most prominent drawback of such a traditional distribution channel is its inherent sluggishness, which tends to prevent rapid change. Extreme forms of decentralisation make the network vulnerable to fundamental alterations in the underlying production technology. Without clear leadership, subsystems in a long and intricate channel of interfirm relationships cannot restructure themselves swiftly. In some cases, changes require abolishing some or all of the subsystems as a matter of life or death for the small firms involved. Networks of interfirm relationships in these channels are nothing but collections of long-term bilateral transaction relations. Without clear initiatives, any particular firm in the system will find it almost impossible to renegotiate all the outstanding contracts, even if the firm perceives the changes to be ultimately beneficial overall. This is precisely the hallmark of extreme decentralisation, and is found in many stagnant distribution channels.

Restructuring of traditional distribution channels has continued from the 1960s to the present. Efforts to restructure have come from two directions: from manufacturers with a wide range of products who organised their own vertical distribution networks; and from large-scale retailers operating nationwide chains. Technological advances and industry lifecycles have influenced the course of changes in the distribution system, with the development of manufacturers' distribution networks mirroring these underlying factors. *Keiretsu* (affiliated) distributors have grown rapidly, along with the growth of the market.

Far more fundamental changes, however, have come from downstream. The rapid modernisation of Japanese society has dramatically changed the consumption basket as well as the modes and frequency of shopping. Above all, it has accelerated integration of segmented local retail markets. Large-scale retailers and convenience stores with nationwide networks have steadily increased their market share. From the viewpoint of these retailers, both traditional and *keiretsu* networks are too narrowly specialised in terms of both geographic coverage and product range. They are also ill-suited to take full advantage of the first-hand information that these retailers collect at store level.

Distribution channels organised by manufacturers

The rapid expansion of markets and the introduction of new products have given rise to distribution channels organised by manufacturers — channels that are much simpler and shorter than the traditional ones.

There is one important exception, however. In the case of industrial raw materials and intermediate goods, manufacturers have continued to rely on wholesalers for distribution — large-scale general trading companies in particular play an essential role as market makers.[5] Even today, firms in these industries have only limited experience in marketing and distribution. Markets for these homogeneous intermediate goods and raw materials are highly competitive and have several layers of distributors. Typically only a few wholesalers trade directly with a manufacturer, and they are usually the general trading companies. In the next layer, we find wholesalers who specialise either in a narrower range of products or by region. In a larger market there may exist a third layer of even smaller wholesalers. Prices are determined within each layer fairly competitively in a middleman's market. Wholesalers use these markets to adjust inventories.

Representing the other extreme are the manufacturers who invest in and are deeply committed to the distribution channel. The most typical case is automobile distribution, in which wholesale activities are completely merged into the assembler's internal organisation. The sales divisions of the auto makers control exclusive dealership networks through varying degrees of ownership and agency controls.

At first glance, short and simple distribution channels seem to be more efficient than complicated multistage ones. But this impression is misleading. For one thing, there are clear differences between the products distributed in the two kinds of channels. In the shorter channels organised by manufacturers, the goods traded are typically highly differentiated. The sales risks are far more idiosyncratic to particular brands, so that the risk absorbing and inventory adjusting functions of independent wholesalers are of less importance. Economies of scope and scale are perhaps also less important in the distribution of highly differentiated products.

What are the distinguishing characteristics of industries which have organised their own distribution channels? Most have experienced rapid technological progress; the automobile and consumer electronics industries, for example, were of negligible size at the beginning of the postwar period. Much of their merchandise was entirely new to the market, and properly trained distributors were simply not available. The explosion in market size induced heavy and hurried investment in marketing channels. The extent to which these industries could rely on existing distributors determined the nature and degree of the manufacturers' involvement in distribution. The more an industry relied upon extant distributors, the less involvement it had in distribution activities.

In the auto industry, for instance, the majority of retailers (dealers) deal exclusively in the products of a particular assembler and adhere strictly to the pricing, marketing, territorial restrictions and policies set by that firm. In the consumer electronics industry retail outlets are far more diversified, comprising regular general merchandise stores (GMSs), specialised discounters and department stores, in addition to the manufacturers' retail outlets (*keiretsu-ten*). In the drug industry, some manufacturers have vertically integrated systems without independent wholesalers, while others use independent wholesalers but at the same time operate their own chain stores at the retail level. At the other end of the spectrum, many drug firms — typically small ones specialising in a narrow range of products — rely entirely upon the distribution channels of a larger drug firm.

Retail market integration and new types of retailers

The rapid shift of population to urban and suburban areas, along with the increased use of private vehicles, has led to an expansion in the size of local retail markets. Whereas on the one hand this created the momentum for large-scale mass merchandising, on the other it induced retail shops to differentiate and specialise in other aspects of retail competition. The number of specialist shops grew rapidly. Needless to say, the increase in supermarkets met fierce resistance from local retailers, in turn giving rise to the infamous *Daiten-Hō* (*Daikibo Kouri Tenpo Hō*, or Large-Scale Retail Stores Law). Even so, the underlying current of change steadily altered the shape of local retail markets virtually all over Japan. It is clear that the multitude of changes in retail markets demanded a complete restructuring of distribution channels.

This time, the initiative was in the hands of large-scale retailers and convenience store chains. Adjusting distribution channels to the more integrated and larger retail markets mainly entailed:

- reorganisation of the wholesaler network;[6]
- realignment of the incentive structure, especially retail margins, which had become grossly out of line with the widening cost differences among retailers; and
- coordination of investments by wholesalers and manufacturers in computerised inventory/order/settlement network systems, especially point of sale (POS) recording systems.

In the existing channels, neither wholesalers nor manufacturers had strong enough incentives or the capability to handle these matters by themselves. For these firms, the expected cost of change was too large and benefits spread too broadly over a wide range of merchandise. Consequently the changes were introduced, from the late 1970s throughout the 1980s, by major chain store retailers.

The last few years have witnessed not only the acceleration of change but also the emergence of new types of retailers.[7] Three factors have played a major, if not decisive, role in shaping these developments. First, entry regulations against large-scale retail stores were relaxed substantially; the Diet amended the *Daiten-Hō* in January 1992. Second, the yen has continued to appreciate since the latter half of the 1980s. Compared with the yen–dollar exchange rate in the mid 1980s, the value of the yen in terms of the US dollar has roughly tripled. With the explosive growth of tourism to foreign countries, the gap between domestic and international prices has become increasingly apparent. Third, the recession that started in 1991 deepened in the following years. Retail sectors faced shrinking markets for the first time in postwar history.

The changes that we are witnessing today are too widespread and too deeply structural for a full account here. We can only comment on the most noteworthy aspects. First, the acceleration of these changes started in the 1980s. The sales share of large-scale retailers and convenience store chains continues to increase. The shift in commerce concentration from inner cities to suburban areas is occurring on several fronts, and is evident in the construction of large shopping centres; the concentration of sales in a few of the largest shopping districts in the inner city; and the emergence of roadside retail concentrations. In inner city areas, traditional 'mom and pop' shops are rapidly being replaced by convenience stores.

Developments in the last few years have also given rise to a proliferation of new kinds of retail outlets, most of them mirroring those found in the United States: large-scale specialty stores, such as do-it-yourself stores, bookshops and stores selling outdoor recreational goods; discount houses; wholesale clubs; and many more. As a result of this proliferation a far-reaching restructuring of the industry is under way. The bypassing of wholesalers is forcing them to redirect their activities away from the more traditional ones of delivery, sorting and trade finance, towards providing consulting, information processing and marketing services to small and medium-scale retailers.

The appreciation of the yen, shrinking markets and the emergence of new competitors induced many major GMS chains to implement an aggressive pricing strategy. They introduced private brands and started to sell at prices roughly half those of comparable national brands. This introduction of private brands along with large price cuts in some imported goods, mistakenly dubbed *kakaku hakai* ('price destruction'), accelerated the shift from brand name, high-quality line products to generic, highly standardised ones. In spite of these developments, in our study of prices we failed to find at an aggregate level any tendency for domestic prices to follow more closely the rapid decline in the prices of imported goods, as we will see later. *Kakaku hakai* has so far been limited to a relatively narrow range of products and is found only in a subset of retailers.[8]

Typology of distribution channels

In this section, we will identify four basic types of distribution channel and offer a simple framework to analyse major differences between them from the viewpoint of transaction cost (broadly defined) minimisation. We try to understand the basic architecture of each type as the solution to (constrained) minimisation of transaction costs, given the nature of the industry, its prior history and the regulatory framework in which it is set.

Length of distribution channel

A distribution channel is said to be long if the number of agents or distributing firms involved in handling the merchandise is large. It seems that the two most important factors favouring lengthy channels are risk shifting/dispersion and technological factors favouring specialisation and division of labour. The principal means through which risks are shifted are the holding of inventories by middlemen, and various fee systems for subcontractors.

Major factors favouring shorter distribution channels are related to various kinds of agency costs and comparative advantages in information gathering. For example, even in the textile industry — which we used earlier as an example of a traditional distribution channel — the distribution channels for final products, especially fashion wear, are almost always short and directly controlled by apparel makers. Sales risks are large in the marketing of these goods, and information asymmetry between apparel maker and retailer is likely to be important. In such a case, it makes sense to allocate more of the sales risk to the apparel makers than to the distributors.

Direct control of downstream distributors in a shorter channel also alleviates many of the problems faced by newcomer manufacturers. The success of newcomers in a consumer goods industry often depends upon the extent to which distributors are willing to trade their products. Each distributor's decision depends, in turn, upon other distributors because market-wide recognition of newcomers or new products is a critical factor for sales volume. If a retailer believes that other retailers will not sell the products of a newcomer, it makes sense for it not to invest its time and effort (however small) to trade the products. Such interdependence among retailers' decision making often leads to flat refusal by distributors to deal with a newcomer unless it can convince them of its products' benefits and of a firm prospect for success. It makes sense in such a case that the manufacturer directly control the distributors, especially retailers. Delegation of these sales promotion activities to wholesalers creates the same kind of problem at the wholesale level.

The scope of retailer discretion is another factor. For most items sold in GMSs, consumers require little advice in selecting a brand. But on the other hand, sales of non-prescription drugs, for example, are very sensitive to the advice given by individual pharmacists, who therefore have much discretion. Manufacturers have to invest heavily in advertising and/or use shorter distribution channels so as to exercise more direct control over the sales policies of pharmacists.

Commodities sold in shorter channels need to be differentiated and have clearly identifiable brand names. Shorter channels are often preferred because long ones may not adequately allow risks to be shifted or provide finely adjusted incentive schemes. This is because the products carry (by definition) idiosyncratic sales risks that may not be reallocated effectively in the competitive middleman markets.

Common or sole agents?

If distributors handle only the products of a particular manufacturer, the distribution channel can be said to be exclusive. Strictly speaking, there are hardly any industries in Japan which have totally exclusive distribution systems. Only automobile dealer networks are approximately so, but even this is changing rapidly. On the other hand, there are many industries in which some (but not all) of the manufacturers use exclusive distribution channels.

These examples aside, distribution channels are predominantly open in the sense that distributors are agents for more than one manufacturer. Economies of scale and scope are the most important reasons. The distribution system in Japan, like those in other countries, is used and shared by many manufacturers; that is, the majority of distributors are common agents.

What are the factors favouring an exclusive distribution network? The logic of transaction cost economics predicts a few important factors, all of which have to do with imperfect information, joint commitment and/or investment in transaction specific capital (broadly defined).[9] A manufacturer may want to maintain an exclusive distribution channel in order to better monitor performance, to provide incentives for sales promotion effort and the making of shared sunk investments, to promote brand loyalty or to prevent free-riding by downstream agents.

An exclusive distribution network can also be built for strategic reasons. For example, preventing rival firms from using existing distributors raises the costs incurred by rivals, which can lead to higher mark-ups and profits. Unfortunately, we do not know to what extent these considerations influence manufacturers' decisions in building their distribution channels. What we do know is that, if a manufacturer uses an exclusive distribution channel for such a reason alone, there is no intrinsic reason to apply exclusion beyond the line of its products and against firms in different industries. Partial exclusion — excluding some products but allowing others — is commonly observed: for example, most pharmacies in Japan sell both cosmetics and medicines. In this sense these shops are common agents. On the other hand, many of them sell the products of only one cosmetics or medicinal company. Although we cannot tell whether or not such a practice is done for strategic reasons, partial exclusion is quite common and is likely to relax competition among retailers in the local markets by, in effect, increasing the number of entry points.[10]

A simple typology

Here we offer a simple taxonomy of the types of vertical relationships, as shown in Figure 3.1 (see Appendix 3.1 for details of the classification). Table 3.1 shows the major cost characteristics of each type of distributor.

Type I involves a general trading company acting as the key organiser of the distribution system. Most typically, imported raw materials, intermediate goods and capital equipment are traded in this way. As shown in Figure 3.1, virtually all of these goods are sold only to firms. Their share in the consumer consumption basket is negligible and thus ignored.

Table 3.1   Cost characteristics of four types of distribution channel

	I	II	III	IV	Total
Wholesalers					
Average cost elasticity of sales	0.75	0.90	0.82	0.84	0.83
Scale difference in wage/sales ratio	15.3	4.87	10.09	6.98	9.84
Average margin (%)	13.3	18.8	12.1	12.9	15.9
Average sales (¥ billion)	98	61	228	62	74
Retailers					
Average cost elasticity of sales (1)	–	0.97	0.91	0.96	0.96
Scale difference in wage/sales ratio (2)	–	5.02	9.25	6.03	5.90
Correlation between (1) and (2)	–	–0.55	–0.58	–0.59	–0.59
Average margin (%)	–	33.5	23.5	25.6	29.5
Average sales (¥ billion)		5.1	9.7	7.2	6.5

Source: Ariga, Namikawa and Ohkusa (1991), Table 12.

PRICE FORMATION AND THE STRUCTURE OF THE DISTRIBUTION SYSTEM

Figure 3.1   **Prototypes of vertical transactions**

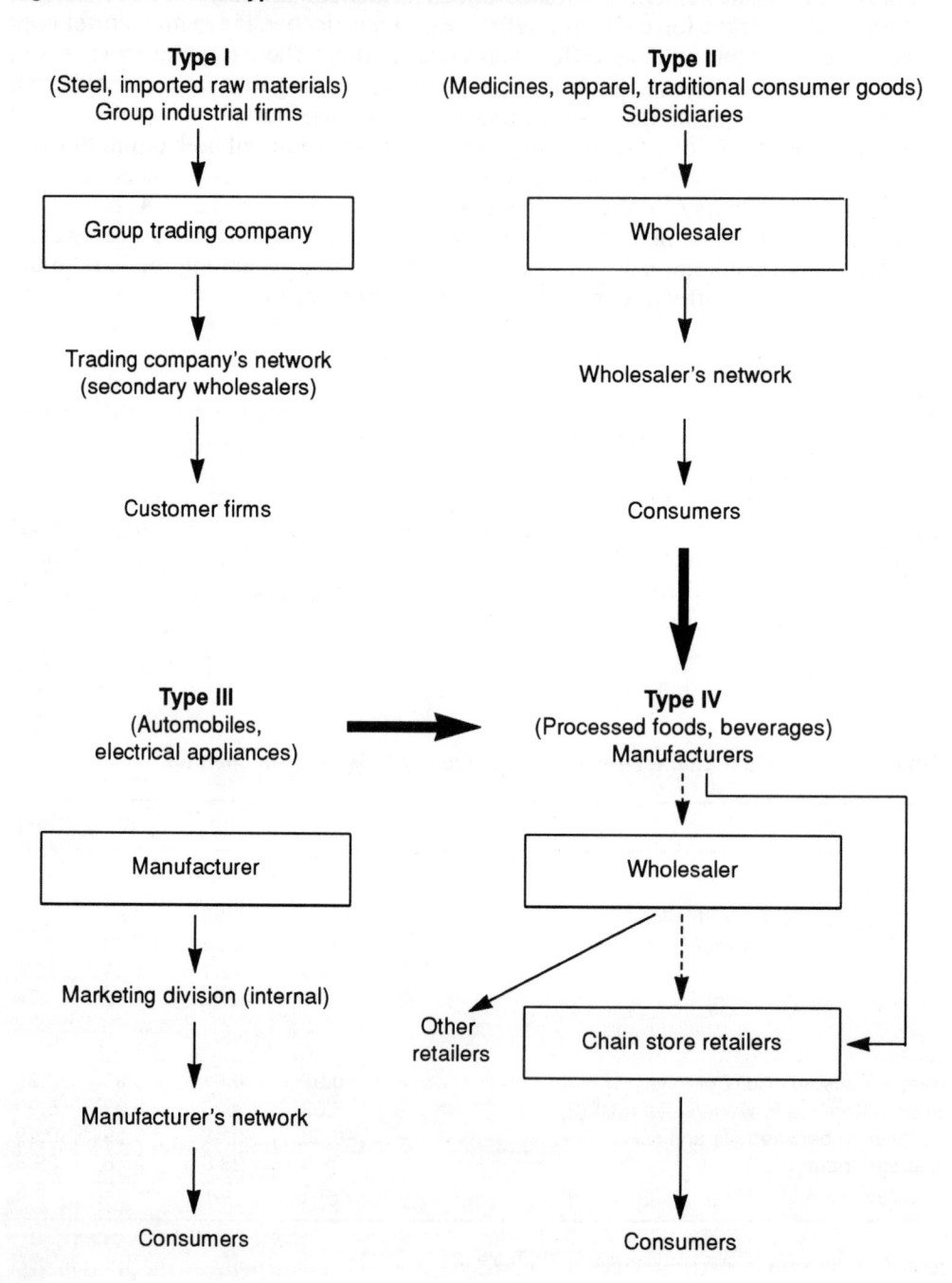

Type I
(Steel, imported raw materials)
Group industrial firms

↓

Group trading company

↓

Trading company's network
(secondary wholesalers)

↓

Customer firms

Type II
(Medicines, apparel, traditional consumer goods)
Subsidiaries

↓

Wholesaler

↓

Wholesaler's network

↓

Consumers

Type III
(Automobiles,
electrical appliances)

Manufacturer

↓

Marketing division (internal)

↓

Manufacturer's network

↓

Consumers

Type IV
(Processed foods, beverages)
Manufacturers

↓

Wholesaler

↓

Other retailers   Chain store retailers

↓

Consumers

64

The type II transaction system is the traditional channel in which the key organiser of the system is a large (typically independent) wholesaler with a nationwide network of secondary distributors. The difference between types I and II appears most clearly in the size of manufacturers: in many type II channels, manufacturers are small and in some cases close to being subsidiaries of major wholesalers.

Type III channels are the most typical *keiretsu* in the distribution system. The key organiser of the distribution system here is the manufacturer or its subsidiary marketing (trading) firms. Type III channels are commonly found in industries which grew rapidly in the high growth era. Automobiles and consumer electronics are the best-known examples.

Type IV is the newest among the four types and is limited to a narrow range of consumer goods. In this system, there are two major flows: one organised by the wholesaler, and the other by large (chain store) retailers. The transactions organised by wholesalers are similar to those of type II, but the wholesaler's influence is limited to independent (and mostly small) retailers. In the other type of transaction, the key organiser is a large chain store equipped with customised local distribution centres; it coordinates all incoming deliveries directly from manufacturers as well as outgoing shipments into its franchise stores. As we have indicated with large arrows in Figure 3.1, some of the type II and III channels are coming to more closely resemble type IV channels.

In type I transactions, the most distinctive characteristic is the decisive role of large trading companies in price formation and the organisation of the distribution network. Interfirm trading in semicentralised markets is quite common and, for some of the key commodities, institutionalised wholesale markets exist. Agency cost considerations in the distribution channel are minimal, and technology factors favouring large-scale transactions dominate.

In type II, markets are typically small in size and no single item constitutes a well-defined industry or market. Vertical relationships are organised mainly by large wholesalers across a wide range of related groups of commodities. Product differentiation can be seen in some cases, but the market size of each item is too small to warrant a manufacturer's direct investment in the distribution network.

In type III, commodities are highly differentiated and interbrand non-price competition is important. Repair and various after-services are important elements of marketing. Manufacturer-organised vertical systems are firmly established, and independent common agencies are rare. Agency cost considerations greatly influence the design of the distribution system. Territory assignment is rigidly applied, and, to overcome various kinds of retailer moral hazard, standardised training in retail marketing is commonly observed.

The main differences between types II and III on the one hand, and type IV on the other, stem from information considerations. In types II and III, retailers have substantial discretionary power to influence consumer choice; medicines, clothing and electrical appliances are the most typical products. Consumers often consult the retailers for advice on the selection of brands. In type IV, advertising in the mass media shapes consumer selections. For retailers, responding quickly to changing consumer preferences, selecting items, and keeping an optimal size and variety of inventory are important.

Price formation and performance in the distribution channel

Although stylised facts concerning the cost structure of the Japanese distribution system are beginning to accumulate, there has been little quantitative analysis of the system's performance. The difficulty stems in part from conceptual issues concerning exactly what role the distribution system plays and how to measure performance. The lack of data that can be used directly as a proxy for measuring performance also presents a difficulty. In this section, we use the responsiveness of prices as one of the most fundamental performance measures of the distribution system. Judging from the preceding analysis, it is unlikely that any manufacturer can independently control the entire system of product prices (wholesale, retail list prices, margins); price formation must be one of the most fundamental and common functions performed by the distributors. The process of price formation is modelled formally and estimated in two stages. (The full details of the model and estimation procedure are set out in Appendixes 3.2 and 3.3.) In this section we present the results and discuss the price performance of different channels.

Summary of the results

Using the estimated quadruple of probability densities, we computed the average price responses to changes in p^*, the target price for distributors in the vertical channel. Notice that in the estimation of p^* we have already netted out all of the factors which directly influence the cost of distribution services. Hence the estimated responses of p, the actual price, to p^* measure the price rigidity due solely to the cost of changing prices. (Both prices are measured in logs.)

We used three benchmarks: price changes when the deviation in the previous period was zero; price changes when the deviation in the previous period was 0.2; and price changes when the deviation in the previous period was −0.2 — in other words, price changes when the price in the previous period was above or below the target level by roughly 20 per cent. To derive the average responses of the distributors in each type, we used log linear aggregations of the probability densities, based on the weights used for the aggregation of each price index.

Let us start with the overall price responses to the deviations of the price from the target level. To shorten the expression, we will call this 'responsiveness'. Table 3.2 presents a summary of the estimation for 347 pairs of price indices. It is apparent from the second and third rows that prices are far more responsive upward than downward; roughly speaking, the upward responsiveness is about seven times the downward responsiveness. Much of this asymmetry stems from the size of the price change conditional upon a price change occurring, rather than the probability of a price

Table 3.2   Summary statistics of estimation

	All samples	1970–79	1980–92
Average inflation rate (%)	3.38	7.70	0.11
Average elasticity of price response at $p = p^* - 0.2$	0.303	0.300	0.368
Average elasticity of price response at $p = p^* + 0.2$	0.045	0.041	0.057
Probability of price increase at $p = p^* - 0.2$	0.512	0.521	0.500
Probability of price decrease at $p = p^* + 0.2$	0.400	0.384	0.456
Number of price pairs	347	100	137

change occurring. Price responses are often highly non-linear. The elasticity of the price response with respect to the deviation from the target level generally rises as the absolute size of the deviation increases. Typically, therefore, prices appear to be quite flexible in stable and relatively high inflation. Prices appear to be very inflexible in unstable deflation.[11]

When we compare price responsiveness in the 1970s and 1980s, it appears that some improvement in overall responsiveness occurred during the period. The difference is minor, however. Overall, at an aggregate level, responsiveness has not changed very much in the last 20 years.

Table 3.3 compares the aggregates for the consumer price index (CPI) and wholesale price index (WPI). It is clear that asymmetry is far more pronounced at the CPI level. Again, the difference between the two can be attributed to the size rather than the probability of a price change. Overall, the WPI is far more flexible downward, but

Table 3.3   Wholesale price index versus consumer price index

	CPI 1970–79	CPI 1980–92	WPI 1970–79	WPI 1980–92
Average inflation rate (%)	7.48	1.57	8.29	−1.32
Average elasticity of price response at $p = p^* - 0.2$	0.329	0.470	0.222	0.177
Average elasticity of price response at $p = p^* + 0.2$	0.022	0.029	0.091	0.102
Probability of price increase at $p = p^* - 0.2$	0.541	0.492	0.467	0.409
Probability of price decrease at $p = p^* + 0.2$	0.380	0.476	0.397	0.421

Notes: CPI = consumer price index.
WPI = wholesale price index.

Figure 3.2 Impulse response: aggregate wholesale price index, measured as deviation from base run (per cent)

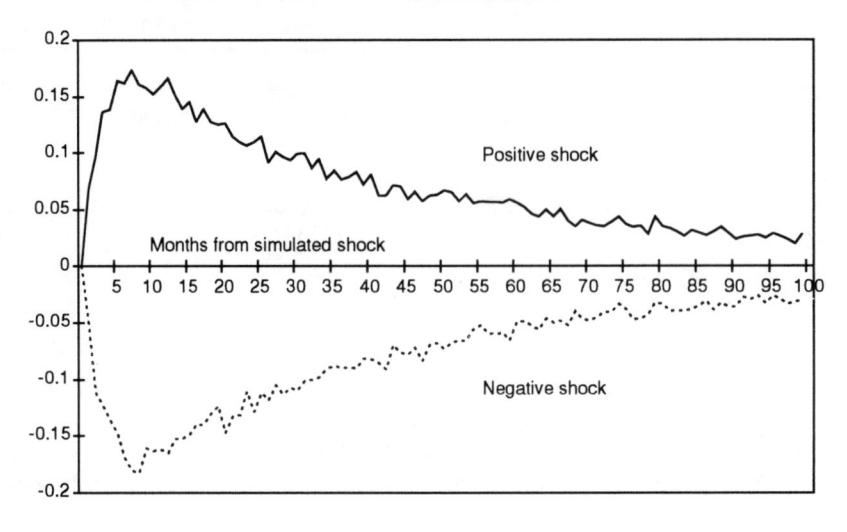

Figure 3.3 Impulse response: aggregate consumer price index, measured as deviation from base run (per cent)

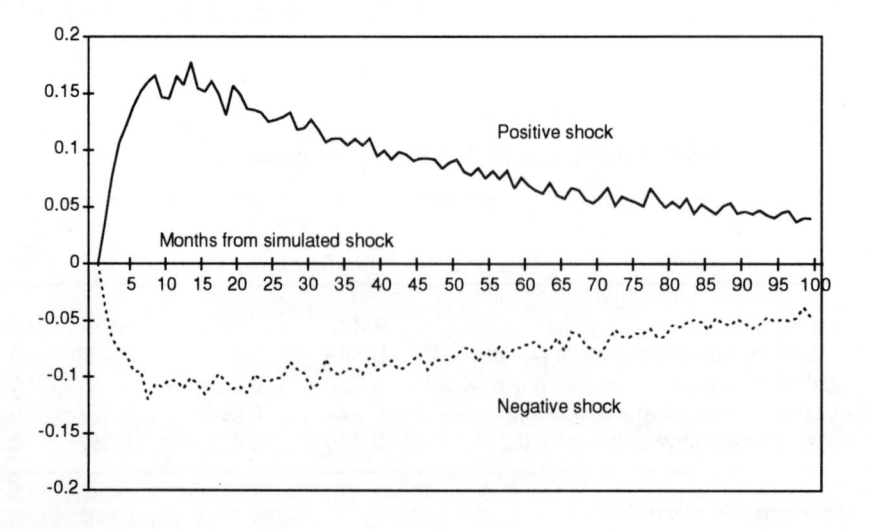

less flexible upward, than the CPI.[12] Note that all the probabilities of price changes are estimated for monthly data. Even a 0.05 per cent monthly probability translates into a 46 per cent probability of a price change within a year. In two years, the probability of a price change exceeds 75 per cent. Although a 20 per cent deviation from the target level is fairly large — typically in the order of three times the standard errors of the first-stage regressions — our estimations suggest that the sluggish response of a price to its target level is due to the slow speed of adjustment rather than a low frequency of price changes.

Figures 3.2 and 3.3 provide some simulation results.[13] The figures trace the impulse response of the downstream price to a shock in the target price. The size of the shock is equal to the weighted average of the standard deviations of the first-stage regressions. Starting from the peak effect, it takes about two years for the deviation in the WPI to be reduced to half. In the case of the CPI, it takes roughly three years for upward adjustment, and about five years for downward adjustment.

Types of distribution channels and their performance

Table 3.4 compares the price responsiveness of the four different types of distribution channel. For retail prices, the type III (*keiretsu*) distribution channel stands out clearly as the least responsive. Again, the rigidity compared with the other types is due mainly to the size of the response, although the probability of price changes is also substantially smaller in this type. Although retail prices generally exhibit downward rigidity, type II is the most rigid downward. Type IV has the highest price flexibility upward, but its downward responsiveness does not differ very much from the others. In short, differences among distribution types are seen most clearly in the size of upward price changes. As noted above, price responses are typically non-linear. In some cases, the response elasticity rises quite rapidly as the size of the deviation increases. (Figures 3.4 through 3.8 display these elasticities.) Type III is again the exception in this respect. Response elasticity is approximately constant in this type. In other types, response elasticity increases quite noticeably as the positive deviation increases. Price elasticity is approximately constant in the downward direction.

Turning to the wholesale level, we immediately notice that price responses are roughly symmetrical. The only exception is the miscellaneous category, and even in this case the asymmetry is minor. In type I, prices are substantially more flexible downward. Overall, type II wholesale prices are the least flexible. Again, except for type III, wholesale prices are less flexible upward than retail prices of the same type. They are more flexible downward.

To sum up, price responses are roughly symmetrical at the wholesale level; a substantial asymmetry appears only at the retail level, especially in consumer non-durables. These results seem to suggest that differences in the structure of distribution channels influence performance in terms of price adjustments. It is not clear, however, whether or not these differences simply reflect differences in the behaviour of the target prices. Indeed, the first row in Table 3.4 shows that the average inflation rates of the target prices differ considerably.

PRICE FORMATION AND THE STRUCTURE OF THE DISTRIBUTION SYSTEM

Figure 3.4   Average elasticity of price responses: type I sector

$E(\Delta p_t)/dp_{t-1}$

Wholesale price index

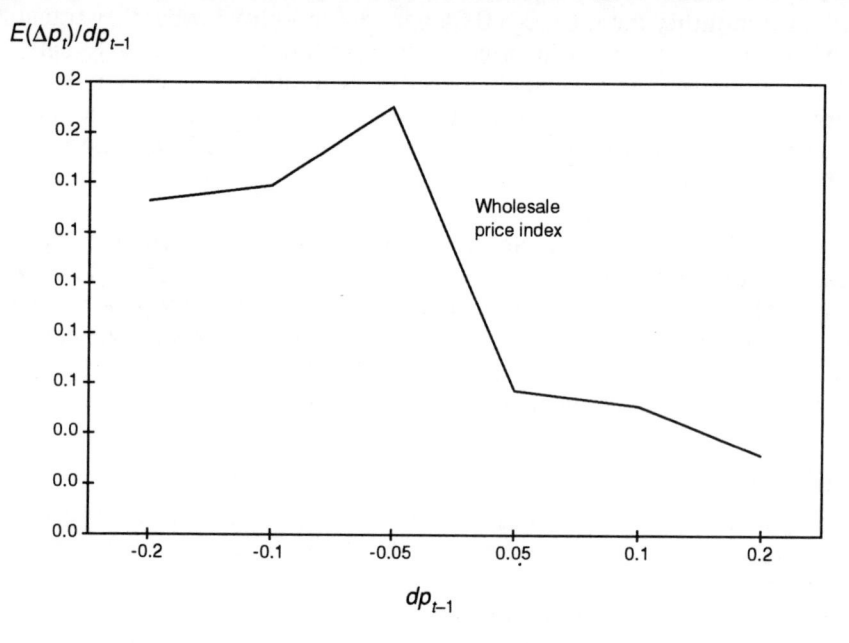

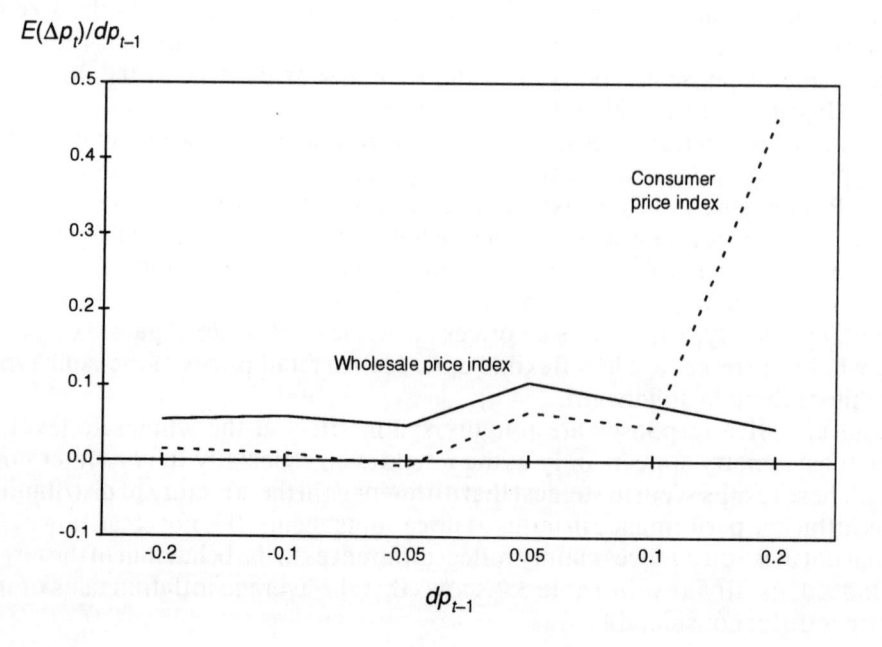

dp_{t-1}

Figure 3.5   Average elasticity of price responses: type II sector

$E(\Delta p_t)/dp_{t-1}$

Consumer price index

Wholesale price index

dp_{t-1}

JAPANESE FIRMS, FINANCE AND MARKETS

Figure 3.6   Average elasticity of price responses: type III sector

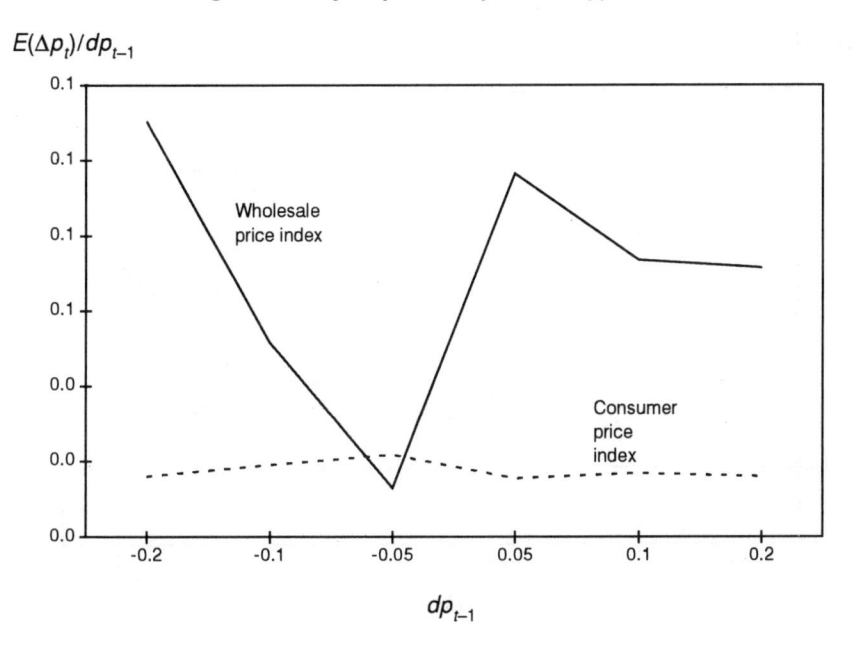

Figure 3.7   Average elasticity of price responses: type IV sector

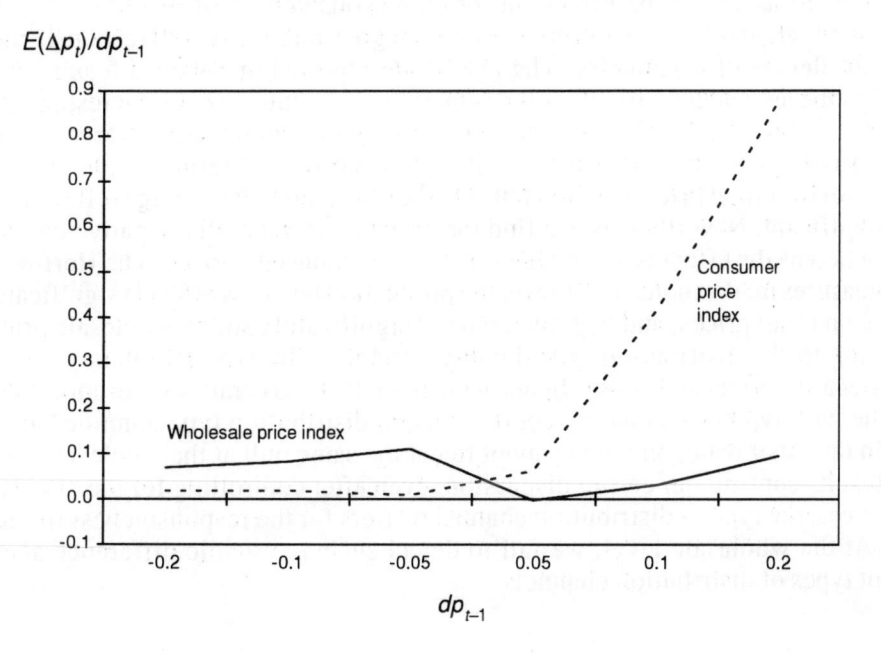

Figure 3.8   Average elasticity of price responses: miscellaneous

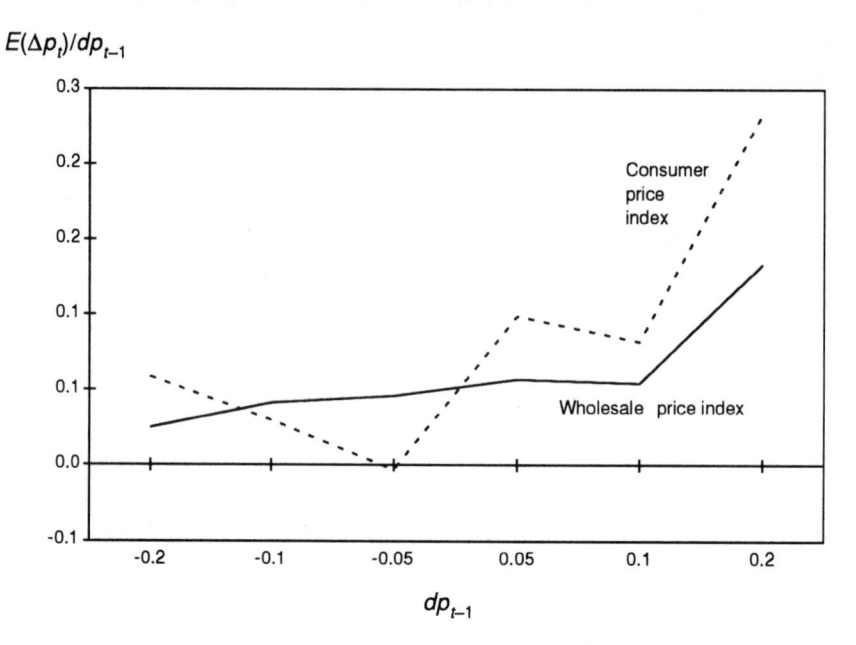

$E(\Delta p_t)/dp_{t-1}$

[Figure: plot showing Consumer price index (dashed) and Wholesale price index (solid) curves against dp_{t-1} ranging from -0.2 to 0.2]

In order to ascertain the effects on price responsiveness of differences in the behaviour of target prices, we ran cross-section regressions on overall responsiveness and on the degree of asymmetry. The results are reported in Tables 3.5 and 3.6. In Table 3.5, the dependent variable is the sum of the (absolute) size of the responses at $p = p^* + 0.2$ and $p = p^* - 0.2$. Overall, the most significant negative effect is found in the variability of the target price, which is measured in terms of the standard deviation of the target price inflation rate. On the other hand, the average inflation rate is not significant. Nevertheless, we find the effect to be generally negative on retail prices, whereas the effect is somewhat positive on wholesale prices. The Herfindahl index measures market concentration at the production level. Its effect is significantly negative on retail prices, and negative, but not significantly so, on wholesale prices.

Turning to the distribution type dummy variables, the type III dummy has the largest negative effect and is significant at the retail level. Overall, we can confidently reject the null hypothesis that the coefficients on distribution type dummies are all zero. On the other hand, an F test cannot reject the same null at the wholesale level. These results confirm our earlier discussion: even after controlling for the effects of target prices, the type of distribution channel matters for the responsiveness of retail prices. At the wholesale level, we fail to detect such a systemic difference across different types of distribution channels.

Table 3.4 Type of distribution channel and price responsiveness

	Type I CPI*	Type I WPI	Type II CPI	Type II WPI	Type III CPI	Type III WPI	Type IV CPI	Type IV WPI	Miscellaneous CPI	Miscellaneous WPI
Average inflation rate		na	1.41	5.54	0.79	1.80	5.12	4.79	0.96	2.13	0.84
Average elasticity of price response at $dp = 0.2$	na	0.082	0.455	0.044	0.016	0.072	0.882	0.096	0.233	0.133
Average elasticity of price response at $dp = 0.1$	na	0.051	0.065	0.075	0.017	0.074	0.416	0.032	0.082	0.054
Average elasticity of price response at $dp = -0.2$	na	0.133	0.015	0.054	0.016	0.110	0.018	0.069	0.059	0.025
Average elasticity of price response at $dp = -0.1$	na	0.139	0.010	0.058	0.019	0.052	0.019	0.083	0.030	0.041
Probability of price increase at $dp = 0.2$	na	0.983	0.971	0.961	0.625	0.508	0.961	0.727	0.983	0.796
Probability of price increase at $dp = 0.1$	na	0.873	0.878	0.820	0.466	0.349	0.833	0.585	0.907	0.591
Probability of price decrease at $dp = -0.2$	na	0.987	0.601	0.478	0.562	0.420	0.737	0.697	0.720	0.989
Probability of price decrease at $dp = -0.1$	na	0.903	0.453	0.400	0.426	0.199	0.522	0.553	0.502	0.851

Notes: * Merchandise in the type I sector is mainly for industrial use and the weights in the CPI are negligible.
CPI = consumer price index; WPI = wholesale price index; na = not available.

Table 3.5 Cross-section regressions: price responsiveness

	Data set A		Data sets B, C		Data sets B, C, D	
	CPI	WPI	CPI	WPI	CPI	WPI
Constant	0.268**	0.899×10^{-3}	0.193**	−0.011	0.0747*	0.0453*
$E(\Delta p^*)^a$	−5.725	2.433*	0.199	3.719	−1.364	1.872
$\sigma(\Delta p^*)^b$	−4.420**	−0.127*	−3.973**	−0.752	−2.426*	−0.610*
Herfindahl index	-0.169×10^{-4}	-0.923×10^{-5}	-0.18×10^{-4}	-0.18×10^{-3}	-0.52×10^{-4}	-0.114×10^{-4}
Dummy I	–	0.638×10^{-2}	–	–	–	−0.039
Dummy II	−0.113*	0.614×10^{-3}	−0.031	–	0.050	0.024
Dummy III	−0.158**	0.0330**	−0.093*	–	−0.0856*	0.00492
Dummy IV	−0.086	0.16	−0.016	–	0.0480	0.0227
1980s dummy	–	–	0.310×10^{-2}	0.037*	0.065	0.038*
Adjusted R^2	0.26	0.52	0.44	0.21	0.26	0.29
F test^c	Reject**	No	Reject*	–	Reject*	No

Notes:
 ** Significant at 1% level (t-value).
  * Significant at 5% level (t-value).
  a Average inflation rate of the target price level.
  b Standard deviation of 1.
  c Reject**: rejects at 1% confidence level the null hypothesis that all the types of dummies are insignificant.
     Reject*: rejects the null hypothesis at 5% confidence level.
     No: cannot reject the null hypothesis.

Table 3.6 Cross-section regressions: asymmetry in price adjustments

	Data set A CPI	Data set A WPI	Data sets B, C CPI	Data sets B, C WPI	Data sets B, C, D CPI	Data sets B, C, D WPI
Constant	8.180**	1.223**	−4.39**	0.807	−8.338*	1.714*
$E(\Delta p^*)$[a]	47.09*	81.35**	39.43*	56.31*	33.43*	19.10*
$\sigma(\Delta p^*)$[b]	−22.27**	−29.39**	−16.43**	−10.98*	−12.17**	−5.30*
Herfindahl index	−0.38 × 10^{-4}*	0.120 × 10^{-4}	−0.17 × 10^{-4}	−0.56 × 10^{-3}*	−0.46 × 10^{-4}	−0.31 × 10^{-4}*
		0.638 × 10^{-2}				−0.039
Dummy I	—	0.174	0.127	—	0.093	−0.122
Dummy II	0.221*	−0.233*	0.395*	—	0.395*	−0.291
Dummy III	0.425*	−0.632*	0.236*	—	0.236*	−0.029
Dummy IV	0.476*	—	0.221	−0.121	0.052	0.17*
1980s dummy	—	—				
Adjusted R^2	0.68	0.87	0.56	0.49	0.39	0.43
F test[c]	Reject**	Reject**	Reject*	na	Reject*	Reject**

Notes: na not available.
       ** Significant at 1% level (t-value).
       *   Significant at 5% level (t-value).
       [a] Average inflation rate of the target price level.
       [b] Standard deviation of 1.
       [c] Reject**: rejects at 1% confidence level the null hypothesis that all the types of dummies are insignificant.
           Reject*: rejects the null hypothesis at 5% confidence level.
           No: cannot reject the null hypothesis.

75

Table 3.6 reports the regression results on the degree of asymmetry measured in terms of the difference in the responses at $p = p^* + 0.2$ and $p = p^* - 0.2$ divided by the sum of the two. Again the results are similar: the effect of variability in the inflation rate is consistently negative. The Herfindahl index also has a largely negative effect on the asymmetry. The difference appears in the effect of inflation: inflation of the target price significantly aggravates the asymmetry at the retail as well as the wholesale level. The dummy variables are generally significant and negative at the retail level, indicating that the degree of asymmetry is significantly smaller than the miscellaneous (which is the default). The results are mixed at the wholesale level. In general, however, the null hypotheses are also rejected at the wholesale level.

Discussion

Earlier we argued that much of the difference in the structure of distribution channels can be attributed to differences in the underlying factors which determine the nature and the magnitude of transaction costs. Do these explanations support our findings on differences in pricing behaviour? We believe so.

Type III is the only channel in which resale price maintenance is commonly practised. In type III sectors, diversity in the scale and cost structure of distributors is the largest among the four types. Price changes require comprehensive rescheduling of list prices and rebates of various kinds at different levels of distribution. Not surprisingly, prices are most rigid in this type of distribution channel.

In type I, prices respond fairly smoothly to changes in the target level. In particular, we find no evidence of downward rigidity, consistent with the competitive market structure found in this type. It is important to note, however, that the competitive and open organisation in this type closely mirrors the particular (and rather limited) functions of this type of distribution channel. Its major transaction costs consist of the costs of coordinating delivery, inventory adjustment and trade finance, all of which are relatively free from agency cost considerations. As shown in Table 3.1, economies of scale are quite significant in this channel. All these factors are amenable to the formation of a competitive middleman's market wherein risk shifting, price formation and inventory adjustments are performed relatively efficiently.

In type II, downward rigidity is the largest. In this type of distribution channel, secular increases in distribution costs at smaller retail stores tend to be accommodated by across-the-board price increases in the retail market. For a large-scale retailer with a cost advantage, it is generally best to increase retail prices when the small-scale retailers increase their prices. Such accommodative behaviour at the retail level is facilitated partially by regulations limiting the entry of large-scale retailers into local retail markets. This has allowed segmentation of retail markets into geographically small units. By so doing, large retailers can avoid direct competition against other large-scale retailers, which makes such accommodative behaviour credible. The situation is much the same in type IV. The difference between types II and IV is more pronounced in cost structure than in price performance.

Extreme decentralisation in distribution channels is closely related to the predominance of small-scale retailers. The intricate and complex structure of the channels reflects the variety of functions expected of distributors. In distribution channels characterised by a predominance of small retailers, the allocative role of prices seems quite limited and the price adjustment function is often in conflict with the other functions of prices. Prices and margins are the most important devices for aligning the incentives of small distributors.

It seems that type III channels fare no better in this regard. The significant feature of this channel is its dual structure. Upward price adjustments tend to be checked by the existence of aggressive large-scale independent retailers, whereas for small-scale retailers price reductions are a matter of life or death.

A general conclusion that emerges from the above is that there is an inherent sluggishness in prices as a whole, which seems to reflect internal conflicts and coordination problems in distribution channels.

Further results on retail price rigidity[14]

The results shown above focused upon the timing and the magnitude of price changes in response to the deviation of the price from the target level. An alternative to this approach is to investigate the long-term response of prices to changes in costs and to estimate the extent to which the observed price changes are due to cost changes. The remainder will be due to changes in mark-ups. For this purpose, we estimated the (marginal) cost function for 31 subsectors of the CPI and regressed the observed price changes on the changes in respective marginal costs. The residuals are, by definition, changes in mark-ups. Table 3.7 shows the breakdown of the price changes into these two components during the two most recent episodes of yen appreciation. Reductions in marginal cost are substantial in both periods. Nevertheless, only three out of 31 sectors in the CPI registered declines in price indices during the more recent period of yen appreciation, and even in the previous episode, only 10 sectors experienced declines in price indices.

These results confirm our conclusions in the last section. The lack of response in the CPI is not due to the sluggishness of WPI response to the appreciation of the yen. Decline in marginal cost is almost totally due to the decline in the WPI. Our estimation in the last section has shown that price response is roughly symmetrical, and the size of the response is, on average, substantial at the WPI level. It is the sluggishness of retail prices that accounts for the stubbornness of domestic prices. As we have seen above, differences between sectors are not apparent. The differences in responsiveness are far more pronounced in the upward than in the downward direction.

Conclusion

The chapter has investigated the performance of Japanese distribution channels in terms of price adjustments. Available evidence suggests that the predominance of

Table 3.7 Response of prices, marginal costs and mark-ups to yen appreciation, 1985–88 and 1990–93 (per cent change during period)

	1985–88			1990–93		
	Price	Marginal cost	Mark-up	Price	Marginal cost	Mark-up
Cereals	0.154	−0.165	0.150	0.094	−0.061	0.076
Fish	0.126	−0.165	0.168	0.113	−0.061	0.111
Meat	0.043	−0.147	0.137	0.090	−0.044	0.112
Dairy products	0.040	−0.165	0.150	0.094	−0.061	0.132
Vegetables	0.005	−0.077	0.049	0.126	−0.100	0.202
Fruits	−0.001	−0.191	0.160	0.045	−0.156	0.189
Oils	−0.048	−0.217	0.135	0.039	−0.171	0.180
Confectionery	−0.066	−0.114	0.017	0.013	−0.113	0.103
Precooked food	0.184	−0.112	0.340	0.053	−0.113	0.240
Beverages	0.210	−0.131	−0.075	−0.116	−0.119	0.020
Liquor	0.035	−0.131	0.073	0.081	−0.119	0.181
Furniture	−0.023	−0.139	0.100	0.035	0.014	0.022
Clothing	−0.147	−0.108	−0.081	0.011	−0.091	0.088
Underwear	−0.664	−0.140	−0.562	0.144	−0.148	0.262
Footwear	0.078	−0.108	0.133	0.077	−0.091	0.141
Fabric	−0.058	−0.051	−0.024	−0.062	−0.108	0.030
Medicines	0.018	−0.091	0.070	0.045	−0.125	0.141
Sanitary goods	0.048	−0.003	0.009	0.008	−0.036	0.010
Autos and auto repairs	0.023	−0.219	0.189	0.003	−0.200	0.166
Consumer durables	−0.251	−0.049	−0.197	−0.086	−0.146	0.052
Personal effects	−0.016	−0.142	0.090	0.062	−0.190	0.221
Tobacco	0.105	−0.143	0.192	0.009	−0.139	0.094

Source: Ariga and Ohkusa (1995).

small-scale retailers has exerted an important influence not only on the structure but also on the performance of distribution channels. Obviously, size per se cannot be the real cause. We believe that it lies rather in the nature of the retail market competition that has allowed the survival of these stores. Small-scale retailers owe their survival mainly to the geographical segmentation of local retail markets. The regulatory framework, *keiretsu* marketing policies aimed at helping retailers, and the unique sociocultural background in which stores operate have, to varying degrees, all helped these small retailers to survive.

The recent relaxation of the *Daiten-Hō* and of a host of other regulations is likely to further accelerate the integration of local retail markets. We are beginning to witness such changes: rapid growth of suburban shopping centres, specialty shops and discount stores, and a shift towards more aggressive pricing policies. As far as price responsiveness is concerned, it is yet to be seen what (if any) ramifications these changes will have. It is unlikely, however, that they will wipe out all the factors that differentiate the structure and performance of various distribution channels.[15] We do not expect that increased competition at the retail level will reshape distribution channels so that, in the end, they will all look like type I. What we can hope for is that increased competition will force small as well as large-scale retailers to compete along dimensions other than location. Geographical segmentation has overly restricted the viable means for retailers to differentiate themselves.

We end this chapter on an obvious but important cautionary note. Our analysis of price adjustment captures only one of the many functions distribution systems are expected to perform. The value of price information varies from one commodity to another, and from one distribution channel to another. Our analysis indicates that the relative performance measurements in price formation reflect the relative importance of the allocative roles of the prices in various distribution channels. Investigation of possible trade-offs between the various other functions of distribution channels is important for future research.

Appendix 3.1: Data selection and classification

Selection of price indices

We obtained 380 pairs from the list of price indices in the WPI, CPI and MPI. The list of final pairs used in the analysis is available upon request. We used 110 pairs for the estimation spanning the entire period (January 1970 to September 1992: data set A). Among these 110 pairs, 100 pairs were chosen for the estimation of the first half (January 1970 to December 1979: data set B), and 78 pairs were chosen for the estimation of the second half (January 1980 to September 1992: data set C). We also selected 58 different pairs for the second half for which data were not available before 1980 (data set D).

Distribution types

The CPI and WPI price series used in the analysis were sorted into either the 29 (retail) or 38 (wholesale) divisions, by consulting Japanese Standard Industry Classification Codes (*Nihon Hyōjun Sangyō Bunrui*) published by the Japanese Management and Coordination Agency (Sōmuchō). We decided to group 29 CPI series and 31 WPI series as a miscellaneous category. Most of these were non-manufactured commodities that were not amenable to our type classifications. The remainder of the series was then further aggregated into four prototype groups, as shown in Table A3.1.1.

Table A3.1.1 Classification by type of transaction

Wholesale price index

Type I (15)
General merchandise
Paints, dyestuffs
Chemical products, misc.
Iron and steel
Minerals and metals
Precision machinery
Machinery, misc.
Sheet glass
Misc. building materials
Recovered materials
Rice, barley and wheat
Meat and poultry
Fresh fish and shellfish
Farm, livestock, misc.
Paper and paper products

Type III (4)
Petroleum
Motor vehicles
Motor vehicles, parts and accessories
Electrical machinery

Type II (14)
Textiles
Textiles, misc.
Men's clothing
Women's and children's clothing
Underwear
Shoes
Misc. apparel accessories
Bakery and confectionery products
Drugs
Toiletries
Furniture and fixtures
Chinaware and glassware
Household furnishings, misc.
Hardware

Type IV (5)
Vegetables and fruits
Beverages
Cured foods
Canned and bottled foods
Food and beverages, misc.

Consumer price index

Type II (17)
Misc. general merchandise stores
Dry goods, dress materials stores
Men's ready-made suits
Women's and children's dress stores
Footwear
Apparel accessories
Misc. retail trade — apparel
Meat and poultry
Fresh fish
Confectionery and bakery stores
Furniture, fixtures and straw mats
Hardware and kitchenware
Misc. household products
Drugs and toiletries
Books and stationery
Watches, spectacles and optical goods stores
Misc. retail trade, not elsewhere classified

Type III (4)
Motor vehicles
Motorcycles and bicycles
Household appliances
Fuel stores

Type IV (7)
Grocery stores
Beverage and seasoning stores
Cured food stores
Misc. retail food and beverage stores
Vegetable and fruit stores
Sporting goods, toys and amusement goods
Cameras and photographic supplies

Note: The names of divisions of wholesale and retail trades are taken from Ministry of International Trade and Industry (1987), *5th Survey of Commercial Structure and Activity*, Tokyo.

Appendix 3.2: Model and estimation procedure

A simple model

We will consider the following simple model of a distribution channel. A distributor purchases its merchandise from upstream firms (a manufacturer or upstream distributor) at price q. The distributor sells the merchandise to consumers or downstream distributors at price p. The distributor's activity can be considered as a production process in which the distributor purchases merchandise from upstream firms and provides services, the combination of which results in trade of the merchandise to downstream firms or to consumers. We assume a conventional neoclassical production function, which is strictly increasing and concave in inputs (commodities purchased from upstream firms and distributive services generated by labour) and which exhibits non-increasing returns to scale. Then the cost of distributing y units of the merchandise is given by:

$$C = y \, \phi(y) \, \psi(w, q),$$

where $\phi(y)$ is non-decreasing in y and ψ is concave and linear homogeneous in w, the wage rate, and q. (That is, doubling w and q doubles the unit cost). The distributor faces the demand function given by:

$$D = D(p/\bar{P}, Z)$$

where $\bar{P}$ is the appropriate general price level and Z is a vector of exogenous variables affecting demand. The target price which maximises the gross profit, $\pi \equiv pD - C$, is given by:

$$p^* = p^*(w, q, \bar{P})$$

where p^* is linear homogeneous in w, q and $\bar{P}$. If the firm can instantaneously change its price without cost, the actual price must always be equal to the target price. Deviation of the price from the target reduces the gross profit. After taking a linear approximation around $p = p^*$, the gross profit function can be given by:

$$\pi(p_t) \cong \pi(p_t^*) - L_1(dp_t), \quad dp_t \equiv p_t^* - p_t$$

L_1 is strictly increasing and convex in the absolute value of the deviation of the actual price from p^*, where we use the property that the derivative of the profit at $p = p^*$ is zero.

We assume that the firm does not always set the price at the target level because changing prices is costly. There are various reasons why a firm might find it costly to change its price, even apart from the purely physical costs of doing so. Given that there is no way to model them all precisely, in the analysis below all of these potentially diverse sources of costs are summarily represented by L_2:

$$L_2 = L_2(\Delta p_t), \Delta p_t = p_t - p_{t-1}$$

The firm maximises profit net of the cost of price changes. That is, the firm sets the price in such a way that the price minimises the sum of the cost of price changes (L_2) and the loss of profit due to the deviation (L_1). Therefore, the optimal pricing policy which maximises the present value of the net profit stream solves:

$$V_s = \text{Min} \sum_{t=s}^{\infty} \rho^{t-s} E[L_1(dp_t) + L_2(\Delta p_t) \mid \Omega_s]$$

where ρ is the discount factor and the expectation is conditional upon Ω_s, the set of information available to the firm at the beginning of each period, s. The resulting optimal pricing policy is a mapping from the vector of exogenous variables and the price in the previous period to the current period price.

Estimation procedure

There are several ways to estimate empirically the optimal pricing policy. One is to estimate directly the fully fledged optimal solution. This procedure requires specification and estimation of the probability distribution over which the expectation is taken in the equation above; in particular, it requires estimation of the joint probability distribution of all the variables in Ω_0. We use an alternative procedure. Suppose that the firm sets the price at the beginning of each period before observing values of exogenous variables, $\{w_t, q_t, \bar{P}_t, Z_t\}$. The optimal policy is written generically as:

$$p_t = \xi(p_{t-1}, w_{t-1}, w_{t-2}, ..., q_{t-1}, q_{t-2}, ..., \bar{P}_{t-1}, \bar{P}_{t-2}, ..., Z_{t-1}, Z_{t-2}, ...)$$

Since we do not directly observe the vector of exogenous variables Z, the resulting optimal policy is a probability distribution conditional upon the observable state variables: that is, the price set in the previous period, and the past realisations of $\{w, q, \bar{P}\}$.[16] The latter is represented concisely by $dp_{t-1} = p^*_{t-1} - p_{t-1}$.

Consider a vertical distribution channel in which product price at each stage of distribution is determined in the manner described above. To estimate the pricing policy, we need a vector of prices of the same product at different stages of distribution. To approximate actual transaction prices, we used three price indices: consumer price index (CPI), wholesale price index (WPI) and imported price index (MPI). For each CPI of a commodity or a commodity group, we looked for the corresponding WPI as the upstream price. Similarly, we used the MPI of each commodity as the upstream price for WPI. We were able to find 380 pairs; of these,

30 were taken out due to an insufficient number of observations. (Some of the series start at the beginning of 1990.) This left us with 350 matched pairs of upstream and downstream prices for the same commodity or commodity group.

In the first stage, we obtained ordinary least squares (OLS) estimates of the target price level for each pair of upstream and downstream price indices:

$$p_t^{i*} = \alpha^i q_t^i + \beta^i w_t + \gamma^i \bar{P}_t + \delta^i + u_t^i$$

where p_t^{i*} is the target price of commodity i in period t, q_t^i is the relevant upstream price, w_t is the average monthly wage rate in the distribution sector, $\bar{P}_t$ is the relevant general (aggregate) price level (WPI if p_t^i is a WPI index, CPI if p_t^i is a CPI index), δ^i is the constant (intercept) and u_t^i is a disturbance term. We ran OLS regressions of p_t^i and used the estimated regressions to generate p_t^{i*}. We further deleted three pairs whose OLS estimates of α^i were negative (they were probably incorrectly matched). Among the 347 pairs that we used, the longest span of available data are for January 1970 to September 1992. For about 150 pairs, the data are available for this entire period. In most of the remaining pairs, the data start from January 1980. Consequently, we divided the sample period into two sets: January 1970 to December 1979, and January 1980 to September 1992. Depending upon the pairs and data availability, we obtained four different sets of OLS estimates. The first-stage results are summarised in Table A3.2.1.

Table A3.2.1 Summary statistics for first-stage regressions

	Data set A		Data set B		Data set C		Data set D	
Constant	0.236	−0.066	0.016	−0.290	0.818	−2.168	0.662	2.17
	(1.31)	(2.33)	(1.61)	(2.57)	(3.28)	(5.93)	(3.41)	(6.82)
$\bar{P}$ (general price level)	0.274	0.219	0.226	0.314	0.880	0.375	0.920	0.089
	(0.758)	(0.276)	(0.749)	(0.790)	(1.68)	(0.505)	(1.79)	(1.09)
q (upstream price)	0.544	0.517	0.578	0.483	0.483	0.463	0.536	0.461
	(0.448)	(0.376)	(0.353)	(0.336)	(0.448)	(0.240)	(0.456)	(0.283)
w (wage rate)	0.088	0.194	0.138	0.184	−0.378	0.434	−0.117	−0.014
	(0.563)	(0.447)	(0.473)	(0.456)	(1.24)	(0.556)	(1.33)	(0.662)
Adjusted R^2	0.93	0.89	0.94	0.90	0.84	0.82	0.84	0.84

Notes: Sample period is January 1970 to September 1992 for data set A; January 1970 to December 1979 for data set B; January 1980 to September 1992 for data set C; and January 1980 to September 1992 for data set D.

Data sets B and C are obtained by dividing data set A into two subperiods. Data set D contains pairs of prices available only after January 1980 (Appendix 3.1). Numbers shown are averages and standard deviations (in brackets) of estimated coefficients over each set of regressions. Results for the 347 individual regressions are available from the authors upon request.

In the second stage, we estimated the probability distribution of price changes conditional upon the deviation and the price in the previous period. Upon inspection of matched pairs, we found that a large fraction of observations was concentrated on zero price changes. To incorporate this feature, we used the following estimation procedure. First we estimated the probability of price changes; that is, the probability of a price increase, a price decrease and zero price change. Next, we estimated the probability distribution of the size *conditional upon* the price change, using the maximum likelihood estimation method (see Appendix 3.3). The estimated probabilities are:

$Prob.[\Delta p_t^i > 0 | dp_{t-1}^i] = f_i^1(dp_{t-1}^i)$ (probability of price increase)

$Prob.[\Delta p_t^i < 0 | dp_{t-1}^i] = f_i^2(dp_{t-1}^i)$ (probability of price decrease)

$Prob.[\Delta p_t^i \leq x | dp_{t-1}^i, \Delta p_t^i > 0] = g_i^1(x | dp_{t-1}^i)$ (conditional distribution of price increase)

$Prob.[\Delta p_t^i \leq x | dp_{t-1}^i, \Delta p_t^i < 0] = g_i^2(x | dp_{t-1}^i)$ (conditional distribution of price decrease)

where $dp_{t-1}^i \equiv p_{t-1}^{i*} - p_{t-1}^i$

$$f_i^k = \frac{\exp.[a_{i1}^k + a_{i2}^k dp_{t-1}^i]}{1 + \sum_{j=1}^{2} \exp.[a_{i1}^j + a_{i2}^j dp_{t-1}^i]}, \quad k=1,2$$

$$g_i^k \sim N(b_{i1}^k + b_{i2}^k dp_{t-1}^i, \sigma_{ik}^2), \quad k=1,2$$

where $n(\mu, \sigma^2)$ is the normal density function with mean μ and variance σ^2. In short, we obtained for the *i*th pair the estimates of $\{a_{i1}^1, a_{i2}^1, a_{i1}^2, a_{i2}^2, b_{i1}^1, b_{i2}^1, b_{i1}^2, b_{i2}^2, \sigma_{i1}, \sigma_{i2}\}$.

Appendix 3.3: Estimation method

The quadruple of conditional probabilities for each pair of price indices was estimated as follows. Given the first stage estimate of the target price $\{p_t^*\}$ and the actual price $\{p_t\}$ (both in logs), we compute:

$\Delta p_t^i = p_t^i - p_{t-1}^i$

$dp_t^i = p_t^{i*} - p_t^i$

Our objective is to estimate the density of Δp_t^i conditional upon dp_{t-1}^i. For this purpose, we introduce:

$$y_t^i = \text{sign}(\Delta p_t^i)$$

which takes the value of one, zero and minus one when (respectively) Δp_t^i is positive, zero and negative. Consider the following model:

(#) $\begin{cases} Prob.[\Delta p_t^i > 0 | dp_{t-1}^i] = a_{i1}^1 + a_{i2}^1 dp_{t-1}^i + u_t^{i1} \equiv f_i^1(dp_{t-1}^i) + u_t^{i1} \\ Prob.[\Delta p_t^i < 0 | dp_{t-1}^i] = a_{i1}^2 + a_{i2}^2 dp_{t-1}^i + u_t^{i2} \equiv f_i^2(dp_{t-1}^i) + u_t^{i2} \\ \Delta p_t^i \big|_{\Delta p_t^i > 0} = b_{i1}^1 + b_{i2}^1 dp_{t-1}^i + v_t^{i1} \equiv g_i^1(dp_{t-1}^i | \Delta p_t^i > 0) \\ \Delta p_t^i \big|_{\Delta p_t^i < 0} = b_{i1}^2 + b_{i2}^2 dp_{t-1}^i + v_t^{i2} \equiv g_i^2(dp_{t-1}^i | \Delta p_t^i < 0) \end{cases}$

where $g_i^k \sim N(b_{i1}^k + b_{i2}^k dp_{t-1}^i, \sigma_{ik}^2)$, $k = 1, 2$.

The entire system (#) can be estimated as a mixture of the multilogit model for y_t^i and the truncated regressions for Δp_t^i (the size of the price changes). We first obtained the initial parameter values by running regressions separately for each of the four equations in (#). With first-stage estimates as the initial values, we simultaneously estimated the system (#) using the maximum likelihood method. The likelihood function is:

$$L \equiv \frac{1}{1 + \exp.[f_i^1(dp_{t-1}^i)] + \exp.[f_i^2(dp_{t-1}^i)]}$$

$$\times \Pi_1 \exp.[f_i^1(dp_{t-1}^i)] \times \frac{\phi\left(\frac{v_t^{i1}}{\sigma_{i1}}\right)}{\sigma_{i1} \Phi\left(\frac{-g_i^1(dp_{t-1}^i | \Delta p_t^i > 0)}{\sigma_{i1}}\right)}$$

$$\times \Pi_2 \exp.[f_1^2(dp_{t-1}^i)] \times \frac{\phi\left(\frac{v_t^{i2}}{\sigma_{i2}}\right)}{\sigma_{i2} \Phi\left(\frac{-g_i^2(dp_{t-1}^i | \Delta p_t^i < 0)}{\sigma_{i2}}\right)}$$

where ϕ and Φ are standard normal density and cumulative density functions. Π_1 (Π_2) are moments which are applicable only when Δp_t^i is positive (negative).

Notes

1. Flath and Nariu (1994) show that the density of small-scale retailers in Japan can be explained by the relative smallness of dwellings, geographic concentration and the high number of commercial vehicles relative to private ones, controlling for the effects of population density.

2. For example, shops with fewer than 10 workers (including the owner) register 54.8 per cent of total sales in Japan, compared with 29.2 per cent in the United States, 51.5 per cent in France, 44.2 per cent in Germany and 26.2 per cent in the United Kingdom.

3. For a comprehensive international comparison of the Japanese distribution system, see Maruyama (1993).

4. Trade finance also has an insurance function; in many cases upstream manufacturers must start accumulating product inventory to meet seasonal demand from downstream. At this point, however, final demand is quite uncertain and manufacturers face risks on top of financing costs. By offering advance payments and ordering predetermined amounts, wholesalers are able to absorb these risks.

5. See Sheard (1989) for the role of trading companies in these types of transactions. Emery and Ariga (1993) offer some econometric analysis of the determinants of trade credit.

6. The rapid growth of independent retailers and the stagnation of *keiretsu* retailers necessitated the reshuffling and integration of wholesalers, most of which enjoyed an exclusive trading relationship with one manufacturer. For example, Matsushita (Panasonic), which had 230 regional wholesalers in the early 1970s, now has 80 and is believed to be planning further reshuffling and integration.

7. The description in this paragraph relates to changes that have occurred in the last two to three years (and which are still continuing). Due to the unprecedented pace of change, uncertainty surrounding the industry is unusually large. Description and assessment are therefore necessarily tentative.

8. Even some of the largest GMS chains expressly announced that they would not pursue an aggressive pricing strategy.

9. Examples include automobile dealers (investments in service and repair facilities, coordinated investments in advertising, common sharing of personnel); customised eye glass chain stores (standardised marketing strategy, access to lists of potential customers and customer information); shared investment in the Just In Time (JIT) inventory ordering system; and express mail networks. They all have features in common with the more well-known examples from manufacturing industries (Asanuma 1989).

10. The predominance of small-scale retailers is also an important factor. Partial exclusion is common among such retailers.

11. Caballero and Engel (1992) obtain similar results with US data for aggregate price levels.

12 Carlton (1986) fails to detect downward rigidity over samples of individual commodity prices. His samples are industrial intermediate goods. Perhaps downward rigidity is more pronounced at the retail level in other countries too. Borenstein, Cameron and Gilbert (1992) find substantial downward rigidity in retail gasoline prices.

13 We used the estimated quadruple of the probability distribution of price changes. To simulate responses to shocks, we obtained numerically the conditional distribution of price changes from the estimated quadruple and then simulated a response for 1,000 replica firms, the results of which were averaged to obtain the final result. Details are available upon request.

14 This section is based on our unpublished work on retail mark-ups in Japan. The original paper is available from the authors upon request.

15 For example, Yamashita, Iba and Arai (1992) report that an increase in the share of large-scale retailers in each regional market reduces average retail prices at small retailers for consumer durables and processed foods. On the other hand, they find that the effect is precisely the opposite for fresh foods. Clearly, increased competition sometimes alters the principal means of competition.

16 There is, in principle, no presumption that w, q and $\bar{P}$ enter into the policy function in this particular way. Neither is it legitimate to exclude *a priori* the realisations of these variables two or more periods before. Our choice is made for two reasons. First, each exogenous variable requires five free parameters to be estimated. Given the limited number of observations, it is imperative to limit the number of right-hand side variables to only a few. Second, our specification is natural and easier to interpret economically.

References

Ariga, K. (ed.) (1993), *Nihon-teki Ryūtsū no Keizaigaku* [Economic Analysis of the Japanese Distribution System], Tokyo: Nihon Keizai Shinbunsha.

Ariga, K., H. Namikawa and Y. Ohkusa (1991), 'The Japanese Distribution System', *Ricerche Economiche*, 45 (2–3), pp. 185–230.

Ariga, K. and Y. Ohkusa (1995), Retail Price Markups in Japan, Tokyo: Institute for Price Formation (mimeo).

Asanuma, B. (1989), 'Manufacturer–Supplier Relationships in Japan and the Concept of Relation-Specific Skill', *Journal of the Japanese and International Economies*, 3, pp. 1–30.

Ball, L.N., G. Mankiw and D. Romer (1988), 'The New Keynesian Economics and the Output Inflation Trade-Off', *Brookings Papers on Economic Activity*, 1, pp. 1–65.

Borenstein, S., A.C. Cameron and R. Gilbert (1992), 'Do Gasoline Prices Respond Asymmetrically to Crude Oil Price Changes?', NBER Working Paper No. 4138, Cambridge, MA.

Caballero, R.J. (1992), 'A Fallacy of Composition', *American Economic Review*, 82 (5), pp. 1,279–92.

Caballero, R.J. and E. Engel (1991), 'Dynamic S-s economies', *Econometrica*, 59, pp. 1,659–86.

—— (1992), 'Microeconomic Rigidities and Aggregate Price Dynamics', NBER Working Paper No. 4162, Cambridge, MA.

Caplin, A.S. and D.F. Spulber (1987), 'Menu Costs and the Neutrality of Money', *Quarterly Journal of Economics*, 102, pp. 703–26.

Carlton, D.W. (1986), 'The Rigidity of Prices', *American Economic Review*, 76, pp. 637–58.

Emery, G.W. and K. Ariga (1993), 'Kigyō-kan Shinyō to Kigyō-kan Kankei no Bunseki' [An Analysis of Interfirm Credit and Interfirm Relations], *Financial Review*, 27, pp. 165–81.

Flath, D. and T. Nariu (1994), Is Japan's Retail Sector Truly Distinctive?, Paper presented to the Seventh Annual Meeting of Association of Japanese Business Studies, Vancouver.

Itoh, M. (1993), 'Organizational Transactions and Access to the Japanese Import Market', in Paul Sheard (ed.), *International Adjustment and the Japanese Firm*, Sydney: Allen and Unwin.

Kurasawa, Y. (1991), 'Ryūtsū no Tadankai-sei to Henpin-sei' [Multistage Distribution Channels and Returns], in Y. Miwa and K.G. Nishimura (eds), *Nihon no Ryūtsū* [The Japanese Distribution System], Tokyo: University of Tokyo Press.

Maruyama, M. (1993), *A Study on the Distribution System in Japan*, Paris: OECD.

Sheard, P. (1989), 'The Japanese General Trading Companies as an Aspect of Inter-Firm Risk Sharing', *Journal of the Japanese and International Economies*, 3, pp. 308–22.

Yamashita, M., H. Iba and K. Arai (1992),'Ōgata Kouriten no Sannyū Kisei to Kouri Kakaku no Hendō [Entry Regulations for Large-Scale Retailers and Their Effects on Retail Prices], *Keizai Bunseki*, 127.

Part II

Corporate Governance Structures

4 Corporate governance and employment incentives: is the Japanese system really different?

Gerald T. Garvey and Peter L. Swan*

Corporate governance is an issue of immense importance both to policy makers and to individual firms. The past few years has seen a flood of articles in the business and popular press wrestling with the question of what 'good' governance is and how to achieve it (*Harvard Business Review*, November–December 1991, pp. 136–43; *Business Week*, 15 March 1993, pp. 38–45). A recent survey in *The Economist* (29 January 1994, pp. S1–S18) summarises the popular and political debate in the United States, Japan and Europe. Some commentators have even attributed the successes of the Japanese and German economies to their unique systems of corporate governance, and urged their transmission to Anglo-American corporations.[1] This chapter summarises past achievements and future research opportunities in the comparative corporate governance area.

Webster's International Dictionary (1971) defines the term 'governance' as follows: 'to exercise arbitrarily or by established rules continuous sovereign authority over'; and 'to rule without sovereign power; to implement and carry into effect policy decisions without having the power to determine basic policy'.

In the corporate context, governance issues are thrown into stark relief by events such as takeovers, shareholder meetings and proxy contests, as well as controversies surrounding board composition and executive compensation. More mundane decisions involving the allocation of physical, human and financial resources, capital budgeting, expansion or contraction of the firm's boundaries, and labour negotiations are also strongly affected by governance.

Despite the significance of these questions, governance has not occupied a central place in economic theory, reflecting the more general tendency of economics to neglect

---

* This chapter is a revised version of 'The Economics of Corporate Governance: Beyond the Marshallian Firm', originally published in the *Journal of Corporate Finance* (1994, 1 [2], pp. 139–74). The authors would like to thank Elsevier Science B.V., Amsterdam, for kind permission to reprint the article.

the theory of the firm.[2] As Demsetz (1982) points out, the perfect competition model of microeconomics is actually a model of perfect decentralisation, in which no one exercises any authority or power over anyone else. Governance has no content in such a world. Hart (1988) sharpens this argument by stressing that both the general equilibrium model of Arrow and Debreu (1954) and the more recent models of incentive problems under asymmetric information assume complete contracts, which leave no role for governance. Governance is irrelevant because a comprehensive set of rules and policies is negotiated in the markets where the firm secures its inputs and sells its output.

Governance matters only when contracts are incomplete. A key implication — and one which has not been widely recognised in the literature — is that the parties who make the decisions that fill in the details of the incomplete contract ('executives') cannot have the same incentives as the 'entrepreneur' who populates microeconomics textbooks. Even if an executive held 100 per cent of the firm's equity shares, his/her wealth would not reflect the firm's net contribution to social welfare. This is because the executive's decisions affect the welfare of *other* members of the firm (investors, workers, managers and/or customers), at least in an *ex post* sense.[3] The case of bond covenants provides a convenient illustration. At the time bonds are sold, the firm will often promise, not only to make fixed payments, but also to restrict its dividends, to maintain liquidity and sometimes even to refrain from investing in certain areas (Smith and Warner 1979). But corporate decision makers are free to take a whole range of actions not covered by the covenants but which may nonetheless affect the welfare of bondholders. The bondholders bear any losses and enjoy any gains that flow from alterations in the riskiness or, indeed, the expected value of the firm's return profile. This simply says that bond prices will move for reasons other than exogenous realisations of states of nature.

The firm's actions are not perfectly controlled, but loosely guided, by rules negotiated in arm's-length markets, and the costs and benefits of its actions are *not* borne entirely by shareholders. To understand the operations of such firms, we must look beyond the markets in which they do business to the incentives and objectives of the executives who make the 'filling-in' decisions. This chapter surveys attempts to endogenise these objectives. It contrasts two approaches: rent seeking theories that focus, explicitly or implicitly, on the ways in which executives extract wealth from other agents in the economy; and efficiency theories which stress that executives help internalise the externalities inherent in a world of incomplete contracts.

An informal model

The basic theoretical framework that underpins most economic analysis of governance issues was first outlined by Jensen and Meckling (1976). The firm begins with a single founder or entrepreneur who wishes to secure additional resources, including capital, labour and perhaps managerial talent. The founder is assumed unable to write contracts that fully map out the firm's future for every conceivable circumstance, such as booms or recessions, war or peace, or the presence or absence of major technological innovations. The contract will be completed by the discretionary actions of other parties, including but not restricted to 'nature' (which mechanically resolves uncertainty). These actions are discretionary in that there will be decisions on which the contract is silent. Essentially, the founder chooses the firm's charter provisions, its top executives and the terms of its contracts with suppliers of capital and labour. In a federal system such as that of the United States, the founder may also select the set of corporate laws by choosing the firm's state of incorporation. Clearly, such choices do not determine fully the firm's response to a hostile takeover bid, the pay and promotion of future workers and managers, the resolution of financial distress and the raising of new capital, or future joint ventures and acquisitions.

While the charter and other *ex ante* contractual features do not set out in detail specific actions to be taken, the founder can influence indirectly the identity and incentives of the parties who will make decisions. Some decisions are subject to a vote of shareholders, others are made by the board, and others are essentially left to managerial discretion.[4] (Except where otherwise indicated, we will refer to the firm's board and top management interchangeably as 'executives'.)

Although many decisions are subject to the discretion of shareholders and/or managers, we assume that *expectations* of all such actions are priced *ex ante*; that is, all affected parties form rational expectations about the actions the relevant decision makers will take while insisting on receiving at least their expected utility levels *ex ante*. With the exception of the public choice approach summarised later in the chapter, it is generally assumed that the founder will choose to set up efficient structures in order to pre-commit executives to use decision making authority in ways that take account of the costs and benefits that the decisions will confer.

This model of governance involves an *ex ante* stage in which market prices and contracts are formed, and an *ex post* stage in which actual decisions are made (Williamson 1988). In technical terms, we focus on the subgame perfect equilibria of contracting games, all of which share the following basic structure. The founder first chooses the legal jurisdiction plus key elements of the firm's charter; investors, workers and other parties then decide whether or not to participate; workers and others choose actions; executives (the founder's delegates) take some other action (decisions on investment and/or promotion, for example); and finally, nature resolves uncertainty and legally binding elements of any agreement are executed. This model incorporates nearly all the theories summarised in this chapter (the exceptions being those in which nature reveals information earlier to some parties than to others, that is, signalling models). No methodological advances beyond those surveyed in Hart and Holmstrom (1987) are involved. Indeed, a central message of this chapter is that governance is an area where we can fruitfully apply techniques that have been well known since the early 1980s.

The specific form of the model is dictated by the problem at hand and by findings based on the existing literature. There is in fact a great deal of evidence to guide theoretical models, even though many studies are themselves only loosely guided by modern theory.[5] The next section presents a picture of the causes and consequences of corporate governance structures based on existing studies. It is necessarily interpretative and is meant to stimulate further research. Our rather bald assertions about the world of corporate governance are deliberately intended to suggest the type of theoretical and empirical work we think would be most valuable.

Our basic empirical contention is that most large firms are managerial,[6] in the sense that often decisions are *not* made primarily in the interests of shareholders (who are, at least legally, the equivalent of Marshall's residual claimant entrepreneur).[7] In other words, the separation of share ownership and firm control highlighted by Berle and Means in the early 1930s is real. We believe, moreover, that there are substantially greater departures from shareholder wealth maximisation than are suggested by the costs of risk aversion and monitoring stressed in the traditional principal–agent models. To use the jargon, the direct costs of reducing the degree to which many managers are entrenched and insulated from pressures to maximise shareholder wealth are not prohibitive. Many decisions heavily weight the interests of parties other than shareholders, even though it would be relatively easy to give shareholders a greater role.

This assertion is controversial, particularly among Chicago-style economists, because it seems to imply that governance is inefficient in the sense that government intervention to specify certain practices or structures would improve social welfare.[8] Our contention is that, in a world of incomplete contracts, there is no reason why the entrenchment of management should be construed as inefficient. A useful analogy is with what Williamson (1985) termed the 'inhospitality tradition' in antitrust, whereby business practices that did not conform with textbook theory were immediately interpreted as monopolistic and counter to the public interest. As the courts have come increasingly to recognise, the point is that, *in order to be efficient*, businesses operating under conditions that differ from those in the textbooks must adopt practices that similarly differ from those in the texts (Coase 1972). In a world of positive transaction costs, it is efficient for many firms to adopt practices that do not resemble textbook, arm's-length transactions. By the same token, if the world of corporate governance is accurately depicted as a standard principal–agent problem involving only shareholders and a top manager, then the observed decoupling of managers' and shareholders' wealth would be inefficient.

A portrait of the typical corporation

This section summarises recent empirical studies that investigate whether the typical large corporation is run mainly in the shareholder's interests and, if not, in whose interests it is in fact run. Reflecting the bias in the literature, our portrait will be most accurate for the case of the United States.

How important are shareholders?

Top management compensation

A multitude of studies has examined the correlation between top managers' wealth and various measures of the firm's financial performance. The best known of the recent work is Jensen and Murphy (1990), who conclude that the average US chief executive officer (CEO) receives less than five cents for every thousand dollar increase in shareholder wealth, even taking into account managerial stock holdings, options, and the linkage between the likelihood of dismissal and share price (see also Warner, Watts and Wruck 1988). Kato and Rockel (1992a) find a similar pattern for Japanese CEOs. While their pay is on average far less that that of US CEOs, the correlation with shareholder wealth is if anything somewhat weaker.

Compounding the relatively weak linkage between managerial and shareholder wealth is the common finding that top executives' pay is approximately three times more sensitive to firm size (measured as total assets or sales) than to shareholder wealth. Murphy (1985) finds that this correlation holds over time as well as cross-sectionally, suggesting that the size–pay relationship is not simply due to large firms hiring more able executives, as suggested by Rosen (1982). Kato (1995) finds that firm size and investment levels are also positively associated with CEO compensation in Japan.

Reputation effects

The assumption that managers act in the shareholder's interests is not always justified by reference to their explicit financial incentives. Fama (1980) takes the extreme view that even if management compensation were formally unrelated to share price, top managers would still seek to maximise shareholder wealth in order to protect or enhance their reputations in the managerial labour market. Holmstrom (1982) shows that this conclusion is optimistic and that reputation will rarely reduce agency costs to zero. Gibbons and Murphy (1992a, 1992b) find evidence consistent with the conclusion that while reputation may go some way towards aligning the interests of managers and shareholders, the effects are not overwhelmingly strong, particularly for managers near the end of their careers.

More recent theoretical research casts further doubt on the notion that reputational concerns drive managers to act in the shareholder's interests. Holmstrom and Ricart i Costa (1986) and others show how reputation can take the form of career concerns that actually *encourage* managers to act counter to the interests of their shareholders (see Borland 1992 for a survey). A related weakness with the reputational story is that it must assume that hiring decisions are always made in the interests of shareholders. Reputation induced distortions will be far greater if executives believe their future employers may be Berle–Means type firms, interested more in how their talents will contribute to the utility of incumbent managers than in whether they serve the interests of shareholders. It should be noted that career concerns are likely to be far weaker in

Japan, where most CEOs are promoted from within the firm and overall turnover is much lower (Kato and Rockel 1992b).

The threat of takeover
An early commentator on the question of whether or not corporations are run in shareholder interests made no reference to managerial reputation and only passing reference to compensation. Manne (1965) argued that competition for the votes generally attached to equity shares (or the 'market for corporate control') was the most important force driving managers to maximise shareholder wealth. Certainly many takeovers in the 1980s bear out his view that gross managerial slack can be pruned by hostile takeovers or the threat thereof (Agrawal and Walkling 1991; Jensen 1988; Martin and McConnell 1991; Davis and Stout 1992; Morck, Shleifer and Vishney 1988a, 1988b).

While the takeover threat is clearly a force that motivates managers to look after their shareholders, it has distinct limitations. Hostile takeovers are, after all, rare in Germany and Japan (Kester 1991a, 1991c). Even in the United States, regulatory developments and the chilling of the junk bond market have substantially dampened the takeover market (see, for example, Jensen 1991). But even before this there were sizeable cost barriers to hostile takeovers that served to insulate or even entrench incumbent managers. Bradley, Desai and Kim (1988) report that the price paid for shares in a successful takeover bid was on average 20–30 per cent higher than the pre-bid price, and that the shareholders of some 'successful' bidder firms actually lost money because of the takeover. While it would be an overstatement to claim that the market for corporate control actually exacerbates managerialism on the part of acquirers (Mitchell and Lehn 1991), there is scope for this view. It is clear that the threat of hostile takeover places only broad limits on the degree to which managers can run the firm in the interests of parties other than shareholders.

Proxy fights and shareholder 'voice'
Shareholders do not, in principle, need to sell to hostile bidders in order to influence management policy. They can exercise their voting rights to elect a new slate of directors, or even in some cases to recommend that explicit actions be taken by managers (see DeAngelo and DeAngelo 1989 for some instances).

With the chilling of the corporate control market in the 1990s, many large institutional shareholders, including public pension funds, have attempted — sometimes successfully — to influence corporate decisions (Pound 1992a). But those who would mount a challenge are at a severe disadvantage relative to management, not only in terms of their own knowledge of the corporation's real situation but also in terms of their ability to communicate with fellow shareholders and finance a campaign (Pound 1991; Roe 1990). Class action suits brought by shareholders are even less rewarding for the participants (Romano 1991).

At present large shareholders face enormous costs in influencing the behaviour of executives. Some commentators claim that this will change with the appearance of large pension funds and other potential 'relationship investors', who participate actively in the corporate governance decisions of the companies they own shares in, and are able to exert a major influence over corporate policies (*Harvard Business Review*, September–October 1990, pp. 70–82, and March–April 1991, pp. 106–14), but to date there is little systematic evidence of such a trend. While institutional investors now have substantial holdings in many firms, the institutions are themselves large organisations. It is not at all clear that the managers of these institutions are willing to push corporate managers to maximise the wealth of their beneficiaries. Lakonishok, Shleifer and Vishny (1992) argue that large pension funds tend to underperform the market, and Murphy and Van Nuys (1993) provide evidence that pension fund managers have little incentive to monitor actively the firms in which they invest. This suggests that the highly publicised incidents of institutional activism may be the exception rather than the rule.

Anecdotal evidence
The preceding sketch of available evidence has of necessity featured a great deal of interpretation. The importance of reputation and the threat of takeover are particularly difficult to identify in statistical studies. Given these ambiguities, softer evidence such as the views of those who advise top executives can make at least some contribution. While many statements that are flagrantly inconsistent with maximising shareholder wealth can be found in the popular press, we will mention two that have appeared in mainstream finance journals.

The first was made by a practising corporate lawyer who was invited to comment on conference papers published in the *Journal of Financial Economics* (Herzel 1990). Herzel focused on statistical studies aimed at discovering whether employee share ownership plans (ESOPs) and related devices are intended to increase shareholder wealth or protect management from takeover. He says:

> ... that leveraged ESOPs are being used as an anti-takeover device should surprise no one. In fact, that is how investment bankers sell leveraged ESOPs to prospective clients ... Courts and everyone else involved understand that leveraged ESOPs are being used as an anti takeover device (Herzel 1990, p. 582).

Herzel thus argues that US courts uphold management actions explicitly recognised as aimed at defeating and deferring takeover bids, not at extracting a higher price for shareholders. Such explicit recognition of acts against shareholder interests has since become unfashionable in the United States, with most managers at least avowing that, despite appearances, their actions were intended to maximise shareholder wealth (see, for instance, the panel discussions in Continental Bank Roundtable 1991, 1992).

A refreshingly candid exception is provided by Prahalad (1993, pp. 34–5), whose work on management strategy is widely acknowledged as highly influential:

> ... in the future, the scarce resource is not going to be capital but human talent. Shouldn't we now be using talent accumulation as one of our major criteria for judging corporate success ... as we enter this new world of global competition, I think we will be forced to re-examine our theory of wealth creation and its assumption of the primacy of shareholder value.

Do other constituencies matter?

The idea that corporate managers do not always act in shareholder interests is not new. The obvious problem that confronts any managerial model of corporate behaviour is to specify the objectives that executives actually pursue. Alchian (1965) summarises an earlier literature positing such alternative objectives as sales maximisation and consumption of perquisites. The incomplete contracts approach suggests that a more explicitly 'public choice' view of corporate objectives is appropriate, since members of the firm other than shareholders are affected by executive decisions (see Meyer, Milgrom and Roberts 1992 for one such theoretical treatment). We have little theory or direct evidence as yet to suggest how effective these other parties are in influencing managerial decisions. This section summarises recent evidence on the relative influence of non-shareholder constituencies.

The influence of senior claimants

Early agency models either focus on the relationship between managers and shareholders or assume that managers act in the interests of shareholders at the expense of bondholders (Jensen and Meckling 1976; Myers 1977). The key idea behind the latter class of models is that shareholders with limited liability receive all the residual gains to firm decisions when share prices increase, while bondholders bear some of the losses associated with poor performance (as in a bankruptcy). Problems attendant to downside losses, such as asset substitution and underinvestment, certainly do exist in cases such as the US savings and loans associations that were protected by deposit insurance (Kane 1989). But in general, the assumption that executives treat bankruptcy or financial distress lightly is implausible, as well as being inconsistent with new evidence for the United States. Gilson (1989) studied a large random sample of underperforming firms, of which only a fraction had sufficient debt in their capital structures to go into default. He found that management turnover in the distressed subsample was over three times as great as in the solvent subsample, even though losses borne by investors as a whole were similar in both subsamples. He also found that neither top managers nor 'outside' board members displaced by insolvency subsequently found similar positions in listed firms. Lo Pucki and Whitford (1990) showed that only three CEOs of a sample of 43 large firms that entered bankruptcy proceedings in the United States in 1979–88 retained their jobs through the ensuing negotiations. Gilson and Vetsuypens (1993) found that the CEOs of almost one-third of 77 American firms in financial distress were replaced; CEOs who kept their jobs usually experienced large reductions in salary and bonuses. Newly appointed CEOs associated with previous management were generally paid 35 per cent less than those they replaced, while CEOs brought in from outside were paid 36 per cent more.

Although the resolution of financial distress raises many important research issues (see Aghion, Hart and Moore 1992 for a recent contribution and summary), we wish to stress the obvious implication for solvent firms: that a key objective of management must be to avoid financial distress and ensure that creditors are paid. De Fusco, Johnson and Zorn (1990) find that the introduction of managerial stock option plans — which benefit managers by increasing the gains to asset substitution and underinvestment — raises equity prices but significantly reduces the wealth of bondholders. The implication is that managerial incentives are 'naturally' aligned with the interests of bondholders in the absence of explicit incentive schemes to make managers act against these interests (see Coffee 1986 for further discussion of this question). This story is altered somewhat for the Japanese case since leading creditors are often substantial shareholders. Nonetheless, as Aoki (1988) indicates, such investors are more active in defence of their bondholdings than of their shareholdings.

The influence of labour

Statements to the effect that the interests of workers, or of some subset of workers, are of importance to top managers are easy to find; the quote from Prahalad (1993) given earlier is just one example. The notion that higher pay for workers is somehow a 'good' to managers appears in the early managerial theories surveyed in Alchian (1965). Jensen (1986) justifies the idea that managers tend to overinvest in part on the grounds that expanding the firm provides more top management positions to which favoured subordinates can be promoted. Brumagin (1991) reports intriguing evidence consistent with the general argument. He shows that large conglomerates operating in unrelated businesses according to traditional measures of output are in fact closely related if we focus on the use of labour skills (measured in terms of occupational categories). Aoki (1988) argues that the tendency to invest 'with labour in mind' is even more pronounced in large Japanese firms.

The presence of an interindustry wage structure in which the employees of large firms and firms in concentrated industries receive higher pay (Krueger and Summers 1988) is certainly consistent with the idea that workers exert considerable influence over management decisions. But as Krueger and Summers themselves stress, it is difficult to interpret their findings in terms of a strategy to maximise shareholder wealth by paying workers an 'efficiency wage' (a higher wage than that prevailing in the competitive market, designed to generate greater worker effort).

Further evidence of the relative influence of workers and investors on management decisions is provided by DeAngelo and DeAngelo (1991), who document the effect of collective bargaining on dividend and investment policy, and by Bronars and Deere

(1991), who find that unionised firms tend to have more debt in their capital structures, arguably to pre-empt concessions to excessive union wage demands.

Summary

The picture that has emerged here is certainly *not* that top managers' decisions, in any economy, will entirely neglect considerations of shareholder wealth. Managerial compensation, dismissal through takeover or board action, and reputation are to some extent linked to share price. But the evidence also suggests that creditors (through the threat of creating financial distress) and a subset of workers also exert strong influence on management decisions.

The implicit theoretical lens used in most studies is the legal and economic model, which assumes that efficiency increases uniformly with the degree to which actions are made in shareholder interests; that is, that shareholders are the only constituency that should matter. This view reflects the assumption that all other corporate constituencies have fully specified contractual claims, or at least that shareholders are a decent approximation of a full residual claimant. We return to this assumption in the next section. The main argument here has been that it is far easier to interpret the evidence as reflecting a world in which managers have considerable leeway, at least *ex post*, to depart from the maximisation of shareholder wealth. Moreover, other claimants appear to exert substantial influence over firms' policy choices.

The next section is devoted to assessing the efficiency of this situation. If the practices documented here are in fact efficient, then they serve to maximise the *ex ante* wealth of shareholders as well as that of society. If they are inefficient, then wealth is transferred from shareholders both *ex ante* and *ex post*, and some reform of governance is warranted.

The consistency of theoretical models with the facts

Wealth redistribution theories

Extracting rents from bidders

The potential conflict between managers' and shareholders' interests is thrown into stark relief by an unsolicited tender offer for the firm. Managers often vigorously resist takeover even though successful acquisition almost invariably increases shareholder wealth. It has been pointed out, however, that while resistance to takeovers certainly serves the interests of managers in the target firm, it may also serve the interests of shareholders by inducing bidders to pay a higher premium (Gilson 1986; Shleifer and Vishny 1986; Berkovitch and Khanna 1990).

While it is true that refusal to accept an initial bid can, and sometimes does, cause the bidder to pay more, or may encourage others to bid, it is difficult to accept this as a general explanation for the amount of resistance observed. While early studies of takeover defences found that they had little effect on target shareholder wealth

(Bradley and Wakeman 1983), more recent defences, particularly those that do not require shareholder approval, such as 'poison pills', have in many cases clearly harmed shareholders. Poison pills are charter amendments that increase the cost of a takeover — usually by instigating some action which reduces the value of the target in the event of a successful hostile takeover — and which do not require a shareholder vote. As Herzel (1990) points out, poison pills and ESOPs are often explicitly intended to lower the probability of a successful bid. Much of the new activism of institutional shareholders has been directed towards revoking poison pills (*Business Week*, 15 March 1993, pp. 38–45). Dann and DeAngelo (1988) and Ryngaert (1988) both find that poison pill and related defences tend to reduce shareholder wealth.

There are as well two theoretical problems with the argument that takeover defences extract a higher price from bidders. First, earlier models of takeover bids (such as that of Grossman and Hart 1980) argue that, left to their own devices, shareholders would be reluctant to tender, rather than anxious as is assumed in the models summarised so far. Grossman and Hart's model suggests that dilution measures, which deprive minority shareholders of some of their voting rights in non-tendered shares after the takeover, and which are aimed at lowering the premium that target shareholders demand, would in fact be wealth increasing. While this conclusion has still not been settled theoretically (see, for example, Holmstrom and Nalebuff 1992), Easterbrook and Fischel (1981) raise another objection with particular relevance for a world of diversified shareholders. They point out that an investor who holds shares in both the bidding and the target firm may not gain anything from defensive actions that extract a higher price from the bidder. This last problem is consistent with the active opposition to takeover defences of shareholders holding sizeable stakes in many firms, such as public pension funds.

Extracting rents from product market rivals

Another rationale for management entrenchment focuses on competition in product markets. The argument is that, by pre-committing to a more aggressive strategy than that implied by profit maximisation, a firm can pre-empt rivals and expand its profits (Sklivas 1987; Fershtman and Judd 1987). While the published research has the appealing feature that managers' pay increases with firm size (as it appears to do in the real world), this result only holds if the firm competes successfully in the quantities of goods sold. If competition is in prices, the authors demonstrate the counterfactual implication that managers' pay should decrease as firm size increases. Katz (1991) points out that the models all rely on the assumption that the key parameters of management compensation are common knowledge among rivals. In addition, Fumas (1992) describes how rewarding managers according to firm performance relative to rival firms can provide effort incentives, insurance and a more aggressive output market strategy than could be achieved through size based pay.

These models all assume that corporate governance is used to sharpen competition. As Sheard (1994a) points out, many commentators on Japanese governance and ownership structures take the opposite viewpoint: that practices such as cross-shareholding are intended to facilitate collusion and weaken product market competition. However, as Sheard also stresses, most of the linkages between firms are vertical rather than horizontal, and are more properly viewed through the efficiency lens which we adopt later on.

Public choice theories: corporate managers as a powerful interest group
This final set of wealth redistribution theories drops the idea that managers extract rents from others on behalf of their shareholders. Rather, the argument is that top managers use the political and regulatory process to tip the scales in their favour, against the interests of shareholders. The broad contours of the theory, outlined in Grundfest (1990) and Roe (1990), follow a straightforward public choice approach. Corporate managers are argued to represent a concentrated and organised interest group which took advantage of the popular suspicion of bankers and financiers in the 1930s to 1970s effectively to free themselves from control by their investors. Roe (1993a, pp. 123–4) asserts:

> ... one must look beyond economics to explain the American results: America's politics of financial fragmentation, rooted in federalism, populism, and interest group pressures, pulverised American financial institutions, contributing heavily to the rise of the Berle–Means corporation.

As is the case with many public choice accounts of regulation, the argument is relatively plausible overall and provides a compelling explanation of certain regulations, such as some of the state based legislation featured in the second wave of antitakeover legislation in the late 1980s (see Karpoff and Malatesta 1989, but also Jahera and Pugh 1991).

In its current state of development, however, it also exhibits the characteristic weaknesses of public choice theories of regulation. The underlying determinants of political power (such as the ability to overcome free-rider problems) are often casually spelled out, leaving open the question of why managers and other parties who might be harmed by takeovers should form a more coherent political group than large institutional shareholders (see Roe 1993b and the ensuing discussion). The theory also relies to some extent on a pre-existing public animosity toward 'Wall Street' that may or may not be grounded in fact. Finally, the theory makes little headway in predicting the actual forms that pro-management regulation will take. To take a particularly anomalous example, Jensen and Murphy (1990) argue that the political process places inefficiently tight constraints on financial rewards to top management — that politics and the media make it impossible for corporations to compensate excellent managers as they deserve. Instead, the political process ensures that managers are well paid regardless of how well they have performed, so that there is neglible linking of pay to performance. While outstanding managers are rewarded poorly in terms of what they have contributed, poorly performing managers may be overcompensated. No straightforward model of individual utility maximising behaviour would suggest that managers prefer insulation from takeovers to immense personal wealth, and of course if managers truly were powerful they need not even trade one for the other. Despite such anomalies, there is little doubt that the public choice approach to finance has much to contribute to our understanding of corporate governance in the real world, and represents a fertile field for more careful and focused theoretical and empirical work.

Efficiency theories

The models sketched so far in this section have described existing corporate governance and management objectives in terms of wealth redistribution. We now turn to theories that explain the suppression of shareholder interests in terms of efficiency.

Direct monitoring cost explanation

The first explanation is essentially tautological: that it must be too costly to align the interests of managers and shareholders more closely than they are at present. Principal–agent theory directs our attention to the costs of having managers rather than diversified shareholders bear risk. As Baker, Jensen and Murphy (1988) stress, the standard principal–agent model of, say, Holmstrom (1979) is, unfortunately, imprecise in assessing the degree to which managers' pay should be linked to shareholder wealth. The predictions of the model depend on the exact nature of managerial risk preferences as well as the statistical association between profit and executive effort.

Measurement problems

One explanation for why managers' objectives are not more closely aligned with those of shareholders refines the popular notion that stock prices reflect short-term interests and are therefore not a good guide to managerial behaviour. The general contention is that managers who are solely concerned with their firm's stock price will take inefficient actions aimed at increasing this price. While this argument is often based on the dubious notion that equities are systematically mispriced, it need not be. The basic insight is that investors are more interested in predicting future dividends than in monitoring managerial effort or efficiency per se. Paul (1992) provides a host of examples (and references) to show that managers who are paid solely according to share price will allocate their effort and time inefficiently, both between projects and between effort and leisure. The models surveyed by Paul help rationalise the weak observed linkage between share price and managerial wealth, and also the use of company profit/loss statements as a performance indicator even when the stock market's assessment of corporate assets (as reflected in the firm's share price) is unbiased.

These studies have provided important insights and may, indeed, have gone nearly as far as is possible within the basic principal–agent framework. We now turn to theories that explicitly recognise that the corporation's productive actions are not taken by a single top manager, but rather by a hierarchy of managers, employees and suppliers.

Models of the large corporation

To the lay person, the notion that corporations should be run in the interests of shareholders may seem odd: should not other investors, workers, suppliers and local communities also have a legitimate voice? Fama (1990) points out that 90 per cent of the cash flows of the average US corporation go to parties other than shareholders. From the perspective of traditional corporate finance, of course, this is confusing totals and margins; the remaining 10 per cent of cash flows are, after all, the risky ones and those that are affected by effort choices. But, as mentioned before, this line of argument effectively assumes a world of complete contracts; when contracts are incomplete, residual claimant status is a matter of degree and is not restricted to shareholders. In such a world it pays to pre-commit to actions that take account of the interests of parties other than shareholders, *ex ante*. Brander and Poitevin (1992) and John and John (1992), who focus on debtholders, demonstrate how the 'low-powered' incentive schemes documented by Jensen and Murphy (1990), which appear to provide very little in the way of incentives, can be optimal for shareholders. Garvey (1994) shows the critical role of basing managers' pay on firm size as opposed to shareholder wealth (as observed in the empirical research for both Japan and the United States) in achieving an efficient outcome from the perspective of the firm/shareholders.

Shleifer and Summers (1988) focus on losses experienced by long-term employees and suppliers in the context of a hostile takeover, which they portray as an event that reasserts the interests of shareholders to a degree not contemplated in the original contract. There is some evidence for the Shleifer–Summers view of takeovers.[9] But it is also clear that wealth transfers from employees to the takeover agent do not explain the premium on shares paid in most hostile takeovers (Palepu 1990).

The Shleifer–Summers argument is also questionable on *a priori* grounds. As Holmstrom (1988) points out, the authors assume that entrenched managers will strike efficient bargains in updating incomplete contracts with employees and suppliers simply because they are insulated from shareholder demands. Garvey and Gaston (1991) present some evidence that Shleifer and Summers' leap of faith may be justified, at least for employees; they find that earnings growth and non-vested pensions are significantly negatively related to the concentration of institutional shareholdings in a small sample of Australian firms. Lazear (1979) shows how earnings growth and non-vested pensions constitute an incentive scheme for employees that requires them to trust the firm not to dismiss them unless they underperform. Garvey and Gaston (1991) find that such schemes are more prevalent in diffusely held, managerial firms.[10] However, in addition to problems of small sample size and highly imperfect proxies for ownership, Garvey and Gaston's study fails to identify *why* managerial firms appear to behave in a more trustworthy fashion towards their labour force.

One key issue raised by the Shleifer–Summers argument is that the incentives and decisions of top managers are of concern to the firm's employees and trading partners, as well as its shareholders. The idea that management may involve more than simply exerting effort or choosing investment projects was confronted in early attempts to apply the principal–agent model to the relationship between manager and shareholder. According to Diamond and Verrecchia (1982, p. 278):

> It is probably inaccurate to model all of a firm's employees as agents directly for the stockholders. This is because information on which most employees' compensation is based is not observed by stockholders but rather by their direct supervisors. That is, most firms have a hierarchical structure. Much of the information relevant for supervised employees is observed only within the firm. Incentive schemes for supervised employees should be designed using information produced internally by the firm. This however merely shifts the problem back one level, as someone within the firm must construct the incentives for its employees. How this someone makes these decisions depends on his incentives.

Despite this recognition, Diamond and Verrecchia and others effectively assume that designing and implementing an incentive scheme for subordinates is formally identical to exerting costly effort. Demski and Sappington (1992) show that this presumption is generally incorrect. They examine the key problem of inducing a manager to reveal accurately private information about a subordinate's performance. Assuming that the manager is a risk neutral, 100 per cent residual claimant (and therefore a perfect agent of stockholders!), they show that it is usually impossible to design a contract that induces managers to reveal such information. This is because, by acknowledging the performance of subordinates, the manager reduces his/her wealth and hence always has an incentive to underreport effort.

Prendergast and Topel (1993) discuss the related but more general problem of biased supervision ratings, pointing out that it may be better for a manager *not* to be a residual claimant.[11] Garvey and Swan (1992a) show that in fact the optimal situation is for the manager of a subordinate to be completely unconcerned with shareholder wealth, to have some propensity to transfer wealth to the subordinate, and to face a hefty penalty in the event of defaulting on a moderate fixed financial claim. The authors' intuition is that, by performing well, the subordinate gives the manager some 'slack' which can be used to claim higher compensation, whereas if the subordinate performs badly the manager has no room to be generous. This mechanism requires on the one hand that default be costly for the top manager, and on the other that the manager actively use slack to reward employees. The model is consistent with the evidence documented earlier in the chapter, and is extended to a multilayered hierarchy in Garvey and Swan (1992b). It also endogenises the view of managerial incentives featured in important work on capital structure by Grossman and Hart (1982) and Hart (1993). By contrast, in the standard principal–agency literature (Mirrlees 1976, for example), reliable third parties observe the performance of workers so that the problem of underpayment cannot arise.

A weakness of the theory is that it proves too much: that it is optimal both for shareholders to be completely passive and for managers to be fully entrenched. Garvey and Swan (1995) readmit shareholders to an active role by making the model more 'dynamic' in the sense that the firm's performance can be affected by random shocks which, from the top manager's point of view, mimic good subordinate performance. Hence, for example, if an investment turns out well then subordinates know that the CEO has breathing space and that they need not work as hard to secure rewards. This leads to a situation analogous to Jensen's (1986) notion of free cash flow, but without having to rely on exogenously imposed inefficiencies in management compensation. Rather, inefficient executive behaviour can develop naturally in an *ex ante* optimal world, and is redressed by the threat of takeover or shareholder activism. The intuition of the static model implies, however, that the cost barriers to hostile takeover should be substantial, but not prohibitive.

Assessment of the various theories

The common theme in all the models discussed in this section is the recognition that shareholders are not 100 per cent residual claimants surrounded by competitive input and output markets and completely specified contracts. Theories that stress the extraction of rents from bidders or rivals in product markets rely on specific departures from perfect competition, and have received the bulk of attention in recent years. We suspect that this will not always be the case, however. Public choice is, to us, the most promising of the wealth redistribution approaches, in part because of its novelty and undeveloped nature. Our suspicion that it has substantial empirical relevance could be tested through more careful identification of the precise conditions under which managers form a powerful interest group.

Efficiency theories have, we believe, at least equivalent empirical importance. Our view reflects, in part, a faith in the power of competition to reject via a Darwinian process of natural selection those institutional forms that are most closely associated with rent seeking. We have argued that a great deal of evidence which seems to suggest inefficiency in governance is in fact consistent with a world in which the major task of managers is to administer labour contracts (that is, to manage human resources). A more convincing case would involve establishing the empirical implications of efficiency versus rent seeking approaches, in the context either of a particular institutional feature (such as board composition, state of incorporation, voting status of equity shares or structure of the firm's internal labour and capital markets) or of a key corporate decision (such as adoption of antitakeover measures or the setting of compensation policy).

Selected topics

International differences: the Japanese-German model

It is now common to distinguish between two distinct forms of governance system for large corporations in developed economies: the Anglo-American type and the Japanese-German type (Aoki 1992, p. 44; *The Economist*, 29 January 1994, pp. S5–S11). Some argue that the Anglo-American type is dominated by shareholder interests through the market for corporate control (takeovers), boards of directors and direct intervention by large stockholders. This view has recently been questioned by Roe (1993a), who believes that managers control the reins of power because stock is diffusely held by individuals and institutions. By contrast, in the Japanese-German type, the large block of stable shareholding by financial institutions (the main bank system as described in Sheard 1989) and the prevalence of interlocking shareholding (Sheard 1991) effectively prevent hostile takeovers, and hence the average shareholder would seem to have very little influence. Nonetheless, as Roe (1993a) points out, senior managers in Japan and Germany are not all-powerful, with power actually being shared by managers and active financial intermediaries. Ownership of corporations does not appear to be more concentrated in Japan than in the United States, but the composition of ownership is different; in Japan banks have much larger shareholdings (Kester 1986).

In Germany as well, a high proportion of firms' shares are held by large banks and other stable shareholders. While the individual shareholder may effectively be locked out in Japan and in Germany, both workers (Aoki 1992), and debtholders together with institutional shareholders (main banks), exercise considerable influence. Suppression of the voice of the individual shareholder is associated with main bank control within a *keiretsu* grouping of firms in Japan (Kester 1991b) and, similarly, with strong links between banks and firms in Germany (Kester 1992). In the latter country, there is also evidence to suggest that bank involvement contributes significantly to the firm's financial performance (Cable 1985).

Traditional explanations for the success of the Japanese main bank system stress that financial intermediaries such as banks can serve a monitoring role, and that they provide a substitute for the external capital market and the market for corporate control (Stiglitz 1985; Sheard 1989). The main bank controls both equity and debt, and its influence helps to overcome the free-riding problem confronting small shareholders and creditors. As well, the bank can obtain access to the firm's informational and decision making mechanisms that is generally unavailable to participants in the external capital market (Sheard 1989, p. 403).

While the informational based argument sounds plausible, it is not obvious why this role should be played by banks rather than by large investors who hold only equity. Why would it not be just as efficient, for example, for conglomerates to provide an internal capital market? And if conglomerates could fulfil this role efficiently, why were so many broken up during the wave of management buyouts in the 1980s in the United States?

The monitoring argument presents an additional puzzle. A large financial intermediary such as a main bank is hardly an individual person for whom, by assumption, there are no agency costs in making decisions. A bank is subject to all the same internal monitoring, informational and control problems as the corporations it is supposed to be monitoring. Who, then, monitors the main banks? Berglof and Perotti (1994) and Sheard (Ch. 5, this volume) provide a potential answer to this question, emphasising the importance of reciprocal monitoring by the large banks underpinned by a reputational mechanism. While this argument undoubtedly has merit, much remains to be done to explain why such forces should be stronger in Japan than in the United States. Further development of recent models will, we hope, help provide a more fundamental explanation for the success of main banks, perhaps related to the specific rights they exercise and the regulatory environment in which they operate.[12]

Another, more cogent, explanation links investor monitoring to the operation of internal labour markets in Japan and Germany. In Japan, workers can expect to be employed with one firm for a much longer period than is the case in the United States (Hashimoto 1989, p. 249). While in Japan lifetime employment with a single firm may be restricted to large, highly successful firms, the employment relationship is a long-term implicit contract to a far greater degree than in the Anglo-American model.

Important differences in the internal labour market are also reflected in the two countries' age–earnings profiles. While with the firm, a typical Japanese worker will experience a much greater rise in earnings than will the worker in the United States (Hashimoto 1989, pp. 255–6). This rising age–earnings profile in Japan is more closely associated with firm-specific experience than with overall experience, whereas the reverse is the case in the United States.

A rising age–earnings profile may be associated with underpayment of workers when they are young, relative to marginal product and overpayment in later years, given that productivity will not always continue to rise with age. Deferring compensation in this way means that employees are rewarded *after* their efforts have been made. However, there is no contractual obligation on the part of the firm to identify and subsequently reward superior performance, and hence the contract is implicit rather than explicit (Becker and Stigler 1974; Lazear 1979).

Alternatively, a rising age–earnings profile may reflect rising productivity levels as workers within the firm acquire skills. Because of the firm-specific nature of these skills, workers cannot expect to get higher wages elsewhere, but they will not invest in such training unless they can expect to be rewarded with higher wages. The firm-specific capital and effort stories are, therefore, almost identical (Kanemoto and MacLeod 1991).

It is generally impossible for courts or other outsiders to assess accurately the past and present contributions of workers, or the costs they have incurred in undertaking firm-specific investments. In the Marshallian firm — in which the employer is the residual claimant — the boss has a strong incentive to understate the worker's past or present performance so as to reduce the firm's wage or bonus bill and increase profitability. The employer may refuse to pay deferred compensation or to reward employees who have incurred firm-specific training costs with a higher wage. Unless outsiders know exactly what has transpired, the employer's reputation will not be much tarnished by such behaviour. This makes reputational explanations somewhat doubtful.

One way in which an owner-managed firm may be able to recompense its workers more equitably is to commit to a fixed total wage bill to be allocated according to relative performance (Malcolmson 1984). Since it is difficult, if not impossible, for a manager to observe the assistance that one worker provides to another, evaluation of relative performance based on a rank order tournament between workers will have the severe drawback of discouraging cooperative behaviour; indeed, it may even encourage active sabotage of coworkers. A partial solution to this problem involves the narrowing of the difference between the winner's prize and the loser's prize (Lazear 1989), although clearly this will reduce the incentive for individuals to perform well.

Relative performance evaluation is therefore most appropriate when agents are separate, with little opportunity for either sabotage or helping. Unless interactions between firms are important, as with a cartel, it seems likely that relative performance evaluation would be used mostly to reward CEOs, an assumption which tends to be borne out in empirical work (Antle and Smith 1986; Gibbons and Murphy 1990).

Japanese firms, however, employ a tournament system which extends throughout the hierarchy and within which each worker has a well-defined grade and rank (Aoki 1988; Kanemoto and MacLeod 1991, p. 165). In contrast to the Anglo-American model, in which workers are assigned to jobs, in Japan both rank and pay are independent of present position. Depending on both seniority and performance, a Japanese worker's income will increase as he/she moves up the promotional ladder. The coexistence of this system with extensive cooperation and teamwork in Japan (Kanemoto and MacLeod 1991, p. 166) is certainly puzzling given Lazear's (1989) demonstration that relative performance evaluation encourages outright sabotage of coworkers.

An important clue to this puzzle is provided in a field study conducted by Kester (1991a, p. 92), who finds evidence of a link between the financial and employment policies of large Japanese firms:

> Maintaining substantial cash balances may have been a means of making credible a company's commitment to implicit contracts with some of its major stakeholders. The promises of lifetime employment and future retirement benefits are good examples. When queried about why so much cash and marketable securities were being held, managers in the field sample most frequently cited labor considerations. As one manager put it, 'If we began paying out the cash as dividends, the employees would probably become angry and frightened. "You are spending our future", they would say. "Why are you draining the company of funds rather than keeping it inside and securing our welfare?" I am sure their concerns would ultimately prevent us from giving the cash to shareholders.'

Garvey and Swan (1992c) draw on this link between, on the one hand, retained cash and corporate governance more generally and, on the other hand, internal labour markets, to propose a hybrid system made up of a labour market tournament as well as a group performance bonus implemented by a manager who is not concerned with share price. The manager does, however, wish to avoid both pay inequality and financial distress. Concern with the former leads to a compressed pay scale and hence greater efficiency when cooperation between workers is important. Concern with the latter because of the costs the manager will bear in case of bankruptcy may encourage the distribution of a group bonus. This will increase when the team of employees performs well, thus reducing the risk of bankruptcy. This hybrid scheme is better than the pure tournament when cooperation among coworkers is important. The model is thus consistent with those described earlier in having an efficiency explanation for manager concerns with constituencies other than shareholders.

The Japanese corporate governance system seems extreme in the extent to which the linkage between shareholder rewards and bonuses to managers is suppressed. While some senior managers in Japanese firms hold equity in their employer, officers are prohibited from owning stock options. Furthermore, while managers' bonuses are often withheld if dividends are not maintained, they are not increased when dividends are raised (Kester 1986, p. 15). Kaplan (1994) gives further details on the small differences and substantial similarities between the compensation of Japanese and US CEOs.

Garvey and Swan (1992d) build an explicit model of the Japanese corporation which rationalises these features of the Japanese firm. A hybrid incentive scheme featuring both tournament based worker compensation and a group piece rate can only be implemented if managers stress employee and debtholder interests over those of the shareholder. The model also implies that shareholdings should be relatively diffuse and takeover difficult so that shareholders cannot intervene to extract cash needed to reward employees.

The predictions of this model are borne out by Sheard (1989), who documents the Japanese main bank interventions which occur in the event of financial distress, and by Aoki (1990), who observes that the power of Japanese banks only becomes visible when the firm is in difficulty. More systematic studies of management compensation (Kaplan 1994) and of the influence of banks on firms' boards of directors and top management (Kaplan and Minton 1994; Sheard 1994b) tend to confirm the view of 'contingent' corporate governance in which managers have substantial discretion when the firm is solvent but lose control and bear large costs if the firm appears likely to default on its fixed obligations to creditors.

Garvey and Swan's (1992d) model also predicts that the hybrid scheme will be most beneficial where cooperation among coworkers is important and where workers are organised into relatively small teams. (The free-riding problem becomes more acute for larger teams.) Such small teams with a relatively homogenous membership of between three and ten workers (Hashimoto 1989, p. 276) are the most common form of organisation within the Japanese corporation.

In the incentive design literature, alternatives to rank order tournaments have been considered when cooperation is required. One response has been to make agents jointly responsible for output, with a group piece rate being offered to encourage cooperation.[13] This approach is similar to Garvey and Swan (1992b), but without the labour tournament and debt mechanism.

Developments in the United States

Some commentators infer that the separation of ownership and control documented earlier in the chapter is so inefficient that the corporation as an institution will decline sharply in importance. Jensen asserts that the massive changes observed in the US economy in the 1980s — including takeovers, corporate break-ups, divisional spin-offs, leveraged buyouts and going private transactions — spell the eclipse of the public corporation (*Harvard Business Review*, September–October 1989, pp. 60–70). The basic cause, he says, is conflict between shareholders and managers over the control and use of resources.

In Jensen's (1986) framework, the manager makes investment decisions on behalf of shareholders. Where internally generated cash flows are excessive, managers interested in self-aggrandisement will tend to invest even though external investment prospects at the time may be poor. The classic example is the US oil industry, which benefited from a tenfold increase in oil prices from 1973 to 1981. It used the funds to invest massively in oil exploration, although the prospects of a major discovery were poor. The solution, according to Jensen, is increased leverage to force managers to direct excessive cash flows to creditors rather than to value destroying investment projects.

The problem with tying the hands of managers by denying them cash is that *ex ante* the investment prospects of a project are not always easy to foresee. Excessive debt will cause a good investment project as well as a poor one to fail (Stulz 1990; Hart and Moore 1990). In fact, if the key to corporate governance lay simply in encouraging managers to make sound investment decisions, the solution would be relatively simple: either 'sell' the corporation to management so that at the margin the manager would suffer the same loss of wealth as the shareholder should the investment founder, or at least ensure maximum exposure to the takeover market. The owner-managed firm portrayed in basic microeconomics texts, rather than the highly leveraged firm financed by junk bonds, reasserts itself as the solution to Jensen's free cash flow problem. Of course there are limits to such links between manager and shareholder wealth, depending on the manager's wealth constraint, degree of risk aversion and so on. As was noted earlier, the observed linkage of managerial and shareholder rewards is too weak to overcome the problem described by Jensen.

There is an alternative explanation for what Jensen calls the conventional model of corporate governance with a moderate debt level and without manager income being tied to shareholder income (*Harvard Business Review*, September–October 1989). The role of the CEO is not only to make investment decisions, but also to manage the firm's internal labour market (Garvey and Swan 1992a, 1992b). The more important is activity lower down in the employment hierarchy relative to the entrepreneurial efforts of the CEO, the less onerous the firm's debt level should be (Garvey and Swan 1992a): that is, large hierarchical organisations should be 'blue chip', because a high risk of default on promised payments to debtholders would place an excessive 'bonus squeeze' on employees at the bottom of the hierarchy.

Despite these criticisms, Jensen (1986, *Harvard Business Review*, September–October 1989) seems to have described accurately the behaviour of cashed up oil companies in the post-1973 period. While some degree of management entrenchment may be optimal, barriers to takeover should not be prohibitive (Garvey and Swan 1993). To stave off takeover, oil companies would have had to disgorge cash to shareholders in the form of dividends or share repurchases, and this would have tended to restore debt–equity ratios to what they were before the oil price increases. This ultimately happened, but with a considerable time lag. The implicit contracts story in Garvey and Swan (199) provides one rationalisation of Jensen's free cash flow mechanism.

Additional support for the role of creditors in disciplining management is provided by Maloney, McCormick and Mitchell (1993), who find that a favourable share price reaction to the acquirer when a merger is announced is positively associated with the leverage of the acquiring firm. Firms which restructure by increasing leverage also improve their acquisition performance.

Rappaport (*Harvard Business Review*, January–February 1990, pp. 96–104) believes that the corporation will survive, with its salvation ultimately depending on management compensation being linked to share value. Once again, such links restore the textbook firm — at the expense of sunk efforts by labour within the hierarchy, who will be right to fear that their future rewards may be threatened.

Perhaps more damaging to Jensen's belief in the eclipse of the public corporation is the finding that the percentage of leveraged buyouts returning to public ownership increases over time (Kaplan 1991). Leveraged buyouts, which remain private for a medium time of 6.8 years, may simply be a transitional phenomenon (see also Bhagat, Shleifer and Vishny 1990). An interesting empirical question for future research is whether these re-corporatised leveraged buyouts correspond more to Rappaport's model, with management compensation being tied to share value, or whether management interests are linked instead to labour and debtholders, as in the Japanese model.

Boards of directors

The basic findings about board composition are unsurprising: insiders depart when stock returns are poor and when the CEO nears retirement. Presumably, when a winning candidate is announced, losing candidates depart. Moreover, insiders are added shortly before a CEO retires, probably as part of a grooming period. Outsiders are more likely to join the board when a new CEO is appointed and when the firm is performing poorly (Hermalin and Weisbach 1988).

More controversial are the reasons for the departure of insiders and arrival of outsiders following poor firm performance. Is there a monitoring explanation, with outsiders disciplining poor performance, or do insiders, who presumably are more influential in decision making, value the advice and counsel of outsiders more highly when they themselves are not getting it right?

The most visible act the board performs in its monitoring role is the removal of an underperforming CEO. As one might expect, the probability of a US CEO's departure rises when stock performance is poor. Board type influences the outcome; the CEO is three times as likely to be removed when outsiders form a majority on the board (more than 60 per cent of directors are outsiders) (Weisbach 1988, p. 441). However, the statistical significance of the difference is relatively small, as is the absolute relation (Warner, Smith and Wruck 1988). When accounting earnings are used as the measure of performance, there is a statistically significant effect for outside but not inside boards. This evidence is consistent with outside directors undertaking more monitoring of CEO performance than inside directors. An alternative explanation is that powerful CEOs tend to appoint internal boards, while weaker CEOs mainly appoint boards composed of outsiders. Nonetheless, share price reacts favourably to replacement of the CEO following poor stock performance only in the case of outside boards, which thus would seem to displace the CEO more effectively than inside or mixed boards (Weisbach 1988, pp. 458–9).

More recent studies distinguish 'independent' from 'affiliated' outside directors (Byrd and Hickman 1992a). (Affiliated outsiders are those having links, such as legal, banking or consulting relationships, with insiders.) In a study of the independence of audit committees, Byrd and Hickman (1992a) found that the committees of over 25 per cent of the firms sampled were dominated by affiliated as opposed to independent outsiders. Another study by Byrd and Hickman (1992b) found that share market response to companies announcing tender offers was slightly more favourable when the company had a board comprised of independent directors. Firms with independent boards also tended to pursue proportionately smaller firms and offer lower premiums.

Recent surveys of the academic literature on the impact of executive compensation on the investment decisions of boards and executives (Jarrell 1993; Gibbons and Murphy 1992a, 1992b) are more optimistic that executive incentive schemes are structured sensibly to achieve efficient outcomes than is suggested by the popular critique (Crystal 1991, for instance). But as Jensen and Murphy (1990) and Kaplan (1994) stress, the effect is small.

Directions for future research

The central contention of this chapter has been that corporate governance cannot be understood in a world where property rights are perfectly defined to make shareholders, as the residual claimants, the only group worthy of consideration. Only when contracts are incomplete do the problems of management and comparative governance become interesting, but as a consequence shareholders lose their standing as true residual claimants. From this follows a fundamental recommendation for comparative studies of Japanese and Anglo-American forms of corporate governance: stop searching for ways in which managers are led to maximise shareholder wealth. Appearances are not misleading, and in any system there are compelling efficiency reasons why the shareholder's voice in corporate affairs should be muted.[14] More importantly, the extent to which shareholder voice should be suppressed in favour of employee and creditor voice varies across firms according to production and employment structure.

One new and exciting area opened up for empirical research by recent developments is the relationship between the firm's capital structure and the implicit contracts linking its governance structure with its internal labour market. Fascinating recent empirical research (Lazear 1992; Baker, Gibbs and Holmstrom 1993) provides details of the internal labour markets of individual US corporations. One obvious step would be to study matching Japanese firms and contrast the ownership and governance structures of the two sets of corporations.

Undoubtedly there are lessons to be learned from comparing the recent evolution of the Japanese and Anglo-American systems. Shareholder activism is certainly on the rise worldwide, to judge from the extent of media attention and evidence from Kester (1991c). Hoshi, Kashyap and Scharfstein (1990) suggest that such traditionally Anglo-American features as public equity sales and takeovers are becoming more prevalent in Japan. The connection between these developments and the pressure on long-term employment structures in both systems is an immensely important topic for further study.

Notes

1 See, for example, Roe (1993a) and the associated comments in the same journal.
2 An exception to this is the contracting framework of Alchian and Demsetz (1972), in which management acts as monitor of a team of workers.
3 The existence of competition generally ensures that these parties expect to receive at least their next best alternative *ex ante*, that is, before joining the firm.
4 See Clark (1985) for a description of the standard assignment of corporate decision rights.
5 For example, Scharfstein (1988) represents the sole published analytical model of the notion that takeovers serve to reduce agency problems between managers and shareholders!
6 A managerial firm is one in which the managers appear to act for interests other than those of the shareholder: for themselves, employees or other stakeholders, for example.
7 In the magnum opus of the famous British economist, Alfred Marshall, the founder, shareholders and executives of the firm are all rolled into one person known as the 'entrepreneur'. This individual receives any revenues left over after meeting all payments which are contractual in nature (Marshall 1948).

8   Berle and Means (1932) pointed out that the management of most large firms is quite distinct from the shareholders, who, for publicly listed firms, are generally quite diffuse and lacking in any direct say in management. The authors not only drew attention to the managerialism thesis but also argued for a widespread socialisation of corporate assets.

9   See particularly the work of Ippolito and James (1992), Petersen (1992), Middlestaedt (1989), Pontiff, Shleifer and Weisback (1990) and Thomas (1989) on the deleterious effects of hostile takeovers and management buyouts on non-vested employee pensions.

10 Management shareholdings are essentially zero in their sample.

11 They also summarise ways in which the internal labour market can be designed to reduce the problem of morally hazardous evaluations (see also Malcolmson 1984 and Prendergast 1993 on this issue). We focus on the role of governance and endogenous management objectives.

12 Aoki, Patrick and Sheard (1994) give some key descriptive details.

13 In the principal–agent model of Holmstrom and Milgrom (1991), free-riding behaviour reduces the effectiveness of the strategy of joint responsibility. As in Garvey and Swan (1992a), the benefits of a group piece rate diminish if the team is large. Itoh (1992) assumes that a little bit of helping is relatively costless at the margin. He shows that joint responsibility is more likely to be optimal when agents must interact with each other: they are less risk averse, and there is less correlation between performance measurement errors. See Aoki (1992) for a more extensive survey of these and related features of the internal structure of the enterprise.

14 Gilson and Roe (1993, pp. 874–5) offer a similar view.

References

Aghion, P., O. Hart and J. Moore (1992), 'The Economics of Bankruptcy Reform', *Journal of Law, Economics, and Organization*, 8, pp. 523–46.

Agrawal, A. and R. Walkling (1991), 'Ex Post Settling Up: The Effect of Acquisition Bids on Executive Turnover and Compensation', Working Paper, Ohio State University Graduate School of Business, Ohio.

Alchian, A. (1965), 'The Basis of Some Recent Advances in the Theory of Management of the Firm', *Journal of Industrial Economics*, 7, pp. 30–41.

Alchian, A. and H. Demsetz (1972), 'Production, Information Costs, and Economic Organization', *American Economic Review*, 62 (5), pp. 777–95.

Antle, R. and A. Smith (1986), 'An Empirical Investigation of the Relative Performance Evaluation of Corporate Executives', *Journal of Accounting Research*, 24, pp. 1–39.

Aoki, M. (1988), *Information, Incentives, and Bargaining in the Japanese Economy*, Cambridge, MA: Cambridge University Press.

—— (1990), 'Toward an Economic Model of the Japanese Firm', *Journal of Economic Literature*, 28, pp. 1–27.

—— (1992), The Internal Structure of the Enterprise: A Partial Survey from a Comparative Perspective, Paper presented to the IEA Tenth World Congress, Session on the Internal Structure of the Enterprise, Moscow.

Aoki, M., H. Patrick and P. Sheard (1994), 'The Japanese Main Bank System: An Introductory Overview', in M. Aoki and H. Patrick (eds), *Main Bank System: Its Relevancy for Developing and Transforming Economies,* Oxford: Oxford University Press, pp. 3–50.

Arrow, K. and G. Debreu (1954), 'Existence of an Equilibrium for a Competitive Economy', *Econometrica,* 22, pp. 265–90.

Baker, G., M. Gibbs and B. Holmstrom (1993), 'Hierarchies and Compensation: A Case Study', *European Economic Review,* 37, pp. 366–78.

Baker, G., M.C. Jensen and K.J. Murphy (1988), 'Compensation and Incentives: Practice vs. Theory', *Journal of Finance,* 43, pp. 593–616.

Becker, Gary S. and George J. Stigler (1974), 'Law Enforcement, Malfeasance, and the Compensation of Enforcers', *Journal of Legal Studies,* 3, January, pp. 1–18.

Berglof, E. and E. Perotti (1994), 'The Governance Structure of Japanese Financial Keiretsu', *Journal of Financial Economics,* 36, pp. 259–84.

Berkovitch, E. and N. Khanna (1990), 'How Target Shareholders Benefit from Value-Reducing Defensive Strategies in Takeovers', *Journal of Finance,* 45, pp. 673–91.

Berle, A. and G.C. Means (1932), *The Modern Corporation and Private Property,* New York, NY: Macmillan.

Bhagat, S., A. Shleifer and R. Vishny (1990), 'Hostile Takeovers in the 1980's: The Return to Corporate Specialization', *Brookings Papers on Economic Activity: Microeconomics,* pp. 1–84.

Borland, J. (1992), 'Career Concerns: Incentives and Endogenous Learning in Labor Markets', *Journal of Economic Surveys,* 6, pp. 251–70.

Bradley, M., A. Desai and E.H. Kim (1988), 'Synergistic Gains from Corporate Acquisitions and Their Division between the Shareholders of Target and Acquiring Firms', *Journal of Financial Economics,* 21, pp. 3–40.

Bradley, M. and L.M. Wakeman (1983), 'The Wealth Effects of Targeted Share Repurchases', *Journal of Financial Economics,* 11, pp. 275–300.

Brander, J. and M. Poitevin (1992), 'Managerial Compensation and the Agency Cost of Debt', *Managerial and Decision Economics,* 13, pp. 55–64.

Bronars, S. and D. Deere (1991), 'The Threat of Unionization, the Use of Debt, and the Preservation of Shareholder Wealth', *Quarterly Journal of Economics,* 106, pp. 231–54.

Brumagin, A. (1991), 'Occupational Skills Linkages: A Resource-Based Investigation of Conglomerates', *Academy of Management Proceedings: Best Papers,* pp. 7–11.

Byrd, J. and K. Hickman (1992a), 'The Case for Independent Outside Directors', *Continental Bank Journal of Applied Corporate Finance,* 5 (3), Fall, pp. 78–82.

—— (1992b), 'Do Outside Directors Monitor Managers?: Evidence from Tender Offer Bids', *Journal of Financial Economics,* 32, pp. 195–221.

Cable, J. (1985), 'Capital Market Information and Industrial Performance: The Role of West German Banks', *The Economic Journal*, 95, pp. 118–32.

Clark, R. (1985), 'Agency Costs and Fiduciary Duties', in J. Pratt and R. Zeckhauser (eds), *Principals and Agents: The Structure of Business*, Cambridge, MA: Harvard Business School Press, pp. 123–45.

Coase, R. (1972), 'Industrial Organization: A Proposal for Research', in V. Fuchs (ed.), *Policy Issues and Research Opportunities in Industrial Organization*, New York, NY: National Bureau of Economic Research, pp. 87–103.

Coffee, J.C. (1986), 'Shareholders versus Managers: The Strain in the Corporate Web', *Michigan Law Review*, 85, pp. 1–109.

Continental Bank Roundtable (1991), 'Corporate Performance and Management Incentives', *Continental Bank Journal of Applied Corporate Finance*, 4, pp. 24–48.

Continental Bank (Stern Stewart) Roundtable (1992), 'Management Incentive Compensation and Shareholder Value', *Journal of Applied Corporate Finance*, 5, pp. 110–30.

Crystal, G. (1991), *In Search of Excess*, New York, NY: W.W. Norton.

Dann, L. and H. DeAngelo (1988), 'Corporate Financial Policy and Corporate Control: A Study of Defensive Adjustments in Asset and Ownership Structure', *Journal of Financial Economics*, 20, pp, 87–128.

Davis, G.F. and S.K. Stout (1992), 'Organisational Theory and the Market for Corporate Control: A Dynamic Analysis of the Characteristics of Large Takeover Targets, 1980–1990', *Administrative Science Quarterly*, 37, pp. 605–33.

DeAngelo, H. and L. DeAngelo (1989), 'Proxy Contests and the Governance of Publicly Held Corporations', *Journal of Financial Economics*, 23, pp. 29–59.

—— (1991), 'Union Negotiations and Corporate Policy', *Journal of Financial Economics*, 30, pp. 3–43.

De Fusco, R., R. Johnson and T. Zorn (1990), 'The Effect of Executive Stock Option Plans on Stockholders and Bondholders', *Journal of Finance*, 45, pp. 617–27.

Demsetz, H. (1982), *Economic, Legal, and Political Dimensions of Competition*, Amsterdam: North-Holland.

Demski, J. and D.E.M. Sappington (1992), 'The Make-or-Buy Decision with Unverifiable Public Information', Working Paper, University of Florida, Gainesville.

Diamond, D. and R. Verrecchia (1982), 'Optimal Managerial Contracts and Equilibrium Security Prices', *Journal of Finance*, 37, pp. 275–88.

Easterbrook, F. and D. Fischel (1981), 'The Proper Role of a Target's Management in Responding to a Tender Offer', *Harvard Law Review*, 94, pp. 1,161–95.

Fama, E.F. (1980), 'Agency Problems and the Theory of the Firm', *Journal of Political Economy*, 88, pp. 288–307.

—— (1990), 'Contract Costs and Financing Decisions, *Journal of Business*, 63, pp. 571–91.

Fershtman, C. and K. Judd (1987), 'Equilibrium Incentives in Oligopoly', *American Economic Review*, 77, pp. 927–40.

Fumas, X. (1992), 'Relative Performance Evaluation of Management', *International Journal of Industrial Organization*, 10, pp. 473–89.

Garvey, G.T. (1994), 'Should Corporate Managers Maximize Firm Size or Shareholder Wealth? A Theory of an Optimal Tradeoff', *Journal of the Japanese and International Economies*, 8, pp. 343–52.

Garvey, G.T. and N.G. Gaston (1991), 'Delegation, the Role of Managerial Discretion as a Bonding Device, and the Enforcement of Implicit Contracts', *Advances in Econometrics*, 9, pp. 87–119.

Garvey, G.T. and P.L. Swan (1992a), 'Optimal Capital Structure for a Hierarchical Firm', *Journal of Financial Intermediation*, 2, pp. 376–400.

—— (1992b), 'The Disciplinary Role of Debt in a Hierarchical Organization', *Research in Finance*, 10, pp. 1–40.

—— (1992c), 'Managerial Objectives, Capital Structure, and the Provision of Worker Incentives', *Journal of Labor Economics*, 10, pp. 357–79.

—— (1992d), 'The Interaction between Financial and Employment Contracts: A Formal Model of Japanese Corporate Governance', *Journal of the Japanese and International Economies*, 6, pp. 247–74.

—— (1995), 'Shareholder Activism, "Voluntary" Restructuring, and the Management of Labor', *Journal of Economics and Management Strategy*, 4 (4).

Gibbons, R. and K.J. Murphy (1990), 'Relative Performance Evaluation for Chief Executive Officers', *Industrial and Labor Relations Review*, 43, pp. 30S–51S.

—— (1992a), 'Optimal Incentive Contracts in the Presence of Career Concerns: Theory and Evidence', *Journal of Political Economy*, 100, pp. 468–505.

—— (1992b), 'Does Executive Compensation Affect Investment?', *Continental Bank Journal of Applied Corporate Finance*, 5, pp. 99–109.

Gilson, R. (1986), *The Law and Finance of Corporate Acquisitions*, Mineola, NY: Foundation Press.

Gilson, R. and M. Roe (1993), 'Understanding the Financial *Keiretsu*: Overlaps between Corporate Governance and Industrial Organization', *Yale Law Journal*, 102, pp. 871–906.

Gilson, S.C. (1989), 'Management Turnover and Financial Distress', *Journal of Financial Economics*, 25, pp. 241–62.

Gilson, S.C. and M.R. Vetsuypens (1993), 'CEO Compensation in Financially Distressed Firms: An Empirical Analysis', *Journal of Finance*, 48, pp. 425–58.

Grossman, S. and O.D. Hart (1980), 'Takeover Bids, the Free-Rider Problem, and the Theory of the Corporation', *Bell Journal of Economics*, 11, pp. 42–64.

—— (1982), 'Corporate Financial Structure and Managerial Incentives', in J.J. McCall (ed.), *The Economics of Information and Uncertainty*, Chicago, IL: University of Chicago Press for the National Bureau of Economic Research, pp. 123–55.

Grundfest, J. (1990), 'Subordination of American Capital', *Journal of Financial Economics*, 27, pp. 89–114.

Hart, O.D. (1988), 'Incomplete Contracts and the Theory of the Firm', *Journal of Law, Economics, and Organization*, 4, pp. 119–40.

—— (1993), 'Theories of Optimal Capital Structure: A Managerial Discretion Perspective', in M. Blair (ed.), *The Deal Decade*, Washington DC: Brookings Institution, pp. 203–33.

Hart, O.D. and B. Holmstrom (1987), 'The Theory of Contracts', in T. Bewley (ed.), *Advances in Economic Theory*, Cambridge, UK: Cambridge University Press, pp. 294–351.

Hart, O.D. and J. Moore (1990), 'A Theory of Corporate Financial Structure Based on the Seniority of Claims', NBER Working Paper No. 3431, Cambridge, MA.

Hashimoto, M. (1989), 'Employment and the Wages System in Japan and Their Implications for Productivity', in A. Blinder (ed.), *Paying for Productivity: A Look at the Evidence*, Washington DC, Brookings Institution.

Hermalin, B. and M.S. Weisbach (1988), 'The Determinants of Board Composition', *Rand Journal of Economics*, 19, pp. 589–97.

Herzel, L. (1990), 'Corporate Governance through Statistical Eyes', *Journal of Financial Economics*, 27, pp. 581–94.

Holmstrom, B. (1979), 'Moral Hazard and Observability', *Bell Journal of Economics*, 10, pp. 4–29.

—— (1982), 'Managerial Incentive Problems: A Dynamic Perspective', in *Essays in Economics and Management in Honor of Lars Wahlbeck*, Helsinki: Swedish School of Economics, pp. 210–35.

—— (1988), 'Comment on Shleifer and Summers', in A.J. Auerbach (ed), *Corporate Takeovers: Causes and Consequences*, Chicago, IL: University of Chicago Press for the National Bureau of Economic Research, pp. 211–13.

Holmstrom, B. and P. Milgrom (1991), 'Multitask Principal–Agent Analyses: Incentive Contracts, Asset Ownership, and Job Design', *Journal of Law, Economics, and Organization*, 7, pp. 524–52.

Holmstrom, B. and B. Nalebuff (1992), 'To the Raider Goes the Surplus? A Reexamination of the Free-Rider Problem', *Journal of Economics and Management Strategy*, 1, pp. 37–62.

Holmstrom, B. and J. Ricart i Costa (1986), 'Managerial Incentives and Capital Management', *Quarterly Journal of Economics*, 101, pp. 835–60.

Hoshi, T., A. Kashyap and D. Scharfstein (1990), 'Bank Monitoring and Investment: Evidence from the Changing Structure of Japanese Corporate Banking Relationships', in R. Glen Hubbard (ed.), *Asymmetric Information, Corporate Finance, and Investment*, Chicago, IL: University of Chicago Press, pp. 121–55.

Ippolito, R. and W. James (1992), 'LBO's, Reversions and Implicit Contracts', *Journal of Finance*, 47, pp. 139–67.

Itoh, H. (1992), 'Cooperation in Hierarchical Organizations: An Incentive Perspective', *Journal of Law, Economics, and Organization*, 8, pp. 321–45.

Jahera, J.S. and W. Pugh (1991), 'State Takeover Legislation: The Case of Delaware', *Journal of Law, Economics, and Organization*, 7, pp. 410–28.

Jarrell, G.A. (1993), 'An Overview of the Executive Compensation Debate', *Continental Bank Journal of Applied Corporate Finance*, 5, pp. 35–43.

Jensen, M.C. (1986), 'Agency Costs of Free Cash Flow, Corporate Finance and Takeovers', *American Economic Review*, 76, pp. 323–9.

—— (1988), 'Takeovers: Their Causes and Consequences', *Journal of Economic Perspectives*, 2, pp. 21–48.

—— (1991), 'Corporate Control and the Politics of Finance', *Continental Bank Journal of Applied Corporate Finance*, 4, pp. 13–33.

Jensen, M.C. and W.R. Meckling (1976), 'Theory of the Firm: Managerial Behavior, Agency Costs and Financial Structure', *Journal of Financial Economics*, 3, pp. 35–60.

Jensen, M.C. and K.J. Murphy (1990), 'Performance Pay and Top Management Incentives', *Journal of Political Economy*, 98, pp. 225–63.

John, K. and T. John (1992), 'Top-Management Compensation and Capital Structure', Working Paper, Stern School of Business, New York University, New York.

Kane, E.J. (1989), *The S&L Insurance Mess: How Did It Happen?*, Washington DC: Urban Institute Press.

Kanemoto, Y. and W.B. MacLeod (1991), 'The Theory of Contracts and Labor Practices in Japan and the United States', *Managerial and Decision Economics*, 12, pp. 159–70.

Kaplan, S. (1991), 'The Staying Power of Leveraged Buyouts', *Journal of Financial Economics*, 29, pp. 287–313.

—— (1994), 'Top Executive Rewards and Firm Performance: A Comparison of Japan and the United States', *Journal of Political Economy*, 102, pp. 510–46.

Kaplan, S. and B. Minton (1994), 'Appointments of Outsiders to Japanese Corporate Boards: Determinants and Implications for Managers', *Journal of Financial Economics*, 36, pp. 225–58.

Karpoff, Jonathon M. and Paul H. Malatesta (1989), 'The Wealth Effects of Second-Generation State Takeover Legislation', *Journal of Financial Economics*, 25, pp. 291–322.

Kato, T. (1996), 'Chief Executive Compensation and Corporate Groups in Japan: New Evidence from Micro Data', *International Journal of Industrial Organization* (forthcoming).

Kato, T. and M. Rockel (1992a), 'Experience, Credentials, and Compensation in the Japanese and US Managerial Labor Markets: Evidence from New Micro Data', *Journal of the Japanese and International Economies*, 6, pp. 30–51.

—— (1992b), 'The Importance of Company Breeding in the US and Japanese Managerial Labor Markets: A Statistical Comparison', *Japan and the World Economy*, 4, pp. 331–47.

Katz, M. (1991), 'Game Playing Agents: Unobservable Contracts as Precommitments', *Rand Journal of Economics*, 22, pp. 307–28.

Kester, W.C. (1986), 'Capital and Ownership Structure: A Comparison of United States and Japanese Manufacturing Corporations', *Financial Management*, Spring, pp. 5–16.

—— (1991a), 'The Hidden Costs of Japanese Success', *Continental Bank Journal of Applied Corporate Finance*, 3, pp. 90–7.

—— (1991b), 'Japanese Corporate Governance and the Conservation of Value in Financial Distress, *Continental Bank Journal of Applied Corporate Finance*, 4, pp. 98–104.

—— (1991c), *Japanese Takeovers: The Global Contest for Corporate Control*, Cambridge, MA: Harvard Business School Press.

—— (1992), 'Governance, Contracting, and Investment Horizons: A Look at Japan and Germany', *Continental Bank Journal of Applied Corporate Finance*, 5, pp. 83–98.

Krueger, Alan and Lawrence Summers (1988), 'Efficiency Wages and the Inter-Industry Wage Structure', *Econometrica*, 56, March, pp. 259–93.

Lakonishok, J., A. Shleifer and R. Vishny (1992), 'The Structure and Performance of the Money Management Industry', *Brookings Papers on Economic Activity: Microeconomics*, pp. 339–92.

Lazear, E.P. (1979), 'Why Is there Mandatory Retirement?', *Journal of Political Economy*, 87, pp. 36–54.

—— (1989), 'Pay Equality and Industrial Politics', *Journal of Political Economy*, 97, pp. 561–80.

—— (1992), 'The Job as a Concept', in W. Bruns (ed.), *Performance Measurement, Evaluation, and Incentives*, Cambridge, MA: Harvard Business School Press, pp. 9–42.

Lo Pucki, L. and W. Whitford (1990), 'Bargaining over Equity's Share in the Bankruptcy Reorganization of Large, Publicly Held Companies', *Pennsylvania Law Review*, 134, pp. 125–73.

Malcolmson, J.M. (1984), 'Work Incentives, Hierarchy, and Internal Labor Markets', *Journal of Political Economy*, 92, pp. 486–507.

Maloney, M.T., R.E. McCormick and M.L. Mitchell (1993), 'Managerial Decision Making and Capital Structure', *Journal of Business*, 66, pp. 189–217.

Manne, H.G. (1965), 'Mergers and the Market for Corporate Control', *Journal of Political Economy*, 75, pp. 110–26.

Marshall, Alfred (1948), *Principles of Economics*, New York, NY: Macmillan (8th edition).

Martin, K. and J. McConnell (1991), 'Corporate Performance, Corporate Takeovers and Management Turnover', *Journal of Finance*, 46, pp. 671–87.

Meyer, M., P. Milgrom and J. Roberts (1992), 'Organizational Prospects, Influence Costs, and Ownership Changes', *Journal of Economics and Management Strategy*, 1, pp. 9–36.

Middlestaedt, H. F. (1989), 'An Empirical Analysis of the Factors Underlying the Decision to Remove Excess Assets from Overfunded Pension Plans', *Journal of Accounting and Economics*, 11, pp. 394–418.

Mirrlees, J. (1976), 'The Optimal Structure of Incentives and Authority within an Organization', *Bell Journal of Economics*, 7, pp. 105–31.

Mitchell, M. and K. Lehn (1991), 'Do Bad Bidders Become Good Targets?', *Journal of Political Economy*, 99, pp. 237–61.

Morck, R., A. Shleifer and R. Vishny (1988a), 'Characteristics of Hostile and Friendly Takeovers', in A.J. Auerbach (ed.), *Corporate Takeovers: Causes and Consequences*, Chicago, IL: University of Chicago Press for the National Bureau of Economic Research, pp. 301–27.

—— (1988b), 'Management Ownership and Market Valuation: An Empirical Analysis', *Journal of Financial Economics*, 20, pp. 293–315.

Murphy, K.J. (1985), 'Corporate Performance and Managerial Remuneration: An Empirical Analysis', *Journal of Accounting and Economics*, 7, pp. 11–42.

Murphy, K.J. and K. Van Nuys (1993), 'Public Pension Funds: Ark of the Lost Raiders?', Working Paper, Harvard Business School, Cambridge, MA.

Myers, S. (1977), 'Determinants of Corporate Borrowing', *Journal of Financial Economics*, 9, pp. 147–75.

Palepu, K. (1990), 'Consequences of Leveraged Buyouts', *Journal of Financial Economics*, 27, pp. 247–61.

Paul, J. (1992), 'On the Efficiency of Stock-Based Compensation', *Review of Financial Studies*, 5, pp. 471–502.

Petersen, M. (1992), 'Pension Reversions and Worker–Stockholder Wealth Transfers', *Quarterly Journal of Economics*, 108, pp. 1,032–55.

Pontiff, J., A. Shleifer and M. Weisbach (1990), 'Revisions of Excess Pension Assets after Takeovers', *Rand Journal of Economics*, 8, pp. 600–13.

Pound, J. (1991), 'Proxy Voting and the SEC', *Journal of Financial Economics*, 29, pp. 241–85.

—— (1992a), 'Raiders, Targets and Politics', *Continental Bank Journal of Applied Corporate Finance*, 5 (3), pp. 6–18.

—— (1992b), 'On the Motives for Choosing a Corporate Governance Structure: A Study of Corporate Reaction to the Pennsylvania Takeover Law', *Journal of Law, Economics, and Organization*, 8, pp. 656–72.

Prahalad, C.K. (1993), 'Comments', *Continental Bank Journal of Applied Corporate Finance*, 6, pp. 38–54.

Prendergast, C. (1993), 'The Role of Promotion in Inducing Specific Human Capital Acquisition', *Quarterly Journal of Economics*, 108, pp. 523–34.

Prendergast, C. and R. Topel (1993), 'Discretion and Bias in Performance Evaluation', *European Economic Review*, 37, pp. 355–65.

Roe, M. (1990), 'Political and Legal Restraints on Ownership and Control of Public Companies', *Journal of Financial Economics*, 27, pp. 7–41.

—— (1993a), 'Some Differences in Corporate Structure in Germany, Japan, and the U.S.', *Yale Law Journal*, 102, pp. 1–137.

—— (1993b), 'Takeover Politics', in M. Blair (ed.), *The Deal Decade*, Washington DC: Brookings Institution, pp. 321–47.

Romano, R. (1991), 'The Shareholder Suit: Litigation without Foundation?', *Journal of Law, Economics, and Organization*, 7, pp. 55–88.

Rosen, S. (1982), 'Hierarchy, Control, and the Distribution of Earnings', *Bell Journal of Economics*, 13, pp. 77–98.

Ryngaert, M. (1988), 'The Effect of Poison Pill Securities on Shareholder Wealth', *Journal of Financial Economics*, 20, pp. 377–418.

Scharfstein, D.S. (1988), 'The Disciplinary Role of Takeovers', *Review of Economic Studies*, 45, pp. 185–99.

Sheard, P. (1989), 'The Main Bank System and Corporate Monitoring and Control in Japan', *Journal of Economic Behavior and Organization*, 11, pp. 399–422.

—— (1991), 'The Economics of Interlocking Shareholding in Japan', *Ricerche Economiche*, 45 (2–3), pp. 421–48.

—— (1994a), '*Keiretsu*, Competition and Market Access', Discussion Paper 94-17, Faculty of Economics, Osaka University, Osaka.

—— (1994b), 'Bank Executives on Japanese Corporate Boards', *Bank of Japan Monetary and Economic Studies*, 12 (2), pp. 85–121.

Shleifer, A. and L. Summers (1988), 'Hostile Takeovers as Breaches of Trust', in A.J. Auerbach (ed), *Corporate Takeovers: Causes and Consequences*, Chicago, IL: University of Chicago Press for the National Bureau for Economic Research, pp. 65–88.

Shleifer, A. and R. Vishny (1986), 'Greenmail, White Knights, and Shareholder's Interest', *Rand Journal of Economics*, 17, pp. 293–309.

Sklivas, S. (1987), 'The Strategic Choice of Managerial Incentives', *Rand Journal of Economics*, 18, pp. 452–8.

Smith, C. and J. Warner (1979), 'On Financial Contracting: An Analysis of Bond Covenants', *Journal of Financial Economics*, 7, pp. 117–61.

Stiglitz, J.E. (1985), 'Credit Markets and the Control of Capital', *Journal of Money, Credit, and Banking*, 17, pp. 133–52.

Stulz, R. (1990), 'Managerial Discretion and Optimal Financing Policies', *Journal of Financial Economics*, 26, pp. 3–27.

Thomas, J. K. (1989), 'Why Do Firms Terminate their Overfunded Pension Plans?', *Journal of Accounting and Economics*, 11, pp. 418–37.

Warner, J., R. Watts and K. Wruck (1988), 'Stock Prices and Top Management Changes', *Journal of Financial Economics*, 20, pp. 461–92.

Weisbach, M.S. (1988), 'Outside Directors and CEO Turnover', *Journal of Financial Economics*, 20, pp. 431–60.

Williamson, O. (1985), *The Economic Institutions of Capitalism*, New York, NY: The Free Press.

—— (1988), 'Corporate Finance and Corporate Governance', *Journal of Finance*, 43, pp. 567–92.

5 Reciprocal delegated monitoring in the main bank system

*Paul Sheard**

A feature of Japanese corporate finance is that most large firms maintain a close relationship with one of the commercial banks, this bank being known as the firm's 'main bank'. The main bank is usually a principal shareholder in the firm, and if, as is normally the case, the firm has bank borrowings, the main bank usually has the largest single loan share among lenders to the firm. A noteworthy aspect of the main bank system is that the main bank appears to play an important role in monitoring the firm and, in the case of managerial crisis or financial failure, in carrying out rescue operations and informal reorganisations of the firm (Sheard 1985, 1989, 1994b; Aoki 1988, Ch. 4, 1994a).[1]

The purpose of this chapter is to explore further the idea that the main bank system serves as an institutional arrangement that allows banks to engage in delegated monitoring among themselves with respect to the monitoring of a set of corporate borrowers. Three stylised facts about the main bank system are particularly relevant to the analysis. The first is that the main bank's monitoring role appears disproportionately large relative to its role as a lender. A firm typically borrows from a large number of financial institutions, generally from 30 to 50. The main bank has the largest loan share, usually in the range of 10 to 20 per cent, but it is only one of many financial institutions lending to the firm. It can be thought of as the bank that is delegated the

---

* This chapter is reprinted from the *Journal of the Japanese and International Economies*, (1994, 8 [1], pp. 1–21). I wrote it while visiting the Department of Economics and Asia/Pacific Research Center, Stanford University, and revised it while at the Institute of Social and Economic Research, Osaka University. I am grateful for financial support from the Program on the Economy of Japan at the Center for Economic Policy Research, Stanford University, and the Daiwa Bank Foundation for Asia and Oceania. I would like to thank Masahiko Aoki, Paul Milgrom, Masahiro Okuno-Fujiwara, Patrick Bolton, Colin Mayer, Mark Ramseyer and two anonymous referees, as well as seminar participants at a number of universities, for their helpful comments. Any deficiencies remain my responsibility.

task of monitoring the firm on behalf of all lenders, given that monitoring has the characteristics of a public good (Stiglitz 1985). The second is that there is a considerable degree of reciprocity among the major banks in terms of who assumes the main bank role and who the non-main bank role across the set of borrowing firms. Roughly speaking, each of the principal commercial banks lends to the same set of firms, but does so as a main bank to some and as a non-main bank to the others. Thus banks A and B may both lend to firms X and Y, but A may do so to X as main bank and to Y as non-main bank, while for B the reverse is the case.[2] A third stylised fact is that, when a firm is in financial distress or fails, the main bank tends to bear a disproportionately large share of any assistance burden or bank losses that are sustained (numerous examples are cited in Sheard 1985, 1989, 1992, 1994b).

These institutional aspects of the main bank system appear at first glance to present some theoretical puzzles. Why doesn't the main bank have a bigger loan share, more commensurate with its supposed corporate governance role? Why does a particular bank lend sometimes as a main bank and other times as a non-main bank, rather than specialising in either role? Why does the main bank assume such a large share of losses, even though it has a relatively low loan share?

This chapter develops a simple model of bank lending that aims to capture the above features of the main bank system and that goes some way towards providing an explanation for these theoretical puzzles. The argument rests on two key ideas. One is that, given the (local) public good nature of monitoring, reciprocal delegated monitoring provides a mechanism for a set of lending banks to ensure that the public good of monitoring is provided, while avoiding costly duplication and maintaining a high level of transactional and risk diversification. The second is that monitoring by the delegated bank is likely to be unobservable to the other banks, leading to the development of a principal–agent relationship between the non-main banks and the main bank. Extending the argument in Sheard (1989, p. 413), the convention that the main bank bears a disproportionate share of bank losses is viewed as being part of a contractual arrangement among banks designed to give the main bank adequate incentives to act as delegated monitor. Although motivated by an interest in the Japanese main bank system, the analysis has relevance to the expanding literature on the theory of financial intermediation (Bizer and DeMarzo 1992; Diamond 1984, 1991a; Dewatripont and Maskin 1990; Hellwig 1990; Krasa and Villamil 1992; Mayer 1988; Von Thadden 1990; Yanelle 1989).

Simple model of bank monitoring

Consider the following simple model of an economy in which there are n identical banks that have loaned funds to m identical firms, where $1 < n < m$. For simplicity, assume that each firm i, having borrowed funds, has incurred an obligation to repay Z dollars of debt.[3] Each firm is engaged in a risky activity so that the actual funds available for repayment to the banks, Y, are a random variable with probability density function $f(Y)$ on support $[0,Z]$, with associated cumulative density function $F(Y)$. In other words, Y is defined so that it cannot exceed Z, although the firm's actual return may exceed Z, with the residual accruing to shareholders.[4] At $Y = Z$, $f(Y)$ (denoted by $f(Z)$ below) is strictly positive but less than one, capturing the notion that in many states the firm is able to repay its debt obligations in full but that there are states in which it cannot do so ('default states'). Assume that Y is identically and independently distributed across firms. Thus firms are identical in an *ex ante* sense but *ex post* will tend to have different realisations of Y.

Banks are characterised by a monitoring technology such that an expenditure of K dollars brings about an improvement in firm i's performance in a first-order stochastic dominance sense; that is, bank monitoring increases the probability that the firm will be able to make its repayments in full and lowers the probability that it will default. The economic notion that 'monitoring matters' is captured by the assumption that $f(Z|K) > f(Z|0)$. In line with the literature, 'monitoring' here should be interpreted broadly as any activity that improves the performance of the firm (Hellwig 1990). It could be an *ex ante* screening activity that improves the quality of the pool of firms surviving screening; it could be an *ex ante* monitoring activity that reduces shirking within the firm through incentive effects or that improves expected performance through productive bank inputs; or it could be an *ex post* intervention that is beneficial to the banks' returns, such as auditing of the firm's accounts or the seizing of a defaulting firm's assets.

It is assumed that there is an extreme form of decreasing returns to scale in monitoring, namely that only one expenditure of K is required to bring about the improvement in the firm's performance. Given that K is being expended by one bank in monitoring firm i, further increments of monitoring expenditure by this or other banks would have no further impact on the firm's performance. Banks have an incentive to set up institutional arrangements that economise on monitoring costs by avoiding duplication of monitoring efforts. We assume that monitoring is an all-or-nothing, indivisible activity: two banks each sinking $K/2$ into monitoring has no effect. That is, up until K, there is an extreme form of subadditivity or increasing returns to scale.[5] The purpose of this assumption is to rule out the possibility that the n banks provide the unit of public good by each committing to providing $1/n$ of the input. Thus monitoring is assumed to be a public good, the efficient provision of which requires total specialisation.

Banks are modelled as expected value maximisers.[6] The expected increase in repayments to the banks that comes from having the firm monitored can be denoted by $E(R|K)$, where:

$$E(R|K) \equiv Z[f(Z|K) - f(Z|0)] - \int_0^{Z'} Y[f(Y|0) - f(Y|K)]dY$$

and where Z' equals $Z - \varepsilon$ for an arbitrarily small $\varepsilon > 0$. By construction, $E(R|K)$ is strictly positive as probability weight is taken away from all values less than Z and transferred to Z. To make the analysis non-trivial, assume that $E(R|K) - K$ is strictly positive so that monitoring is collectively beneficial to the banks. The above assumptions model a situation where monitoring is beneficial but joint profit maximisation requires that each firm be monitored by one and only one bank so that there is no duplication of monitoring effort and the total fixed costs of monitoring are minimised at mK.

Exclusive lending

One way to achieve efficient monitoring is to have specialisation in lending. The n banks could divide up the set of m firms so that each bank lent to m/n firms, had a loan share of unity in each firm that it lent to, and monitored those firms. The net benefit to monitoring, $E(R|K) - K$, is positive by assumption, so monitoring occurs and there is no duplication. This arrangement works because exclusivity in monitoring — desirable because of the indivisible public good nature of monitoring — is combined with exclusivity in lending, so that the monitor internalises through its loan share the beneficial externality that would otherwise be conferred on non-monitoring banks.

The exclusive lending case is interesting as a theoretical benchmark (see Diamond 1984, for example), but in order to focus on reciprocal delegated monitoring we rule out this solution on the grounds that either firms or banks prefer diversified borrowing or lending relations. Empirically, firms and banks in Japan are quite diversified in their borrowing and lending sources, so exclusivity, although achieving the first best in this simple model, is of limited practical interest. Japanese firms typically borrow from many banks: according to a survey reported in Horiuchi and Murakami (1991, p. 94), large firms with 10,000 or more employees transact with about 45 banks on average. Typically the bank lending the largest amount to a firm has a relatively small share of the firm's total borrowings: Aoki, Patrick and Sheard (1994) report that the average largest loan share for listed firms in Japan was in the range of 13–16 per cent during the period 1977–91. It is difficult to say whether this transactional diversification reflects firm or bank preferences — presumably the number of lenders and loan shares is determined jointly — but empirically a marked departure from exclusivity is observed.

Although attributed to exogenous preferences here, a number of reasons for firms' and banks' revealed preference for diversified relations can be noted. From the viewpoint of the banks, the desire to diversify risks is an obvious factor.[7] If the banks were even slightly risk averse, optimal risk sharing would be achieved by complete diversification; exclusivity involves the least amount of risk diversification. A second reason is that, by diversifying transactions, banks increase their information sources or contact points in the real economy, helping to create a richer intangible asset base. For example, each bank in a set of banks may want to lend to all (or most) of the firms in a given industry so as to increase the number of information draws that it makes from that industry. It may also want to lend in tandem with other banks in order to facilitate contact with and obtain information from them.[8] It can be posited that the information effect of diversification is quite relevant to Japanese banks given that the lifetime employment system severely limits interbank managerial mobility and thus the scope for information to flow between banks in this way. Third, in a dynamic setting, there may be a kind of 'foothold' or option value effect associated with lending in that establishing a lending relationship puts the bank in a better position to participate in future loan opportunities resulting from the successful growth of the firm. If so, banks may want to diversify, not just to achieve portfolio risk diversification in the current period, but to establish a diversified portfolio of longer term options on business growth opportunities.

There are also factors on the firm side favouring diversification. An obvious one is that firms may want to diversify their borrowing sources to induce competition among lending banks or to avoid the potential delays that could attend an exclusive banking relationship.[9] A second reason is that, by maintaining diversified banking relations, firms can diversify their access to information, given that banks are an economy-wide information intermediary providing productive informational inputs as a joint product with the supply of financial capital and risk bearing services. On theoretical grounds, then, a high degree of diversification in bank–firm relations is to be expected, and this is observed in practice in Japan.

Diversified lending

An important insight is that the incentives for diversification noted above conflict with those for adequate monitoring, as under diversification no single bank is likely to have incentives to provide what is effectively a form of (local) public good. Under diversification there may be a tendency towards free-riding or the underprovision of monitoring services on the one hand, or towards duplication or the overprovision of monitoring services on the other, since if one bank *does* find it in its private interest to incur a monitoring cost it is likely that others will also.

We define a *normal bank contract* as one having the following two features: bank returns are completely specified by loan shares; and banks decide whether or not to monitor non-cooperatively, that is, based on their own profit calculations. The share that bank j is entitled to in firm i's repayment of any fixed obligation is denoted by r_i^j. The normal bank contract specifies that $r_i^j = s_i^j Y$ for all i; banks differ, if at all, in their loan shares only. Thus under the normal bank contract each bank j has an expected return of $s_i^j E(Y)$. Focus on the symmetric benchmark case where all banks have the same loan share, $s_i^j = 1/n$ for all j and i, and the maximum amount of transactional diversification is obtained.

There are two general cases: $K > E(R|K)/n$, in which case no bank monitors, and $K < E(R|K)/n$, in which case too many banks may monitor. In the first case no bank finds it in its own interests to monitor the firm because the bank bears the cost but internalises only part (but not enough) of the benefits. In the second case, because banks are assumed to behave non-cooperatively, there may be duplication of monitoring costs (too many banks monitoring) or coordination failure (none monitoring).

Reciprocal delegated monitoring

There is a way to ensure an efficient level of monitoring that is consistent with complete diversification in lending and borrowing. It is for banks to be completely diversified in their lending but to share the burden of being a monitor by having each be responsible for monitoring m/n firms. Each bank would then lend to m firms, monitor m/n firms, and incur mK/n in monitoring costs. Total monitoring costs would be mK, with all firms being monitored but each being monitored by only one bank.

This arrangement involves free-riding at the level of the individual firm by the $n-1$ banks that lend to the firm as non-monitoring banks. This free-riding is desirable because it is the mechanism by which the banks are able to recover the monitoring costs that they incur when *they* monitor. However, there is no free-riding at the aggregate level as no single bank does a disproportionate amount of monitoring *on average*. Notice that this scheme is equivalent to one in which each of the non-monitoring banks makes a payment to the monitoring bank for its share of the monitoring bank's expenses: monitoring bank k expends K with respect to its monitoring of firm i and receives $(n-1)K/n$ from the non-monitoring banks, making its net payment K/n. This scheme essentially restores the equivalence between loan and monitoring shares at the level of the firm to be monitored, but in terms of monitoring *expenditure* rather than monitoring *activity*.

Notice, however, that such monetary side-payments are completely superfluous since each bank makes a net side-payment of zero: it pays $m(n-1)/n$ times K/n to the other banks in delegated monitoring fees and receives $(n-1)K/n$ times m/n for its monitoring activity from them. So we can assume that no monitoring side-payments are in fact made; rather, the scheme maintains an equivalence between loan shares at the level of the firm and monitoring shares at the aggregate, or effective per firm, level. *Reciprocal* delegated monitoring is the mechanism by which the set of banks can avoid costly duplication of monitoring efforts, preserve the benefits of diversification and ensure that monitoring takes place.

The main bank contract and incentives to monitor

The above scheme can be expected to work well as long as banks are able to observe each other's monitoring. Suppose now that there exists an informational asymmetry between the delegating monitors and the delegated monitor that gives rise to a potential moral hazard problem. Assume that whether or not an individual bank actually monitors a firm that it is responsible for is not observed by the other banks. (It is observed by the firm concerned but is not verifiable to others.) Rather, the banks observe the output or performance of the firm, which is a random variable. This seems to be a fairly reasonable assumption. Given the very nature of the activity we call 'monitoring' — loosely, the bridging of an informational asymmetry between two economic agents — it is reasonable to assume that, without incurring a monitoring cost of their own, agents external to the monitoring activity will find it difficult to know whether the asymmetry has indeed been bridged.

To motivate the analysis, assume that $K > E(R|K)/n$. No bank will monitor under the normal bank contract as described above because the marginal cost of monitoring exceeds the marginal benefit — that part of the improvement in expected performance that accrues to the monitor.[10] No bank will monitor under the reciprocal delegation arrangement either. Given that the sinking of K is unobservable and cannot be contracted upon by the banks, the monitoring bank will have an incentive to shirk on its monitoring expenditure and free-ride on the monitoring that other banks do with respect to other firms. But by construction all banks are identical and so all banks shirk in this simple setup. Monitoring is collectively beneficial here, so banks are caught in a (static) prisoners' dilemma.

A principal–agent interpretation

As suggested in Sheard (1989), the reciprocal delegation setup can be conceptualised in principal–agent theoretic terms. Consider firm i. We can view the non-monitoring banks taken as a whole as the principal, and the monitoring bank (or main bank) as the agent. The principal wishes to delegate to the agent the task of monitoring.[11] This activity benefits the principal but is costly (in a net sense) to the agent and is not observed by the principal. (It benefits the agent as well, but not enough to justify it bearing all of the monitoring cost.) The activity of monitoring is combined with a stochastic activity (the performance of the firm being monitored), so the principal faces a non-trivial signal extraction problem. The principal observes only a noisy signal that reflects both the stochastic nature of the firm's activities and the bank's monitoring input. Poor firm performance, for instance, could imply that the bank monitored but that there was a bad draw from nature, or that the state of nature was more favourable but that the bank shirked on its monitoring; similarly, a firm's performance might be good even though the draw from nature was not so good because the bank monitored, or the bank may have shirked but been lucky.

The problem that the principal faces is to design a contract that gives incentives to the agent to take the action desired by the principal. In the standard principal–agent model, the payment function would be a wage contract or a managerial compensation schedule that the principal (shareholder or manager) used to pay the agent (manager or worker). In the real world the optimal contract is an actual payment scheme offered by the principal to the agent. Here it is not suggested that the non-monitoring banks 'hire' the bank to monitor the firm under a contingent contract. Rather, on a practical level, the payment schedule can be thought of as being induced by the loan arrangements and the legal and implicit conventions that support them.

The normal bank contract is particularly simple. Each bank's share of the total funds available for repayment is state-independent and equal to its loan share; under complete diversification it is also symmetric. *A priori*, however, there is no necessary reason for a bank's share in the funds available for repayment to be equal to its loan share in every state of nature. By making the payoffs of the bank delegated the task of monitoring firm i depend on the state of nature in some way, it may be possible to manipulate the bank's incentives to monitor: the specification of the returns function can serve as a mechanism for the principal to design an implicit payment function for the agent. By having r_i^j deviate from $s_i^j Y$ in some states of the world, the principal can effectively alter the agent's incentives to engage in costly monitoring. In a situation where $K > s_i^j E(R|K)$, the bank may be induced to monitor by introducing a payoff function that alters the right-hand side and in effect reverses the inequality, making it in the monitor's private interests to undertake the monitoring.

Main bank contract

Consider the following candidate for such a payment schedule, which we designate as the 'main bank contract', where 'main bank' is synonymous with 'delegated monitoring bank'. Under the main bank contract one of the banks, denoted by superscript k, is designated as the bank responsible for monitoring the firm. The payoffs are as follows:

$$r_i^k = \begin{cases} s_i^k Y & \text{if } Y = Z \\ Y - \Sigma_j(s_i^j Z) & \text{if } Y<Z \text{ and } \Sigma_j(s_i^j Z) \leq Y \\ 0 & \text{if } Y<Z \text{ and } \Sigma_j(s_i^j Z) > Y \end{cases}$$

for the monitoring bank k; and

$$r_i^j = \begin{cases} s_i^j Y & \text{if } Y = Z \\ s_i^j Z & \text{if } Y<Z \text{ and } \Sigma_j(s_i^j Z) \\ [s_i^j/(1-s_i^k)]Y & \text{if } Y<Z \text{ and } \Sigma_j(s_i^j Z) > Y \end{cases}$$

for $j \neq k$, where $s_i^k = s_i^j = 1/n$ or $s_i^j < 1/n < s_i^k$.

As long as the firm has sufficient returns to meet its loan obligations each bank is repaid in accordance with its loan share. However, if the returns fall short of the repayment obligation the monitoring and the non-monitoring banks are treated differently. If returns fall short but there are sufficient funds to repay the non-monitoring banks in accordance with their loan shares, then this is done, with the main bank receiving the residual, which must by assumption be less than $s_i^k Y$. If returns fall short of the amount needed to repay the non-monitoring banks, the main bank receives nothing and the non-monitoring banks are repaid in accordance with their loan shares, adjusted for the fact that the main bank does not receive any repayment.

This kind of bank contract resembles fairly closely the way that the Japanese main bank system actually appears to operate. In particular, the main bank: (a) is regarded by participants in the capital market as the bank responsible for monitoring the firm and, if a failing firm, for overseeing its rescue, reorganisation or, in the worst case, liquidation; (b) has the largest loan share (but typically not a very large share); and (c) bears a disproportionately large share of the assistance burden or loan losses when the firm requires financial assistance or fails. With regard to the last point, suppose for example that the outcome was $Y = Y'$, where Y' is total promised repayments to the non-main banks. Then the main bank bears 100 per cent of the loss, $Z - Y'$, despite only having a loan share of s_i^k. The arrangement is, moreover, simple to understand and to implement.

We can state the following propositions. (The proofs, derived from simple but tedious algebraic manipulations, are given in Sheard 1991b.)

Proposition 1 The marginal cost of shirking for the monitoring bank under the main bank contract exceeds that under the normal bank contract.

In deciding whether or not to shirk, the bank weighs up the marginal (here, also total) benefits and costs of shirking (equivalently the marginal costs and benefits of monitoring). As under the normal bank contract, the marginal benefit of shirking is just the fixed cost saved, K. Under the normal bank contract the marginal cost was $E(R|K)/n$. Under the main bank contract the marginal cost of shirking is more complicated and becomes:

$$MCS_i^k = s_i^k Z f(Z|K) + \int_{Y'}^{Z'} [Y - \Sigma_j(s_i^j Z)] f(Y|K) dY + 0$$

$$- s_i^k Z f(Z|0) - \int_{Y'}^{Z'} [Y - \Sigma_j(s_i^j Z)] f(Y|0) dY - 0$$

$$= s_i^k Z [f(Z|K) - f(Z|0)] - \int_{Y'}^{Z'} [Y - \Sigma_j(s_i^j Z)][f(Y|0) - f(Y|K)] dY$$

where $Y' \equiv \Sigma_j s_i^j Z = Z \Sigma_j s_i^j = Z(1 - s_i^k)$, and $j \neq k$. It can no longer be written as the simple product of two terms since the bank's share in repayments from the firm depends on the particular state of nature. (Previously it was independent of the state of nature.)

If $s_i^k > 1/n > s_i^j$, then the main bank's loan share will be larger than its share under the symmetric normal contract while the non-monitoring banks' shares will be smaller.[12] This says that, relative to the normal contract benchmark, the main bank is 'rewarded' in the best state ($Y = Z$) by receiving a larger share of Z than other banks and than it would under the normal contract.[13] On the other hand, in bad states the main bank is 'penalised' by being sent to the end of the queue; in sufficiently bad states it receives no repayment at all.[14] The payment schedule is consistent with the prediction of the standard principal–agent model, namely that the agent is rewarded in good states (when it is more likely that effort was supplied) and punished in bad states (when the converse is the case) (Kreps 1990, Ch. 16).

There are two other ways to characterise intuitively this form of contract. One is in terms of loan priority.[15] The main bank contract can be viewed as making the delegated monitoring bank *junior* in priority relative to the non-monitoring banks and, if $s_i^k > 1/n$, as giving the main bank a larger share of returns when priority does not matter, that is, when $Y = Z$. The main bank then has an incentive to reduce the probability of states of nature occurring where it suffers from its junior status and, relative to the case when its loan share is the same as other banks, to bring about a state of nature in which priority does not matter.

A second interpretation concerns risk insurance. The loans of the non-monitoring banks to a particular firm become less risky because the range of states of nature in which these banks are repaid in full is enlarged. In states of nature in which they are not repaid in full they receive more because the main bank foregoes its share of the pie; the converse is true for the main bank. It is as if the main bank is acting as a partial insurance agent for the lending to the firm of the non-main banks. The intuition for the incentive effect is that, as an insurance agent, the main bank has strong incentives to ensure that states of nature in which it would have to pay out do not occur, and conversely that states in which it collects premiums (in the sense of having a larger loan share and so larger payoff) do occur. Of course, in the absence of the monitoring incentive problem, there would be no need for a risk insurance agent as banks could diversify fully through their loan shares. In this setting, however, fully exploiting risk diversification would result in the benefits of monitoring being lost.

The implication of the proposition is that the main bank contract, by increasing the marginal costs of shirking (or marginal benefits of monitoring), will in certain circumstances induce monitoring where the normal bank contract would not. When the marginal benefits of monitoring rise it is in the bank's private interests to monitor rather than shirk, making the bank's commitment to monitor under reciprocal delegation more credible. The proposition does not imply that an arbitrary main bank contract will always induce monitoring since the marginal cost of shirking may not rise enough to reverse the inequality. (Recall that the marginal benefit is constant across the two regimes, being simply K.) What the proposition does show, however, is that there exist values of K such that the main bank contract will induce monitoring where the normal bank contract would not, and this is true even when $s_i^k = s_i^j = 1/n$.[16] Viewed from a different angle, if the main bank contract was constructed so that the designated monitoring bank had only individual incentives to monitor, then switching to the normal bank contract would result in monitoring not taking place.

The above analysis demonstrates that the implementation of the main bank contract may induce the monitoring bank to monitor. We need to check that the principal, the non-monitoring banks, would want to implement such a scheme. This is established in the following proposition.

Proposition 2 The non-monitoring banks of firm i do better in their transactions with firm i under the main bank contract than under the normal bank contract when

$s_i^k = s_i^j = 1/n$. They also do better when $s_i^k > 1/n$ (or $s_i^j < 1/n$) as long as s_i^k does not get 'too large'.

Intuitively, non-monitoring banks enjoy the benefits of free-riding: they do better since monitoring (a desirable activity) takes place; they do not incur the costs of monitoring; and, at least when loan shares are equal, they have a higher share in some states and never have a lower share.

Proposition 3 assesses the same situation from the perspective of the monitoring bank.

Proposition 3 The monitoring bank fares worse in its transactions with firm *i* under the main bank contract than under the normal bank contract in the case that all banks have identical loan shares. It also fares worse when $s_i^k > 1/n$ as long as s_i^k does not get 'too large'.

This proposition shows that, in the simplified setting studied here, the main bank does not benefit *directly* from its main bank relationships. Intuitively this is because the main bank has to incur the monitoring cost itself — a cost which by assumption is not warranted for this particular loan transaction given the posited loan share — whereas it internalises only part of the benefit. However:

Proposition 4 Over all its transactions (as a main bank and as a non-main bank) each bank does better under the main bank contract regime than under the normal bank contract regime.

The intuition behind this proposition is that under the main bank contract regime, over all its transactions each bank derives a net benefit of $E(R|K)-K$, which is positive by the assumption that monitoring is collectively desirable. By operating under the main bank contract regime, each bank becomes better off because in equilibrium monitoring takes place and monitoring costs are minimised.

Discussion

The result that the main bank does not benefit in its capacity as main bank from its position as a main bank follows from the fact that, by definition, it bears the costs of monitoring. The above propositions characterise the extreme case in which there are no direct benefits from being main bank that compensate for these costs. They show that even in this extreme case reciprocal delegation may be collectively beneficial to a set of banks. The costs associated with being main bank to m/n firms are more than compensated for by the benefits that the main bank obtains when it lends as a non-main bank. The main bank confers a beneficial externality on the other non-monitoring banks. It is prepared to do this because it is the recipient of beneficial externalities from the same banks when it lends as a non-monitoring bank.

More realistically, it may be that the main bank derives direct benefits from its position by gaining preferential access to other lucrative financial business generated by the firm: its foreign exchange transactions, for example, or by acting as clearing bank for the firm's promissory notes (Aoki, Patrick and Sheard 1994). Another idea, proposed by Nakatani (1984), is that the main bank benefits from implicitly being able to sell insurance to the firm, thereby receiving insurance premiums in good states even though it may have to pay out in bad states. While these effects are not modelled here, it suffices to say that they would reinforce the incentive properties of the agency arrangement by increasing the marginal cost to the main bank of shirking.[17]

Propositions 2 and 3 together might seem to imply that banks would prefer not to become main banks but rather to specialise in being non-main banks and free-ride on the main banks. There are two kinds of potential free-rider: free-riders from among the n banks, and free-riders from outside the arrangement (in the wider capital market). Free-riding by the former group can be ruled out in the context of the model because in participating in the reciprocal delegation arrangement it is assumed that each bank commits to taking on the role of main bank towards m/n firms. It is not possible to free-ride as part of the reciprocal delegation arrangement because this is tantamount to refusing to participate *ex ante*; if all banks did this monitoring would not take place at all. Given that it is in their collective interests to ensure that monitoring takes place (proposition 4), it can be assumed that banks will be able to agree *ex ante* to exclude free-riders.

Whether or not other banks or lenders outside of the n banks can free-ride depends critically on the attitude and actions of the firms being monitored. Firms can prevent such free-riding by deciding not to borrow from these lenders, and in the case of repeated dealings it may be in their long-run interests to do so even if there are short-term gains to be made from defecting to the free-riders.[18] It might also be that the n core banks can effectively exclude peripheral free-riding banks from gaining significant lending shares to the firms by imposing this as a condition of their lending. Such self or imposed enforcement is most likely to be feasible when the capital market is relatively closed and the number of banks reasonably small, conditions that have characterised the operation of the main bank system in Japan until fairly recently.[19] On the other hand, it may be possible to interpret part of the shift toward more market based instruments that occurred in corporate finance in the 1980s as reflecting firms' decisions to opt out of monitoring under main bank lending arrangements (Hoshi, Kashyap and Scharfstein 1993).

Even if banks can coordinate on an *ex ante* assignment of roles and minimise external free-riding, there may be a problem associated with *ex post* enforcement in bad states. The main bank does rather badly in adverse states of nature even though it may have actually done the required monitoring. (Indeed, in the equilibrium under consideration here this will have been the case.) In the case that $Y \leq \Sigma_j(s_i^j Z)$, the main bank gets no return even though it has a loan share at least as large as that of the non-main banks. The main bank might want to claim *ex post* that it is entitled to $s_i^k Y$ rather than zero (that is, to claim opportunistically that it is operating under the normal bank contract). Since Y is observable and verifiable, and since there is no disagreement *ex ante* about which bank is the main bank, there should be no problem in writing enforceable contracts simply by specifying the difference in priority between the main and non-main banks.

Interestingly, in the Japanese case the main bank contract is not written down in a legally enforceable way (why this is so remains somewhat of a puzzle); rather it is implicit in the conventions surrrounding the main bank system, and those are common knowledge among practitioners (see Sheard 1985, 1989 for more details). Thus as a practical matter the issue of opportunistic *ex post* behaviour by the main bank and enforceability *does* arise. In practice, two kinds of enforcement mechanism seem to be at work. One relates to the self-enforcing nature of the arrangement. Reciprocity, by exposing banks symmetrically to opportunistic hazards, creates an exchange of 'hostages' in the sense described by Williamson (1985, Ch. 8). This serves to curb opportunistic behaviour: a bank contemplating such behaviour *ex post* takes into account the possibility that the other banks may retaliate in their capacity as main banks by taking similar actions against it in its non-main bank dealings. A point to note here is that, given the correlation of risks across firms in a given market, banks often find themselves providing assistance to a number of firms in an industry at the same time: although bank A may be bearing losses on loans to firm X to bank B's benefit, bank B may be incurring losses on loans to firm Y to bank A's benefit.[20] More importantly, perhaps, banks are engaged in a repeated rather than one-shot game with one another, and a bank that violated the implicit norms of main bank behaviour could find itself being excluded from participation in future reciprocal delegation arrangements. Such self-enforcement may not always work, particularly when the present gains from defection loom large. In those cases, the regulatory authorities — the Ministry of Finance and the Bank of Japan — appear to play an important role in enforcing the norms of main bank behaviour by bringing various forms of pressure and moral suasion to bear.[21]

Incentives to intervene

A prominent aspect of the main bank's role, and one which is not adequately captured in the simple model described above, is that the main bank intervenes in and takes control of the management of failing firms in rescue-cum-reorganisation operations (Aoki 1994b; Sheard 1994b). This *ex post* monitoring role can also be viewed as the main bank providing a form of public good to other creditors. It is worth asking how the main bank contractual arrangement influences the incentives of the bank to perform this role.

Suppose that a failing firm is taken to be one for which $Y < Z$. To capture the idea of bank intervention, suppose that a bank can increase the value of the firm's outcome by ΔY by expending K, where $\Delta Y > K$. This K can be thought of as the cost of verifying the *ex post* profit state, or of providing reorganisation or liquidation services; in another setting it could be the costs incurred by a takeover agent. The generation of extra value could reflect a number of things: an increase in the liquidation value of the firm from a carefully managed asset sale as compared to a fire sale of assets; additional funds 'wrested' from incumbents or prevented from being diverted from the firm; or the capitalised value of non-contractible, firm-specific rents which are preserved by a bank rescue that saves the firm from liquidation.

Note that when the outcome, Y, is in (Y',Z), under the main bank contract the main bank is the full residual claimant.[22] If the bank expends K and generates extra value ΔY, it obtains the full amount, given that in this region the non-main banks have a guaranteed return. It is easy to see that there will be cases such that $\Delta Y/n < K < \Delta Y$, that is, cases in which the fully diversified normal bank contract would not provide individual incentives to intervene when the main bank contract would. In this 'failing firm' or financial distress region, the main bank contract mimics an exclusive lending relationship: it is *as if* the bank were the only lender to the firm, which helps to mitigate the free-rider/collective action problems that are thought to characterise financial distress.

An interesting contrast can be drawn with the US bankruptcy doctrine of equitable subordination.[23] Under this doctrine a creditor intervening in a borrower's business may have its claims on the firm subordinated to those of other creditors. This doctrine is felt by some to represent an impediment to bank interventions of the kind seen in Japan by providing disincentives to creditors who might be able to effect beneficial interventions (supply the public good of sorting the firm's affairs out). On the surface, the main bank contract appears to be analogous to the equitable subordination doctrine in that the priority of the main bank, the intervening bank, is implicitly subordinated. An important distinction, however, is that in the main bank's case the subordination is imposed *ex ante* as part of the structuring of incentives rather than being triggered *ex post* by an act of intervention. The intervention of the main bank does not of itself change the priority status of the main bank; at the point of intervention the priority status is sunk. It may be that this arrangement has the opposite effect to that associated with the US doctrine: namely, the main bank has good incentives to intervene because at the point of intervention it is in effect internalising a large share of the benefits thus generated.

Notes

1 For quantitative studies of the effect of main bank monitoring on investment behaviour and behaviour during financial distress, see Hoshi, Kashyap and Scharfstein (1990a, 1990b). On the monitoring role of main banks, see also Aoki, Patrick and Sheard (1994), Aoki (1990, 1994a, 1994b), Corbett (1987) and Hodder and Tschoegl (1985).

2   It should be noted that the rotation of roles is across firms rather than across time for a given firm. Main bank relations appear to be fairly stable across time (Tachibanaki and Taki 1991), although there is some debate about just how stable they are; see the discussion in Horiuchi, Packer and Fukuda (1988).

3   That is, in an earlier period banks lent the firm L dollars, where $(1+r)L < Z$, to allow for default risk (r is the interest rate).

4   Following Aoki (1988, Ch. 4), Diamond (1991a), Stiglitz (1985) and others, it is assumed that monitoring is by banks rather than by stockholders, who in this model are in the background as well-diversified investors specialising in risk bearing over the upper tail of the distribution. Although not explicitly modelled here, the main bank also typically has a shareholding (usually 3–5 per cent) that allows it to internalise some of the beneficial externality that its monitoring confers on shareholders. For more on main bank shareholding, see Aoki, Patrick and Sheard (1994) and Sheard (1991a, 1994a).

5   It is apparent, for example, that if monitoring took the form of carrying out a long calculation using data extracted from the firm, doing half of the calculation only would provide no useful information. Neither can the monitoring bank halt its calculation in midstream and hand over (or sell) its results to another bank for it to continue the calculation. One reason might be that the second bank could not be sure that the first bank had provided truthful data, fearing perhaps that the first bank was in collusion with the firm.

6   This can be justified by arguing that as a result of portfolio diversification banks can be modelled as being approximately risk neutral, even if underlying preferences are risk averse. It can also be justified by appealing to the efficiency argument that maximising expected value is desirable for any given risk level.

7   Indicative of the banks' preference for diversification is the fact that the largest single corporate loan exposure for the six principal banks thought to be at the core of the main bank system was on average 0.65 per cent of their total lending (Tōyō Keizai Shinpōsha 1992, pp. 602–4). This does not preclude the banks from having large loan shares for *particular* firms, though they tend not to. To take two large banks as examples, although Daiichi Kangyō Bank occupied the top lending bank position in 1992 for 191 listed firms, in only 13 cases did it have a loan share of 50 per cent or more; Mitsubishi Bank similarly had a loan share of over 50 per cent in only 15 of 154 cases (Tōyō Keizai Shinpōsha 1992, pp. 639–41, 651–4).

8   It is assumed that such informational effects occur in the normal course of bank lending and are distinct from the monitoring activity studied in this paper.

9   Because of the inherent informational asymmetries, bank lending may be a market where actual and potential competition are less than perfect substitutes.

10 Since $E(R\,|\,K) > K$, there is a loan share $s^* < 1$ such that $s^* E(R\,|\,K) = K$, that is, the bank would monitor under the normal bank contract. We rule out this case by assuming, for the same reasons as those discussed in the text, that such a loan share would involve too little diversification in transactional relations for either the banks or the firms. It is easy to show that for such an s^* there is always a main bank contract with a lower loan share that also induces monitoring by the main bank.

11 The setup here differs from the standard principal–agent theory in that each bank acts as a principal for some transactions and as an agent for others. It is a model in which agency relationships emerge as a set of principals divide up a set of indivisible tasks among themselves, and differs in that sense from the common agency model (many principals–single agent) (Bernheim and Whinston 1986) and the multitask agency model (single principal–many agents) (Holmstrom and Milgrom 1991). Each lending arrangement to a given firm is like a standard, multiple principal–single agent model; because goals are aligned the principals can be treated as a single unit, but because the agent participates in other deals as a principal its participation constraint must be evaluated with respect to participation in the overall syndicate rather than any single lending transaction.

12 For the propositions to be correct, it is not necessary for the loan share of the main bank to be higher than under the normal bank contract. There are two reasons for believing that it will be higher, however. First, by increasing the marginal cost of shirking to the monitoring bank, a larger loan share increases the potency of the main bank contract (proposition 1). Second, a larger loan share clearly identifies the main bank and prevents it from being able to behave opportunistically by claiming *ex post* that it was not the main bank. One way to avoid opportunistic behaviour would be to write a set of bank contracts incorporating explicit priority differences, but such contracts appear not to be written in Japan.

13 The total amount of bank lending is held constant at mL/n regardless of the particular contractual arrangement. A larger loan share can then be interpreted as serving to 'reward' the bank in the best state since it signifies a higher payoff in that state.

14 In the model, the worst that can happen is that the main bank receives a zero payoff. Case evidence (for example, Sheard 1989, 1994b) suggests that the main bank may on occasion do worse (receive a negative payoff) because it may assume some of the loans of other banks. Introducing this possibility would reinforce the incentive effect of the main bank contract.

15 See Diamond (1991b) for an analysis of the role of priority structure in bank lending.

16 Note that this is the simplest form of the main bank contract where the contract penalises bad outcomes but does not reward a good outcome.

17 If the direct benefits were too large, this might imply that banks would only want to act as main banks. But again this is not an issue in the context of the model as in forming the reciprocal delegation arrangement it is assumed that banks are able to commit to an allocation of main bank and non-main bank roles.

18 Although not considered explicitly in this paper, firms may derive advantages (relating to corporate governance and possible assistance in financial distress) from operating under the main bank system, which will make it incentive compatible for them to cooperate with the banks in excluding free-riders (Aoki, Patrick and Sheard 1994; Hoshi, Kashyap and Scharfstein 1990a, 1990b; Sheard 1994b). More intense monitoring may be a price firms have to pay in order to obtain these benefits.

19 Seven large banks — six city banks and one long-term credit bank — form the core of the Japanese main bank system (Aoki, Patrick and Sheard 1994). Hoshi, Kashyap and Loveman (1992) found that for the core firms associated with these respective

main banks, 40–45 per cent of total loans were provided by the seven banks. This rose to 51–59 per cent when associated trust banks were included.

20 Two notable examples are the aluminium industry in the late 1970s and early 1980s (Sheard 1991c) and the real estate sector in the early 1990s (Sheard 1992).

21 It is well known that the banking authorities closely monitor and exercise guidance over corporate rescues and reorganisations led by main banks. See Aoki (1994a) and Aoki, Patrick and Sheard (1994) for further discussion of the enforcement issue and the role of the regulators.

22 When $Y < Y'$, the main bank may still have an incentive to expend K, but only if $Y > Y_C$, where $Y_C \equiv Y' - (\Delta Y - K)$. Then $(Y' - Y)$ of the ΔY that is generated goes to non-main banks, K is absorbed as cost, but $\Delta Y - (Y' - Y) - K > 0$ accrues to the main bank; otherwise it would not be worth the bank's while to expend K.

23 I am grateful to Mark Ramseyer for drawing my attention to this doctrine; I benefited from discussions with him in writing this section. On these issues see also Roe (1990, 1991) and Ramseyer's (1991) analysis of Japanese banking.

References

Aoki, M. (1988), *Information, Incentives and Bargaining in the Japanese Economy*, Cambridge, MA: Cambridge University Press.

—— (1990), 'Toward an Economic Model of the Japanese Firm', *Journal of Economic Literature*, 28, pp. 1–27.

—— (1994a), 'Monitoring Characteristics of the Main Bank System: An Analytical and Developmental View', in M. Aoki and H. Patrick (eds), *The Japanese Main Bank System: Its Relevancy for Developing and Transforming Economies*, Oxford: Oxford University Press, pp. 109–41.

—— (1994b), 'The Contingent Governance Structure of Teams: Analysis of Institutional Complementarity', *International Economic Review*, 35, pp. 657–76.

Aoki, M., H. Patrick and P. Sheard (1994), 'The Japanese Main Bank System: An Introductory Overview', in M. Aoki and H. Patrick (eds), *The Japanese Main Bank System: Its Relevancy for Developing and Transforming Economies*, Oxford: Oxford University Press, pp. 3–50.

Bernheim, B.D. and M.D. Whinston (1986), 'Common Agency', *Econometrica*, 54, pp. 923–42.

Bizer, D.S. and P.M. DeMarzo (1992), 'Sequential Banking', *Journal of Political Economy*, 100, pp. 41–61.

Corbett, J. (1987), 'International Perspectives on Financing: Evidence from Japan', *Oxford Review of Economic Policy*, 3, pp. 30–55.

Dewatripont, M. and E. Maskin (1990), 'Credit and Efficiency in Centralized and Decentralized Economies', Discussion Paper Number 1512, Harvard Institute of Economic Research, Boston.

Diamond, D.W. (1984), 'Financial Intermediation and Delegated Monitoring', *Review of Economic Studies*, 51, pp. 393–414.

—— (1991a), 'Monitoring and Reputation: The Choice between Bank Loans and Directly Placed Debt', *Journal of Political Economy*, 99, pp. 689–721.

—— (1991b), 'Debt Maturity Structure and Liquidity Risk', *Quarterly Journal of Economics*, 106, pp. 709–37.

Hellwig, M. (1990), Banking, Financial Intermediation and Corporate Finance, University of Basel, Basel (mimeo).

Hodder, J.E. and A.E. Tschoegl (1985), 'Some Aspects of Japanese Corporate Finance', *Journal of Financial and Quantitative Analysis*, 20, pp. 173–91.

Holmstrom, B. and P. Milgrom (1991), 'Multitask Principal–Agent Analyses: Incentive Contracts, Asset Ownership, and Job Design', *Journal of Law, Economics and Organization*, 7, Special issue, pp. 24–52.

Horiuchi, A., F. Packer and S. Fukuda (1988), 'What Role Has the "Main Bank" Played in Japan?', *Journal of the Japanese and International Economies*, 2, pp. 159–80.

Horiuchi, T. and E. Murakami (1991), 'Wagakuni ni okeru Mein Banku Torihiki Jittai: Ankēto Kekka kara Mita Kigyō Kin'yū no Sugata' [The State of Main Bank Transactions in Japan: The Shape of Corporate Finance as Seen from Questionnaire Results], in T. Horiuchi (ed.), *Jiyūka/Kokusaika Jidai no Kigyō Kin'yū no Henbō: Mein Banku no Kinō to Hensei* [Transformation of Corporate Finance in the Era of Liberalisation and Internationalisation: The Function and Transformation of the Main Bank], Nihon Keizai Kenkyū Sentā Kenkyū Hōkoku No.75, Tokyo: Nihon Keizai Kenkyū Sentā, pp. 91–150.

Hoshi, T., A. Kashyap and G. Loveman (1992), Lessons from the Japanese Main Bank System for Financial System Reform in Poland, University of California, San Diego, (mimeo).

Hoshi, T., A. Kashyap and D. Scharfstein (1990a), 'Bank Monitoring and Investment: Evidence from the Changing Structure of Japanese Corporate Banking Relationships', in R.G. Hubbard (ed.), *Asymmetric Information, Corporate Finance, and Investment*, Chicago, IL: University of Chicago Press, pp. 105–26.

—— (1990b), 'The Role of Banks in Reducing the Costs of Financial Distress in Japan', *Journal of Financial Economics*, 27, pp. 67–88.

—— (1993), The Choice between Public and Private Debt: An Analysis of Post-Deregulation Corporate Financing in Japan, University of California, San Diego (mimeo).

Krasa, S. and A.P. Villamil (1992), 'Monitoring the Monitor: An Incentive Structure for a Financial Intermediary', *Journal of Economic Theory*, 57, pp. 197–221.

Kreps, D. (1990), *A Course in Microeconomic Theory*, Princeton, NJ: Princeton University Press.

Mayer, C. (1988), 'New Issues in Corporate Finance', *European Economic Review*, 32, pp. 1,167–89.

Nakatani, I. (1984), 'The Economic Role of the Financial Corporate Grouping', in M. Aoki (ed.), *The Economic Analysis of the Japanese Firm*, Amsterdam: North-Holland, pp. 227–58.

Ramseyer, J.M. (1991), 'Legal Rules in Repeated Deals: Banking in the Shadow of Defection in Japan', *Journal of Legal Studies*, 20, pp. 91–117.

Roe, M.J. (1990), 'Political and Legal Restraints on Ownership and Control of Public Corporations', *Journal of Financial Economics*, 27, pp. 7–41.

—— (1991), 'A Political Theory of American Corporate Finance', *Columbia Law Review*, 91, pp. 10–67.

Sheard, P. (1985), 'Main Banks and Structural Adjustment in Japan', *Pacific Economic Papers*, 129, Australia–Japan Research Centre, Australian National University, Canberra.

—— (1989), 'The Main Bank System and Corporate Monitoring and Control in Japan', *Journal of Economic Behavior and Organization*, 11, pp. 399–422.

—— (1991a), 'The Economics of Interlocking Shareholding in Japan', *Ricerche Economiche*, 45, pp. 321–47.

—— (1991b), 'Delegated Monitoring among Delegated Monitors: Principal–Agent Aspects of the Japanese Main Bank System', Center for Economic Policy Research Publication No. 274, Stanford University, Palo Alto.

—— (1991c), ' The Role of Firm Organization in the Adjustment of a Declining Industry in Japan: The Case of Aluminum', *Journal of the Japanese and International Economies*, 5, pp. 14–40.

—— (1992), 'The Role of the Japanese Main Bank when Borrowing Firms Are in Financial Distress', Center for Economic Policy Research Publication No. 330, Stanford University, Palo Alto.

—— (1994a), 'Interlocking Shareholdings and Corporate Governance, in M. Aoki and R. Dore (eds), *The Japanese Firm: The Sources of Competitive Strength*, Oxford: Oxford University Press, pp. 310–49.

—— (1994b), 'Main Banks and the Governance of Financial Distress', in M. Aoki and H. Patrick (eds), *The Japanese Main Bank System: Its Relevancy for Developing and Transforming Economies*, Oxford: Oxford University Press, pp. 188–230.

Stiglitz, J.E. (1985), 'Credit Markets and the Control of Capital', *Journal of Money, Credit, and Banking*, 17, pp. 133–52.

Tachibanaki, T. and A. Taki (1991), 'Shareholding and Lending Activity of Financial Institutions in Japan', *Bank of Japan Monetary and Economic Studies*, 9, pp. 23–60.

Tōyō Keizai Shinpōsha (1992), *Kigyō Keiretsu Sōran* [Directory of Corporate Affiliations], Tokyo: Tōyō Keizai Shinpōsha.

Von Thadden, E-L. (1990), 'Bank Finance and Long Term Investment', WWZ Discussion Paper 9010, University of Basel, Basel.

Williamson, O.E. (1985), *The Economic Institutions of Capitalism*, New York, NY: The Free Press.

Yanelle, M-O. (1989), 'Increasing Returns to Scale and Endogenous Intermediation', WWZ Discussion Paper 8908, University of Basel, Basel.

6 Moral hazard and main bank monitoring

*Luke Gower**

In *The General Theory of Employment, Interest and Money*, Keynes (1936, p. 157) observed that those banks which are the most responsible for the public interest are also the most vulnerable to public contempt during cyclical downturns. His hypothesis appears to have won some support from recent Japanese experience with the business cycle. When heady growth and asset price inflation ended abruptly in the recession of the early 1990s, the banks became magnets for public outrage.

This episode of bank bashing might be unremarkable if it did not stand in stark contrast with an enduring consensus among corporate finance theorists that Japan is blessed with the kind of financial institutions that promote high and stable growth. At the core of this consensus is Japan's main bank system. This form of relationship banking is often thought to have been a cornerstone of the so-called 'Japanese miracle', and some scholars have been so certain of its efficiency as to suggest that it may be an appropriate model for countries with less developed systems of financial intermediation.[1]

The collapsed 'bubble economy' and the recent epidemic of bad debts in Japan imply that analysis of main banking may need to be more circumspect than it has been to date. At the very least, it now seems necessary to ask if the main bank system, which once delivered corporate stability and growth in Japan, can continue to do so in its

---

* This chapter is a substantially revised version of Gower (1995). It was written while I was a PhD scholar at the Australian National University and a visiting researcher at the Bank of Japan's Institute for Monetary and Economic Studies. I would like to thank the Bank for providing excellent research facilities. The project was funded with generous financial support from the Japan Foundation, Sanwa Bank and the Academy of the Social Sciences in Australia. I am grateful for advice from Peter Drysdale, Gerald Garvey, Akiyoshi Horiuchi, Warwick McKibbin, Hugh Patrick, John Pitchford, Paul Sheard, Naoyuki Yoshino and an anonymous referee of *Pacific Economic Papers*. Any errors which remain are mine.

present form. After all, if the main banks provide such a worthy model of the way in which lending risks should be managed, then why have they been so heavily implicated in Japan's most severe postwar economic slump?

After examining the broad profile of the banking sector, a number of analysts have concluded that the banks themselves may only indirectly be at fault for the failure of their lending. According to this argument, financial deregulation throughout the 1980s heightened the contestability of the corporate finance market, forcing banks to compete more strenuously in the lending market.[2] Banks appear to have cut corners by economising on expenditure devoted to the monitoring and screening of borrowers.

The goal of this chapter is to pursue this theory of the bad debt crisis in Japan by showing that it has particular force in the context of Japan's main bank system. Main banking is just like other forms of financial intermediation in that it depends for its viability on a sufficient return to the banks. But it is also distinctive in that main banks involve themselves in the monitoring of their client firms to an unusual degree. The banks require customised incentives in order to fulfil their monitoring role properly, and these incentives depend on a certain degree of insulation from competition in the lending market. When main banks are introduced to competition from other financial intermediaries, the pricing behaviour of the new entrants may induce the main bank to shirk its monitoring of borrowers.

Several characteristics of main bank behaviour are shown to support this result. Most important is the peculiar extent to which they monitor. Main banks not only monitor borrowers that are in good financial health, they also have a major role in rescuing or liquidating them when they are financially distressed. This convention raises the price that a main bank charges for its loans, and it sets the main bank at a competitive disadvantage vis à vis other suppliers of finance in the capital market. Competition between main banks and non-main banks on the basis of this priority structure can lead the main bank to price finance in ways that are inconsistent with a comprehensive provision of monitoring services.

This argument poses some challenges to existing theories of the main bank system. Specifically, it qualifies the commonly held view that assigning junior claimant status to the main bank encourages monitoring by that bank. The assignment of junior claimant status may not necessarily strengthen the main bank's incentives to monitor if it implies seniority for non-main bank intermediaries, whose behaviour affects the price of debt.

Similarly, I question the view that low funding costs for financial intermediaries enhance the incentives for monitoring. In brief, reduced funding costs lower the price which the main bank's competitors could charge borrowers for debt. However, they have a similar effect on the pricing behaviour of the main bank only up to a point, because the main bank has monitoring costs to meet. It turns out that, beyond this point, the optimal response of the main bank to falling funding costs is to match the price of its competitors by shirking its monitoring obligations. This in turn is conducive to an increased probability of financial distress for the borrower and a greater risk of bad debts for the bank. As I show later, it is possible to interpret this kind of mechanism in terms of moral hazard.

Background

One of the main purposes of a bank is to act as an intermediary between borrowers (usually firms) and lenders (usually depositors). Through its monitoring and controlling of borrowers, a bank dissolves the informational asymmetries that often hinder more direct interactions between these two parties. In modern times, this idea is attributable to Schumpeter (1939). More recently, it has been refined and empirically verified through the works of Fama (1985), Diamond (1984), Mayer (1988), Stiglitz (1985) and James (1987), to name just a few.

In Japan, this role of the banks is thought to be acutely important. Japanese banks are often deeply involved in the operations of the corporations that borrow from them.[3] They feature in the lives of firms not just as creditors but also as shareholders, and their representatives even appear as corporate directors. When one bank is particularly active in these roles with respect to a certain firm, it is often held to be that firm's main bank.[4]

Much of a main bank's involvement with a firm is directed toward monitoring the behaviour of the borrower from the position of what Fama (1985) might call an inside creditor.[5] When a firm is in good financial health, a main bank will usually monitor in an *ex ante* and in an interim sense. The former activity involves the bank screening new borrowing that the firm may wish to undertake; the latter involves it monitoring the firm's position on a more regular and ongoing basis, both on its own behalf and on behalf of other actors who may have interests in the firm.

However, the role of a main bank does not end with interim monitoring. Indeed, case study evidence suggests that one of the most striking features of the main bank system is that a bank which is main for a firm often monitors *ex post* — that is to say, it intervenes heavily in the management of firms in order to resolve situations in which the firm cannot meet its contractual obligations. A particularly noteworthy feature of this activity is that the main bank may well incur expenses which far exceed its nominal exposure to the distressed borrower, and it may cushion other constituents of the firm against the adverse effects of financial distress. To ensure that this role is performed properly, firms generally reward their main bank well. This has traditionally taken the form of the bank managing a substantial share of the firm's debt, on which it earns a generous rate of return.[6]

Academic assessments of this symbiotic relationship have, on the whole, been quite positive. Nakatani (1984) pointed out that the role of the main bank as a rescuer of financially distressed firms is an important means by which firms insure their viability across different states of nature. His argument has been extended in numerous directions. Studies such as Hoshi, Kashyap and Scharfstein (1990) and Horiuchi (1993) have subsequently confirmed that firms with main banks do indeed benefit substantially from having a main bank manage their temporary crises. There has also been reasonably widespread agreement that main banks perform extremely efficiently in terms of monitoring borrowers in order to prevent financial distress in the first place.

In dramatic contrast to such positive assessments of the role played by the banks, public perceptions of bank monitoring have been highly negative in the wake of Japan's 'economic bubble'. Importantly, public criticism of financial intermediation has cut across a range of financial institutions without sparing the banks which lie at the heart of the main bank system. The following editorial opinion from *The Daily Yomiuri* (24 May 1991, p. 5) expresses the sentiment well.

> Now that the bubble has popped, financial institutions are facing difficult times. As a result, they have been rethinking their deeply-rooted profit-oriented drive. It is no longer OK to do anything to make a profit and banks are tightening their lenient screening of large-scale borrowers. The environment surrounding the financial world will also become tighter as the coming few years bring the complete liberalization of deposit interest rates and further reviews of the banking business. It is high time that financial institutes recognize their public responsibility and the necessity of having trustworthy management. Banks should make their two biggest assets confidence and trust.

Even certain sections of the public sector have been critical of the banks. For example, the Institute of Fiscal and Monetary Policy claims of the 'bubble economy' period that:

> Many banks were in fact careless about lending substantially larger sums than before, and thus ended up saddled with huge, irrecoverable debts. Such practices drew attention to the deficiencies of the internal management structures in place at many financial institutions, as well as to an erosion in bankers' ethical standards and rules of conduct (Ministry of Finance 1993, p. 40).

Stripped of some of their value judgements, these critiques amount to a perception that the banks have failed to carry out sufficient *ex ante* and interim monitoring of their borrowers. In the absence of any other form of discipline on borrowers, a deficiency of either activity will raise the probability of financial distress for the borrower and bad debts for the intermediary.

Serious inquiries are now being made into the factors underlying this change in bank behaviour. Many commentators have been content to ascribe the phenomenon to the 'animal spirits' of bankers, which are thought to generate perilous optimism about lending opportunities and dangerous complacency toward monitoring during periods of economic expansion. But in recent Japanese experience there is the added dimension of structural change in the banking environment to be considered. According to Nakajima and Taguchi (1995), financial deregulation may have increased competition in the bank lending market and undermined the franchise values of banking. The squeeze on bank margins that this implied encouraged banks to cut corners on their monitoring.[7]

Trends in the profitability of lending supply the impetus for this theory. As far back as 1984, it was apparent that the gross margin which separates commercial banks' cost of funds from their effective lending rates was being compressed.[8] From the 1970s, much of the pressure on bank lending margins seems to have been applied by sustained reductions in compensating balances. Once an important means by which the effective lending rate of interest was raised above the face or notional rate, these balances have been declining for some time and appear not to have been offset by higher average face lending rates. Figures 6.1 to 6.3 provide evidence of this.

In the course of the 1980s, the trend toward slimmer margins on commercial bank loans was severely exacerbated by the deregulation of the financial sector.[9] The particular intensity of the pressure on margins in this period was due to the fact that both deposit and lending markets were simultaneously being deregulated, so that margins were compressed from two directions at once. The consequence was a sharp decline in the profitability of the banks. The Bank of Japan (1993) has noted that bank profitability, as measured by the rate on equity, has been falling for several decades. However, the drop was noticeably steeper in the late 1980s, with the rate falling from around 11 per cent in 1987 to about 3 per cent in 1992.

It is difficult to be certain that this pressure translated directly into weaker monitoring performances by banks. Nevertheless, enough informed opinion is circulating to encourage the idea. For instance, the Economic Planning Agency (1993, p. 148) acknowledges that inadequate information collection and provision by banks contributed to the failure of much lending during the boom years of the late 1980s. The

Figure 6.1   Estimates of compensating balances as a proportion of total loans, May 1973 – May 1988 (per cent)

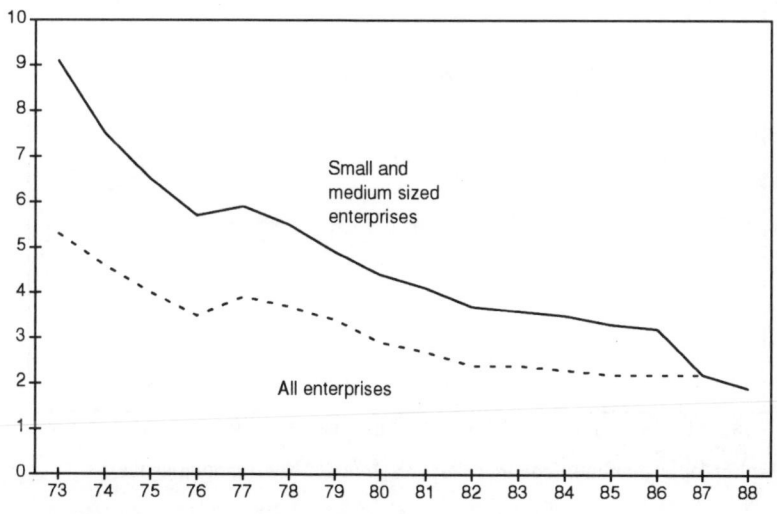

Source: Ministry of Finance (1993), *Financial Statistics Monthly*, 467, Tokyo.

Figure 6.2 Estimates of compensating balances, May 1973 – May 1988 (per cent)

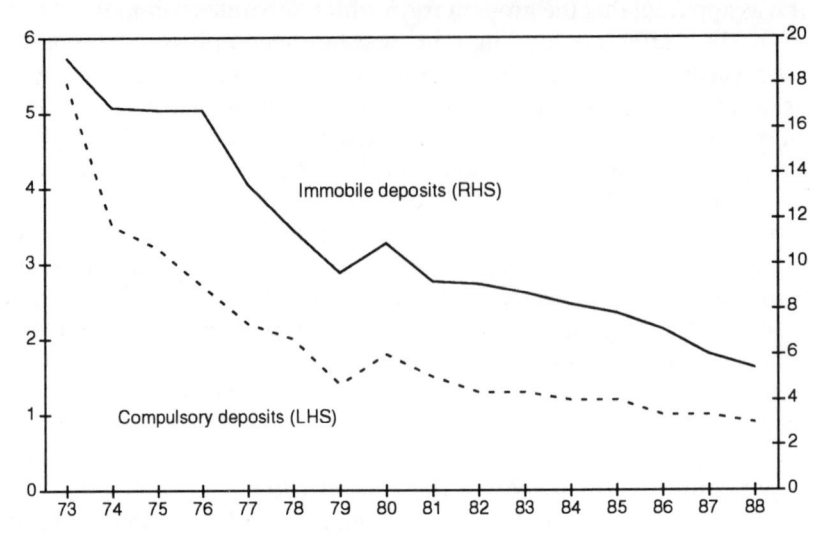

Source: Ministry of Finance (1993), *Financial Statistics Monthly*, 467, Tokyo.

Figure 6.3 Average contracted loan rates of city banks, 1973–88 (per cent)

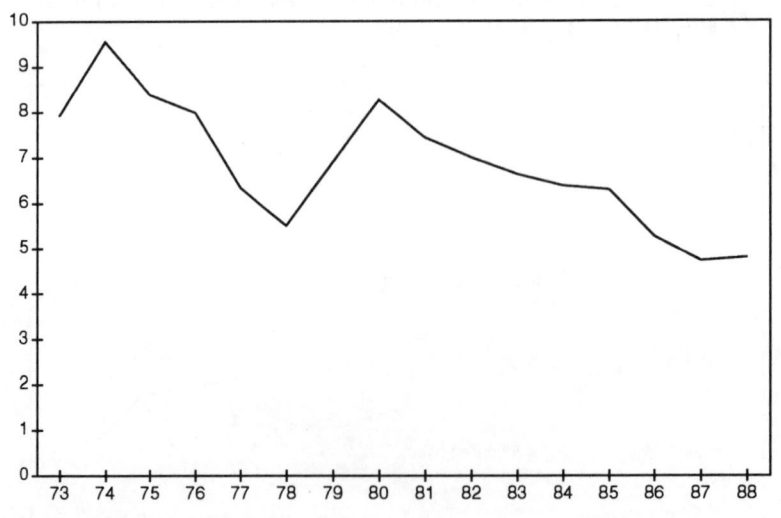

Source: Bank of Japan (annual), *Economic Statistics Annual*, Tokyo (various issues).

Bank of Japan (1991,1992) has reached a similar conclusion, arguing that risk management and credit analysis in major banks were downgraded during the 1980s. Furthermore, it has suggested that banks did not adequately monitor the use to which their loans were put. Horiuchi (Ch. 10, this volume) endorses this view and provides a number of examples of developments which seem to embody the trend toward weaker monitoring and greater risk taking by the banks.

Aoki (1994) offers an interesting insight into why this analysis may be important in the context of a main bank relationship. He makes the point that the returns to main banks, which he calls main bank rents, are particularly necessary for the proper functioning of capital markets when they support an *integrated* monitoring structure. In other words, the fact that the main bank monitors at all stages of a borrower's life-cycle means that it requires a customised set of incentives. A main bank will only monitor if the return from doing so and the price of not doing so are sufficiently high.

This insight into the dependence of main bank monitoring on rents is highly plausible, but it is incomplete for a number of reasons. One of these is that it is not yet fully linked to the way in which rents are appropriated. Rents that are meant to support integrated monitoring may conceivably be appropriated by players against which the main bank competes in lending markets, and so the main bank's commitment to *ex ante* and interim monitoring could be undermined by free-riding. This would seem to be a particularly pressing consideration given the extent to which entry barriers to the capital market in Japan have recently been relaxed. An analysis that juxtaposes the incentives of non-main bank intermediaries against those of the main bank will reveal the conditions under which the free-riding question is a legitimate threat to monitoring.

Another issue that needs to be explored further is the state contingency of main bank returns. Aoki (1994, p. 15) argues that low deposit rates of interest have underpinned integrated monitoring by widening lending margins and thus providing main banks with the *ex ante* rents that form the incentive to monitor.[10] However, a deposit contract is not state contingent; depositors are entitled to a return both *ex ante* and *ex post* of a borrower's financial distress. As a result, the conditions under which deposit costs should influence the bank's preference for a monitored borrower over an unmonitored one are slightly obscure.

A final incentive for developing Aoki's model further is that, in its present form, it does not examine the way in which main bank rents are determined. As it stands, Aoki's theory states only that successfully integrated monitoring requires that certain rents be generated for the main bank; it is incomplete in explaining how conditions in the capital market might determine these returns.

A simple model of main bank monitoring

In this section, a very simple model of main banking is developed to explore some of the issues discussed above in a unified way. I draw heavily on a technique that was developed by Shapiro and Stiglitz (1984) for their analysis of labour markets. In this financial context, the key optimising agents consist of a representative main bank and a non-main bank financial intermediary. A risk neutral final borrower is used to fix the equilibrium.

The main bank

In this model, the main bank is a large city bank which maximises its profit in continuous time over an infinite horizon by acting as a delegated monitor. The central bank requires it, under the terms of a franchise contract, to accept an interest bearing deposit (of given size), to lend that deposit to an infinitely lived borrower and to monitor that borrower. The deposit contract is strictly enforceable, and its cost is determined exogenously by the central bank through its monetary policy. The interest payments on deposits appear as d per unit time. The repayments by the firm amount to bank receipts of r_M per unit time.

The bank's income and deposit liability flows occur indefinitely unless the borrower encounters financial distress. In this case, financial distress implies the application of *ex post* monitoring by the main bank to restore the borrower to a condition in which it is able to meet debt repayments.[11] There are two sets of circumstances under which this *ex post* monitoring might be required: either the borrower has an unforeseeable accident, or it fails because the main bank neglected to monitor it. The former type of failure happens to monitored and unmonitored firms alike with simple probability b per unit time.

The chance that a firm will fail through the neglect of the bank follows a Poisson process; it is given by the rate of that process, which I denote with q. The choice of a Poisson process means that, in long-run equilibrium, all unmonitored projects encounter financial distress at least once. This is a fairly easy assumption to justify if the final borrower operates in a sufficiently competitive final product market. If *ex ante* and interim monitoring improve the position of the borrowing firm in some way, then analytically speaking they form part of the technology of that firm. Thus monitored firms have a technological advantage over unmonitored firms. Those that enjoy this advantage should eventually drive into distress those that do not. Through such a process, the long-run financial distress of unmonitored borrowers is inevitable.[12]

To avoid exposure to q, the main bank must monitor the firm at a cost per unit time of c. By incurring c, it can identify projects which are sound and force the borrower to undertake them. This cost is best thought of as interim monitoring but, under some circumstances, it could also include a component of *ex ante* monitoring. If a borrower finishes a project at some point and then begins a new one, the bank's task will momentarily switch from interim to *ex ante* monitoring and then back again. Provided that neither c nor r_M change in the course of this transient disturbance, the model will be unaffected.

If financial distress occurs for any reason then the bank will be required to resolve it. While the borrower is financially distressed, the bank will earn no interest on the loan (although it will still have to meet its commitments to depositors) and it will incur *ex post* monitoring costs of f per unit time. The probability that the firm will be restored to financial health in any small interval is given by α. This term is perhaps best thought of as the expected speed at which banks can repair their financially distressed borrowers. Once restored to financial health, a loan is treated as it was before the financial distress.[13] In other words, loans that failed because of shirking are once again subject to shirking after the borrower has recovered, while loans that failed by accident are again monitored after the financial distress has passed.

This assumes, of course, that the main bank will always opt to undertake, rather than shirk, its *ex post* monitoring. Numerous justifications for this position have emerged in the literature and I provide five of them here.[14] First, financial distress is highly visible. A bank that repeatedly shirks its *ex post* monitoring would therefore expose itself to sanctions by the monetary authorities. Second, Japanese banks secure scant tax relief for bad debts. They therefore have strong incentives to resolve privately the financial distress of debtors rather than concede that a loan is non-performing and suffer the taxation consequences (*The Economist*, 2 May 1992, p. 36). Third, there is the possibility of retribution by other creditors. Sheard (Ch. 5, this volume) suggests that there is a particularly compelling incentive to undertake *ex post* monitoring where the main bank participates in a reciprocal delegated monitoring arrangement. Fourth, as Hoshi, Kashyap and Scharfstein (1990) point out, the main bank is a prominent provider of finance for the firm. It is therefore likely to have sufficient private incentive to intervene to restore the firm to a profitable position. Finally, I accept the arguments of Packer and Ryser (1992) that the Japanese legal system is sufficiently costly that banks frequently find it optimal to manage financial distress privately.

Given these conditions, the problem for the bank is to decide whether or not it ought to shirk its *ex ante*/interim monitoring obligations; that is, whether or not it is optimal to incur c.[15] From the assumptions, the value of the loan in its different states is:

$$R_S^M = \int_0^\infty (b+q)e^{-(b+q)T}\left[\int_0^T e^{-\delta t}(r_M - d)dt + e^{-\delta T} R_{CS}^M\right] dT \qquad (1a)$$

$$R_{CS}^M = \int_0^\infty \alpha e^{-\alpha T}\left[\int_0^T e^{-\delta t}(-f - d)dt + e^{-\delta T} R_S^M\right] dT \qquad (1b)$$

$$R_N^M = \int_0^\infty b e^{-bT}\left[\int_0^T e^{-\delta t}(r_M - d - c)dt + e^{-\delta T} R_{CN}^M\right] dT \qquad (1c)$$

$$R_{CN}^M = \int_0^\infty \alpha e^{-\alpha T}\left[\int_0^T e^{-\delta t}(-f - d)dt + e^{-\delta T} R_N^M\right] dT \qquad (1d)$$

where

δ = discount rate;

T = stochastically determined time at which the state of the loan changes;

R_S^M = the value of a loan that is not being monitored;

R_{CS}^M = the value of an unmonitored loan that is financially distressed;

R_N^M = the value of a loan which is being monitored; and

R_{CN}^M = the value of a monitored loan that is financially distressed.

Evaluating (1a) through (1d) gives the following:[16]

$$\delta R_S^M = r_M + (b+q)(R_{CS}^M - R_S^M) - d \tag{2a}$$

$$\delta R_{CS}^M = \alpha(R_S^M - R_{CS}^M) - f - d \tag{2b}$$

$$\delta R_N^M = r_M + b(R_{CN}^M - R_N^M) - c - d \tag{3a}$$

$$\delta R_{CN}^M = \alpha(R_N^M - R_{CN}^M) - f - d \tag{3b}$$

The main bank will shirk its *ex ante* or interim monitoring if and only if $R_S^M > R_N^M$. From equations (2) and (3), this is true when:

$$f < \frac{c(\alpha + \delta + b + q)}{q} - r_M \tag{4}$$

Inequality (4) has several obvious features. First, if *ex post* monitoring is expensive, then the main bank will not require a great inducement to monitor. In these circumstances, it would monitor in return for a very low value of r_M, and the pressure for monitored debt in equilibrium would therefore be strong. Conversely, the higher the cost of *ex ante* and interim monitoring, and the greater the probability of accidental failure, the greater is the inducement that the main bank will require in order to monitor. It goes almost without mention that a high discount rate is also conducive to unmonitored debt.

A more novel aspect of (4) is that the cost of deposits does not directly influence the bank's decision as to whether or not it ought to shirk its *ex ante* and interim monitoring responsibilities. The reason is simply that the bank's deposit contract is independent of the financial condition of the borrower. While an increase in deposit costs may lower the profitability that flows from a monitored borrower and seem to activate the incentive to shirk (Aoki's point), it also makes less attractive a situation in which the borrower produces no return at all, and so it simultaneously discourages shirking. These considerations perfectly counterbalance one another in the bank's behaviour, and the cost of deposits is therefore irrelevant to the monitoring decision.[17]

If the capital markets were closed by regulation and r_M were somehow fixed, then inequality (4) would be the end of the matter. Main banks would always monitor borrowers, provided that conditions in the capital market ensured that their returns from doing so, and the penalties for not doing so, were sufficiently high and probable. However, the deregulation of Japanese capital markets that has taken place since the 1980s has introduced to some borrowers a new set of potential intermediaries whose behaviour can influence the price of finance to the borrower.

The non-main bank intermediary

Suppose that the capital market is contestable by a non-main bank financial intermediary. This intermediary exists in a perfectly competitive market, and it optimises intertemporally by offering a debt contract to borrowers at a contracted rate of return per unit time, r_F. For the purpose of fixing ideas, it may be helpful to think of this intermediary as an institutional holder of corporate bonds.

There are several respects in which this intermediary differs from the main bank. First, I assume that it is not obliged to monitor the behaviour of borrowing firms and that it would, in any case, be unable to do so at reasonable cost. This is a common assumption about the holders of public debt. Fama (1985) offers some empirical justification for it, and it is used by Hoshi, Kashyap and Scharfstein (1993) and Diamond (1991), among many others.

Second, assume that the deposit expenses of the non-main bank intermediary are higher than those of the main bank.[18] Let the cost of funds to the non-main bank intermediary be θd, and assume $\theta > 1$. This assumption simply suggests that the city banks are more efficient than their competitors in the collection and management of deposits, and there are several justifications for it. First, cheaper deposit costs for the large city banks have flowed from the so-called convoy system. This arrangement has meant that a restricted number of large commercial banks has enjoyed preferential access to funds from the monetary authorities. A particular example is that, in much of the earlier high growth period, those banks had preferential access to the Bank of Japan's reserve facility at artificially low rates of interest.[19] There are, of course, other reasons why main banks might be able to secure deposits more efficiently than some of their competitors. For instance, they often have firms, for which they are main, deposit their employees' payrolls with them. More generally, it is worth noting that the city banks are, by definition, very large. They are therefore able to exploit any economies of scale in deposit collection and management to an extent that might lie beyond the reach of other intermediaries. Taken together, these considerations mean that non-main banks are at something of a disadvantage in the cost of their funds.

Third, the debt of the non-main bank financial intermediary is assumed to be senior to that of the main bank. In normal states, the non-main bank receives its contracted rate of return of r_F. However, if the borrower becomes financially distressed, then the non-main bank intermediary would still receive a fraction, γ, of its return as a result of the main bank's *ex post* monitoring.

The assumption that the non-main bank can rely on the main bank for *ex post* monitoring in the event of the borrower's financial distress is admittedly awkward, when there is only one debt contract for sale. It might well be argued that, if the non-main bank earns the (sole) debt contract, then the main bank has no financial commitment to the borrower, and so the main bank tie dissolves completely. But if such a dissolution occurs, then the non-main bank cannot reasonably expect the main bank to undertake any *ex post* monitoring. Therefore, it is difficult to imagine a situation in which main bank *ex post* monitoring means that the non-main bank can price on the basis that $\gamma > 0$.

Fortunately, this conjecture presents no serious problems. The model will still work even if the non-main bank cannot depend upon the main bank for *ex post* monitoring. It is merely necessary to suppose that, if the main bank does not undertake *ex post* monitoring on behalf of the non-main bank, there is an alternative process for managing financially distressed borrowers. For example, financial distress might be resolved either by judicial means or by the joint actions of a number of other constituents of the firm. It is not even necessary for any such alternative process of distress resolution to respect the seniority of the non-main bank intermediary. It will become evident that, even if $\gamma = 0$, the model will still operate properly.[20]

Given these conditions and the assumption that the borrower knows the values of b and q,[21] the value of a loan in its various states is:

$$R_S^F = \int_0^\infty (b+q)e^{-(b+q)T}\left[\int_0^T e^{-\phi t}(r_F - \theta d)dt + e^{-\phi T}R_{CS}^F\right]dT \tag{5a}$$

$$R_{CS}^F = \int_0^\infty \alpha e^{-\alpha T}\left[\int_0^T e^{-\phi t}(\gamma r_F - \theta d)dt + e^{-\phi T}R_S^F\right]dT \tag{5b}$$

where

ϕ = discount rate;

R_S^F = the value of a loan that is not financially distressed; and

R_{CS}^F = the value of a loan that is financially distressed.

Evaluating (5a) and (5b) gives the following:

$$\phi R_S^F = r_F + (b+q)(R_{CS}^F - R_S^F) - \theta d \tag{6a}$$

$$\phi R_{CS}^F = \alpha(R_S^F - R_{CS}^F) + \gamma r_F - \theta d \tag{6b}$$

We can determine the price that the non-main bank intermediary would charge for the loan by solving (6a) and (6b) for r_F under the perfectly competitive condition that $R_S^F = 0$. Equation (7) gives this simple solution.

$$r = \frac{\theta d(\phi + \alpha + b + q)}{\gamma(b+q) + (\phi + \alpha)} \tag{7}$$

Equation (7) can be used to determine whether or not the main bank monitors. Implicit in (4) and (7) is the notion that the borrower has a choice about the terms on which it borrows. It could borrow funds at the level of r_M, which means that (4) holds with equality, thus ensuring that it is monitored. Alternatively, it could compel its main bank to match the price, r_F, being offered by the non-main bank intermediary. To determine the outcome of this choice, assume that the final borrower is risk neutral and that it will reject monitoring if the cost of finance associated with it is strictly greater than r_F. Under this assumption, the condition under which monitoring does not take place is given by:

$$f < \frac{c(\alpha + \delta + b + q)}{q} - \frac{\theta d(\alpha + \phi + b + q)}{\gamma(b+q) + \alpha + \phi} \tag{8}$$

Before discussing the properties of (8) in detail, I will pause to define the limits to the main bank's participation in the market. It is quite possible that the non-main bank intermediary could price finance such that $R_S^M < 0$; that is, the main bank earns negative equilibrium profit. The situation in which this occurs is obtained by determining the level of r_M that sets $R_S^M = 0$. If r_F is less than that value, then the main bank is unable to lend to the firm and the main bank lending market collapses. This eventuates when the following condition is met:

$$\frac{d(\alpha + \delta)}{b+q} \left[\frac{\theta(b + q + \alpha + \phi)}{\gamma(b+q) + (\phi + \alpha)} - 1 - \frac{b+q}{\alpha + \delta} \right] < f \tag{9}$$

Discussion

Not all of the variables in (8) carry unambiguous implications for the provision of monitoring. Nevertheless, several of them have clear and revealing effects. These more interesting influences ultimately reduce to the terms of the franchise agreements that the intermediaries hold with the monetary authorities. As the implicit terms of these agreements change, either through adjustments to monetary policy or through capital market regulation, the relative competitive positions of the different classes of financial intermediary also change. In consequence, so too does the pressure for monitored debt.

Consider these factors individually, beginning with the cost of deposits, d. The implications of the model regarding the effect of deposit costs on the conduct of monitoring are at odds with some earlier studies, such as Aoki (1988). Aoki has contended that the rent from main banking underpins monitoring and that lower deposit costs raise the incentive of the main bank to undertake *ex ante* and interim monitoring by increasing main bank rents *ex ante* of financial distress.

The present model suggests that this reasoning focuses too heavily on the *ex ante* significance of deposit costs. As condition (9) shows, rising deposit costs can (but need not necessarily) cause the main bank system to collapse as Aoki claims, but this is only because lending is unprofitable on any terms. As inequality (4) shows, when borrower–intermediary relations are viable for the main bank, lower deposit costs do not inspire integrated monitoring because they apply *ex post* and *ex ante* of financial distress.

The argument that low deposit costs enhance the incentives for *ex ante* and interim monitoring is even more seriously disabled when non-main bank intermediaries are admitted to the analysis. The extra returns that seem to flow from lower deposit costs may not directly affect the main bank's monitoring incentives. However, as inequality (8) reveals, lower deposit costs exert an indirect effect through the pricing behaviour of the non-main bank intermediary. The senior claimant status of these intermediaries, measured by γ, means that they have incentives to ignore the risk that is associated with their pricing decisions. Therefore, as deposit costs decline, non-main bank intermediaries are more prone to price funds so cheaply as to make *ex ante* and interim monitoring inconsistent with profit maximisation by the main bank. In short, far from increasing the incentives of main banks to conduct *ex ante* and interim monitoring, low deposit costs actually reduce them.

This resembles a moral hazard of insurance problem, in which insurance takes the form of seniority. The greater is the seniority of non-main bank intermediaries (that is, the greater is their insurance against financial distress), the stronger is their power to generate pricing outcomes that make more likely the adverse states against which they are insured. Contrary to existing theory on the main bank system, low deposit costs help to enable this mechanism.

A moral hazard problem of this sort takes as its starting point the moral hazards that often appear in other delegated monitoring models. As Stiglitz (1985) argues, monitoring has public good properties, and so it is possible that no single provider of finance will have the incentives to undertake monitoring on behalf of the others. Delegated monitoring appears to be one solution to the problem. But this is pregnant with moral hazard since anyone who delegates monitoring implicitly signals that they cannot observe compliance with the delegated monitoring contract at reasonable cost.

The present model shows that this moral hazard problem is not necessarily eradicated by integrating monitoring and assigning junior claimant status to the main bank. Assigning claims to distressed borrowers in this way may appear to be a good method for eliminating property rights problems in *ex ante* and interim monitoring because it raises the penalties associated with shirking and so gives the main bank sufficient private incentives to monitor on behalf of either depositors or other creditors. However, this strategy is only effective up to a point. When deposit costs are low and γ is high, it simply shifts some of the moral hazard away from the main bank and onto non-main bank financial intermediaries.

Recent Japanese commercial experience seems consistent with such an idea. In particular, moral hazards may partly explain why an accommodating monetary policy seemed to coexist with successful corporate performance in the high growth period of the Japanese economy (the late 1950s through to the early 1970s) but why it also coincided with an apparent breakdown in monitoring arrangements in the late 1980s and early 1990s. In the former period, monetary policy did not compromise monitoring arrangements (neither, however, was it as supportive as is commonly argued) because entry to the market in financial intermediation was regulated and non-main bank intermediaries were in no position to undercut the main bank. In such an environment, the monetary authorities were able to maintain low deposit rates in order to achieve macroeconomic objectives without fear of the corporate governance implications of their actions. In contrast, in the latter 1980s such a policy was not viable. Non-main bank financial intermediaries were more competitive, and thus the moral hazards to which they are inherently susceptible became potent when policy once again turned accommodating around the time of the 1985 Plaza Accord. Viewed in these terms, the recent outbreak of financial distress in the corporate sector and the subsequent criticism of the screening and monitoring performances of major Japanese banks are hardly surprising.

Deposit costs are not the only dimension of the problem to have adjusted in the Japanese economy lately. Foremost among the other variables to have changed is the cost of financial recontracting, f. As I have shown, the main bank will offer finance to the final borrower at a lower price when financial distress is expensive and will thus be more likely to capture the debt contract of the firm on terms that guarantee monitoring.

The capital adequacy requirements of the Bank for International Settlements (BIS) might be viewed as one mechanism by which monetary authorities can raise the cost of financial recontracting in order to stimulate monitoring. Under these requirements, bad debts damage a bank's capital adequacy. To the extent that this capital adequacy is costly to repair in the subordinated loan markets, financial contracting will be higher under the regulations than it would otherwise be.

By way of aside, it is worth noting that the model is able to explain the apparent tendency of the BIS regulations to reduce lending by the major commercial banks. Note from inequality (9) that higher values of f reduce the ability of the main bank to lend profitably. Thus, while higher monitoring costs increase the incentive of the main bank to monitor, they paradoxically undermine its capacity to lend at all. This might partially explain why commercial bank lending has apparently been slower and more cautious since the introduction of the requirements.[22]

Another variable that might have altered is the cost of *ex ante* and interim monitoring, c, but in this case it is more hazardous to speculate on the direction of the change. On the one hand, the broader spectrum of investment opportunities that economic liberalisation has introduced must surely have made monitoring fundamentally more complex and expensive. On the other hand, as the Bank of Japan (1992) has pointed out, in recent years there have been substantial improvements in banking technology which should have reduced the expense of monitoring.

Movements in θ are also interesting. With the steady progress of Japanese financial liberalisation, it becomes likely that the difference in the cost of funds to major commercial banks and other types of financial intermediary should gradually be compressed. This being the case, θ should have declined toward, or even below, unity. This would raise the ability of the non-main bank intermediaries to induce shirking by the main bank and, by inequality (9), it would weaken the viability of the main bank system.

A final point embedded in (8) and (9) is that discount rates can influence monitoring. In particular, long planning horizons are important to the maintenance of debt that is main bank monitored. On its own, this verification of a popular belief about the underpinnings of the main bank system is not very interesting; it follows almost directly from the model's simple set-up. More noteworthy is the finding that an increase in the discount rate of the main bank does not affect the equilibrium to the same extent as an increase in the discount rate of the non-main bank intermediary.

Conclusion

In the literature on delegated monitoring, much is made of the possibility that monitors might shirk their monitoring and in doing so fall prey to moral hazard. In this chapter, I have shown that whether or not this happens to Japanese main banks depends in part on the pricing behaviour of their competitors. If non-main banks are well insured by integrated main bank monitoring, then the debt contracts that they offer to borrowers may be priced in such a way as to ensure the potency of the moral hazard that confronts the main bank. Since the non-main banks realise this when they act, they are effectively surrendering to the very different moral hazard that they confront by virtue of their status as senior claimants against the final borrower.

This reasoning has clear applications for Japan. As new forms of finance emerged and non-main bank intermediaries flourished in the late 1980s, commercial bank margins declined; at about the same time, monitoring standards appeared to deteriorate. As suggested earlier, certain aspects of the main bank system could have contributed to this turn of events.

Whether or not any policy prescriptions can be drawn from such conjectures is a difficult question. On the one hand, main bank monitoring evolved in Japan partly because the various participants in the corporate finance market once found it to be a workable mode of corporate governance. If the lesson of bad debts from the 'bubble economy' is that the system is now less reliable in the wake of financial deregulation, then we may anticipate that private transactions will adjust to accommodate the new realities.

On the other hand, much research attests to the importance of Japan's legal and monetary systems as underpinning main banking. These institutions were conducive to the provision of main bank monitoring when capital markets were tightly regulated. If they are the real glue that continues to hold the system of main bank monitoring together, then they may need to be re-examined. There is a strong message in this chapter that the old system of main bank monitoring is fragile in the face of highly contestable capital markets. To the extent that this is the fault of residual regulation of markets which affect main bank monitoring, further efforts to deregulate the banking environment may be warranted.

The model through which these ideas are expressed is still very basic, and there are many ways in which it might be improved and its implications refined. In closing, I list a few of the more pressing considerations. First, it would be interesting to model the final borrower more thoroughly and to incorporate into this model findings such as those by Hoshi, Kashyap and Scharfstein (1993). For various reasons, borrowers may be risk averse and so may be willing to pay their main bank for monitoring even when $r_M > r_F$. Also, a final borrower may wish to diversify its borrowing in ways that allow it to reward its main bank for monitoring, while taking advantage of any cheaper funds that may be available elsewhere.

Diversification is also important from the viewpoint of the main bank. A number of studies in the delegated monitoring literature rely on diversification as a key element in the delegated monitor's behaviour.[23] In this model I have not allowed the main bank to diversify its risk, even though this will undoubtedly affect its monitoring incentives.

Yet another aspect of the model that needs improvement is the treatment of financial distress. There are two obvious extensions to be made. First, as much research points out, whether and to what extent a monitor ought to intervene in the affairs of a borrower is often taken optimally by the monitor and need not automatically be triggered by some state of the world. Although I have ignored this issue here, further work on the subject might seek to address it.

Second, it would be interesting to model explicitly the incentives that the main bank has to undertake *ex post* monitoring. I have assumed that the main bank can simply be compelled to perform *ex post* monitoring by the central bank. In reality, though, pressures to resolve financial distress probably emanate from sources other than the central bank. In particular, if these pressures are applied by non-main bank intermediaries, as Sheard's reciprocal delegated monitoring hypothesis suggests (Ch. 5), then they may impinge on the incentives for monitoring in ways that the present model obscures.

Finally, future work might allow non-main bank finance in the form of equity as well as debt. Such an extension promises a more realistic portrayal of the changes in financing techniques that have taken place in Japan over the last decade. Moreover, a formal study of the significance of financial leverage in relation to integrated monitoring would be a valuable extension of Aoki's (1984) analysis of the tension between banks and corporate shareholders.

Appendix 6.1: Derivation of the asset equations

In this appendix, I derive equation (2a) from equation (1a). It is possible to derive the other equations by an analogous process. Equation (1a) is reproduced here for convenience as (A1):

$$R_S^M = \int_0^\infty (b+q)e^{-(b+q)T}\left[\int_0^T e^{-\delta t}(r_M-d)dt + e^{-\delta T}R_{CS}^M\right]dT \qquad (A1)$$

Decomposing this, we have:

$$R_S^M = \int_0^\infty (b+q)e^{-(b+q)T}\left[\int_0^T e^{-\delta t}(r_M-d)dt\right]dT + \int_0^\infty (b+q)e^{-(b+q+\delta)T}R_{CS}^M dT \qquad (A2)$$

The second integral on the right-hand side of (A2) can be written as:

$$\int_0^\infty (b+q)e^{-(b+q+\delta)T}R_{CS}^M dT = (b+q)R_{CS}^M \int_0^\infty e^{-(b+q+\delta)T} dT \qquad (A3)$$

Evaluating the right-hand side of (A3) gives:

$$(b+q)R_{CS}^M \int_0^\infty e^{-(b+q+\delta)T} dT = \frac{b+q}{b+q+\delta}R_{CS}^M \qquad (A4)$$

The first integral on the right-hand side of (A2) can be integrated by parts. Rewrite it as:

$$\int_0^\infty (b+q)e^{-(b+q)T}\left[\int_0^T e^{-\delta t}(r_M-d)dt\right]dT = \int_0^\infty U(T)V(T)dT \qquad (A5)$$

or

$$\int_0^\infty (b+q)e^{-(b+q)T}\left[\int_0^T e^{-\delta t}(r_M-d)dt\right]dT = G(T)V(T)\Big|_0^\infty - \int_0^\infty G(T)V'(T)dT \qquad (A6)$$

where

$$\left.\begin{aligned} U(T) &= (b+q)e^{-(b+q)T} \\ V(T) &= \int_0^T e^{-\delta T}(r_M-d)dt \\ V'(T) &= (r_M-d)e^{-\delta T} \end{aligned}\right\} \qquad (A7)$$

and where

$$G(T) = \int_0^T U(Z)dZ = -e^{-(b+q)Z}\Big|_0^T = 1 - e^{-(b+q)T} \qquad (A8)$$

Using (A7) and (A8), equation (A5) can be rewritten as follows:

$$\int_0^\infty U(T)V(T)dT = \left(1 - e^{-(b+q)T}\right)V(T)\Big|_0^\infty - \int_0^\infty \left(1 - e^{-(b+q)T}\right)(r_M - d)e^{-\delta T}dT \qquad (A9)$$

Evaluating the right-hand side of (A9) gives:

$$\int_0^\infty (b+q)e^{-(b+q)T}\left[\int_0^T e^{-\delta t}(r_M - d)dt\right]dT = \frac{r_M - d}{\delta + b + q} \qquad (A10)$$

Substituting (A4) and (A10) into (A2) gives:

$$R_S^M = \frac{b+q}{b+q+\delta}R_{CS}^M + \frac{(r_M - d)}{b+q+\delta} \qquad (A11)$$

or

$$(b+q+\delta)R_S^M = (b+q)R_{CS}^M + r_M - d \qquad (A12)$$

Simple rearrangement of (A12) gives equation (2a).

Notes

1. The Economic Development Institute of the World Bank commissioned a study of the Japanese main bank system and its possible relevance for transforming socialist economies (Aoki and Patrick 1994).
2. For an excellent chronology of this deregulation, see Takeda and Turner (1992).
3. One of the best descriptions of this involvement is provided by Aoki, Patrick and Sheard (1994).
4. Usually, the main bank is the one which lends the most to the firm, with short-term loans being a particularly salient indicator. Nevertheless, this is only a rule of thumb and it becomes problematic when the firm has slight or no dependence on external debt. In this chapter, I observe the convention of reserving the term 'main bank' for a subset of Japan's major commercial banks. It is between large firms and large banks that financial relationships are at their most complex and that the evidence of main bank related phenomena is most striking.

5   Whether or not main banks intervene as creditors or shareholders is admittedly still in dispute. Sheard's (1994a) results tentatively indicate that they may intervene as creditors.

6   More recently, however, other forms of income have become important for the main bank as many firms have reduced their reliance on debt finance.

7   Nakajima and Taguchi (1995) argue that the safety net placed under the banks by the monetary authorities encouraged them in this activity.

8   This seems to be the major implication of the graph in Aoki (1984, p. 212).

9   The Bank of Japan's (1991) study confirms this, as does the work of Ueda (1994, Chart 7).

10 In Aoki (1988, p. 148) the suggestion is made that the returns to banks form the basis for integrated monitoring. In the model which was developed in that work, it can be shown that main bank rents are negatively related to deposit costs.

11 The association between financial distress and continuation of the firm is for ease of exposition. It is possible to construct a scenario in which financial distress amounts to liquidation of the borrower. This depends, among other things, on the bank's experiencing a delay in recruiting a new borrower and on the management of liquidation being costly for the main bank.

12 A variation on this argument uses the familiar assumption that managers of unmonitored borrowing firms use firm assets to consume private perquisites. In the long run, competition in the borrower's final product market means that firms which are 'immunised' by main bank monitoring against such 'cancerous' management should drive into difficulty, if not out of existence, those borrowers not so protected.

13 Under appropriate assumptions about the relative magnitudes of the variables and parameters of the model, this will be the optimal policy of the bank. Less realistic equilibria are also possible, but I do not explore them here.

14 See Aoki, Patrick and Sheard (1994, p. 15) and Sheard (1994b) for a discussion of the difficulties that main banks have in shirking their *ex post* monitoring.

15 The main bank's choice over monitoring expenditure could be continuous rather than binary, but it is not strictly necessary to present the problem in these terms. Suppose that c is the minimum level of monitoring expenditure that is required to eradicate such borrower failure as is driven by q. The main bank could spend some amount on monitoring that is less than c, but it would not benefit by doing so. Likewise, it could spend an amount on monitoring that exceeds c, but this increment would not reduce the prospect of borrower failure below b. It is therefore reasonable to present the main bank's choice as being binary.

16 A sample of the working is provided in Appendix 6.1.

17 This is not to deny that deposit costs are relevant to bank profit. The role of deposit costs as an influence on bank profit is dealt with next.

18 This assumption is necessary in order for there to be an equilibrium in which the main bank can compete with non-main bank intermediaries.

19 See Ito (1992) for a discussion of the overloan phenomenon and Aoki, Patrick and Sheard (1994, p. 17) for a more general discussion of the privileged access of main banks to cheap funding.

20 Note that we are assuming that the resolution of financial distress by a party other than the main bank still takes place at speed α. This assumption can be relaxed with a simple respecification of (5b).

21 It is not strictly necessary that the non-main bank know these parameters. It could merely guess at them, and the core results of the model would still hold.

22 That the BIS's capital adequacy requirements constrict bank lending is a widely held belief among practitioners in Japan. See, for example, *The Economist* (23 April 1994, p. 73).

23 See, for example, Diamond (1984) and, for a treatment of the Japanese main bank case, Sheard (Ch. 5, this volume).

References

Aoki, Masahiko (1984), 'Shareholders' Non-Unanimity on Investment Financing: Banks vs Individual Investors', in Masahiko Aoki (ed.), *The Economic Analysis of the Japanese Firm*, Amsterdam: North-Holland, pp. 193–224.

—— (1988), *Information, Incentives and Bargaining in the Japanese Economy*, Cambridge, MA: Cambridge University Press.

—— (1994), 'Monitoring Characteristics of the Main Bank System: An Analytical and Developmental View', in Masahiko Aoki and Hugh Patrick (eds), *The Japanese Main Bank System: Its Relevancy for Developing and Transforming Economies*, Oxford: Oxford University Press, pp. 109–41.

Aoki, Masahiko and Hugh Patrick (eds) (1994), *The Japanese Main Bank System: Its Relevancy for Developing and Transforming Economies*, Oxford: Oxford University Press.

Aoki, Masahiko, Hugh Patrick and Paul Sheard (1994), 'The Japanese Main Bank System: An Introductory Overview', in M. Aoki and H. Patrick (eds), *The Japanese Main Bank System: Its Relevancy for Developing and Transforming Economies*, Oxford: Oxford University Press, pp. 3–50.

Bank of Japan, (1991), 'Recent Developments in Lending Rates: Changing Behavior of Banks under Interest Rate Liberalization', Bank of Japan Special Paper No. 206, Bank of Japan, Tokyo.

—— (1992), 'Deregulation, Technical Progress and the Efficiency of the Banking Industry in Japan', Bank of Japan Special Paper No. 211, Bank of Japan, Tokyo.

—— (1993), 'Japanese Banks' Capital Ratio and Their Earnings Trend: An ROE Analysis', Bank of Japan Special Paper No. 230, Bank of Japan, Tokyo.

Diamond, D. (1984), 'Financial Intermediation and Delegated Monitoring', *Review of Economic Studies*, 51, pp. 393–414.

—— (1991), 'Monitoring and Reputation: The Choice between Bank Loans and Directly Placed Debt', *Journal of Political Economy*, 99, pp. 689–721.

Economic Planning Agency (1993), *Economic Survey of Japan 1992–93*, Tokyo: Economic Planning Agency.

Fama, E. (1985), 'What's Different about Banks?', *Journal of Monetary Economics*, 15 (1), pp. 29–39.

Gower, Luke (1995), 'A Simple Model of Main Bank Monitoring in Japan', *Pacific Economic Papers*, 240, Australia–Japan Research Centre, The Australian National University, Canberra.

Horiuchi, Akiyoshi (1993), 'Functions of the Japanese Capital Market', *Japanese Economic Studies*, 21 (3), pp. 66–95.

Hoshi, T., A. Kashyap and D. Scharfstein (1990), 'The Role of Banks in Reducing the Costs of Financial Distress in Japan', *Journal of Financial Economics*, 27, pp. 67–88.

—— (1993), 'The Choice Between Public and Private Debt: An Analysis of Post-Regulation Corporate Finance in Japan', Graduate School of International Relations and Pacific Studies Research Report 93–02, University of California, San Diego.

Ito, T. (1992), *The Japanese Economy*, Cambridge, MA: MIT Press.

James, C. (1987), 'Some Evidence on the Uniqueness of Bank Loans', *Journal of Financial Economics*, 19, pp. 217–35.

Keynes, J. (1936), *The General Theory of Employment, Interest and Money*, London: Macmillan and Cambridge University Press (1973 edition).

Mayer, C. (1988), 'New Issues in Corporate Finance', *European Economic Review*, 32 (5), pp. 1,167–82.

Ministry of Finance (1993), *The Mechanism and Economic Effects of Asset Price Fluctuations: A Report of the Research Committee*, Tokyo: Institute of Fiscal and Monetary Policy, Japanese Ministry of Finance.

Nakajima, Z. and H. Taguchi (1995), ' Toward a More Stable Financial Framework: Long-Term Alternatives', in Z. Nakajima and M. Sawada (eds), *Financial Stability in a Changing Environment*, London: Macmillan.

Nakatani, Iwao (1984), 'The Economic Role of Financial Corporate Grouping', in Masahiko Aoki (ed.), *The Economic Analysis of the Japanese Firm*, Amsterdam: North-Holland, pp. 227–58.

Packer, F. and M. Ryser (1992), 'The Governance of Failure: An Anatomy of Corporate Bankruptcy in Japan', Working Paper Series, 62, Center on Japanese Economy and Business, Graduate School of Business, Columbia University, New York.

Schumpeter, J. (1939), *Business Cycles*, New York, NY: McGraw-Hill.

Shapiro, C. and J. Stiglitz (1984), 'Equilibrium Unemployment as a Worker Discipline Device', *American Economic Review*, 74 (3), pp. 433–44.

Sheard, Paul (1994a), 'Bank Executives on Japanese Corporate Boards', *Bank of Japan Monetary and Economic Studies*, 12 (2), pp. 85–121.

—— (1994b), 'Main Banks and the Governance of Financial Distress', in Masahiko Aoki and Hugh Patrick (eds), *The Japanese Main Bank System: Its Relevancy for Developing and Transforming Economies*, Oxford: Oxford University Press, pp. 188–230.

Stiglitz, J. (1985), 'Credit Markets and the Control of Capital', *Journal of Money, Credit and Banking*, 17 (2), pp. 133–52.

Takeda, M. and P. Turner (1992), 'The Liberalisation of Japan's Financial Markets: Some Major Themes', BIS Economic Papers No. 34, Bank for International Settlements, Basle.

Ueda, K. (1994), 'Institutional and Regulatory Frameworks for the Main Bank System', in Masahiko Aoki and Hugh Patrick (eds), *The Japanese Main Bank System: Its Relevancy for Developing and Transforming Economies*, Oxford: Oxford University Press, pp. 89–108.

7 Banks, blockholders and corporate governance: the role of external appointees to the board

Paul Sheard*

The mechanisms that exist for intervening in the top management of corporations, and their effectiveness, constitute an important aspect of any system of corporate governance. The much studied principal–agent conflict between financiers and managers is probably most acute when the optimal action required of a top management team is to sack itself. Naturally enough managers may be reluctant to do this, and yet on occasion this is precisely what may be called for. It is now realised that in theory and in practice a variety of intervention mechanisms exists. This in part recognises the fact that the firm sits at the intersection of a number of different markets, with pressure on managers coming through each of these market channels, but it also reflects crossnational differences in institutions, conventions and legal frameworks.

While the real world differences are probably a matter of degree rather than absolute, it is convenient to distinguish between two polar modes, which I will term 'insider based' and 'open bidding' systems. They differ in the mechanisms used to effect *ex post* reallocations of corporate control and in the identity of the potential agents involved. In an insider based system, corporate control is exercised by financiers, such as banks or large shareholders, who have pre-existing, ongoing relations with the firm. In an open bidding system, bidding for control is more open and new agents may enter *ex post* to bid for the control rights. Japan and much of continental Europe are often thought of as typifying the insider based mode, while the United States and the United Kingdom are viewed more as open bidding systems (Roe 1993). Corporate control is contingent in nature. In normal times or 'default' states

---

* I would like to thank Colin McKenzie and seminar participants at the Australian National University, Humboldt University and Oxford University for their valuable comments. The Institute for Monetary and Economic Studies, Bank of Japan, and the International Cooperation (Osaka Gas) Research Fund at Osaka University generously provided research support.

of nature, control rests with incumbent management, in either kind of system. The two systems can be said to differ, however, in how control shifts in extraordinary times, such as when the firm suffers a financial setback, when it is performing below potential even though performing well in absolute terms, or when the capital market and the firm's management disagree about what is best for the firm. When control shifts in an insider based system, it does so to an insider; the control shift may be indistinguishable from a large shareholder exercising its latent control rights, or it may be more dramatic, as when a Japanese main bank intervenes in a troubled client firm. In an open bidding system it may be impossible to predict *ex ante* and even close to the event, not only whether or not a control shift will occur, but who will bid for and perhaps gain control: an existing shareholder or creditor, a third party takeover agent, or even the incumbent management in the case of a management buyout.

The distinction between the two systems is sometimes made in terms of whether or not there is an active takeover market. This is a useful distinction, but it does cloud the fact that in an insider based system a form of takeover mechanism operates — if 'takeover' is taken to mean intervention from outside the firm through the exercise of control rights attached to securities — albeit in a more circumscribed and often less transparent form.

A more useful distinction that is relevant to understanding why equilibrium outcomes differ concerns the degree of liquidity: there is a high degree of liquidity in an open bidding system and a reduced degree in an insider based system (Coffee 1991). At the risk of oversimplification the following generalisation can be made. In an open bidding system investors are arm's-length and well diversified, and hence have relatively small individual holdings; secondary markets for securities are active and well developed. In an insider based system, investors have large holdings and hold instruments that are either inherently less liquid or are so in equilibrium.

Diversification and liquidity are complementary, and conducive to the operation of a price taking market. If investors are diversified, then for given investment levels they will have small individual holdings; if they have small holdings they will have little incentive to monitor individual corporate managements in an active way, and less means of doing so. Their monitoring will be more arm's-length and arbitrage driven in nature, aimed at moving funds from lower to higher yielding firms.

The above distinctions have implications for the nature of intervention or the form that takeovers will take. Large blockholders have greater means and incentives to intervene directly in firms. Having less liquidity means that, when they are dissatisfied with incumbent management, they are less likely and able to exercise the exit (sell) option that investors with small holdings enjoy. They have less liquidity for two reasons. First, by virtue of their large holding, there is a smaller residual market of actively traded stocks. Second, they will generally have access to information not available to diversified arm's-length investors (by occupying a seat on the board, for instance). This information access will reduce their liquidity for adverse selection reasons: unless carefully managed, an attempt to sell a large block of stocks could be interpreted as bad news by the liquid part of the market, leading to a sharp decline in the price. A large blockholder is therefore unlikely to be a price-taker. On the other hand, having a large holding makes direct intervention a sensible strategy: externality effects can be partially internalised, while information access and an accumulated information base provide the large blockholder with an inherent comparative advantage as a takeover agent.

Japan offers an example of a prototypical insider based system. Although a large stock market exists, the takeover market is largely inactive; corporate governance is exercised by large blockholders — main banks and parent firms — in the context of extensive interlocking shareholdings. This chapter adds to the growing literature on Japanese corporate governance from a comparative institutional and theoretic perspective by focusing on the phenomenon of 'outside directors' on Japanese corporate boards. These are directors who have entered from outside the firm rather than being internally promoted, long-term employees of the firm. A brief overview of the Japanese corporate governance system is followed by a model of the determinants of outside director presence on the board. This is then extended by estimating a logit model of the likelihood of an external appointee occupying the key president position.

Japan's insider based system of corporate governance

Two pivotal elements in the Japanese system of corporate governance are the role played by leading banks, known as 'main banks', and the high degree of corporate shareholding. Typically, shareholdings take the form of cross-holdings between pairs of firms, and banks themselves occupy a central place in these. These are the building blocks of insider corporate governance in Japan.

Japanese banks are limited to holding 5 per cent of an individual firm's equity unless an exemption is obtained. Most listed firms maintain a close relationship with a particular main bank, which holds close to the 5 per cent limit, supplies the largest share of bank loans (traditionally the main source of external finance), in many cases places bank executives on the firm's board, and expects to garner a high share of various banking business. This includes handling the firm's settlement accounts and thereby gaining a window on the firm's cash flow position (Aoki, Patrick and Sheard 1994). In theoretical terms, the main bank can be viewed as providing a delegated monitoring arrangement in the capital market. In particular, the prominent part that the main bank plays in coordinating rescue-cum-reorganisation operations of troubled client firms has received much attention in the literature (Aoki 1994; Hoshi, Kashyap and Scharfstein 1990; Sheard 1989, 1994b).

The role of the main bank is complementary to and set in the context of the corporate shareholding structure, which has three noteworthy features. One is that there is a high level of corporate and institutional shareholding: 27 per cent of listed stocks are held by domestic non-financial corporations and another 42 per cent by financial institutions. A second feature is that top shareholding is quite concentrated, with the main blockholder often being another, larger, listed firm. For firms listed on the first section of the stock exchange in Japan, on average the largest shareholder holds 15 per cent of the stock, the top three shareholders together hold 25.5 per cent, and the top ten shareholders account for 45 per cent of the stock.[1] These averages mask significant variation, particularly in the top shareholding position. For 26 per cent of firms, the top shareholder had a holding of 20 per cent or more, while in 44 per cent of cases the top shareholding was between 5 and 10 per cent (Sheard 1994c).

A third feature is the extensive interlocking shareholding engaged in by Japanese firms (Sheard 1994a), which tend to own parcels of shares in their own corporate shareholders. Two points are noteworthy. Interlocking shareholdings, which probably constitute the majority of the top 50 to 100 shareholdings, are not arm's-length. The firms involved are typically transaction partners in such input or output markets as loans, business services, insurance and physical products. Financial ties are thus bundled together with product market ties (Flath 1996). Moreover, Japanese firms typically implement strategies known as 'stable shareholding arrangements' (*antei kabunushi kōsaku*), whereby interlocked firms agree to hold the shares as insiders friendly to incumbent management and not to sell their shares to external takeover raiders. A second point is that banks, who play a key role in corporate governance as main banks, are themselves deeply embedded in the stable interlocking shareholding arrangements (Sheard 1994a).

Although having its own distinctive features, the board of directors is at the centre of corporate governance in Japan as elsewhere. Ostensibly directors are chosen by, and charged with representing the interests of, shareholders. However, directors in Japan are generally full-time officers of the corporation, and the board is effectively the top layer of senior management (Aoki 1988, p. 144). The board is hierarchically structured from junior to increasingly senior positions, culminating in the chief executive officer (CEO) position of president (*shachō*); above the president is the chairperson, who is usually the previous president. The board of directors is effectively the pinnacle of the internal promotion track for lifetime employees, who typically join the corporation after graduating from university.

Not all directors are internally bred, however: about 25 per cent are executives who rise up through (and usually separate from) the internal promotion hierarchy of other corporations (or organisations) to enter the firm late in their careers. Of these, 5.3 per cent come from banks and other financial institutions, 16.5 per cent from non-financial corporations and 2.6 per cent from government and public sector organisations. In labour market terms these top executive movements are separations followed by new matches between employer and employee, but from a corporate governance perspective it is noteworthy that they take place in an interfirm context as placements from one firm to another. As shown in Sheard (1994c), the main source of late entry executives is firms with leading ownership and financial ties to the firm.

The literature on Japanese corporate governance has tended to emphasise that top management enjoys a high degree of autonomy, pointing to the fact that directors are internally promoted managerial employees and that managers are free from external takeover pressure. The above discussion suggests two qualifications to this view.

First, Japanese managers operate in the purview of an insider based system of corporate governance in which main banks and large blockholders, rather than new entrants to the market for corporate control, are key players. Second, while most directors are internally bred, a substantial fraction has entered from outside the firm. It is well documented that main banks commonly intervene in the management of troubled corporations by despatching executives into senior positions as part of rescue-cum-reorganisation operations. Even in normal times, however, there is a substantial flow of executives between firms which, even if low key and routine in nature, can be regarded as a form of intervention in senior management by the capital market (Kaplan 1994; Kaplan and Minton 1994; Morck and Nakamura 1992).

Table 7.1 provides data on the distribution of directors drawn from outside the firm according to position on the board. It can be seen that outsiders are more concentrated than insiders in senior positions, particularly the posts of president and chairperson, and in the position of statutory auditor. (The statutory auditor is charged with overseeing the board of directors.) Relative to entrants from non-financial firms, bank directors are concentrated in the senior positions below president and in the statutory auditor role.

Table 7.1 Indexes of distribution of board positions by background status[a]

Position	Outsider/ total	Outsider/ insider	Bank/ total	Bank/ insider	Bank/ other firm
Chair	1.57	1.94	1.14	1.43	0.71
President	1.49	1.77	1.19	1.41	0.73
Vice-president	1.19	1.27	1.61	1.72	1.76
Executive director	1.06	1.07	1.51	1.53	1.81
Managing director	0.93	0.91	1.06	1.06	1.33
Director	0.80	0.75	0.59	0.55	0.27
Auditor	1.37	1.53	1.60	1.81	1.18

Note: a Each index is constructed as the ratio of the respective category's fraction of directors in that position.

Source: Compiled from Tōyō Keizai Shinpōsha 1991, p. 90.

Determinants of external appointees to the board

The discussion so far points to the fact that Japanese corporate governance operates through an insider based set of mechanisms rather than through an open bidding market for corporate control.[2] Movement of executives at senior levels from parent firms and financial institutions to affiliated firms is one important facet of the system.

This section aims to cast light on this phenomenon by estimating a model of the determinants of external presence on Japanese corporate boards.

Variables used

The dependent variable in the initial regression is the percentage of the membership of the board that has entered the firm in mid or late career from another firm or organisation. A number of financial and ownership related variables are included as explanatory variables. (See Appendix 7.1 for a full description of the variables and data sources used.)

ASSETS, the total assets of the firm, is included to see whether there is a firm size effect. A negative sign is expected on two grounds. From a managerial labour market perspective, the smaller the firm the more likely that it can garner superior top executive resources from larger firms, which under the Japanese system may have had an edge in initial hiring. There may be a rank hierarchy aspect to corporate control in Japan, with larger firms enjoying a greater degree of managerial autonomy, at least in normal times, and smaller firms being subject to a greater degree of managerial supervision and control by larger firms. On such corporate governance grounds as well, a negative sign would be expected.

LEVERAGE is the ratio of bank borrowings to total assets. A positive sign is expected. It is often argued that by placing executives in senior management positions in client firms banks are better able to monitor client firms and influence corporate decision making. Case study evidence strongly indicates that banks tend to despatch directors when firms are in financial distress.

BANKSHARE is the proportion of the firm's shares owned by banks and other financial institutions, on average 41 per cent in the sample. There are no strong grounds for predicting the sign, but it is an interesting variable to include. A positive sign would be expected if, put simply, banks supplied directors as equity holders. On the other hand, high levels of BANKSHARE could well be indicative of the firm's enjoying a high degree of managerial autonomy, suggesting a negative sign for the coefficient. In other studies the coefficient has often failed to be significant, and a negative sign would not be surprising here given that bank directors are only one component of external appointees.

Several measures of top shareholding concentration are included. SHARE(1), SHARE(2–3), and SHARE(4–10) measure the percentage shareholdings of the number one, numbers two and three, and numbers four to ten top shareholders respectively. A positive sign is expected, and would indicate that large blockholders are able to exercise a high degree of control over the senior management of listed firms in which they hold shares. It would provide evidence for the argument that, along with main banks, parent firm blockholders play a significant role in the corporate governance of listed firms in Japan. The inclusion of these three measures is aimed at determining how far down the share register this share concentration effect extends.

Several variables are included to capture loan concentration effects. LOANSHARE(1) and LOANSHARE(2–3) are the loan shares of the number one lender and the numbers two and three lenders respectively. TOPLENDER is the ratio of the number one lender's loans to total assets. LOANSHARE(1) and TOPLENDER both provide measures of the extent to which there is dependence on a major single lender. As with LEVERAGE, a positive sign is expected. LOANSHARE(2–3) captures effects coming from the presence of other major lenders. It is an interesting variable to include, although there are reasons for expecting either sign. Partly it can be thought of as casting light on the delegated monitoring hypothesis (Sheard, Ch. 5, this volume). Significant positive signs for LEVERAGE and LOANSHARE(1) but not for LOANSHARE(2–3) would lend support to the delegated monitoring hypothesis. It would indicate that a high level of bank presence on boards (assuming that this translates into high levels of the dependent variable) is associated with a high level of bank loan exposure overall and with evidence of the presence of a main bank, but that the distribution of loan exposures among non-main banks is not so important. A positive sign for LOANSHARE(2–3) would be expected if there was a strong 'multiple main bank' aspect to the main bank system, as some observers have suggested; higher levels would be indicative of the second and third lenders rivalling the top lender in terms of loan importance. But a negative sign is also plausible: higher levels of LOANSHARE(2–3) might reflect a strategy on the part of the firm of maintaining arm's-length relations with banks by diversifying key banking relationships, which might be associated with lower levels of bank presence on the board.

PROFIT(1) is a dummy variable equal to one if the firm has had negative operating profits in any of the five years prior to 1991. The expected sign is positive. Deteriorating financial performance should be associated with increased intervention from the capital market, and this should be reflected in higher levels of outside presence on the board. However, part of the intervention by main banks and parent firms, known from the case study literature and other recent empirical studies to occur, will be reflected in qualitative changes in board composition (director replacements and turnover) and will not be captured in the quantitative measure of the dependent variable.

INSIDER is a dummy variable capturing the presence of residual founding figure or family influence in the management or ownership of the firm. Surprisingly, in the full sample of 1,064 first-section listed firms, residual family control was found in 36 per cent of cases. In some cases there may be little or no substantive effect, but in 25 per cent of cases the president was identified as a founding family figure and in 12 per cent of cases the top shareholding was associated with the founding family. Although this is clearly a key characteristic of corporate governance, it has largely been overlooked in the literature. Following Nakatani (1984), a long line of studies has tested for various differences between group affiliated and independent firms by employing some variant of the Keizai Chōsa Kyōkai (annual) or Dodwell Marketing classifications of listed firms; strangely enough, though, insider entrepreneur or family presence is not used as an explicit criterion in forming these lists. This is a weakness in the existing line of studies, avoided here. A negative sign for the coefficient is expected, given that inside family figures are likely to try to maintain high levels of managerial autonomy by not accepting as many placements into senior management from outside the company. Such a result would lend some economic content to the notion of an independent firm, as it would indicate that firms with family influence maintain a higher level of independence from the capital market.[3]

FIRMAGE, the number of years since the firm was established, is included to control for a possible firm age effect. A negative sign is expected given that older firms may have accumulated deeper managerial resources and so need fewer resources from outside the firm or require less capital market monitoring due to the reputation they have built up for creditworthiness.

Dummy variables for industry sector and membership of one of the six enterprise group presidents' clubs are also included. It is often claimed that firms affiliated with the six big bank-centred groups have a high level of interlocking directorates. It is of interest to test whether this is so, particularly after controlling for other determinants of outside directors.

Regression results: external appointees

The results of one-sided Tobit regressions are presented in Table 7.2. Results for three versions of the model are presented: one containing all the explanatory variables, one containing significant variables only, and one containing only those variables about which there are fairly strong theoretical priors. Tobit regression is used because the dependent variable is censored at values of zero, 10 per cent of the sample taking on this value. Reported t-statistics are heteroscedastic consistent. OLS regressions, which were also run, yielded very similar results in terms of coefficient values and significance judgements. The OLS regressions explained about 40 per cent of the variation in the extent of outside presence on boards in the sample of 1,016 firms listed on the first section of the stock exchange.

ASSETS, LEVERAGE, SHARE(1), SHARE(2–3), LOANSHARE(1), INSIDER and FIRMAGE all have the expected sign and are significant. Firms have a higher proportion of externally sourced directors the more highly levered they are, the larger the loan share of the top lender, the larger the top shareholding, and the larger the top two and three shareholdings; they have a smaller proportion the bigger they are in size, the older they are and when there is residual family control.

The coefficient for BANKSHARE is negative and significant at the 1 per cent level. Higher aggregate shareholdings by banks and other financial institutions (basically life and property insurance companies) translates into less apparent intervention from the capital market in top management. The coefficient for LOANSHARE(2–3) is negative and significant at the 5 per cent level. Loosely speaking, firms are less reliant on external directors when the closest rivals for the main bank slot have large loan shares.

Table 7.2 Tobit estimation of proportion of directors entering from other firms for listed Japanese firms, 1991

	Variables with theoretical priors (model 7.2.1)	Significant variables only (model 7.2.2)	All explanatory variables (model 7.2.3)
CONSTANT	32.55***	33.03***	32.75***
	(7.51)	(7.18)	(6.85)
ASSETS	−1.95***	−2.03***	−2.08***
	(−2.97)	(−3.04)	(−2.99)
LEVERAGE	0.21***	0.22***	0.26***
	(5.28)	(5.39)	(3.69)
BANKSHARE	−0.25***	−0.25***	−0.28***
	(−4.41)	(−4.41)	(−4.32)
SHARE(1)	0.40***	0.40***	0.40***
	(6.54)	(6.60)	(6.57)
SHARE(2–3)	0.48***	0.49***	0.47***
	(3.19)	(3.22)	(2.89)
INSIDER	−6.21***	−6.28***	−6.37***
	(−4.90)	(−4.98)	(−4.97)
FIRMAGE	−0.18***	−0.17***	−0.17***
	(−4.73)	(−4.57)	(−4.56)
LOANSHARE(1)		0.04*	0.06*
		(1.37)	(1.62)
LOANSHARE(2–3)		−0.08*	−0.09**
		(−1.96)	(−2.08)
SHARE(4–10)			0.07
			(0.46)
PROFIT(1)			−1.16
			(−0.66)
TOPLENDER			−0.16
			(−0.78)
MITSUI	−15.93***	−15.89***	−15.64***
	(−4.33)	(−4.34)	(−4.20)
MITSUBISHI	−5.49*	−5.25*	−5.21*
	(−1.93)	(−1.81)	(−1.80)
SUMITOMO	−7.75**	−7.81**	−7.78**
	(−2.03)	(−2.05)	(−2.05)
FUYO	−2.62	−2.67	−2.48
	(−1.27)	(−1.30)	(−1.21)
SANWA	−5.69**	−5.68**	−5.65**
	(−2.16)	(−2.19)	(−2.15)
DKB	−4.22*	−4.31*	−4.20*
	(−1.70)	(−1.72)	(−1.67)
Log likelihood	−3,938.9	−3,936.5	−3,935.8
No. of observations	1,016	1,016	1,016

Notes: Industry dummies are included in all regressions; heteroscedastic consistent t-ratios are in brackets. *** Significant at 1 per cent confidence level; ** significant at 5 per cent level; * significant at 10 per cent level (one-sided or two-sided test as appropriate).

The sign of the SHARE(4–10) coefficient is positive but not significant. The share concentration effects appear to be in the top three positions. The sign for TOPLENDER is negative. This is unexpected, but the sign is not significant.

The sign of the PROFIT(1) coefficient is negative — the opposite of what was expected — but not significant. Other case study and quantitative studies find that a deterioration in performance triggers director interventions from main banks and parent firms as well as increased director turnover. The result obtained here may be suggesting that, dramatic and effective though these interventions may be, they do not necessarily show up in this kind of cross-sectional analysis. Alternatively it may be that the measure of profit performance is not a good one.

A curious result is obtained for the presidents' club dummy variables. All have negative coefficients and five are significant, most notably MITSUI. Contrary to the widespread belief, core firms in bank-centred groupings appear to be less characterised by interlocking directorates. The industry dummies, which are included in all regressions but with results suppressed, reveal that belonging to the construction industry or the real estate or service industries raises the proportion of external appointees to the board by about 8 per cent, relative to the machinery industry, while being in the textile industry lowers it by about 11 per cent.

Taken together, the results for the lending and ownership variables are interesting. In the case of LEVERAGE, BANKSHARE, LOANSHARE(1) and LOANSHARE (2–3), the results seem to support the delegated monitoring view of the main bank system and the view, put too simply perhaps, that banks monitor firms as lenders rather than as equity holders. However, the theoretical grounds for including the loan share variables are not strong, and a likelihood ratio test accepts the restriction that they can be omitted (model 7.2.1). The robust results are that high leverage and high concentration of top equity positions, particularly the presence of a large top shareholder, increase the presence of externally sourced directors, while a high financial institution shareholding reduces it, as do being large, old or having residual family control. Combined with the fact that external appointees predominantly come from firms or banks with close financial and ownership ties (Sheard 1994c), the evidence is consistent with the view that late career director placements are an important mechanism of corporate governance in Japan, if less spectacular or transparent than similar mechanisms in more open corporate control environments.

Regression results: bank appointees

This section reports the results of similar analysis, but with attention restricted to external appointees to the board who come from banks. The analysis differs from Sheard (1994c) in that the dependent variable is the fraction of the board entering the firm from a bank rather than a dummy variable for one or more bank directors being present. Here, account is taken of the number of bank executives on the board relative to the size of the board. Because bank executives form a subset of externally sourced directors, there is more bunching of the dependent variable at zero (44 per cent of observations). The explanatory variables are a subset of the ones used in the previous section.

The results are reported in Table 7.3. The most satisfactory results are obtained for LEVERAGE, SHARE(1) and LOANSHARE(1): the more highly levered and the larger the loan share of the top lender, the greater the presence of banks on the boards; the larger the top shareholding the less the presence. Insider ownership and firm size reduce the presence of banks, but the coefficients are significant only at the 10 per cent level. Interestingly, BANKSHARE fails to be significant, casting doubt on the result obtained in the previous section.

PROFIT(1) has the correct sign but is not significant. Another measure of profit was tried, PROFIT(2), the ratio of operating income to total assets for the financial year in which the latest bank director entered. This measure has the correct sign and is significant at the 1 per cent level.

Presidents from outside the firm

The most critical director position from a corporate control and managerial incentive perspective is that of president (*shachō*). In 67 per cent of firms listed on the first section of the stock exchange, the president came from the internal promotion hierarchy; in the other 33 per cent of cases the president had entered in mid or late career from outside the firm, sometimes directly into the president's position.

Regression results: logit analysis

This section examines the factors determining whether a firm has an internally or externally sourced president by estimating a logit model for 1991 cross-sectional data. The dependent variable is one if the president came from outside the firm and zero otherwise. (This is extended to the multinomial case in the next section.)[4] The sample consists of 589 first-section listed firms which have experienced a change in president since 1985.

Table 7.4 presents the results of a logit analysis using a number of explanatory variables employed in the earlier analysis. To test whether the appointment of an internal or external president is sensitive to profit performance, a new profit variable is assembled, PROFIT(3), the percentage ratio of operating income to total assets in the financial year immediately preceding the change in president. ASSETS, BANKSHARE, SHARE(1) and INSIDER are the only significant variables in the broadest specification, and all have the expected sign. LEVERAGE, PROFIT(3), FIRMAGE, SHARE(2–3), TOPLENDER and LOANSHARE(1) have the expected signs but are not significant. When an alternative measure of profit performance is used (model 7.4.4), the regression results are only slightly affected, but PROFIT(1) is significant and of the right sign. LEVERAGE becomes significant at the 5 per cent level when the insignificant variables are dropped (models 7.4.1–7.4.3).

Table 7.3 Tobit estimation of proportion of directors entering from banks for listed Japanese firms, 1991

	Significant variables only (model 7.3.1)	Modified model (model 7.3.2)	All explanatory variables (model 7.3.3)
CONSTANT	6.59***	5.92*	5.06*
	(3.05)	(1.93)	(1.83)
ASSETS	−1.46**	−1.43**	−1.09*
	(−1.77)	(−1.70)	(−1.55)
LEVERAGE	0.24***	0.20*	0.18***
	(6.09)	(2.84)	(2.99)
SHARE(1)	−0.33***	−0.31***	−0.28***
	(−7.73)	(−6.45)	(−6.31)
INSIDER	−1.31*	−1.27*	−1.27*
	(−1.38)	(−1.35)	(−1.53)
FIRMAGE	−0.07**	−0.07*	−0.05*
	(−2.29)	(−1.35)	(−1.53)
PROFIT(1)			0.30
			(0.26)
PROFIT(2)	−0.30***	−0.30***	
	(−3.02)	(−2.97)	
BANKSHARE			0.02
			(0.59)
LOANSHARE(1)	0.06***	0.05*	0.03
	(2.80)	(1.62)	(1.26)
LOANSHARE(2–3)		−0.04	−0.05
		(−1.19)	(−1.61)
TOPLENDER		0.22	0.26*
		(1.07)	(1.43)
MITSUI	−8.85***	−8.83***	−7.69***
	(−3.02)	(−3.05)	(−2.93)
MITSUBISHI	3.61*	3.65*	2.83
	(1.68)	(1.67)	(1.60)
SUMITOMO	−4.31	−4.25	−3.02
	(−0.91)	(−0.89)	(−0.70)
FUYO	−0.57	−0.94	−0.83
	(−0.29)	(−0.46)	(−0.51)
SANWA	0.52	0.30	0.20
	(0.32)	(0.19)	(0.14)
DKB	2.45	2.25	1.46
	(1.09)	(0.99)	(0.72)
Log likelihood	−2,141.3	−2,138.9	−2,409.7
No. of observations	940	940	1,016

Notes: Industry dummies are included in all regressions; heteroscedastic consistent t-ratios are in brackets.
*** Significant at 1 per cent confidence level; ** significant at 5 per cent level; * significant at 10 per cent level (one-sided or two-sided test as appropriate).

Table 7.4 Logit estimation of likelihood of president having come from outside firm for listed Japanese firms, 1991

	Dropping profit variable (model 7.4.1)	Changing profit variable (model 7.4.2)	Dropping variables without strong priors (model 7.4.3)	All explanatory variables (model 7.4.4)	All explanatory variables (model 7.4.5)
CONSTANT	0.87	0.61	0.92	0.31	0.62
	(1.37)	(0.92)	(1.42)	(0.36)	(0.72)
ASSETS	−0.37*	−0.35*	−0.37*	−0.32*	−0.34*
	(−1.43)	(−1.46)	(−1.45)	(−1.36)	(−1.35)
LEVERAGE	0.01**	0.01**	0.01**	0.01	0.01
	(2.28)	(1.73)	(1.99)	(0.82)	(0.87)
BANKSHARE	−0.05***	−0.05***	−0.05***	−0.04***	−0.04***
	(−4.55)	(−4.09)	(−4.43)	(−3.71)	(−3.98)
SHARE(1)	0.03***	0.03***	0.03***	0.04***	0.03***
	(2.64)	(2.79)	(2.72)	(3.00)	(2.94)
INSIDER	−0.89***	−0.89***	−0.88***	−0.93***	−0.90***
	(−3.41)	(−3.39)	(−3.34)	(−3.45)	(−3.39)
PROFIT(1)		0.46*		0.46*	
		(1.58)		(1.57)	
PROFIT(3)			−0.02		−0.02
			(−0.64)		(−0.69)
FIRMAGE				−0.00	−0.00
				(−0.67)	(−0.67)
SHARE(2–3)				0.02	0.02
				(0.70)	(0.73)
TOPLENDER				0.01	0.02
				(0.25)	(0.41)
LOANSHARE(1)				0.00	0.00
				(0.62)	(0.50)
LOANSHARE(2–3)				0.00	0.00
				(0.27)	(0.28)
Log likelihood	−294.6	−293.3	−294.4	−292.3	−293.2
No. of observations	589	589	589	589	589

Notes: Industry dummies are included in all regressions; heteroscedastic consistent t-ratios are in brackets. *** Significant at 1 per cent confidence level; ** significant at 5 per cent level; * significant at 10 per cent level (one-sided or two-sided test as appropriate).

Overall the results suggest the following. Firms with a dominant shareholder are more likely to have a president from outside the firm (in most cases from the parent company), while larger firms, firms in which the founding family is still present and firms with high levels of financial institution shareholding are less likely to. There is some evidence that higher leverage and poor profit performance increase the likelihood of having an externally sourced president.

Regression results: multinomial logit analysis

The above analysis does not distinguish between the backgrounds of presidents who have entered from outside the firm. Presidents come from three main sources: non-financial corporations (24.9 per cent of presidents in first-section listed firms); banks and other financial institutions (6.5 per cent); and government bureaucracy and public sector organisations (1.6 per cent). This section extends the binomial logit analysis to the multinomial case in order to see if different factors are at work depending on the source of the outside president. The multinomial analysis allows the coefficients to differ depending on the categories specified.

Table 7.5 presents the results.[5] Less than half of the coefficients are significant, perhaps partly reflecting the low number of occurrences for two of the categories. In the case of presidents who were formerly bank executives, most of the coefficients are of the expected sign, but only LEVERAGE and SHARE(1) are significant. Being more highly levered and not having a dominant top shareholder increased the likelihood of the firm having a former bank executive as president. For presidents who were previously in non-financial corporations, better results are obtained. All of the coefficients (about which there are strong priors) are of the expected sign, and most are significant. Firms with a dominant top shareholder are more likely to have a president from a non-financial corporation, while larger, older firms, firms with high levels of financial shareholding and those with residual family control are less likely to do so.

Focusing on the significant variables, overall the following picture emerges from Table 7.5. Large firms tend to supply presidents to smaller firms (negative sign for ASSETS) in which they have significant top shareholder positions (positive sign for SHARE(1)). Banks tend to supply presidents to firms in which they are large lenders and to firms that do not have a dominant shareholder (negative sign for SHARE(1)).

Interestingly, the sign for BANKSHARE is negative, although it is not significant under a two-sided test in the case of former bank executive presidents. This permits an interesting interpretation, albeit a somewhat speculative one, in the context of these results. If we associate appointments of presidents from outside the firm with capital market intervention — a reasonable interpretation given the institutional facts in Japan — it suggests that to the extent that equity is active it is through the large blockholder effect. There is some support for the stable shareholding view of interlocking shareholdings: high levels of financial institution shareholding in particular work in the direction of increasing incumbent managerial autonomy, at least in normal times (Aoki, Patrick and Sheard 1994; Sheard 1991, 1994a). When banks intervene by supplying a president, it is to firms with large loan exposures relative to their assets, consistent with what we know about the bank intervention function from the case study literature (Sheard 1994b).

Table 7.5 Multinomial logit estimation of background of president for listed Japanese firms, 1991

	Financial institution	Non-financial corporation	Government body
CONSTANT	−0.36	1.93**	−2.55
	(−0.31)	(2.52)	(−1.20)
ASSETS	−0.05	−2.53***	0.12
	(−0.25)	(−2.79)	(0.50)
LEVERAGE	0.02**	0.01	−0.01
	(1.85)	(1.32)	(−0.53)
BANKSHARE	−0.03	−0.05***	−0.07***
	(−1.55)	(−3.93)	(−3.27)
SHARE(1)	−0.08***	0.05***	−0.01
	(−2.54)	(3.79)	(−0.41)
PROFIT(3)	−0.05	−0.04	0.09
	(−0.99)	(−1.19)	(0.90)
INSIDER	−0.53	−1.00***	1.00
	(−1.05)	(−3.33)	(0.90)
FIRMAGE	−0.00	−0.02***	0.02
	(−0.01)	(−2.46)	(0.75)
Number of ones	32	175	10
Log likelihood	−388.3		
No. of observations	589		

Notes: Sample is first-section listed firms whose president as of 1991 had assumed the position since 1985.
Coefficients for internal promotions to president normalised to zero.
Industry and presidents' club dummies not included.
Heteroscedastic consistent t-ratios in brackets.
*** Significant at 1 per cent confidence level.
** Significant at 5 per cent level.
* Significant at 10 per cent level (one-sided or two-sided test as appropriate).

Conclusion

Most directors and CEOs in Japan have risen up through internal promotion hierarchies as lifetime managerial employees. At the same time, Japanese firms implement stable shareholding arrangements which appear to insulate them successfully from the direct threat of external takeovers. Taken together, these two stylised facts might suggest significant scope for managerial moral hazard, at least if one has an open bidding model of corporate control in mind.

What prevents this from occurring? A large part of the answer seems to lie in the fact that, while Japanese firms may be insulated from direct external takeover threats, they are not free from monitoring and control by inside agents. The very coalition of stable shareholders whose collective actions ensure that outsiders cannot intervene in corporate management also enjoy the latent power to do so themselves. There is abundant evidence that large banks, as main banks, and large shareholders, as parent firms, play a key role as the principal agents of direct corporate governance in Japan (Kaplan and Minton 1994; Morck and Nakamura 1992; Sheard 1985, 1987, 1994b).[6] This chapter has sought to cast further light on this insider based system of corporate governance by focusing on the role of outside directors. It is possible to distinguish three kinds of large listed firm in Japan: firms whose top shareholders are banks and other financial institutions; firms which have non-financial firms as leading blockholding shareholders; and firms where there is founding family residual control.

The locus of corporate control in any capitalist economy is the board of directors of the firm. Decisions about hiring and firing top management are made by the board; board members are chosen or their selection ratified at the stockholders' meeting. Ultimate control rights reside with the body of stockholders. Open bidding and insider based systems of corporate control differ in the mechanisms by which control rights are exercised, rather than in the basic logic of the system. In the former system, rights can be transferred and reallocated through the sale of shares (a takeover) or the gathering of votes into blocks (a proxy battle). In the latter system, the stock market arena and stockholders' meeting are bypassed as a direct means of control. Rather, existing large blockholders and main banks directly exercise 'voice' by supplying managers to the board, usually a regular process but sometimes as part of crisis management.

The empirical results obtained here lend support to this emerging view of Japanese corporate governance. One-quarter of Japanese listed firm directors had entered from outside the firm, as had one-third of CEOs. The regression results suggest that these movements are not random, but can be explained in part by financial, ownership and other factors relating to corporate governance, such as presence of a founding family and the size and age of the firm. Outside presence on the board is more pronounced the more highly levered the firm and the more concentrated the main shareholding positions, particularly the top one, and less pronounced the greater the extent of financial institution shareholding, the larger and older the firm, and when there is residual family presence. Bank presence on the board is more pronounced the more highly levered the firm, the larger the top loan share, and when profitability has been low; it is less pronounced the larger the top shareholding, the larger and older the firm, and when family influence is present. Listed firms are more likely to have taken their president from outside the firm the larger the top shareholding, the more highly they are levered, and the less profitable they are; they are less likely to have an outside president the greater the extent of financial institution shareholding, the larger they are, and when there is residual family presence.

Appendix 7.1: Variables and data sources

List of variables used[7]

Dependent variables

OUTSIDEDIR: fraction of total directors listed by Tōyō Keizai Shinpōsha (annual) as having entered from outside the firm.

BANKDIR: fraction of total directors listed by Tōyō Keizai Shinpōsha (annual) as having entered the firm from a bank (where 'bank' refers to any city, trust, long-term credit or regional bank but does not include government financial institutions, insurance companies, agricultural financing cooperatives or other financial institutions).

OUTSIDEPRES(1): one if the president is listed by Tōyō Keizai Shinpōsha (annual) as having entered from outside the firm; zero otherwise.

OUTSIDEPRES(2): zero if the president was internally promoted, one if the president entered from a financial institution, two if from a non-financial corporation, three if from the government or a public sector agency.

Explanatory variables

ASSETS: total assets of the firm (million million yen).

LEVERAGE: percentage ratio of total bank borrowings to total assets.

BANKSHARE: percentage ratio of total shares of firm held by financial institutions.

DIRECTORSHARE: percentage ratio of total shares of firm held by directors.

SHARE(1): percentage shareholding of number one shareholder.

SHARE(2–3): percentage shareholding of numbers two and three shareholders.

SHARE(4–10): percentage shareholding of numbers four to ten shareholders.

LOANSHARE(1): percentage share of total borrowings supplied by number one lender (zero if no borrowings). (Government financial institutions are excluded from the definition of top three lenders, but their loans are a component of total borrowings.)

LOANSHARE(2–3): percentage share of total borrowings supplied by numbers two and three lenders combined (zero if no borrowings).

PROFIT(1): one if operating income (*eigyō rieki*) negative in one of past five years.

PROFIT(2): percentage ratio of operating income to total assets for financial year prior to latest bank executive becoming director.

PROFIT(3): percentage ratio of operating income to total assets for financial year prior to president assuming office.

INSIDER: one if one or more founding family members present on board or among top 20 shareholders; zero otherwise.

FIRMAGE: number of years since firm was established.

TOPLENDER: percentage ratio of borrowings from number one lender to total assets (=LEVERAGE*LOANSHARE(1)).

Presidents' club dummy variables

MITSUI: member of Mitsui group presidents' club (Nimoku-kai).

MITSUBISHI: member of Mitsubishi group presidents' club (Kin'yō-kai).

SUMITOMO: member of Sumitomo group presidents' club (Hakusui-kai).

FUYO: member of Fuyō (Fuji Bank) group presidents' club (Fuyō-kai).

SANWA: member of Sanwa group presidents' club (Sansui-kai).

DKB: member of DKB (Daiichi Kangyō Bank) group presidents' club (Sankin-kai).

Industry dummy variables

FOOD: food processing and marine products industries.

MINING: mining, petroleum and coal industries.

CONSTRUCT: construction industry.

TEXTILE: textiles industry.

CHEMICAL: chemicals, pharmaceuticals, paper/pulp, rubber and glass industries.

METAL: metal and steel industries.

MACHINE: machinery, electrical, transportation and precision equipment industries.[8]

COMMERCE: commerce, financial and securities industries.

SERVICE: real estate and service industries.

TRANSPORT: transport and utilities industries.

INDUSTRY(1): sum of CONSTRUCT, METAL and MACHINE.

INDUSTRY(2): sum of FOOD, CONSTRUCT, CHEMICAL, METAL, MACHINE, COMMERCE and SERVICE.

Descriptive statistics of variables
Table A7.1.1 Continuous variables[a]

	Mean	Standard deviation	Minimum	Maximum
OUTSIDEDIR	23.840	18.949	0.000	96.667
BANKDIR	5.062	7.235	0.000	82.609
ASSETS	0.352	0.896	0.003	11.088
LEVERAGE	0.170	0.174	0.000	0.936
BANKSHARE	41.204	13.627	1.565	78.344
SHARE(1)	14.843	13.395	2.300	72.030
SHARE(2–3)	10.510	3.602	1.430	35.030
SHARE(4–10)	19.560	4.920	3.090	36.300
FIRMAGE	52.787	16.601	6.000	122.000
LOANSHARE(1)[b]	23.666	17.790	0.000	100.000
LOANSHARE(2–3)[c]	23.374	13.510	0.000	66.667
PROFIT(2)[d]	4.634	4.080	−25.032	53.445
PROFIT(3)[e]	4.513	3.988	−17.031	53.446
TOPLENDER[b]	4.236	5.046	0.000	52.764

Notes:
 a The sample is 1,064 unless otherwise stated.
 b The sample is 1,025.
 c The sample is 1,016.
 d The sample is 985.
 e The sample is 619.

Table A7.1.2 Dummy variables

	Zeros	Ones
OUTSIDEPRES(1)	725	339
INSIDER	683	381
PROFIT(1)	925	139
MITSUI	1,045	19
MITSUBISHI	1,042	22
SUMITOMO	1,048	16
FUYO	1,041	23
SANWA	1,028	36
DKB	1,026	38
FOOD	1,002	62
MINING	1,048	16
CONSTRUCT	967	97
TEXTILE	1,018	46
CHEMICAL	875	189
METAL	977	87
MACHINE	764	300
COMMERCE	916	148
SERVICE	1,019	45

Data sources

Data for the dependent variables, bank borrowings and loan shares, shareholdings of the top shareholder(s), membership of a presidents' club and for the construction of industry dummy variables were obtained from Tōyō Keizai Shinpōsha (1991).

Data on total shareholdings of financial institutions, non-financial corporations and directors, and total assets and operating income were obtained from the NEEDS-Kigyō Zaimu [Corporate Financial] electronic database and from Nihon Keizai Shinbunsha (annual).

Data on the presence of an inside owner and inside owner shareholdings were obtained from Tōyō Keizai Shinpōsha (1991) and Nihon Keizai Shinbunsha (1991a).

Data on the year of establishment of firms and year of stock exchange listing were obtained from Nihon Keizai Shinbunsha (1991a).

Data on the year that the president gained that position as of 1991 were obtained from Nihon Keizai Shinbunsha (1991b).

Notes

1. These figures are computed from a database compiled by the author from Tōyō Keizai Shinpōsha's *Kigyō Keiretsu Sōran*.
2. For an analysis of the role that arm's-length investors play in the Japanese system, see Sheard (1994a).
3. There are alternative explanations: that such firms are less attractive destinations for managers separating from other listed firms and financial institutions; or that they are better run so that there is less need for capital market supervision and intervention. It is hard to distinguish these effects in the current study. Still, the hypothesis in the text seems most compelling, particularly given that many notable cases of failure and bank intervention have involved firms with inside owners — Ataka & Co., Daishowa Paper and Tōyō Kōgyō (Mazda), for instance (see Sheard 1985, 1994b for details).
4. See Kang and Shivdasani (1995) for another recent analysis of this issue.
5. The estimation procedure required that dummy variables be omitted.
6. See Sheard (1994a) for analysis of the important *indirect* role that peripheral investors play in the Japanese system.
7. Unless otherwise stated, all data for variables are for the 1990 financial year, ending in March 1991. Data for the dependent variables are as of July 1991.
8. This is the omitted industry dummy in the regressions, any effect of which is captured in the intercept term.

References

Aoki, Masahiko (1988), *Information, Incentives, and Bargaining in the Japanese Economy*, Cambridge, MA: Cambridge University Press.

—— (1994), 'Monitoring Characteristics of the Main Banks System: An Analytical and Developmental View', in Masahiko Aoki and Hugh Patrick (eds), *The Japanese Main Bank System: Its Relevancy for Developing and Transforming Economies*, Oxford: Oxford University Press, pp. 109–41.

Aoki, Masahiko, Hugh Patrick and Paul Sheard (1994), 'The Japanese Main Bank System: An Introductory Overview', in Masahiko Aoki and Hugh Patrick (eds), *The Japanese Main Bank System: Its Relevancy for Developing and Transforming Economies*, Oxford: Oxford University Press, pp. 3–50.

Coffee, John C., Jr (1991), 'Liquidity versus Control: The Institutional Investor as Corporate Monitor', *Columbia Law Review*, 91, pp. 1,277–368.

Flath, David (1996), 'The *Keiretsu* Puzzle', *Journal of the Japanese and International Economies* (forthcoming).

Hoshi, Takeo, Anil Kashyap and David Scharfstein (1990), 'The Role of Banks in Reducing the Costs of Financial Distress in Japan', *Journal of Financial Economics*, 27 (1), pp. 67–88.

Kang, Jun-Koo and Anil Shivdasani (1995), 'Firm Performance, Corporate Governance, and Top Executive Turnover in Japan', *Journal of Financial Economics*, 38 (1), pp. 29–58.

Kaplan, Steven N. (1994), 'Top Executive Rewards and Firm Performance: A Comparison of Japan and the U.S.', *Journal of Political Economy*, 102 (3), pp. 510–46.

Kaplan, Steven N. and Bernadette Alcamo Minton (1994), 'Appointments of Outsiders to Japanese Boards: Determinants and Implications for Managers', *Journal of Financial Economics*, 36, pp. 225–58.

Keizai Chōsa Kyōkai (annual), *Nenpō Keiretsu no Kenkyū: Daiichibu Jōjō Kigyōhen* [Corporate Affiliation Annual Directory: First-Section Listed Firm Edition], Tokyo: Keizai Chōsa Kyōkai.

Morck, Randall and Masao Nakamura (1992), Banks and Corporate Control in Japan, University of Alberta, Alberta (mimeo).

Nakatani, Iwao (1984), 'The Economic Role of Financial Corporate Grouping', in Masahiko Aoki (ed.), *The Economic Analysis of the Japanese Firm*, Amsterdam: North-Holland, pp. 227–58.

Nihon Keizai Shinbunsha (annual), *Kaisha Nenkan: Jōjō Kaishaban* [Company Annual: Listed Firm Edition], Tokyo: Nihon Keizai Shinbunsha.

—— (1991a), *Nikkei Kaisha Jōhō, '92-I Shinshungō* [Nikkei Corporate Information, 1992/I edition], Tokyo: Nihon Keizai Shinbunsha.

—— (1991b), *Yakuin Shikihō Jōjō Kaishaban, 1992 Nenban* [Quarterly of Directors, 1992 Listed Firm Edition], Tokyo: Nihon Keizai Shinbunsha.

Roe, Mark J. (1993), 'Some Differences in Corporate Structure in Germany, Japan, and the United States', *Yale Law Journal*, 102 (8), pp. 1,927–2,003.

Sheard, Paul (1985), 'Main Banks and Structural Adjustment in Japan', *Pacific Economic Papers*, 129, Australia–Japan Research Centre, Australian National University, Canberra.

—— (1987), 'How Japanese Firms Manage Industrial Adjustment: A Case Study of Aluminium', *Pacific Economic Papers*, 151, Australia–Japan Research Centre, Australian National University, Canberra.

—— (1989), 'The Main Bank System and Corporate Monitoring and Control in Japan', *Journal of Economic Behavior and Organization*, 11, pp. 399–422.

—— (1991), 'The Economics of Interlocking Shareholding', *Ricerche Economiche*, 45 (2–3), pp. 421–48.

—— (1994a), 'Interlocking Shareholdings and Corporate Governance', in Masahiko Aoki and Ronald Dore (eds), *The Japanese Firm: Sources of Competitive Strength*, Oxford: Oxford University Press, pp. 310–49.

—— (1994b), 'Main Banks and the Governance of Financial Distress', in Masahiko Aoki and Hugh Patrick (eds), *The Japanese Main Bank System: Its Relevancy for Developing and Transforming Economies*, Oxford: Oxford University Press, pp. 188–230.

—— (1994c), 'Bank Executives on Japanese Corporate Boards', *Bank of Japan Monetary and Economic Studies*, 12 (2), pp. 85–121.

Tōyō Keizai Shinpōsha (annual), *Kigyō Keiretsu Sōran* [Directory of Corporate Affiliations], Tokyo: Tōyō Keizai Shinpōsha (various issues).

Part III

The Financial System: Present and Future

8 The financial system and corporate competitiveness

Masasuke Ide

Japan's traditional financial system

The 'indirect financing system'

Japan is generally thought of as a capitalistic, market based economy. In terms of its mechanisms for allocating economic resources, however, the Japanese economic system differs significantly from that of the United States. During postwar reconstruction and the period of rapid economic growth that followed, the public and private elites of Japan worked together to establish a consensus concerning the nation's priorities; for better or for worse, they have carried out a strategic allocation of resources according to that consensus. Although the free market approach predominating in the United States has, of course, also been used, the major characteristic of Japanese capitalism has been the strategic allocation, or targeting, of resources by political, bureaucratic and business leaders.

The financial system has been a key component of this resource allocation system. Table 8.1 summarises my view of the characteristics of Japan's traditional financial system and capital market. It shows that free market principles may have been violated or restricted in a wide range of areas. While many restrictions were gradually eased or abolished during the 1980s in the process of the liberalisation and internationalisation of finance, some parts of the traditional system — including the stock ownership structure — are still firmly entrenched. Japan's financial system has been elaborately constructed and controlled; in many ways it is the very opposite of the open US system, which was designed to create the conditions for an efficient market (see, for example, Sharpe and Alexander 1990, pp. 77–8). The large discrepancy in the number of financial organisations in Japan and the United States (Table 8.2) is symbolic of the difference between the two systems. The extremely diversified format of the American system stands in marked contrast to the highly concentrated configuration of the Japanese one.

In contrast to other countries, Japan carried out postwar reconstruction and achieved high economic growth without depending on foreign loans or capital in any

Table 8.1   Characteristics of Japan's traditional financial system

Isolation from the rest of the world	Foreign exchange control laws. Foreign capital laws. Severe restrictions on raising capital from overseas.
High savings policy	Fiscal and institutional incentives for high savings. Emphasis on bank deposits and postal savings. Restraints on consumer credit and home mortgage loans. Underdeveloped welfare programs.
Strategic allocation of capital	Allocation of capital in accordance with the priorities of industrial policy. Strong emphasis on the manufacturing and public utilities industries.
Public financial institutions	Postal savings system supplementing and competing with private financial institutions. Several government banks specialising in non-commercial loans and investments.
Capital allocation through the banking system	Limited choice of financial products for small savers. Underdeveloped money and bond markets.
Tight control of financial institutions	Channelling of savings from household to industrial sector through a small number of financial institutions. Tight control over the activities of financial institutions by the Ministry of Finance and Bank of Japan.
Interest rate controls	Adoption of low interest rate policy. Tight controls on all interest rates and terms of new bond issues.
Emphasis on collateral	Collateral required for all borrowings and bonds.
Interlocking relations between companies and financial institutions	Development of business groups centred around large banks. Main bank system. Stable and cross-ownership of stocks.

Table 8.2   Major financial institutions in Japan and the United States (number)

	Japan	United States
Banks	153	11,449
Life insurance companies	27	1,944
Non-life insurance companies	25	3,914
Securities companies	210	7,805
Investment advisory companies	615	18,000

Note: Figures for Japan are for end of calendar year 1991 (for banks, securities companies and investment advisory companies) and for end of fiscal year 1991 (for life and non-life insurance companies). All US figures are for the end of calendar year 1992.

Source: Japan: Nihon Ginkō (1992), *Economic Statistics Annual 1991*, Tokyo, for all groups except investment advisory companies; Investment Advisory Industry Association of Japan (1992), *1991 Fact Book*, Tokyo, for investment advisory companies.

United States: *FDIC Statistics on Banking* (1994) for banks; American Council of Life Insurance (1994), *1994 Life Insurance Fact Book*, Washington DC, for life insurance companies; Insurance Information Institute (1994), *Property/Casualty Insurance Facts*, New York, for non-life insurance companies; Securities and Exchange Commission (1995), *SEC Annual Report 1994*, for securities companies and investment advisory companies.

significant way. Japanese leaders saw a need to encourage savings by the household sector, to absorb these small parcels of savings efficiently at low cost, and to allocate them strategically in accordance with the nation's priorities. This required the establishment of a system that relied on a limited number of large financial institutions (particularly large commercial banks) to act as intermediaries in the mobilisation and allocation of capital. Suzuki (1974, pp. 18–22) called this the 'indirect financing system'.

Domestic savings alone were not sufficient to overcome the problems of poor endowment of raw materials, limited basic technologies and a scarcity of capital. To fund development, Japan also needed large amounts of foreign exchange, particularly US dollars. Expanding exports became an urgent priority; and strengthening the international competitiveness of major companies constituted the core of the nation's economic policy. To this end, Japanese companies adopted a common competitive strategy of marketing 'high-quality products at low prices', a strategy that required steady access to low-cost capital regardless of the company's short-run financial performance.

Largely because Japan was at the time a relatively small economy, it was not necessary for its leaders to assume that the cost of capital was set by an open market and thus beyond government control. A more rational approach to survival in the international marketplace was to lower the cost of capital for strategically important companies while rationing capital to the rest. These strategically important companies typically belonged to basic manufacturing, transportation, public utilities, or the financial and international trading industries. They were members of established *keiretsu* or business groups, were listed on the first section of the Tokyo and Osaka stock exchanges and had main banks. They enjoyed preferential treatment in public bond offerings, and their stocks were characterised by a high proportion of stable shareholdings, often cross-held by 'relationship' investors.

For a long time Japan openly provided certain industries with debt capital at artificially low interest rates (Suzuki 1974, pp. 38–61). Although it is not the only country to have adopted this strategy to achieve international competitiveness, it is one of the few to have done so extensively and systematically. In his latest book, Calder (1993) also emphasises the role of the capital allocation mechanism in Japan, and in particular the importance of large commercial and industrial banks in the allocation of capital. He pays little attention, however, to the importance of equity capital, share ownership structure and stock valuation in Japan's postwar economic development.

A system which effectively reduces the cost of equity capital below that which would prevail in an open market offers competitive advantages to the corporations operating under it. As discussed in detail later, the unique features of Japan's capital market — such as the main bank system, stable stockholdings and the cross-holding of stocks — have all made it possible for Japan's major companies to reduce substantially their cost of equity capital.

In designing a system that could consistently provide capital on a priority basis to large companies at low cost, Japan adopted the following approach.

- It financed industrial activities primarily through low-cost debt capital while minimising the use of high-cost equity capital.
- Increasing the use of debt while keeping the cost of equity capital low would have been difficult if debt and equity capital were to be raised separately in an open market with a large number of outside investors. Accordingly, a system was developed in which capital was provided primarily by a small number of financial institutions, based on their long-term, interlocking shareholding relationships with the borrowing company. This allowed companies to obtain debt and equity capital on a long-term basis as a package.

Stock ownership structure and the role of main banks

As long as value creation activities are entrusted mainly to investor owned stock companies, all nations — the United States and Japan included — face the challenge of how to lower the cost of equity capital to a reasonable level. Through requiring public disclosure of information and encouraging the development of a large number of investment professionals, US capitalism has tried to achieve this goal by fostering the conditions necessary to create an 'efficient' market. Policy in Japan to achieve the same goal has been geared rather towards constructing longstanding and interlocking relationships among companies, and between companies and major financial institutions. Such arrangements as stable stockholding and the cross-holding of shares are an essential element in this. The stock ownership structures in Japan and the United States clearly reflect the differences in these two approaches.

Table 8.3 Stock ownership structure in Japan and the United States[a] (per cent)

	Japan	United States
Institutional investor	15	44
Relationship investor		
Financial institution	47	12
Other company	11	9
Parent or group company	17	3
Founder or family	4	10
Individual	3	19
Other	4	4
Total	100	100

Note: a   Composition of top five stockholders.
Source: MITI (1989), pp. 100–1.

Table 8.3 shows the results of a survey of the top five stockholders of large Japanese and US companies, conducted by the Ministry of International Trade and Industry. As can be seen, in the United States major stockholders are more likely to be 'pure financial investors': institutions and individuals interested mainly in financial returns. In Japan, ownership is overwhelmingly weighted towards 'relationship stockholding' wherein investment goes hand in hand with a key business relationship. The relationship might be between a parent company and its subsidiaries, a bank and its borrowers, a company and a major customer, or companies within the same business group.

In short, one major difference between the United States and Japan is the preponderance of pure financial investors in the former and of relationship investors in the latter. Indeed, the very concept of stable stockholding in Japan amounts to a company selecting its major stockholders. This clearly contravenes the basic spirit of companies going public; in the United States, stocks are presumably made widely available to general investors. However, the Japanese approach — in which resource allocation and the terms of trade are decided mutually through face-to-face negotiation between the parties concerned — can equally be considered highly rational and consistent with Japan's economic system.

Another major difference between the two countries concerns the extent of cross-holding of shares. Cross-holding occurs when two firms hold shares in each other, either directly, as when firm A holds shares in firm B and firm B holds shares in firm A, or indirectly, as when firm A holds shares in firm B, firm B holds shares in firm C, and firm C holds shares in firm A. Although there are no official statistics on cross-holding (as opposed to shareholding) per se, this practice is widespread among listed companies and banks in Japan. According to a recent Fair Trade Commission report (1994, pp. 22–37) on the six major corporate groups, for example, cross-ownership arrangements existed in 76 per cent of the member companies of the Mitsui, Mitsubishi and Sumitomo groups as at the end of fiscal year 1992. Of the outstanding stocks of these companies, 28 per cent were cross-held among group members.

In contrast, cross-holdings are hardly conceivable in the United States, where managers are evaluated primarily in terms of the company's financial returns. Cross-holding tends to overstate the equity base. If it results in the accommodation of low profitability, as this chapter argues, a low reported return on equity will result. Moreover, if cross-holding relationships involve some kind of reciprocal or preferential business dealings, as is often claimed to be the case in Japan, they could be considered to contravene US antitrust laws. One may therefore conclude that the cross-holding of stocks in the Japanese sense, if it occurs at all, will be marginal in the United States.

A third difference in stock ownership structures concerns the relationship between the issuers of shares and banks and other financial institutions. In the United States and in Japan, large companies have recently substantially diversified their sources of financing, particularly in the area of debt and hybrid securities possessing both debt and equity characteristics. Examples include junk bonds in the United States, and convertible and warrant bonds in Japan. The chief difference between Japanese and American companies lies in the nature of the diversification of sources of capital. In the United States, companies have diversified not only the forms of financing, but also their relationships with creditors and investors, who may have conflicting or competing interests. Companies are creating all kinds of financial 'claims' with differing risk/return characteristics to maximise the market value of the cash flow stream generated by the business; they are selling these to investors who are interested only in one particular slice of the total corporate cash flow pie. These claims essentially represent bundles of contracts that stipulate the conditions and relative seniorities of each claim against the total cash flow. Although this poses no problem when the business is going well, the conflicting interests of creditors and investors may lead to a scramble for a portion of the diminished cash flow if the business turns sour.

In the Japanese case, although major companies have gradually distanced themselves from their banks in recent years, the traditional pattern has been for a small number of large financial institutions to commit themselves, virtually as a package, to the company at all levels of its capital structure. The most notable example is the case of the firm's relationship with a 'main bank', in which a company establishes a particularly close relationship with a large commercial or industrial bank. The main bank usually supplies short and long-term loans to the firm and is often a major holder of straight and convertible bonds. As well, it is a large stockholder in the firm. (This stands in sharp contrast to the US system, where commercial banks are prohibited by banking laws from owning stocks.) This kind of relationship is still maintained (though to a lesser degree than previously) in the dealings with corporate clients of almost all Japan's major financial institutions, including long-term credit banks, trust banks and life insurance companies. As a result, diversification of financing for most large Japanese companies has thus far mainly meant a diversification of the forms of financing, but not of relationships with creditors and investors.

When a financial institution commits itself to meeting all of a company's needs for capital, conflicts of interest among different parts of the total corporate cash flow become much less acute. Both the company's managers and the financial institution can then focus on the growth of the total business at the cost of a relatively low return on equity capital. Moreover, this arrangement means that the company can raise needed debt capital even with a low interest charge coverage or high debt to equity capital ratio. Stock investment motivated by relationships leads to a considerably different stock market from the one that results when pure financial investment is the norm. I call the Japanese approach 'relationship investment' (Ide 1994, p. 87).

Table 8.4 summarises my view of the main characteristics of investors in the United States and Japan. In the US approach, the primary purpose of stock investment is to realise the maximum possible financial returns via dividends and capital gains. In Japan, this is usually not the sole or even necessarily the main purpose of stockholding. Rather, it represents an important device to cement business relationships between two companies, or between a company and a financial institution. Banks hold shares, but they also lend large amounts, hold bonds, manage settlement accounts and provide a range of financial services. Insurance companies are principal shareholders, provide loans and hold bonds, in addition to selling insurance products to the firm, its affiliated companies and its employees. Manufacturing and trading companies hold shares in the firms that they sell to or purchase from. Cross-holding also serves to promote mutual trust, with cooperation between the managements of companies and financial institutions helping to protect both against the threat of takeover (Nakatani 1984).

Such relationships offer an obvious competitive advantage in terms of the cost of capital. When the main purpose of stock investment is to develop and maintain a long-term and interlocking relationship, and when the total return includes non-financial returns from other parts of the relationship for major shareholders, they can more easily tolerate a relatively low return on their equity investment.

Even more important is the day-to-day sharing of business information that goes on between a company and a financial institution. Because of the long-term and

Table 8.4 Characteristics of major shareholders in Japan and the United States

	Japan	United States
Investment objectives	Multiple: integrated financing, business relationships such as insurance, financial services, input–output ties	Purely financial: dividend plus capital gain
Degree of freedom to sell	Small	Large
Relationship with the issuing company	Long-term; interlocking; de facto business partner; de facto insider	Temporary; buy if underpriced, sell if overpriced; arm's-length outsider
Type of risk involved	Business and financial risk	Pure financial market risk
Means to control risk	Sharing of information; strong commitment to management; development of interlocking relations	Public disclosure; fundamental analysis; diversification

comprehensive relationship that is fostered, information is shared at all organisational levels through formal and informal contacts. This is especially important in the company's relationship with its main bank. Main banks not only bear the credit and investment risks of their major clients, but they also essentially share the business risks as well. The main bank is thus for all practical purposes a business partner of the client company. In this role, the main bank naturally commits itself to providing all types of capital. Conversely, it also expects to have full access to information about the company, even posting its own managers to the firm if necessary (Fair Trade Commission 1994, pp. 22–37). Such involvement effectively reduces the business risk for the main bank, thereby lowering the cost of capital, or the minimum required financial return, for the company.

In the US approach, in which companies tap a broad base of creditors and investors, each with separate interests, the oft-cited problem of 'agency costs' may become a serious issue. These are costs that arise from the imperfect monitoring of managers by investors and from conflicts of interest among different classes of investors. The Japanese system may well be effective in reducing agency costs. Bank–company relationships similar to those in Japan can be found in Germany, France and elsewhere. However, the idea of long-term, interlocking relationships runs counter to the philosophy of the US system, which is based on the belief that companies should remain at arm's length from banks and investors.[1]

One of the conditions for efficient stock price formation is an emphasis on pure financial returns rather than on the control aspect of common stock investments. In the relationship investment typical of Japan, the control aspect is of far greater importance than in the United States.

It should be noted that in Japan economic activities are, in large part, carried out by companies that are investor owned and whose shares are traded on the stock exchange; these firms are run by professional managers. In this sense, corporate ownership and management are as fully separated in Japan as in the United States. However, since three-quarters of all outstanding shares of listed companies are held by business partners or financial institutions with which the company maintains close business relations, ownership and management can also be said to be unified in a unique way. Unlike entrepreneur owned companies, which also typically feature unified ownership and management, the top managers of large Japanese companies and banks almost always work on a salaried basis; they do not invest a large amount of their own money in the company or bear much personal risk as owners. As personal risk is not at issue, relationship shareholders can easily sacrifice financial returns on equity investment if other goals, such as expanding the business, increasing exports or maintaining lifelong employment, are considered to have a higher priority.

Stock valuation in Japan

In any well-developed capital market, stock price changes tend to be random; returns usually conform to a normal distribution in the short run and have a positive skewness in the long run.[2] The primary risk of owning common stocks is the high chance of a negative change in stock price. The traditional Japanese financial system faced a fundamental dilemma in that major commercial banks, whose primary source of capital was short-term, fixed interest paying deposits, were expected to have large holdings of common stocks, the riskiest type of financial asset. The book value of the common stock investment of city banks at the end of fiscal year 1994 amounted to ¥23.9 trillion, or approximately 1.6 times the banks' book equity capital (Bank of Japan 1995, p. 32, 35).

From the point of view of the asset liability management of a financial institution with 95 per cent or more of its capital in the form of short-term, fixed interest bearing obligations, it could be fatal to hold a large portfolio of common stocks whose returns fluctuated wildly and which had a high chance in the short run of negative returns. The basic precondition for a bank to play the role of a major, stable shareholder was to make common stock a quasi-fixed income security; ownership would then not jeopardise the main business of commercial and industrial lending.

Financial institutions originally resolved this problem by demanding that borrowing companies commit to stable payment of dividends as long as they were making a profit, and also by asking for preemptive rights to subscribe to any new issue of common stocks at or below par (normally ¥50). The minimum dividend level was set at ¥5, so that stable investors could count on a 10 per cent current return on their common stock portfolio. This was more or less the average effective lending rate for large financial institutions in those days.

Since banks and insurance companies were expected to become stable relationship shareholders, they would not regularly trade stocks purely for financial gain. This does not mean that capital gains were considered unimportant. Unrealised capital gains over and above the historical average book cost of equity investment were important to the management of banks and other financial institutions as a buffer for stabilising their financial results or as a reserve for contingencies. However, capital gains, which might or might not be realised, were an unreliable source of return for these institutions, whose primary source of current return on common stock investment was the dividend yield. The countable or floor value of subscribing to any new issue of common stocks was ¥50: a stable stream of ¥5 dividend for eternity divided by 10 per cent, the opportunity cost of capital.

For borrowing companies, this system meant that an after-tax return of at least 10 per cent was required on their equity capital, a very high cost compared with that of debt capital. It was, however, an essential one if firms were to maintain their relationships with financial institutions, and especially with the main bank, which guaranteed in return stable access to capital, both debt and equity, regardless of short-term financial performance.

As long-term, stable shareholders, the financial institutions were unable to play an active role in stock market pricing of stocks; this was, rather, the role of general, outside investors. However, as well-informed insiders, underwriting the health of borrowing companies through their commitment to remaining stable shareholders (or de facto business partners), large banks were able to act as 'delegated monitors', so to speak, for outside investors.

In the area of lending, the role of main banks as delegated monitors is a well-accepted concept. Representing the group of lenders, main banks are typically expected to monitor the business and financial performances of borrowing companies, assess their creditworthiness and new investment projects, and commit further financial and managerial resources when a firm experiences financial distress (Oba and Horiuchi 1990; Sheard 1994). If main banks, as delegated monitors, play a valuable role in the lending market, which consists of a relatively small number of well-trained and sophisticated professional managers, it is clear that they would play an even more valuable role in the stock market, which consists of a large number of relatively unsophisticated small public investors.

Unlike large financial institutions, outside investors have traditionally lacked investment opportunities beyond postal savings accounts and bank deposits; their opportunity cost of capital was considered to be much lower than that of the institutions. Based on the average available return on a one-year deposit, which was something like 5 per cent for a small investor, a common stock with a strong commitment to a stable ¥5 dividend could be as valuable as ¥100 (¥5 divided by 5 per cent, the small investor's opportunity cost of capital). In other words, for an outside investor the fixed income value of the common stock was ¥100, or twice as much as the par value.

Common stocks also came with a preemptive right for shareholders to buy additional shares at par when companies issued new stocks. As long as the market price of the stock was above ¥50, this option to subscribe to the new share had market value. For a one-to-one new issue, the preemptive right had a market value of ¥50 if the fixed income value of the stock remained at ¥100 before and after the new issue. The most important precondition for allowing companies to make new equity issues was the strong expectation among shareholders that the firm would be able to maintain its current dividend. In those days, the stock price started to rise quickly to reflect the value of the option as soon as news of a new issue reached the market. The theoretical cum-right price was ¥150. If the market anticipated more than one new issue, the stock price would rise even higher.

By adding a strong commitment to a fixed dividend payment to a preemptive right to subscribe to new issues, Japanese common stocks were transmuted to unique option securities: quasi-fixed income securities with warrants to buy future issues of common stocks at an exercise price of ¥50 (par) or less.

This situation was ideal for main banks because it guaranteed the accumulation of unrealised capital gains on their stock investments. Stock prices set in the secondary market were almost always way above the average book costs of stock investment for banks. This meant that during the high economic growth era they could meet the request to subscribe to frequent new issues of stocks to finance the capital hungry business sector without the fear of fluctuations in daily stock prices jeopardising their lending business.

The idea of pricing new issues at or near the market price was introduced around 1970, first by marginal companies in emerging industries and then gradually by many established companies in major industries who were the traditional clients of major banks. This was a clear breach of the traditional (tacit) agreement between banks and major borrowers and created a major difficulty for the banks. Although the marginal cost of subscribing to new equity issues was often 10 or more times the traditional ¥50, the banks were still expected to maintain stable ownership. The system effectively triggered a slow but steady process of 'marking to market' the average cost of banks' stock investments, eliminating most unrealised capital gains and threatening the traditional guarantee against capital losses on stock investment portfolios.

Borrowing companies met this challenge by introducing a voluntary program to distribute systematically the capital surplus raised through new issues of stocks at market price to existing shareholders, in the form of free distributions of stocks on a regular basis, while at the same time promising to maintain stable dividends per share. This program reduced the average book cost of stock investments for banks while increasing the dividend received.

A more fundamental solution was to build in various mechanisms whose combined effect was to limit the downside risk of the stock market while leaving the upward potential wide open. The following were some of the key elements underpinning this effort:

- a general consensus that price stability, and especially avoiding severe drops in price, was desirable;
- main banks as lenders of last resort, and a general consensus that major listed companies should not be allowed to go bankrupt;
- large securities companies acting as floor members on all stock exchanges, if necessary mobilising all their resources to stabilise the market;[3]
- a mechanism to allow 'wash sales' so as to neutralise the market impact of sales of large blocks of stocks by major banks (cross or matched trading) for such reasons as realising capital gains on stock portfolios to boost accounting profit for reporting purposes;
- a lack of instruments, such as stock index futures and options, to systematically bed against the market; and
- a strong commitment by the government to maintaining the stock price index at a certain level, as evidenced by recent widely publicised unofficial and informal efforts by the Ministry of Finance which, as a package, came to be known as price keeping operations.

All of these effectively limited the downside risk of stock investment, especially for investors whose investment horizon was longer than one year. Indeed, over 15 years starting January 1974, an investor who adopted a strategy of buying a complete market portfolio at the beginning of each month and holding it for two years would not on any occasion find the initial investment eroded in the 169 trials during those 15 years. This means that the Japanese stock market behaved during those years as if it was a perfect stock call option with a two-year maturity (as opposed to a common stock) in terms of price changes. Figure 8.1, which compares patterns in price changes of the leading stock market indexes for the United States and Japan, shows that the downside risk was hedged much more effectively in Japan than in the United States for investment time horizons of 12 months and 24 months (see Ide 1993 for further discussion).

A stock call option as compared to a common stock has the following characteristics.

- Holders of a call option do not question whether the price of the underlying asset (in this case a common stock) is higher or lower than its fundamental value.
- The higher the price of the underlying asset, the more valuable is the call option.
- With the downside risk effectively hedged, more volatility in the stock price is a positive rather than a negative factor.

JAPANESE FIRMS, FINANCE AND MARKETS

Figure 8.1   Distribution of stock market returns for different holding periods, January 1974 – December 1989 (per cent net price change per year)

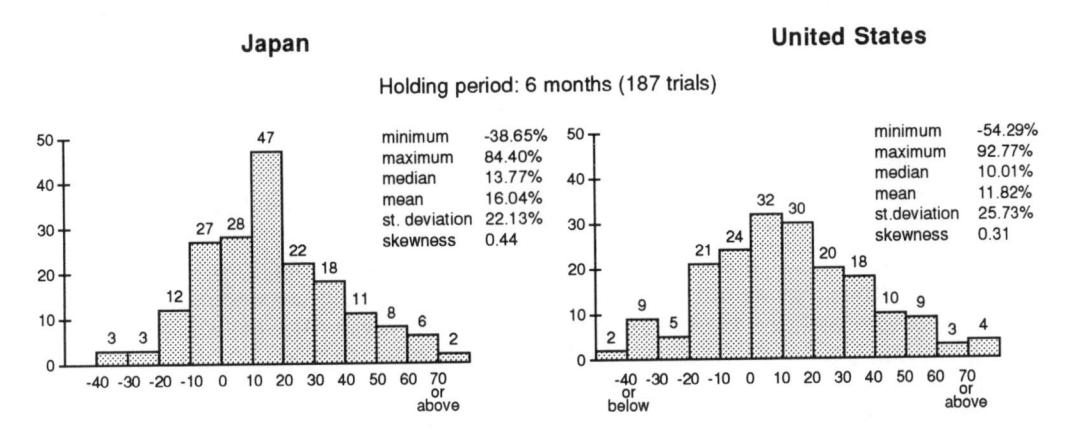

Japan   United States

Holding period: 6 months (187 trials)

Japan:
- minimum: -38.65%
- maximum: 84.40%
- median: 13.77%
- mean: 16.04%
- st. deviation: 22.13%
- skewness: 0.44

United States:
- minimum: -54.29%
- maximum: 92.77%
- median: 10.01%
- mean: 11.82%
- st. deviation: 25.73%
- skewness: 0.31

Holding period: 12 months (181 trials)

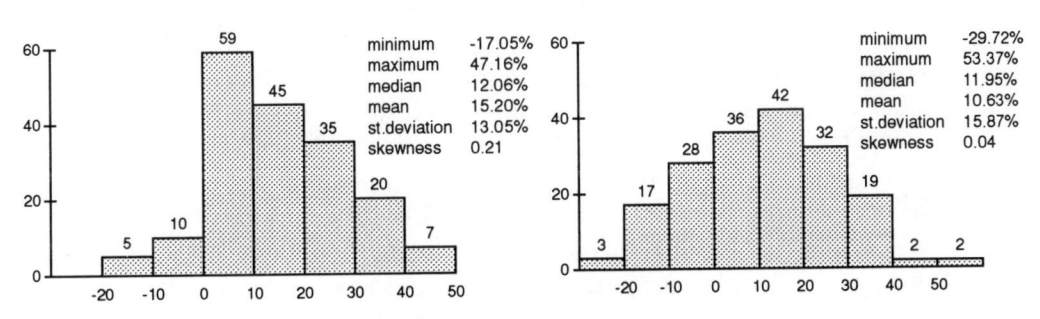

Japan:
- minimum: -17.05%
- maximum: 47.16%
- median: 12.06%
- mean: 15.20%
- st. deviation: 13.05%
- skewness: 0.21

United States:
- minimum: -29.72%
- maximum: 53.37%
- median: 11.95%
- mean: 10.63%
- st. deviation: 15.87%
- skewness: 0.04

Holding period: 24 months (169 trials)

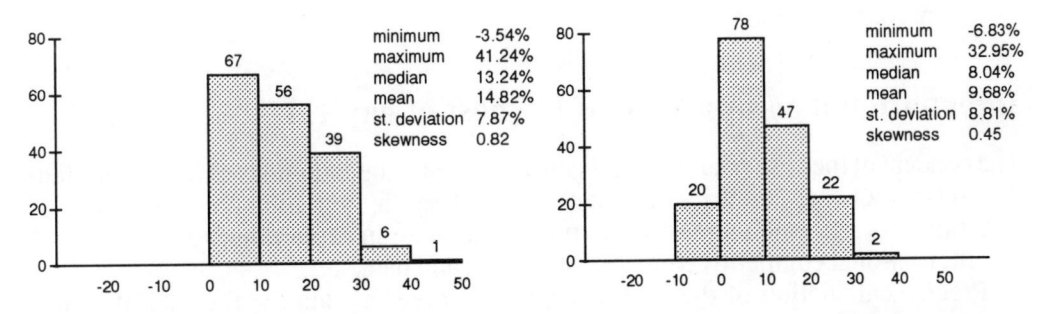

Japan:
- minimum: -3.54%
- maximum: 41.24%
- median: 13.24%
- mean: 14.82%
- st. deviation: 7.87%
- skewness: 0.82

United States:
- minimum: -6.83%
- maximum: 32.95%
- median: 8.04%
- mean: 9.68%
- st. deviation: 8.81%
- skewness: 0.45

Note: Vertical axis shows number of occurrences and horizontal axis annualised per cent net price change. To compute net price change for each holding period, end of month numbers of the NRI 350 composite stock price index (for Japan) and S&P 500 composite stock price index (for the United States) were used.

Source: Japan: Nomura Research Institute (1990), *NRI 400 Handbook*, Tokyo; United States: Standard and Poor's Corporation (1990), *Standard and Poor's Analyst's Handbook*, New York.

In summary, until the market crashed in 1990, the Japanese stock market was designed in such a way that price changes would conform more to the pattern of option securities than to that of pure common stocks. In the first half of the postwar period, the market valued stocks as if they were quasi-fixed income securities with warrants, in the second half as if they were call options based on common stocks. The long-term experience was such that most investors naturally assumed that the stock market would keep going up, with little downside risk. Virtually all parties involved — relationship and outside investors, stockbrokers, banks and other financial institutions, borrowing companies and the government — were beneficiaries of the ever-rising stock market, and there was strong agreement that the higher the stock price, the better for everybody. Until stock index futures and options were introduced in the late 1980s, few investors would have benefited from a stock price decline, nor was it possible to shortsell the market even if stocks were grossly overpriced. The market crash brought a belated adjustment, pulling stock price levels more in line with their fundamental value.

One way to reconcile the unique features of the Japanese stock market with Western financial theory is as follows.

- Main banks and other major financial institutions, whose chief business was to accept deposit type savings and lend them to industrial and commercial companies, occupied the position of holders of both senior debt and common stocks as a package, fully bearing the residual risks of the borrowing companies.
- Outside investors held and traded, not a pure common stock, but a quasi-fixed income security (similar to a preferred stock) with some kind of option feature and without the residual risk inherent in any pure common stock.
- A secondary market for pure common stocks bearing full residual risk and having control rights had not developed far. This is evidenced by the lack of open merger and acquisition or takeover bid activities in the Japanese stock market even today.

International comparison of the cost of capital

The concept of the cost of capital has been used by macroeconomists chiefly to explain differences between countries in the level of fixed capital formation. Recently, the cost of capital has attracted increasing attention as a factor in explaining stock prices and the international competitiveness of companies and banks.

Precise calculation of the cost of capital involves estimating the rate of return expected by investors, as embodied in the market prices of stocks and debt securities; this can then be used to discount the anticipated cash flows generated by companies. As already noted, one characteristic of Japan's stock ownership structure is an acceptance by investors of low profitability on a book basis. Indeed, historical price/earnings ratios suggest that, among industrialised nations, Japan valued low profitability most highly (Table 8.5). If measured in terms of market price, therefore, the cost of equity capital for Japanese companies would have been even lower than that implied by the rate of return on book value.

In determining the weighted average cost of capital, the effective interest rate can be used as an estimate for the cost of debt capital. Estimating the cost of equity capital is more problematic. One approach is to estimate the per share earnings yield (earnings per share divided by the stock price, which is the reciprocal of the price/earnings ratio), making appropriate adjustments for differences in tax rates, depreciation methods and the like, in order to estimate as precisely as possible sustainable economic earnings. Another approach involves calculating the total return expected by investors based on the sum of dividend yield and expected growth in earnings and dividends, using consensus forecasts by professional securities analysts.

Table 8.5   International comparison of price/earnings ratios, 1980–95[a]

	Japan[b]	United States[c]	World average[d]
1980	19.4	8.9	10.0
1981	21.1	7.9	9.7
1982	22.9	10.3	11.7
1983	27.6	11.2	13.2
1984	31.0	9.4	11.9
1985	33.6	12.9	15.3
1986	50.0	13.7	18.5
1987	54.0	12.4	18.3
1988	58.5	11.9	19.5
1989	60.9	14.2	20.8
1990	38.7	14.3	16.2
1991	40.8	19.1	19.9
1992	40.5	20.3	20.5
1993	57.2	19.4	24.0
1994	68.1	15.9	20.5
1995	69.5	17.2	19.9

Note: a Ratio of share price to earnings per share, at end of calendar year.
       b First and second sections of the Tokyo Stock Exchange.
       c All listed companies.
       d Argentina, Australia, Austria, Belgium, Canada, Chile, China, Denmark, Finland, France, Germany, Greece, Hong Kong, Indonesia, Ireland, Italy, Japan, Malaysia, Mexico, Netherlands, New Zealand, Norway, Philippines, Portugal, Singapore, South Africa, South Korea, Spain, Sweden, Switzerland, Taiwan, Thailand, Turkey, United Kingdom, United States.

Source: Datastream International, London.

The former approach was used by McCauley and Zimmer (1989). They concluded that the weighted average real after-tax cost of capital (cost of 'funds', in their terminology) during the 1980s was significantly lower in Japan than in the United States, largely because of the relatively low cost of equity capital in Japan. Malkiel (1992a), who adopted the latter approach, also found that the cost of capital was considerably higher in the United States than in either Japan or Germany during the 1980s. Frankel (1991) concluded that the cost of capital was lower in Japan than in the United States during the 1970s and 1980s, although the gap narrowed in the 1980s as a result of financial deregulation in Japan. These studies on the accounting profitability of Japanese and US companies support my own argument.

It should also be noted that Japan's advantage in the cost of equity was derived primarily from a very high debt leverage in the early years. During this period the required return on equity was relatively high because new equity issues were made at par value with a commitment to maintain current dividends per share. During the 1980s, however, many Japanese companies took advantage of very high price/earnings ratios to expand their equity base through large new stock issues sold at the market price. This ability to issue new equity at high market prices relative to current earnings became their major source of cost of equity advantage.

The cost of capital for large banks

If main banks were to support the low return strategy of the Japanese manufacturing sector, the cost of capital for banks also had to be low. In other words, to complete the full circle, the system had to be able to tolerate a low level of profitability among both companies and large banks. We should not be surprised, then, to find that a common strategy of major Japanese banks has been to sacrifice profitability for growth in size. The banks' average pretax return on assets in recent years has been about half, or less than half, that of the leading US and British banks (*The Banker*, July 1987, pp. 69–179). Major Japanese banks were able to dominate the international lending market in the 1980s — basically by providing high-quality capital with thin spreads — largely because the system tolerated low returns while encouraging growth in size. It should also be noted that Japanese banks, like Japan's non-financial sector, had one of the lowest equity cushions among industrialised countries.

The international competitiveness of large Japanese banks during the 1980s as measured by the cost of capital is more dramatically seen if we measure their cost of equity capital based on stock price. McCauley and Zimmer (1991) discovered that, among industrialised countries, Japan's advantage in cost of equity capital was even more conspicuous in the banking than in the non-financial sector. This is consistent with the fact that large banks have been at the heart of Japan's relationship based financial and business system, and that their shares are among the most heavily cross-held (Sheard 1994). According to the Fair Trade Commission (1994), main banks had cross-holding arrangements with virtually all member companies of the Mitsui, Mitsubishi and Sumitomo groups. Once the practice of cross-holding starts to decline, the safety and stability of commercial banks and other financial institutions may also become questionable.

International competition and the cost of capital

Until recently, the stock markets of different countries — including those of the United States and Japan — operated largely under local rules. Initially this posed no great problem from an international standpoint. With the intensification of global competition among large companies in the 1980s, however, it has become a controversial issue. If a key rule of survival in the open market is that the firm continue to produce returns that exceed the cost of capital, then it clearly follows that a difference in the cost of capital, or in minimum required profitability, can become a very significant factor in international competition.

When US and Japanese firms compete head to head in the open market, the latter have a clear advantage in terms of the cost of capital, mainly because their major investors are willing to tolerate lower levels of corporate profitability. A lower cost of capital has enabled Japanese companies not only to survive in global markets, but also to expand substantially their market share.

Comparison of corporate profitability

The cost of capital reflects the minimum profitability (or return) suppliers of capital are willing to accept when companies go to the market for debt and equity capital. If we assume that the performance of a company is evaluated mainly on the basis of its business results as reported in its financial statements, we can assume that the primary goal for the management of any listed company is to maintain sufficient profitability to satisfy the average supplier of capital.

Table 8.6 compares the profitability of major companies in Japan and the United States. These data are averages based on actual results in the 1980s, using the S&P index of industrial companies for the United States (some 400 companies), and the NRI 350 index of manufacturing and commercial companies for Japan. Data for the Japanese companies were compiled on a parent company basis.

To eliminate discrepancies in the calculation of profitability arising from differences in tax rates, capital structures or depreciation methods, the comparisons were made at four levels of the income statement: after-tax profit margin, pretax profit margin, operating profit margin and operating cash flow margin (the sum of operating profit plus depreciation as a percentage of sales). As a further check against distortion, the data for Japan are provided in two formats: including and excluding the 10 large general trading companies, all of which have extremely low margins. The return on equity in the United States and Japan was then compared before and after tax.

Although some differences in degree are observable depending on the item under consideration, the data in Table 8.6 generally indicate that the profitability of Japanese

Table 8.6 Financial performance of large Japanese and US industrial companies[a] (per cent)

Profitability measure	Japan NRI 350	Japan Excl.10 trading companies	United States S&P industrials
Operating margin	3.2	5.2	9.8
(Operating income + depreciation)/sales	5.0	8.2	13.5
Pretax income/sales	2.8	4.6	8.0
Net income/sales	1.3	2.2	4.5
Return on equity			
Before tax	18.2	18.5	24.5
After tax	8.5	8.6	13.9

Note: a Average for 1980–88 reporting years.

Sources: Japan: Nomura Research Institute (1990), *NRI 400 Handbook*, Tokyo.
United States: Standard and Poor's Corporation (1990), *Standard and Poor's Analyst's Handbook*, New York.

Table 8.7 Minimum required profitability of large Japanese and US industrial companies in the 1980s

	After tax (%)	Before tax (%)	Weight		Minimum required EBIT[a] (%)	(¥)
US company						
Debt[b]		8.0	x 0.5	=	4.0	
Equity[c]	13.9	24.5	x 0.5	=	12.25	
					16.25	16.25
Japanese company						
Debt[b]		7.0	x 0.7	=	4.9	
Equity[c]	8.5	18.2	x 0.3	=	5.46	
					10.36	10.36

Notes: a Earnings before interest and tax (EBIT), assuming asset turnover of one per year.
b Interest rate on debt, set at 8 per cent for US companies and 7 per cent for Japanese companies.
c US companies assumed to procure 50 per cent of capital as equity, and Japanese companies 30 per cent.

Source: Table 8.6.

companies was considerably lower than that of US companies. Specifically, the American firms had an average after-tax return on equity of 13.9 per cent, compared with only 8.5 per cent for Japanese firms, while the pretax return on equity was 24.5 per cent for US companies but only 18.2 per cent for Japanese companies. The Japanese levels of return on equity change only slightly when the general trading companies are included. If we assume that these figures reflect the minimum profitability levels that large corporations must maintain to continue operating as well-managed listed companies, the pretax cost of equity capital for large Japanese companies in the 1980s would be roughly two-thirds that of large American companies.

Low profitability as an international competitive edge

Let us consider the implications for international competition if such a gap in required profitability between US and Japanese companies were to continue over a long period of time.

Based on the historical data given in Table 8.6, Table 8.7 shows the minimum earnings before interest and tax (EBIT) that a large US and Japanese company would have to earn in order to undertake a hypothetical ¥100 investment in new plant and equipment while still providing the minimum return expected by holders of the company's debt and equity capital, under the conditions that prevailed in the two markets during the 1980s. The calculation includes three new assumptions.

- Reflecting the interest rate differential between the United States and Japan in the 1980s, the interest rate on debt is set at 8 per cent for the United States and 7 per cent for Japan.
- Book equity to total capitalisation ratios are set at 50 per cent for US companies and 30 per cent for Japanese companies.
- The asset turnover rate for the new investment is set at one per year, for simplicity of calculation.

As Table 8.7 shows, in this hypothetical case the minimum EBIT that the US company must earn is ¥16.25, compared with only ¥10.36 for the Japanese firm; this is almost 1.6 times more. Indeed, US companies face a clear handicap of about ¥6 for each ¥100 of investment. Note, too, that a large part of the difference is attributable to the equity portion of the capital structure. This structural difference in the cost of capital would give Japanese companies a number of options in competition against US companies in the open market, including at least the following:

- lowering the selling prices of their products;
- absorbing the high cost of importing raw materials and/or basic technologies not available in Japan;

- outspending their American rivals in aggressive capital investments (including more frequent scrapping of existing plants and building of new ones) and/or expanded R&D efforts;
- offering better quality products with additional functions without raising prices, or carrying out more aggressive advertising and sales promotion campaigns;
- maintaining employee morale and loyalty by avoiding layoffs, even at times when the workforce is overly large;
- making large-scale investments in businesses that have stable markets but offer only low returns — businesses in which US companies would have difficulty justifying the investment;
- concentrating on mature product segments that earn low returns but have a stable market size, and which do not involve too much risk in terms of technology or marketing; and
- in situations where prices are set in the open market or where competitors' strategies are known, pursuing a strategy of undercutting prices and/or making incremental quality enhancements to capture market share.

While there are other possibilities, these are the tactics most often cited as typical of the competitive strategies pursued by many large Japanese companies.

Table 8.8   Profitability of cross-country foreign direct investment in the United States and Japan, 1980–88[a] (per cent)

	Japanese direct investment in the US		US direct investment in Japan	
	Manufacturing companies	All companies	Manufacturing companies	All companies
1980	2.7	14.4	13.5	13.4
1985	−7.6	8.9	21.4	17.5
1986	−6.0	3.8	34.2	29.5
1987	3.9	3.5	27.9	25.5
1988	−0.5	3.3	19.9	21.0

Note: a   Profitability is defined as net profit for the period divided by average capital during the period.

Source: Survey of current business by US Department of Commerce, in Masayuki Hara (1990), 'US Direct Investment in Japan', *Journal of Trade and Industry,* 6, MITI, Tokyo, p. 15.

To summarise, the strong competitiveness of Japanese companies in the open international market was attributable mainly to their low cost of capital. Indeed, many of the characteristics of so-called 'Japanese-style' management — such as the emphasis on high quality, low prices and incremental improvements in products and technology, a long-term and aggressive approach to investments in plant and equipment, and 'lifetime' employment — were possible largely because Japanese firms enjoyed a significant advantage in the cost of capital.

Making the Japanese approach even more powerful was its tolerance of low profitability, or even losses, for a sustained period of time if there was a consensus within the system that the investment had strategic importance. Table 8.8, which compares the average returns on foreign direct investment in Japan and the United States of large Japanese and US companies during the 1980s, provides good evidence of the differences between the two systems. There was a consensus within Japan that expanding market share in the United States through direct investment was so important that low profitability would if necessary be tolerated. Thus in sharp contrast to Japanese manufacturers, who on average were barely breaking even on their US investments, American manufacturers were gaining a return of over 20 per cent on their Japanese operations.

Table 8.9, which provides annual data on the profitability of large Japanese and US corporations during the 1970s and 1980s, confirms Japan's advantage. Japanese profitability, whether in terms of operating margin or return on equity, continued to decline during these two decades when Japan was 'winning' against the United States in the international marketplace. In contrast, 'losing' US companies maintained or even improved their profitability during the same period.

It is often claimed that Japanese companies adopt a low return strategy in the short run with the long-run goal of driving out competitors, securing market dominance and reaping high profitability. Tables 8.8 and 8.9 indicate that this is not the case. The profitability of Japanese companies did not increase even after they had expanded their market share. Rather, they forced competitors to accept Japanese levels of profitability. US companies were unable to meet this challenge because the American financial system does not support a low return strategy. In the United States such a strategy would be met by a lower stock price, a reduced bond rating and a loss of competent managers. Before long, any sensible US company would retreat from low return areas to redeploy capital and other resources in businesses where they could expect higher returns.

As a result, Japanese companies almost always conquer the markets they target. From that point of view, Japanese competition based on a low cost of capital has been a very effective — though not necessarily efficient — approach in the open market system.

Table 8.9   Trends in the profitability of large Japanese and US companies, 1971–95[a]

	Japan						United States				
	Gross margin (%)	Operating margin (%)	After tax margin (%)	ROE[b] (%)	EPS[c]	DPS[d]	Operating margin (%)	After tax margin[e] (%)	ROE[b] (%)	EPS[c]	DPS[d]
1971	13.9	5.4	2.1	14.8	8.4	3.5	10.0	5.0	10.8	6.0	3.2
1972	13.2	4.6	1.6	11.2	6.9	3.3	10.6	5.3	11.7	6.8	3.2
1973	13.3	4.8	1.7	11.9	8.0	3.3	11.7	6.0	14.2	8.9	3.5
1974	12.9	5.1	1.7	14.4	10.8	3.8	11.6	5.3	14.2	9.6	3.7
1975	11.6	4.2	1.1	10.0	8.1	3.8	10.4	4.6	12.1	8.6	3.7
1976	11.2	3.3	0.9	7.9	6.6	3.6	10.7	5.3	14.0	10.7	4.2
1977	11.7	3.8	1.1	9.7	8.7	3.9	10.6	5.1	13.9	11.5	5.0
1978	11.7	3.3	1.1	9.3	9.0	3.7	10.6	5.2	14.6	13.0	5.4
1979	12.4	3.6	1.3	9.9	10.4	3.8	10.7	5.6	16.5	16.3	5.9
1980	12.3	4.2	1.5	12.3	14.0	4.2	9.4	4.9	14.9	16.1	6.5
1981	11.6	3.9	1.4	11.7	14.6	4.4	8.9	4.9	14.4	16.7	7.0
1982	11.3	3.6	1.2	9.4	12.9	4.5	8.2	4.0	11.1	13.2	7.1
1983	11.0	3.2	1.2	8.9	13.5	4.5	9.0	4.4	12.1	14.8	7.3
1984	11.4	3.1	1.2	8.3	13.6	4.8	9.3	4.8	14.6	18.1	7.5
1985	11.7	3.4	1.3	9.0	16.1	5.1	8.8	3.8	12.1	15.3	7.9
1986	11.8	2.9	1.3	8.3	15.4	5.2	8.2	3.8	11.6	14.5	8.1
1987	12.0	2.4	1.2	6.0	11.9	5.0	9.0	4.7	15.1	20.3	8.7
1988	12.6	2.9	1.4	6.7	14.1	5.2	10.4	5.5	19.1	26.6	9.8
1989	13.5	3.5	1.6	7.9	18.5	5.8	10.2	5.0	18.5	26.8	12.0
1990	12.5	3.3	1.7	8.1	21.6	6.3	9.5	4.2	16.2	24.8	12.7
1991	13.0	3.3	1.8	7.7	23.0	6.6	8.1	2.9	10.8	16.9	12.5
1992	13.1	2.8	1.5	6.0	18.9	6.7	8.1	3.2	13.4	19.1	13.0
1993	12.9	2.2	1.0	3.7	12.2	6.5	8.9	3.6	16.0	21.9	12.5
1994		2.0	0.9	2.8	9.1	5.7	9.9	5.2	21.9	33.1	13.0
1995		2.5	0.9	2.8	9.2	5.7					

Notes:
     a   Year ending March for Japan; year ending December for the United States. Figures for Japan are averages for NRI 350 companies obtained from NRI 400 series compiled by Nomura Research Institute. Figures for the United States are averages for the companies included in the S&P industrial composite stock index compiled by Standard and Poor's Corporation.
     b   ROE = return on equity.
     c   EPS = earnings per share.
     d   DPS = dividend per share.
     e   After depreciation charges, for consistency with Japanese figures.

Source: Japan: Nomura Research Institute (1995), *NRI 400 Handbook*, Tokyo; United States: Standard and Poor's Corporation (1995), *Standard and Poor's Analyst's Handbook*, New York.

The future: pressure for change

Japan's financial system was designed and developed to support economic development. The acquisition of foreign exchange through exports allowed firms to expand investment in plant and equipment, leading the economy to grow rapidly, employment to expand and national income levels to increase. The system strengthened the international competitiveness of large companies — the key players in this process — and for the most part was supported and considered desirable as long as the consensus, inside and outside Japan, was that the country should prove itself an economic success under the Cold War regime. But in a way the system proved too effective, and its 'legitimacy' then came to be questioned. Although the system was effective in mobilising resources to achieve certain goals at any cost, it was inefficient in that it accommodated low efficiency and profitability. This section discusses the major forces challenging the traditional financial and management system, and the implications for the future.

External imbalances

Viewed from the standpoint of resource allocation, Japan's traditional system had a major weakness. Because the consensus judgement of the ruling elites rather than the strict discipline of financial performance was the basis for determining allocations, the system lacked a built-in mechanism for autonomous correction of major misallocations of capital and other resources.

When a US company decides to invest in new plant and equipment, it typically gives serious consideration to the trade-off between the advantages of expanded scale and the possible drag on financial performance stemming from the new investment. Because the market imposes serious penalties on management if financial performance deteriorates, there is a natural reluctance on the part of managers to undertake new investment unless the anticipated returns are sufficiently attractive to justify the risk.

By contrast, because the traditional Japanese approach attached much greater importance to the economic benefits that came from an expansion in scale, new investments — even those that did not promise to be sufficiently profitable — were approved rather too easily. The system also almost always enabled firms to survive, especially in an open market. Consequently, the Japanese system was strongly biased towards overexpansion. Japanese companies and banks flooded foreign markets with exports and investments, to the point where it became politically difficult for the host country to continue to accept the resulting expansion of scale.

A natural consequence of this has been that Japan runs a substantial surplus in its international balance of payments and has become the world's largest creditor nation. It could be said that the system has succeeded because it lacks an effective braking mechanism, and that its very success is contributing to its breakdown. The accumulation of surplus is rapidly undermining the consensus outside Japan that long provided the underpinning for the Japanese system.

Until quite recently, the Japanese system was tolerated in part because there was a consensus between the United States and other Western nations, forged during the Cold War, that Japan should be encouraged to develop as a peaceful economic nation. Reinforcing this was the very openness of the international market economy and its willingness to accommodate minor differences in national approach; great importance was attached to the notion that accepting new competitive entrants was good for the discipline of the market as well as benefiting consumers. Accordingly, in the days when Japan had a small market presence, its companies were welcomed rather than shunned, and their unique management approach even came in for praise.

It was, however, only a matter of time before the legitimacy of the behaviour of Japanese companies (and of the system supporting them) would be questioned — especially when, one after another, US companies with better financial performance were either driven out of business or acquired by Japanese companies with inferior profitability.

The Cold War is now a relic of the past. Competition among nations is rapidly shifting from military to economic dimensions, as evidenced by recent US opinion polls showing a marked rise in the view that Japan is the 'greatest threat' to the United States (*Yomiuri Shinbun*, 22 July 1992, p. 15). It would not be surprising if this revisionist view were to take hold in other Western nations as the public re-examines Japan in the light of the new economic realities — namely, that Japan's uniqueness is not merely a subtle difference of nuance on the same basic philosophy of capitalism and the market economy, but instead stems from a system based on completely different values and philosophies.

The bursting of the bubble

It is probably fair to say that the Japanese system has attached greater importance to equality of outcomes than does a purely free market system emphasising equality of opportunity to participate, and that on the path to becoming an economic superpower, Japan has created unparalleled economic equality among its people. It is also probably fair to assume that the majority of the population supported the system basically because of this achievement.

Yet even as Japan emerged as a financial powerhouse in the mid 1980s, the domestic conditions supporting the system began to crumble rapidly. Becoming a major financial power meant that there was no longer a need as a nation to absorb capital centrally and channel it back into strategic areas. It heralded the arrival of an economy in which financial institutions, corporations and individual households with ample funds to invest would make their own judgements about risk and return, and manage their own financial affairs. In short, the very economic success of Japan gave rise to the need for a freer and more open financial system.

It seems that nobody — not the politicians, nor the bureaucrats, the bankers or the corporate managers, let alone the general public — was prepared for such a shift. We now know the result: in the latter half of the 1980s vast sums were spent on unsound investments, and the immense liquidity thus created sustained huge speculative bubbles in many areas of the economy. Those who enjoyed the benefits of all this were by no means the wage earners and salaried workers who had sustained Japan's economic growth through sheer hard work. During the bubble years, there was a rapid widening of the relative wealth gap between those with land or assets and those without.

Financial deregulation

The financial deregulation implemented in the 1980s, accelerated by the agreement of the Japan–US Yen–Dollar Committee in 1984, has been the driving force behind several recent developments in the Japanese financial system.

The short-term effect of deregulation was to encourage the development of bubbles in land and stock markets by encouraging performance competition throughout the entire financial services industry. The industry had until then been strictly segmented, and tightly regulated, controlled and protected. Abundant liquidity, declining interest rates and sudden pressure to compete for higher financial returns encouraged speculation in land and stocks on a massive scale — an easy but very risky way to create short-term returns at the expense of the long-term soundness of financial institutions. Speculation spread through the entire economy, involving financial and non-financial companies of all sizes as well as the household sector.

Another short-term effect of financial deregulation was the triggering of systematic arbitrage operations in the Japanese stock market through the introduction of stock index futures and options. In 1987, the Osaka stock exchange began trading stock index futures. In 1988, Osaka introduced the Nikkei index option and Tokyo introduced the TOPIX option. Chicago and Simex also began trading futures and options on Japanese stock indexes. For the first time it became possible for investors to shortsell the entire stock market systematically, thus creating investors (mostly professional) who had an incentive to bet against the market and who would benefit handsomely if it declined. It is generally believed that these stock index futures and options were at least partly responsible for the major stock market adjustment that took place after 1990, marking the beginning of the end of the traditional call option type stock market.

In the long run, financial deregulation and the pressure on banks and other financial institutions to achieve better performance may well have been the single most fundamental force driving the traditional relationship based system towards one based more on arm's-length relations among companies and between companies and financial institutions. Financial institutions seeking higher returns for depositors and investors will find it very difficult to continue to support the low return strategy of their traditional corporate partners. This means that the entire set of traditional relationships will have to be reviewed in the new light of financial returns, including a thorough reassessment of both relationship stock investments and cross-holding arrangements.

Globalisation

Globalisation constitutes one of the basic undercurrents of the economic and business environment in the 1990s and into the 21st century. It is an immense force, not only in absorbing inferior systems into a superior one (as symbolised by the collapse of the former Soviet-led centrally planned economies and the fall of the Berlin Wall), but also in compelling successful but unique systems to conform to the norms of a more widely accepted and more universal system. Japan obviously faces this latter challenge.

The guiding principles in creating a global system are the development of common standards for all important matters and the reciprocal acceptance of local rules for more technical matters. The former group includes harmonisation, at least among industrialised nations, of rules dealing with fair competition, intellectual property rights, environmental issues, financial reporting and disclosure, and bank regulations.

In the context of the discussion in this chapter, the harmonisation of fair trade laws has the potential to affect the Japanese system significantly. The entire concept of the traditional Japanese *keiretsu* and business groups was a key issue at the US–Japan Structural Impediments Initiative talks (SII 1990). More specifically, if the customary long-term, interlocking relationships between main banks and their corporate clients do indeed involve preferential and reciprocal business dealings, as is often claimed, their legitimacy will increasingly come under scrutiny in the light of fair global competition.

The new Bank for International Settlements (BIS) rule on bank equity capital can also be expected to have a substantial impact on Japan's financial system. The BIS rule asks all international banks to maintain an equity capital cushion of at least 8 per cent of risk weighted business loans and investments. Loans and investments to all private companies are classified under the same risk category, no matter whether the borrower is a well-established large company with which the bank has a longstanding relationship. In other words, the BIS rule assumes the relationship with any private company to be an arm's-length one. If they are to abide by the rule, the large banks will have to reassess their entire set of traditional relationships so that they can achieve on average higher returns on assets. This will make it very difficult for them to provide preferential terms of lending or investment to selected corporate customers (Ide 1993).

Japan's ageing society

About the same time as it became an economic and financial superpower, Japan also became one of the lowest growth nations in terms of labour supply. According to the most recent official demographic statistics, the average Japanese woman will have 1.53 children (sometimes referred to as the '1.53 shock'). The Japanese labour force will begin to decline in 2001 and the population will peak in around 2006. The ageing of society will also accelerate. The proportion of the population over 65 years old will exceed 20 per cent by 2010 and will approach 30 per cent by 2020 (Ministry of Welfare 1991).

Together with the longer than average life expectancy, these demographic trends are rapidly turning Japan into a 'pension' state, where life after retirement is a major concern for many citizens. With the stock of household financial assets approaching ¥1,000 trillion, the efficient management of financial assets in general, and of corporate and government pensions in particular, is becoming a very important issue.

These emerging needs of the Japanese people may well affect the behaviour of large companies and financial institutions in such a way as to encourage them to manage much more efficiently the capital entrusted to them.

Restructuring the entire economic system

The traditional financial and management system with its heavy emphasis on economic growth was supported by a general consensus that, above all, Japan needed to fully employ its labour force, the country's most abundant and probably most precious economic resource. It was this consensus that legitimised the strategic allocation of economic resources in general, and of capital in particular. The goal has largely been achieved, creating new demands on Japanese companies from domestic and international stakeholders. Today, expansion of the economic pie, increasing investments, production and exports, and the creation of more jobs are no longer desirable per se. Instead, Japan now needs a system which will make more efficient use of scarce resources while at the same time meeting the new and diversified demands of its people, who are increasingly seeking a better quality of life.

A free market approach guided by the 'invisible hand' seems more compatible with these new economic goals than the traditional system of allocating resources based on the consensus judgements of elites and on long-term, interlocking relationships.

In the open market approach, the primary role of large companies and financial institutions is, as professional management entities, to make best use of scarce economic resources. Financial institutions will be expected to perform as professional managers with fiduciary responsibility for managing the financial assets of their clients. In short, both firms and financial institutions will be judged increasingly in terms of their financial performance.

Some evidence of change

It is uncertain how long it will take for these early signs of change to mature. There will, of course, be a transition period in which forces for and against change may clash. But the fundamental shift from strategic allocation to a more open market system seems inevitable. The following constitute some of the early evidence that such a change is in train.

Disappearance of cost of capital advantage
Mainly due to the major stock market decline since 1990, Japan's cost of capital advantage has largely disappeared. The Economic Planning Agency (1992) estimates that the average cost of capital for Japan had risen to approximately the same level as in the United States by 1991. Malkiel (1992b) agrees that, as of early 1992, the average cost of capital for the United States, Japan and Germany had converged to similar

levels. If this is the case, Japanese companies will be unable to expand any further on the basis of a low cost of capital, marking the end of the low return strategy. Unless they can achieve higher profitability, they will find it increasingly difficult to attract capital for growth.

Breaking down of cross-ownership arrangements
Partly because of the BIS rule and partly because of the current severe recession, both banks and companies are beginning to liquidate part of their relationship equity investment to improve accounting profits and/or cash flows. It seems that the cost of maintaining the cross-ownership arrangement is now becoming too high and the benefits diminishing.

Declining role of main banks as delegated monitors
Traditionally, it was assumed that main banks would always be committed, stable shareholders. This was the premise on which outside investors regarded them as delegated monitors in the stock market. Banks did occasionally sell part of their relationship portfolio in order to realise capital gains for reporting and other purposes. However, they almost always bought back the same number of stocks in the same companies simultaneously at essentially the same prices, through so-called 'cross-transactions' (wash sales).

The assumption of stable ownership on a 'net' basis was the primary rationale for the banks to count 45 per cent of the unrealised capital gains on their equity investments as tier-II equity capital under the BIS rule. However, as the need intensified to write off the large number of bad and non-performing loans that had materialised in 1991 and 1992, banks began to realise capital gains on their relationship equity portfolios on a massive scale. While a large part of these sales was matched by simultaneous repurchases, it was widely reported in the market that some banks had either sold some stocks outright, were trying to get consent from companies to sell outright, or were shortselling stocks to realise capital gains (see, for example, *Nihon Keizai Shinbun*, 4 April 1992; *Yomiuri Shinbun*, 19 August 1992). Indeed, the massive sale of stocks by major banks caused so much concern in the summer of 1992 that the Ministry of Finance, as part of its widely publicised price keeping operations, strongly requested that banks refrain from the outright sale of stocks (*Nihon Keizai Shinbun*, 19 August 1992). The role of main banks as delegated monitors for the stock market also seems to be beginning to decline.

Emphasis on corporate profitability
My paper in Japanese, which won the Tokyo Marine Kagami Memorial Foundation prize in 1991, triggered a discussion in policy circles concerning the low profitability orientation of the Japanese management system (Ide 1991). In February 1992, Akio Morita, chair of Sony Corporation, contributed a controversial article to the monthly

journal, *Bungeishunjū* (pp. 94–103). In it he argued that the traditional Japanese approach of selling high-quality products at low prices might be at the heart of the so-called 'Japan problem' as perceived by the West.

It is now widely recognised that the profitability of Japanese companies needs to be improved. Several major companies have announced that they will raise the hurdle or cut-off rates for their new investment decisions. Some have decided to shut down unprofitable operations in North America and elsewhere. Others are emphasising improvements in profitability even at the risk of shrinking the total size of their business. To some extent, these changes have been made in response to the current severe recession. But they also reflect a fundamental shift in the priorities of large Japanese companies, from growth in size to efficiency of capital utilisation and profitability.

For investors, too, profitability measures — return on equity, dividend payout ratios and so on — are becoming the primary criteria for evaluating stocks. This change may well signal the beginning of an investment approach based on the fundamental value of companies.

Japan's traditional relationship based and stable stock investing, with main banks as delegated monitors, can be characterised as a market with strong asymmetries of information, little attention to fundamental analysis and a lack of appropriate adjustments of portfolio in response to daily stock price changes. According to Sharpe and Alexander (1990, pp. 77–8), market stock prices will become a good indicator of the stock's investment or intrinsic value when all investors have costless access to currently available information about the future, are good (security) analysts, and pay close attention to market prices, adjusting their holdings appropriately. The emphasis on corporate profitability may well be a small but irreversible step towards the emergence of a more efficient stock market in Japan.

Notes

1 It is interesting to note that the concept of 'relationship investing' has been discussed in the United States recently (Porter 1992; *Business Week,* 15 March 1993, pp. 38–45).

2 One of the basic assumptions of modern investment theory is the mean variance postulate of common stock returns, originally developed by Markowitz (1959). Variance is the standardised statistical measurement of the second moment of the deviations from the mean. The positive skewness for a longer time horizon reflects the fact that common stock investment is also a kind of option, with the maximum potential loss being limited to 100 per cent. Skewness is measured by the third moment of the deviations from the mean (see, for example, Elton and Gruber 1987, p. 222).

3 For a comparison of the stock exchange systems of the United States, the United Kingdom and Japan, see Yamashita (1991).

References

Bank of Japan (1995), *Economic Statistics Monthly*, 584, Bank of Japan, Tokyo.

Calder, Kent E. (1993), *Strategic Capitalism: Private Business and Public Purpose in Japanese Industrial Finance*, Princeton, NJ: Princeton University Press.

Economic Planning Agency (1992), *1991 Nendo Keizai Hakusho* [1991 Economic White Paper], Tokyo: Ōkurashō Insatsukyoku.

Elton, Edwin J. and Martin J. Gruber (1987), *Modern Portfolio Theory and Investment Analysis*, New York: Wiley (3rd edition).

Fair Trade Commission (1994), *Report on the Actual Conditions of the Six Major Corporate Groups*, Tokyo: Fair Trade Commission, pp. 22–37.

Frankel, Jeffrey A. (1991), 'Japanese Finance in the 1980s: A Survey', in Paul Krugman (ed.), *Trade with Japan: Has the Door Opened Wider?*, Chicago, IL: University of Chicago Press, pp. 225–70.

Ide, Masasuke (1991), *Nihon Keizai wa Ishitsuka* [Is Japan's Economy Unique?], Tokyo: Tokyo Marine Kagami Memorial Foundation.

—— (1993), 'Waga Kuni no Kabuka Keisei to BIS Kisei' [Stock Valuations in Japan and the Impact of the BIS Rule], *Nihon Keizai Kenkyū*, 26, Japan Center for Economic Research, Tokyo, pp. 127–66.

—— (1994), *Nihon no Kigyō Kin'yū Shisutemu to Kokusai Kyōsō* [The Japanese Corporate Financing System and International Competition], Tokyo: Tōyō Keizai Shinpōsha.

Malkiel, Burton G. (1992a), The Influence of Conditions in Financial Markets on the Time Horizon of Business Managers: An International Comparison, Paper presented to the Osaka University Conference on Corporate Financial Policy and International Competition, Osaka University, Osaka.

—— (1992b), 'Shihon Kosuto no Gainen to Kokusai Hikaku' [The Concept of Cost of Capital and an International Comparison], *Security Analysts Journal*, 30 (3), March, Tokyo, pp. 29–36.

Markowitz, Harry M. (1959), *Portfolio Selection: Efficient Diversification of Investments*, A Cowles Foundation Monograph, New York: J. Wiley.

McCauley, Robert N. and Steven A. Zimmer (1989), 'Explaining International Differences in the Cost of Capital', *Federal Reserve Bank of New York Quarterly Review*, 14 (2), Summer, pp. 7–28.

—— (1991), 'Bank Cost of Capital and International Competition', *Federal Reserve Bank of New York Quarterly Review*, 16 (4), Winter, pp. 33–59.

Ministry of Welfare (1991), *1990 Nendo Jinkō Dōtai Tōkei* [1990 Demographic Statistics Yearbook], Tokyo: Ministry of Welfare.

MITI (Ministry of International Trade and Industry) (ed.) (1989), *Nichibei no Kigyō Kōdō Hikaku* [Comparison of the Behaviour of Japanese and US Firms], Tokyo: NihonNōritsu Kyōkai.

Nakatani, Iwao (1984), 'The Economic Role of Financial Corporate Grouping', in Masahiko Aoki (ed.), *The Economic Analysis of the Japanese Firm*, Amsterdam: North-Holland, pp. 227–58.

Oba, Ryōko and Akiyoshi Horiuchi (1990), 'Honpō Ginkō no Mein Banku Kankei to Setsubi Tōshi Kōdō no Kankei ni tsuite — Rironteki Seiri' [On the Relationship between Main Bank Relations and the Investment Behaviour of Japanese Companies], *Kin'yū Kenkyū*, 9 (4), Institute of Monetary and Economic Studies, Bank of Japan, Tokyo.

Porter, Michael E. (1992), 'Capital Disadvantage: America's Failing Capital Investment System', *Harvard Business Review*, September–October, pp. 65–82.

Sharpe, William F. and Gordon J. Alexander (1990), *Investments*, Englewood Cliffs, NJ: Prentice-Hall (4th edition).

Sheard, Paul (1994), 'Interlocking Shareholding and Corporate Governance', in Masahiko Aoki and Ronald Dore (eds), *The Japanese Firm: The Sources of Competitive Strength*, Oxford: Clarendon Press, pp. 310–49.

SII (Structural Impediments Initiative) (1990), *Final Report*, Tokyo: Japanese Ministry of Foreign Affairs.

Suzuki, Yoshio (1974), *Gendai Nihon Kin'yū Ron* [Money and Banking in Contemporary Japan], Tokyo: Tōyō Keizai Shinpōsha.

Yamashita, Hideaki (1991), 'Puraishingu Shisutemu no Genjō to Kadai' [Stock Pricing System: As It Is Now and in the Future], *Nihon Shōken Keizai Kenkyūjō*, pp. 15–24.

9 The impact of financial deregulation on corporate financing

Takeo Hoshi

The Japanese financial system underwent significant change during the 1980s. Important aspects of these changes can be summarised in two words: internationalisation, and deregulation.

Japan's financial market was effectively isolated from the world financial market until the end of the 1970s. Only a few foreign investors had ventured into the Japanese market, and very few Japanese individuals or corporations were investing or raising funds abroad. The process of internationalisation began in 1980 with the reform of the Foreign Exchange and Foreign Trade Control Law. Foreign exchange transactions, which had been 'forbidden in principle' under the legislation, became 'free unless prohibited'. Internationalisation was further advanced by the abolition in 1984 of the 'real demand principle', which required that foreign exchange transactions be backed by 'real' demand for foreign exchange, such as foreign trade. In line with the recommendations of the Yen–Dollar Committee, the Euromarket was substantially deregulated and a Tokyo offshore market opened in 1986.

Many of the numerous regulations governing domestic financial markets were lifted during the 1980s. The easing of restrictions on deposit rates began with the introduction of certificates of deposit in 1979. The minimum value of this instrument fell gradually over the next decade. Other types of deposit were also introduced, including money market certificates, whose interest rates move with market rates. These were introduced in the 1980s and had expanded to cover even small accounts by the end of the decade. By October 1994, interest rates on all kinds of deposits had been liberalised. A secondary market for government bonds was created in the late 1970s, with some types of government bond being sold at auction. New kinds of corporate bond, such as unsecured bonds or warrant bonds, were introduced, while the criteria that firms had to meet in order to issue bonds were also relaxed. Reform of the Corporate Bonds Act in 1993 further simplified the bond issue process and reduced the cost of bond financing.

Internationalisation and deregulation were closely related, with one driving the other in some cases. Following the development of the Euromarket, for example, which gave Japanese corporations the capacity to issue bonds abroad, deregulation of the domestic bond market became a matter of its survival. The Japanese government also saw deregulation of the domestic market as a tool to advance the internationalisation of the yen. The *March 1985 Report on Internationalisation of the Yen* argued that '[because] international yen-denominated transactions will evolve around Japanese financial and capital markets, where ample yen funds are available, the liberalisation of domestic financial and capital markets is indispensable for the internationalisation of the yen' (Ministry of Finance 1992, pp. 67–8).

This chapter documents how the dual processes of internationalisation and deregulation changed the behaviour of Japanese corporations. Traditionally, Japanese firms had depended heavily on banks for funds. The banks not only provided loans to the firm, but also served as major shareholders. It was not unusual for a bank to dispatch a current or former employee to sit on the board of a corporate client. This close relationship between banks and firms, often called the 'main bank system', was characteristic of Japanese corporate finance throughout much of the postwar period. Responding to greater opportunities in domestic and foreign bond markets, in the 1980s many firms increased their dependence on bonds and reduced their bank borrowing. Others did not greatly reduce their dependence on banks for funding, even though they had the capacity to issue corporate bonds. Increased heterogeneity among firms in their sources of financing is thus another important aspect of the shift in Japanese corporate finance that took place in the 1980s.

The shift from bank to bond financing raises the question of the future of the Japanese financial system. Traditionally, banks have been not just an important source of funds, but have also acted as efficient monitors of firms. They have been aided in this by their close relationships with the firms they monitor. As firms begin to move away from bank financing, will this system change? Will Japanese corporations rely in future primarily on securities market financing and arm's-length banking? This chapter takes up these questions and speculates about the future of Japanese corporate finance.

Deregulation of the corporate bond market

For much of the postwar period, the domestic corporate bond market was heavily regulated; credit was severely rationed. As will be shown, credit rationing favoured the use of government bonds and bank debentures. Corporate bonds were an unreliable source of funds for industrial firms. Japanese corporations had limited access to foreign bond markets and thus were unable to avoid the restrictions associated with the domestic bond market. This situation changed in the 1980s, when the restrictions on firms issuing bonds in foreign and domestic markets were gradually relaxed. This section examines the postwar history of the regulation of corporate bond issues and shows how internationalisation and deregulation broadened the financing opportunities of Japanese corporations.

Regulation of the bond market was a product of two conditions prevailing in the early postwar period. First, household demand for bonds was low. This can be attributed to the low level of household financial assets, which prevented most people from diversifying their financial portfolios beyond safe bank deposits. Financial institutions were the major purchasers of bonds in the early postwar years. Second, the Japanese government pursued a policy of maintaining interest rates at artificially low levels with the goal of lowering the cost of capital. Without a market mechanism to balance demand and supply in the bond market, bond issues had to be rationed; stringent regulation was introduced to establish the rationing mechanism. The low interest rate policy also affected the bank loan market, although banks were able to adjust *effective* loan rates through the practice of 'compensating balances'. By requiring corporations to deposit a portion of their bank loans with the bank as a compensating balance, banks could effectively raise the interest rate on loans above the regulated level. As Teranishi (1982, pp. 538–40) argues, the bank loan market can thus be considered to have been close to equilibrium despite regulation. Because there was no equivalent to compensating balances in the bond market, however, rationing was inevitable.

Under the bond rationing mechanism, corporate bond issues were especially squeezed. Government bonds and government guaranteed bonds issued by public companies received preferential allocation of funds, as did bank debentures sold by long-term financial institutions. These were institutions deemed important to economic growth because they supplied long-term funds to key industries. They were not subject to rationing and were able to place debentures privately with commercial banks.[1]

The rationing mechanism was set up when the corporate bond market first reopened after the war, in 1949 (Kōshasai Hikiuke Kyōkai 1980, pp.166–75, 232–8). The Bond Issuance Round Table (Kisai Kondankai) determined the general terms of corporate bond issues, such as maturity and underwriting fees. This body consisted of staff from the Ministry of Finance, Economic Planning Agency, Home Affairs Agency, Bank of Japan, Reconstruction Bank (forerunner of the Japan Development Bank), Industrial Bank of Japan, Nōrin Chūkin Bank and Nihon Kangyō Bank, along with representatives from city banks, regional banks, trust banks and securities companies. The Bond Issuance Committee (Kisai Uchiawasekai, later Kisaikai) decided the coupon rate, the issue price and the amount of each individual issue. This committee consisted of representatives from the Bank of Japan, the Industrial Bank of Japan, all the trustee banks and the four main securities companies (Nomura, Daiwa, Nikkō and Yamaichi). With the liberal credit policy of 1955–56 making rationing unnecessary for a short time, the Bond Issuance Round Table decided to 'liberalise' bond issues and disband itself in 1956. The Bond Issuance Committee also stopped meeting. But when credit conditions tightened in 1957, the private sector members of the committee (that is, all except the Bank of Japan) regrouped. From this time on, regulation of the domestic corporate bond market was carried out by the Bond Issuance Committee, which was now a group of private financial institutions, without the formal involvement of the government or the central bank. However, the Ministry of Finance and the Bank of

Japan continued to influence the bond issuing process, as the committee made a practice of consulting these bodies before reaching any decision (Kōshasai Hikiuke Kyōkai 1980, pp. 304–5; Teranishi 1982, pp. 455–6).

Credit rationing in the corporate bond market was done by rating each individual issue and allocating available credit preferentially to highly rated ones. Since the rating standard used by the committee relied exclusively on measures of size, such as capital, net worth and outstanding bonds, this system effectively favoured large companies. By 1975 the Bond Issuance Committee had finally abandoned the explicit rationing of bond issues (Gotō 1986, pp. 111–12) in favour of bond issue criteria (*tekisai kijun*) that companies had to satisfy if they were to issue bonds. The criteria thus functioned very much like rationing in that they continued to deny small firms access to the bond market. As discussed below, the bond issue criteria survived well into the 1980s.

The Bond Issuance Committee also insisted that all corporate bonds be secured. This 'collateral principle' has a long history in Japanese finance, going back to an agreement reached among representatives of banks, trust banks and insurance companies in 1931 (Arai 1991, p. 83). The committee established the collateral principle as an explicit rule to be imposed on all bond issues. This severely restricted the ability of firms with a low level of collateralisable assets to issue bonds. Because firms had to pay management fees to the trustee banks that held their collateral, it also raised the costs of issuing bonds. Although relaxed by the introduction of bond issue criteria for unsecured bonds in 1979, the collateral principle continued to be applied even in the 1980s.

The convertible bond market, reintroduced in 1966, was not subject to regulation by the Bond Issuance Committee, and underwriting securities companies had discretion over coupon rates for the convertible bond issues that they placed. Nevertheless, this market faced a different type of self-regulation. The securities companies established bond issue criteria that were similar to but less stringent than those of the Bond Issuance Committee, which firms had to satisfy in order to issue convertible bonds. Collateral was required until 1979, when the bond issue criteria for unsecured convertible bonds were established. Regulation of the market then eased gradually during the 1980s.

Regulation of the corporate bond market meant that Japanese corporations had little choice but to obtain most of their external (non-equity) financing through the banks. Many firms were forced to rely on the banks because they were completely locked out of the corporate bond market or because regulation made the cost of bond financing prohibitively high. The regulatory environment in the corporate bond market began to change in the late 1970s. The government began to run deficits as economic growth slowed and as the social security system expanded. Government bond issues increased, making it impossible for the government to continue to force the syndicate of financial institutions to absorb low-yielding government bonds. The Ministry of Finance was compelled to establish a secondary market for government bonds in 1977, and began to issue some types of bond through public auction in 1978 (Hamada and Horiuchi 1987, pp. 247–9). The opening of the secondary market, combined with the accumulation of financial wealth by households in the 1960s and early 1970s, increased demand for bonds and eliminated one of the two major factors that had necessitated rationing.

The government also relaxed its low interest rate policy: the second reason for credit rationing. Interest rates in the call, *tegata* and *gensaki* markets were freed from all regulation in the late 1970s.[2] All other interest rates except those on deposits were fully liberalised in the 1980s; deposit rates were partially decontrolled in the early 1980s. By June 1993, interest rates on time deposits were totally free of regulation. Interest rates on small deposits (except demand deposits) had been fully deregulated by October 1994 (Bank of Japan Institute of Monetary and Economic Studies 1995, pp. 43–6).

The accumulation of liquidity in the corporate sector during the period of rapid economic growth and the slowing of growth after the first oil crisis helped make credit rationing obsolete. The appetite of corporations for investment funds dwindled, and in any case they were no longer as dependent on external funds. The supply of industrial bonds (demand for funds) by corporations fell, making rationing unnecessary. Rationing in the corporate bond market by the Bond Issuance Committee formally ceased in 1975, when the committee adopted a policy of honouring the amount of bond issues requested by each company. Although companies wishing to issue bonds still had to meet the committee's criteria, once approved they could then issue as many bonds as they liked. The collateral principle also became gradually less important. In 1979, companies were permitted to issue unsecured straight bonds and convertible bonds, but under such stringent criteria that only two companies (Toyota Auto and Matsushita Electric) qualified. The criteria for unsecured bonds were gradually relaxed throughout the 1980s. By the end of the decade, about 300 firms were able to issue unsecured straight bonds and about 500 could issue unsecured convertible bonds in the domestic market (Table 9.1).

Table 9.1   Companies eligible to issue unsecured bonds, 1979–88 (number)

	Straight bonds	Convertible bonds
March 1979	2	2
January 1983	2	25
April 1984	16	97
July 1985	16	175
October 1985	57	175
February 1987	about 120	about 240
November 1988	about 300	about 500

Source: Nomura Securities (1989), *Fainansu Handobukku* [Finance Handbook], Tokyo, pp. 115–17.

In 1981, firms were allowed to issue a new type of bond, called a warrant bond, which came with an option to buy shares at a prespecified price for a certain period. The use of warrant bonds in the domestic market has not been particularly popular. The introduction of this new financing method broadened the financing options of Japanese firms only when it was combined with internationalisation; Japanese firms issued a substantial amount of warrant bonds in foreign markets in the 1980s.

As mentioned earlier, the 1980 reform of the Foreign Exchange and Foreign Trade Control Law made corporate foreign exchange transactions 'free unless prohibited', enabling many Japanese firms to issue bonds abroad. Foreign markets were attractive to Japanese firms because they were less regulated than the domestic market. Even more importantly, they did not require collateral. Their popularity is evident in the increase in foreign issues by Japanese firms in the 1980s. This is seen in Figure 9.1, which shows the proportion of Japanese corporate bonds (convertible, warrant and straight) issued abroad from 1975 to 1993. The share of foreign issues increased rapidly in the early 1980s, to fluctuate at around 50 per cent in the late 1980s.

Figure 9.1   Proportion of bond issues in foreign markets, 1975–93[a]

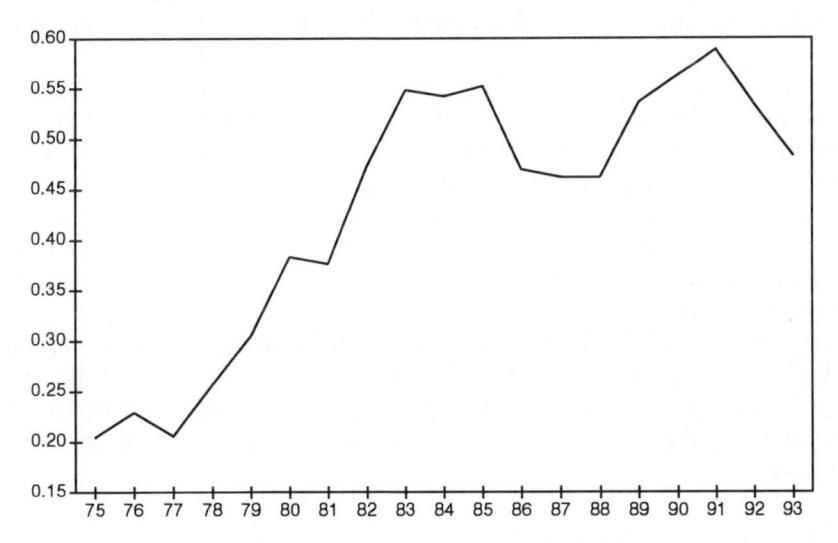

Note: a   Calculated as the ratio of the value of corporate bonds issued abroad (including convertible and warrant bonds) to the total value of corporate bond issues (both domestic and foreign).

Source: Ministry of Finance (annual), *Shōken Kyoku Nenpō* [Annual Report of the Securities Bureau], Tokyo (various issues).

Although foreign markets for corporate bonds were free of regulation by the Bond Issuance Committee, some self-regulation by securities companies continued. Banks, which were central members of the Bond Issuance Committee, were not formally involved in this self-regulation process. Although Japanese banks could legally underwrite the foreign bond issues of Japanese corporations through their subsidiaries, the so-called 'three bureaus agreement', (an agreement reached by the Banking Bureau, the Securities Bureau and the International Finance Bureau of the Ministry of Finance, effective from 1975 to March 1993), made it clear that banks should 'pay due respect to the experience gained by and the mandate given to the Japanese securities firms' (Rosenbluth 1989, p. 152). This agreement has been interpreted as preventing subsidiaries of Japanese banks from becoming the leading underwriters of bond issues by Japanese corporations (Taiyō Kōbe Mitsui Bank 1990, p. 5). Thus the banks have not had much say in the self-regulation of foreign bond issues, and securities companies have continued to impose bond issue criteria on corporate bond issues in foreign markets.

The securities companies applied different criteria according to the type of bond, so that those for convertible bonds differed from those for warrant bonds, for example. Often, the criteria for domestic issues were applied to comparable foreign issues without change; the bond issue criteria for convertible bonds in a foreign market were the same as those for domestic convertible bonds, for instance. The criteria prevented some firms from tapping foreign markets. Other companies could issue only straight or warrant bonds secured by a bank guarantee, for which they had to pay a fee to the guarantor bank.

Table 9.2 outlines changes in the bond issue criteria for domestic (secured) convertible bonds. These also applied to foreign issues of the (unsecured) bonds. The criteria were based on both size measures (such as net worth) and profitability measures (such as dividend per share and profit per share), and have been relaxed substantially over time. Under the rating criteria introduced in 1989, firms were allowed to issue convertible bonds if they had a BB or higher rating, even if they did not satisfy all the accounting criteria. In 1990 the accounting criteria (but not the rating criteria) were abolished.

In order to get an idea of the magnitude of the relaxation of regulation, I checked if the criteria were satisfied for the 577 manufacturing companies in the database constructed by Hoshi and Kashyap (1990). Figure 9.2 shows that the number of companies meeting the criteria in each year increased substantially, from 153 in 1977 to 382 in 1989.

Changes in corporate financing

The internationalisation and deregulation of the Japanese financial system opened new opportunities in corporate funding for many firms and changed their financing behaviour. This section documents some of the notable changes in corporate financing that took place in the 1980s.

Table 9.2   Bond issue criteria for convertible bonds (domestic secured and foreign unsecured), October 1976 – present

October 1976 – July 1987
Accounting criteria
A firm with net worth greater than ¥10 billion can issue if:
- Dividend per share in the most recent accounting period exceeds ¥5;
- Ordinary after-tax profit per share in the most recent accounting period is greater than ¥7; and
- One of the following three conditions is met: Net worth ratio $\geq$ 0.15; Net worth/Paid-in capital $\geq$ 1.2; and Business profit/Total assets $\geq$ 0.04.

A firm with net worth greater than ¥6 billion but less than ¥10 billion can issue if:
- Dividend per share in the most recent accounting period exceeds ¥5;
- Ordinary after-tax profit per share in the most recent accounting period is greater than ¥7; and
- Two of the following three conditions are met: Net worth ratio $\geq$ 0.2; Net worth/Paid-in capital $\geq$ 1.5; Business profit/Total assets $\geq$ 0.05.

Rating criteria: None

July 1987 – May 1989
Accounting criteria
A firm with net worth greater than ¥10 billion can issue if:
- Dividend per share in the most recent accounting period exceeds ¥5;
- Ordinary after-tax profit per share in the most recent accounting period is greater than ¥7; and
- One of the following three conditions is met: Net worth ratio $\geq$ 0.1; Net worth/Paid-in capital $\geq$ 1.2; Business profit/Total assets $\geq$ 0.05.

A firm with net worth greater than ¥6 billion but less than ¥10 billion can issue if:
- Dividend per share in the most recent accounting period exceeds ¥5 yen;
- Ordinary after-tax profit per share in the most recent accounting period is greater than ¥7; and
- Two of the following three conditions are met: Net worth ratio $\geq$ 0.12; Net worth/Paid-in capital $\geq$ 1.5; Business profit/Total assets $\geq$ 0.06.

A firm with net worth greater than ¥3 billion but less than ¥6 billion can issue if:
- Dividend per share in the most recent accounting period exceeds ¥5 yen;
- Ordinary after-tax profit per share in the most recent accounting period is greater than ¥7; and
- Two of the following three conditions are met: Net worth ratio $\geq$ 0.15; Net worth/Paid-in capital $\geq$ 2.0; Business profit/Total assets $\geq$ 0 07.

Rating criteria: None

May 1989 – December 1990
Accounting criteria: As for previous period
Rating criteria
A firm with a BB rating or higher can issue bonds if:
- Dividend per share exceeds ¥5; and
- Ordinary after-tax profit per share is greater than ¥7.

December 1990 – present
Accounting criteria: None
Rating criteria: As for previous period

Notes: Net worth ratio = Shareholders' equity/Total assets; Business profit = Operating income + Interest income + Dividend income; Ordinary after-tax profit = Ordinary income – Tax.
Source: Ministry of Finance (1977, 1991), *Shōken Kyoku Nenpō* [Annual Report of the Securities Bureau], Tokyo; Industrial Bank of Japan (annual), *Shōken Binran* [Securities Handbook], Tokyo (various issues); Nomura Securities (1987, 1989), *Fainansu Handobukku* [Finance Handbook], Tokyo; Industrial Bank of Japan (1987), *Shin Ginkō Jitsumu Kōza: 8, Shōken* [New General Lectures on Banking Business: Vol. 8, Securities], Kin'yū Zaisei Jijō Kenkyūkai, Tokyo.

Figure 9.2 Firms eligible to issue convertible bonds, 1977–89[a] (number)

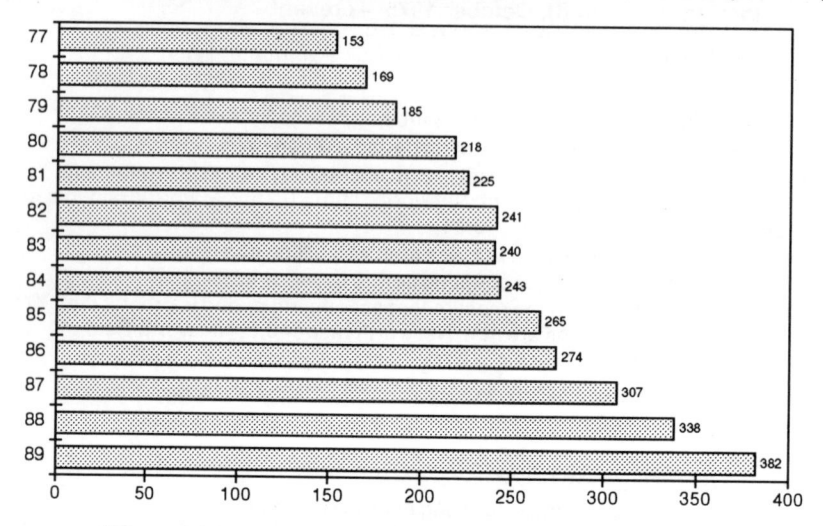

Year	Number
77	153
78	169
79	185
80	218
81	225
82	241
83	240
84	243
85	265
86	274
87	307
88	338
89	382

Note: a Firms satisfying bond issue criteria as of March each year.

Source: Author's estimates, based on Hoshi and Kashyap's (1990) sample.

Table 9.3 gives a breakdown of large Japanese corporations' sources of new funds for the period 1966–90, based on data collected annually by the Bank of Japan. The bank's 1991 survey (Bank of Japan 1992) covered listed firms with capital greater than ¥1 billion and included 638 firms, of which 383 were in manufacturing.[3] The table shows five-year averages in order to eliminate year-to-year fluctuation of funding sources and to focus on long-run changes in financing on a flow basis.[4]

The table documents the increasing dependence of firms on new stock and bond issues and their declining reliance on bank borrowing over time. The proportion of bond issues in total new funds rose from 4.8 per cent in the late 1960s to 16.1 per cent in the late 1980s, while that of stock issues increased from 4.1 per cent to 13.5 per cent. The rise in new share issues is associated with the increased reliance on new bond issues because, as will be shown below, many bonds issued in the 1980s were either convertible or warrant attached. The importance of bank borrowings declined significantly over the 25-year period. Combining short and long-term loans, the proportion of bank borrowings fell from 39.5 per cent in the late 1960s to 8.0 per cent in the late 1980s.

The bottom portion of Table 9.3 shows that these changes affected manufacturing firms disproportionately. Their bond and stock issues increased respectively from 3.0 per cent and 3.2 per cent in the late 1960s to 19.9 per cent and 19.1 per cent in the late

Table 9.3   Sources of funds for large corporations, 1966–90 (per cent)

	Internal funds			External funds					
							Bank borrowings		
	Depre-ciation	Retained earnings	Total	Stock issues	Bond issues	Trade payable	Short term	Long term	Total
All industries
1966–70	24.55	13.70	38.25	4.10	4.79	25.29	16.34	23.14	61.75
1971–75	22.63	10.66	33.29	3.96	6.91	18.11	19.39	22.61	66.71
1976–80	30.06	13.36	43.42	6.89	6.92	14.27	12.19	5.70	56.58
1981–85	45.35	14.26	59.61	11.13	10.24	2.51	8.45	2.94	40.39
1986–90	30.20	12.61	42.81	13.46	16.05	9.58	4.56	3.40	57.19
Manufacturing
1966–70	20.86	12.89	33.75	3.18	3.00	17.30	14.35	16.04	66.25
1971–75	24.13	10.96	35.08	2.90	3.90	13.08	18.54	15.31	64.92
1976–80	36.65	17.63	54.28	7.76	1.04	17.43	12.10	–2.56	45.72
1981–85	49.20	18.76	67.96	12.82	10.32	2.91	6.09	–4.91	32.04
1986–90	35.99	17.85	53.84	19.07	19.89	8.60	–6.17	–3.33	46.16

Source: Bank of Japan (annual), *Shuyō Kigyō Keiei Bunseki* [Financial Statements of Principal Enterprises], Bank of Japan, Tokyo (various issues).

1980s. Bank borrowings, which accounted for 30.4 per cent of total funds in the late 1960s, recorded a net decrease of 9.5 per cent of total funds. These figures suggest that manufacturing firms were especially aggressive in taking advantage of the deregulation of bond markets to reduce their dependence on bank loans.

Figures 9.3 and 9.4, which present the same data in different forms, show that firms preferred some types of bond to others. Convertible bonds in foreign and domestic markets were the most popular instruments in the 1980s, followed by warrant bonds issued in foreign markets. Domestic straight bonds also seem to have been in demand. Included in this category, however, are bonds issued by Nippon Telegraph and Telephone Corporation (NTT) and by the electricity companies. These corporations, which have traditionally been favoured by the Bond Issuance Committee, can be thought to account for a high proportion of straight bonds.

This is confirmed by Figure 9.5, which shows that NTT and the electricity companies together sponsored most domestic straight bond issues in the 1980s. For other industrial firms, domestic straight bond financing did not become common until the 1990s. Domestically issued warrant bonds were another seldom used instrument. Some have argued that this was because warrants were detachable only from bonds issued in foreign markets. But the popularity of domestic warrant bonds has not increased since 1989, when the domestic rules were changed to conform to foreign standards.

Figure 9.6 provides further evidence of the shift in bank financing towards bond issues, based on survey data measured in stock. These data are gathered each quarter by the Ministry of Finance. The ministry's survey differs from that of the Bank of Japan in its broader coverage: it covers a sample of firms with capital greater than ¥10 million but less than ¥1 billion, as well as all firms with capital greater than ¥1 billion. Because of the survey's inclusion of these smaller firms, the shift from bank financing towards bond financing appears less pronounced. Even so, it can be seen that the bank debt ratio had dropped from 95 per cent in the early 1970s to less than 90 per cent by the end of the 1980s. Again the trend is more pronounced for manufacturing firms, with the ratio for these companies dropping from 95 per cent to less than 80 per cent.

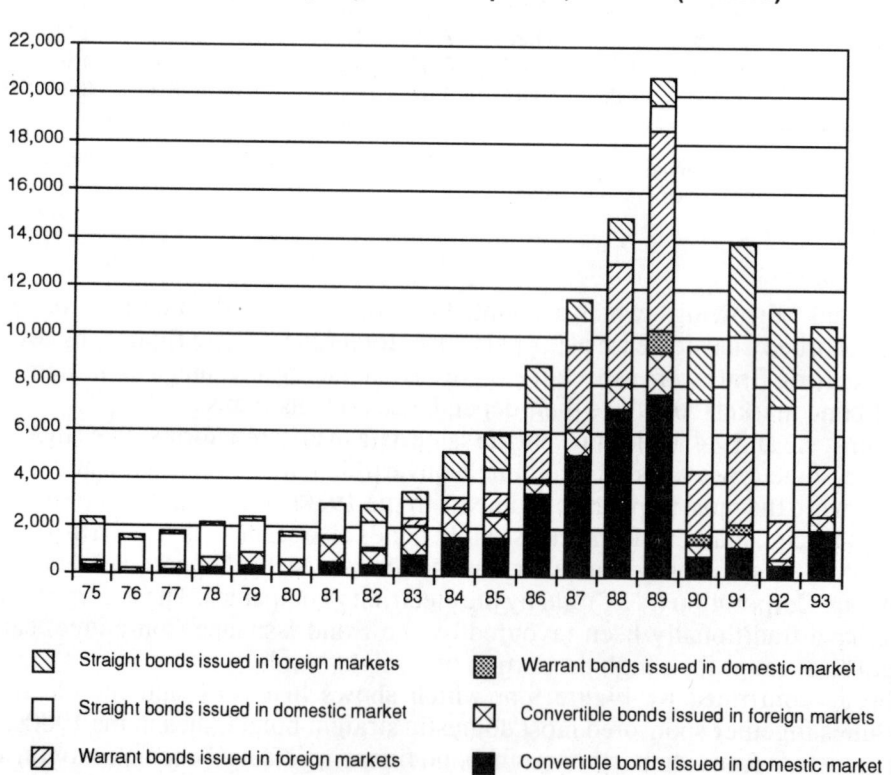

Figure 9.3   Bond issues by Japanese companies, 1975–93 (¥ billion)

- Straight bonds issued in foreign markets
- Straight bonds issued in domestic market
- Warrant bonds issued in foreign markets
- Warrant bonds issued in domestic market
- Convertible bonds issued in foreign markets
- Convertible bonds issued in domestic market

Source: Ministry of Finance (annual), *Shōken Kyoku Nenpō* [Annual Report of the Securities Bureau], Tokyo (various issues).

The magnitude of the changes found in the aggregate data (both flow and stock) is impressive if we remember the gradual nature of deregulation, and that some firms were not able to issue bonds freely even at the end of the 1980s. If we look only at firms that in fact had the choice of substituting bank loans with corporate bonds, we find that the shift has been even greater. Based on the sample used in Figure 9.2, Figure 9.7 compares the average bank debt ratio of two groups: firms that satisfied the bond issue criteria for convertible bonds in every year from 1982 to 1989, and the other firms in the Hoshi–Kashyap sample that did not. (Because both figures use stock measures, the ratios shown in Figures 9.6 and 9.7 are comparable.) Even though both series in Figure 9.7 decline substantially during the 1980s, the drop is much more marked for firms

Figure 9.4   Proportion of bond issues by type of bond, 1975–93

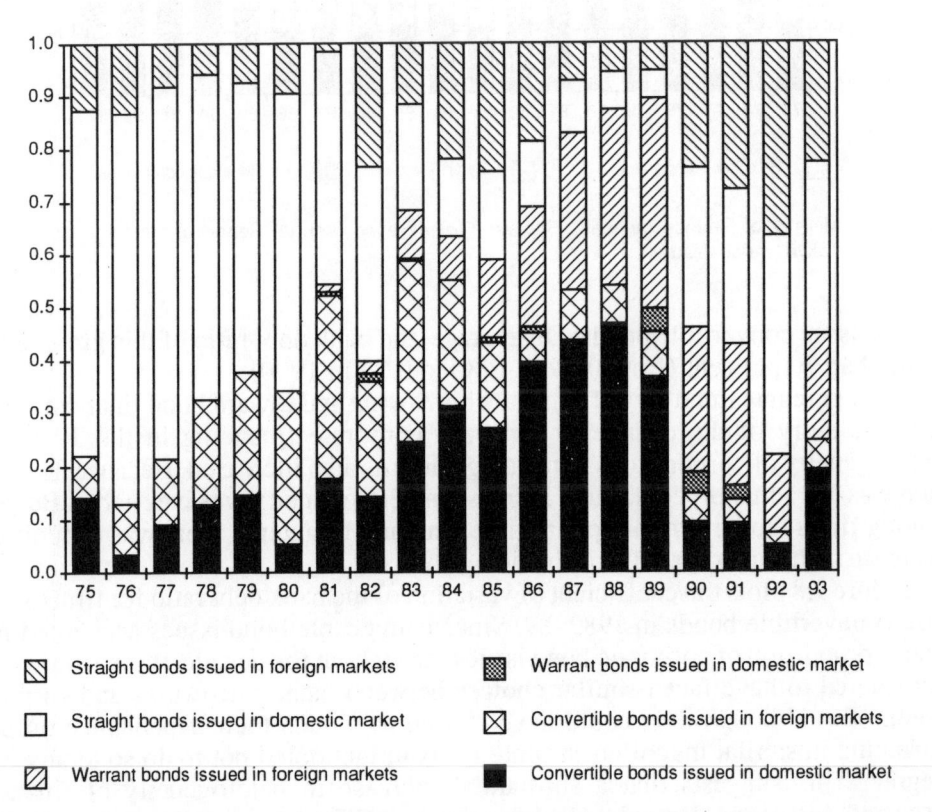

Source: Ministry of Finance (annual), *Shōken Kyoku Nenpō* [Annual Report of the Securities Bureau], Tokyo (various issues).

Figure 9.5 Straight bond issues by NTT, electricity and other companies, 1975–93 (¥100 million)

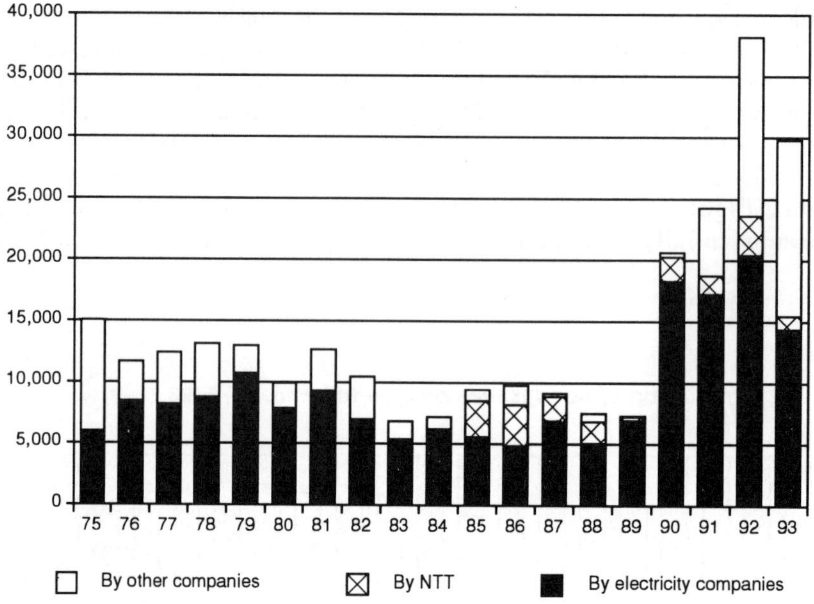

Source: Ministry of Finance (annual), *Shōken Kyoku Nenpō* [Annual Report of the Securities Bureau], Tokyo (various issues).

able to issue convertible bonds. On average, the bank debt ratio of this group fell by more than 70 per cent (from 0.79 in 1980 to 0.23 in 1990).

The aggregate trend away from bank borrowing and toward bond financing is just half the story of the change in Japanese corporate financing in the 1980s; the heterogeneity of corporations' financing patterns also increased. Because deregulation was a gradual process, some increase in heterogeneity was inevitable. But even among firms facing similar opportunities in bond financing, there was a significant increase in the heterogeneity of financing choices.

Figure 9.8 plots the coefficient of variation of the bank debt ratio for firms able to issue convertible bonds in 1982–89. Since convertible bond issues accounted for a major proportion of corporate bond issues throughout the decade, these firms can be considered to have faced similar choices between bank borrowings and corporate bonds. But although they could have chosen to reduce their dependence on bank financing in similar magnitudes, some firms in fact opted not to do so to any great degree. This suggests that a substantial increase in heterogeneity of financing occurred, with firms responding to deregulation in different ways. Even when standard deviations instead of coefficients of variations are calculated (not reported here), we find that the standard deviation increased in the 1980s.

Figure 9.6   Bank debt ratio, 1966–93[a]

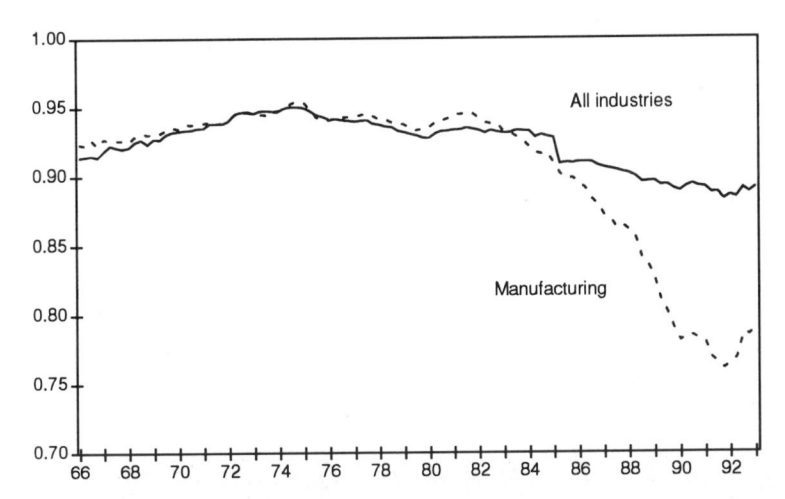

Note: a   The bank debt ratio is defined as the ratio of total bank borrowings to the sum of total bank borrowings and corporate bonds outstanding (including convertible and warrant bonds), calculated quarterly.

Source: Ministry of Finance (quarterly), *Quarterly Reports of Incorporated Enterprise Statistics*, Tokyo.

Figure 9.7   Bank debt ratio for firms eligible to issue convertible bonds, 1975–93[a]

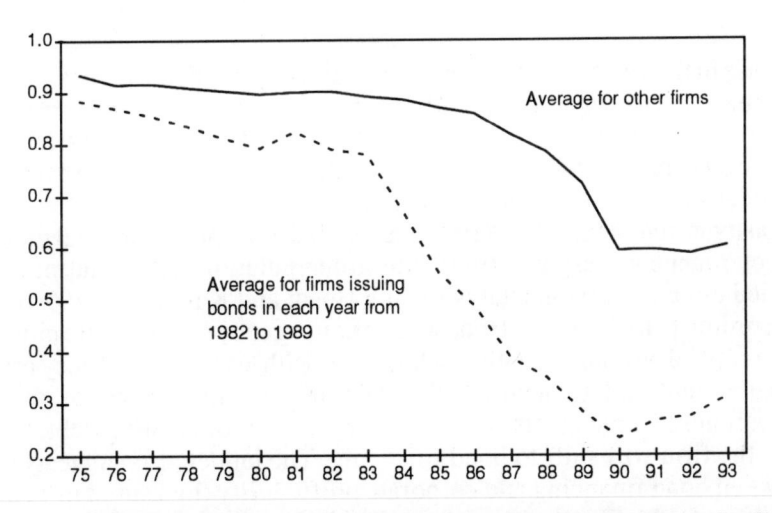

Note: a   The bank debt ratio is defined as the ratio of total bank borrowings to the sum of total bank borrowings and corporate bonds outstanding (including convertible and warrant bonds), calculated as of March. Of the 577 sample firms, 166 were able to issue convertible bonds in each year from 1982 to 1989.

Source: Author's estimates, based on Hoshi and Kashyap's (1990) sample.

Figure 9.8   **Coefficient of variation of bank debt ratio, 1975–93[a]**

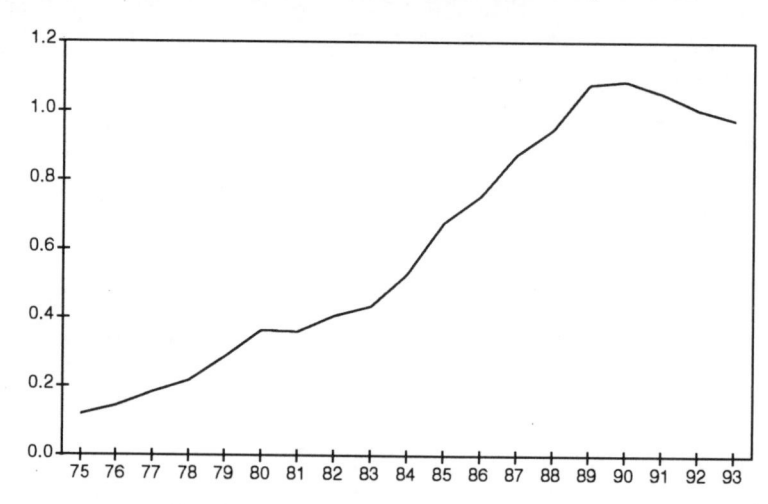

Note: a   The bank debt ratio is defined as the ratio of total bank borrowings to the sum of total bank borrowings and corporate bonds outstanding (including convertible and warrant bonds), calculated as of March each year. Only firms able to issue convertible bonds in each year from 1982 to 1989 were included in the calculation. Sample size differs from year to year; the ratio cannot be calculated for firms with zero debt. Sample size ranges from 141 to 159.

Source: Author's estimates, based on Hoshi and Kashyap's (1990) sample.

The increase in the variation of the bank debt ratio implies that whereas some firms reduced their bank borrowings only slightly, others took full advantage of deregulation to move aggressively away from banks. It is natural to ask what type of firm reduced its dependence on bank borrowings and what type decided to stay with the banks. Some recent empirical studies have addressed this question.

Hoshi, Kashyap and Scharfstein (1993) developed a simple theoretical model that predicted a heterogeneous response from firms to deregulation of the bond market. The authors carried out a regression analysis using Hoshi and Kashyap's (1990) sample of firms. According to their model, firms with serious agency problems are more likely to continue to depend on bank financing, while firms with less serious agency problems will tend to substitute bank financing with bond financing. In other words, the higher the level of collateralisable assets and the lower the level of existing debt, the more aggressively the firm will shift to bond financing. The model also suggests that the relation between bond financing and corporate profitability (measured in Tobin's q) may be non-monotonic. Firms with high profitability are more likely to issue bonds because this reduces the extent of the agency problem. However, those with low profitability may also decide to issue bonds, because their profitability is too low to justify the cost of being monitored by banks.

The authors examined empirically the implications of their model, using data on firms able to issue bonds in each year from 1982 to 1989. It is important that they focused on firms facing similar financing opportunities. If firms not meeting the bond issue criteria had been included in the analysis, their investigation would have revealed only that the firms that were more likely to satisfy the criteria reduced their dependence on bank financing: not an illuminating result. Hoshi, Kashyap and Scharfstein found that firms with a low degree of agency problems are in fact more likely to use bond financing. Although their model predicted a non-monotonic relation between Tobin's q and bond financing, the empirical results suggested that the relation is monotonic for those firms which belong to one of the six largest corporate groups (*keiretsu*). The authors found that high profitability *keiretsu* firms are more likely to issue bonds, suggesting that the second reason for issuing bonds (low profitability) is not important for these firms.

Hsieh and Wells (1992) also investigated the choice between bank financing and bond financing using Japanese data from the 1980s. They found that larger and more profitable firms were more likely to reduce their dependence on bank financing. Their analysis does not, however, exclude from the sample those firms which did not satisfy the bond issue criteria. Their results are therefore likely to be driven by the bond issue criteria, which favour larger and more profitable corporations.

Anderson (1995) carried out a similar exercise, but was careful to choose only those firms which satisfied the bond issue criteria. He found that firms with low agency costs (indicated by larger size, higher profitability, lower operating volatility, lower growth opportunity and a larger amount of collateralisable assets) are more likely to depend on bond financing. His results thus accord with those of Hoshi, Kashyap and Scharfstein (1993).

The heterogeneous reaction to deregulation is explained by the differing extent of agency problems among firms, according to Anderson (1995) and Hoshi, Kashyap and Scharfstein (1993). Campbell and Hamao (1994) suggest a different interpretation. They divided firms into two subgroups: those having one of the 19 major city, trust or long-term credit banks as their largest lender as of 1983, and those having either no bank loans or a different largest lender. The former group was said to consist of firms with a main bank, and the latter of firms without a main bank. This definition of main bank affiliation is not standard: researchers have traditionally looked at the share of the largest lender rather than its identity to separate firms with a strong main bank attachment from those without. Campbell and Hamao found that whereas firms without a main bank have aggressively substituted bank loans with bond issues, those with a main bank did not greatly reduce their dependence on banks. Although their analysis fails to exclude firms that did not satisfy the bond issue criteria, the authors claim to find similar results when they repeat their analysis using the subsample of firms identified by Hoshi, Kashyap and Scharfstein (1993) as being eligible to issue convertible bonds in each year from 1982 to 1989 (Campbell and Hamao 1994, pp. 339–40). Thus, according to Campbell and Hamao (1994), heterogeneity is explained by the historical relations of firms and banks.[5]

Financial deregulation and the main bank system

Following the internationalisation and deregulation of finance in the 1980s, a tremendous shift in financing took place, with bank borrowings being replaced by corporate bonds. Although Campbell and Hamao (1994) play down this shift — arguing that 'the major changes in corporate finance have occurred among unaffiliated firms, not main bank firms' (p. 341) — even their results show that main bank firms satisfying the bond issue criteria shifted toward bond financing (although to a lesser extent than unaffiliated firms). This shift may have important implications for the Japanese system of corporate financing and corporate control, in which banks have traditionally played a significant role. This section considers whether the shift away from bank borrowings by large corporations will eventually lead to a decline of Japan's bank-led financial system.[6]

As is well known, banks have traditionally played an important role in Japanese corporate finance.[7] Many firms have very close relations with their main bank, which is often their largest lender. The main bank almost always holds a substantial parcel of shares in the firm, and often places its employees on the firm's board. It monitors client firms on behalf of other lenders (Schoenholtz and Takeda 1985; Horiuchi 1989), and reduces the incentive and informational problems that would exist with arm's-length banking (Hoshi, Kashyap and Scharfstein 1991). The main bank often seems to be committed to rescuing clients that are in financial trouble (Sheard 1994), and to reducing the cost of financial distress (Hoshi, Kashyap and Scharfstein 1990; Suzuki and Wright 1985). Because rescue operations often include disciplinary measures for current management, the main bank can in effect be said to 'replace the missing takeover market' (Sheard 1989).

The shift away from bank financing by major corporations seems to cast doubt on the future of the main bank system. If banks become unimportant as a source of funds, they may stop acting as efficient monitors of firms and guardians against mismanagement. But does the shift away from bank borrowing to bond financing really imply any significant change in the importance of banks as a source of funds? After all, it has traditionally been banks that were the major buyers and holders of corporate bonds.

Figure 9.9 shows the distribution of corporate bond ownership in 1954–93. The figure is based on data provided by the Bank of Japan on outstanding balances of main financial assets and liabilities, calculated as of the end of March each year. It confirms that Japanese banks were the major holders of corporate bonds until the early 1970s. Bond holdings by banks declined substantially in the 1970s, while those of the household sector increased. The two sectors are now of roughly equal importance in the corporate bond market.

Subscription data reported in Figure 9.10 show that households have been important actors in the convertible bond market in particular. This instrument is also

Figure 9.9 Distribution of corporate bond ownership, 1954–94[a] (per cent)

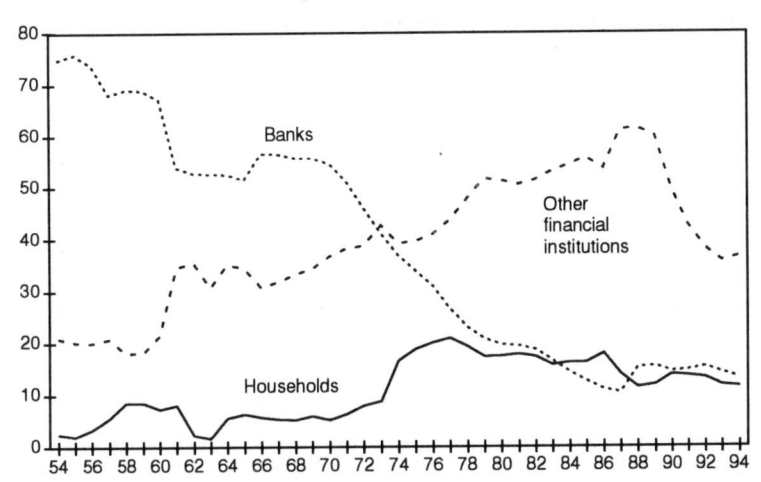

Note: a Calculated by dividing the gross value of corporate bonds held by each sector by total gross corporate bonds outstanding.

Source: Bank of Japan (monthly), *Economic Statistics Monthly*, Bank of Japan, Tokyo (various issues).

Figure 9.10 Convertible bond subscriptions by banks and households, 1969–85[a] (per cent)

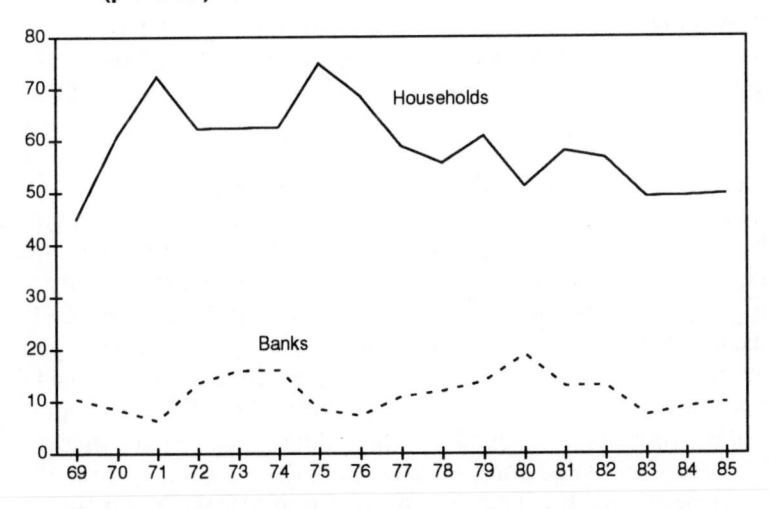

Note: a Based on total amount of convertible bonds initially sold to each sector.

Source: Shimura, Kaichi (ed.) (1986), *Gendai Nihon no Kōshasai Shijō* [Government and Corporate Bond Markets in Contemporary Japan], Tōkyō Daigaku Shuppankai, Tokyo, pp. 288–9, based on original data from Kōshasai Hikiuke Kyōkai.

far more popular with the corporate sector than straight bonds. Since the 1970s, more than half of newly issued convertible bonds have been purchased by individuals; banks have bought only 10–20 per cent of the total value. Figures 9.9 and 9.10 together show that banks now have a relatively minor share of bond financing. This confirms that the shift out of bank loans into corporate bonds in the 1980s reflects real change in the financing habits of Japanese corporations.

How will the shift in corporate financing affect the Japanese financial system? One possibility is that the system will adopt features of the US system, in which bonds and stocks issued in open markets constitute a major source of funds, non-bank institutions such as rating agencies provide monitoring services, and the market for takeovers acts to discipline management. This shift to a market based financial system, if it happens at all, will certainly take time.[8] Rating agencies and the other informational infrastructure of open securities markets, including disclosure rules and regulations on insider trading, are underdeveloped in Japan, as Horiuchi (1992) has pointed out. Hostile takeovers are virtually nonexistent, with greenmailers — who buy up shares in order to force companies to buy them back later at a premium — constituting the closest thing Japan has to a corporate raider (Okumura 1990). The gradual nature of deregulation so far also implies that any transition process will take time. A substantial number of firms have only recently acquired the ability to issue bonds, while others are still as yet unable to satisfy the bond issue criteria.

Another reason why the Japanese system of corporate finance is unlikely to converge quickly towards that of the United States is that Japanese banks still maintain some influence over corporations through their shareholdings and the dispatch of directors. Even though bank loans have become a less important source of funds for large firms, banks continue to be major shareholders of companies and to send many employees to sit on their boards. City banks, as top 20 shareholders, held 7.46 per cent of listed companies' shares in 1994, only a little below the 8.09 per cent they held in 1981 (Tōyō Keizai Shinpōsha 1982, p. 39; 1994, p. 68). The number of directors dispatched from city banks to other listed companies increased from 1,167 in 1981 to 1,559 in 1994 (Tōyō Keizai Shinpōsha 1982, p. 51; 1994, p. 82). Thus as far as the aggregate trend is concerned, no weakening of bank ties is evident. The aggregate data may again, however, hide heterogeneity, and significant changes in bank–firm relations may in fact be occurring among large firms even in the areas of shareholding and director dispatch. Careful study of firm-level data is therefore needed on this issue.

The increased heterogeneity of firms' financing patterns suggests yet another reason why the transition to a securities based system will at the very least take time. The existence of heterogeneity among firms faced with similar financing opportunities implies that some firms have decided not to reduce their dependence on banks, presumably because they value the potential benefits stemming from their close relations with them. Hoshi, Kashyap and Scharfstein (1993) found that the firms which did not greatly reduce their dependence on bank financing were those with a low level of collateralisable assets and high leverage. These are often characteristics of newly established, high-growth companies. As long as there is a supply of such firms in the Japanese economy, demand for the main bank system will continue to exist.

Demand by corporations is not in itself sufficient to guarantee the survival of the main bank system; banks must also be able to supply the services of a main bank. The loss of a large number of clients profitable enough to satisfy the bond issue criteria and issue bonds in the open market may imply a decline in the ability of the banks to fill this role. The departure of worthy companies from the main bank relationship at least means the loss of a source of stable revenue, and hurts bank profitability. Because of the costs involved, banks may become more reluctant to rescue firms experiencing financial difficulty. If, as Nakatani (1984) suggests, the main bank system works as an implicit insurance mechanism in which better performing firms subsidise those performing less well, the loss of the more profitable firms will make such cross-subsidisation impossible.

A finding by Hoshi, Kashyap and Scharfstein (1993) is instructive on this point. They find a positive correlation between the level of Tobin's q and the decline in the bank debt ratio for firms belonging to *keiretsu*. Thus better performing firms in *keiretsu*, where the main bank relation is presumed to be strongest, do indeed seem to be moving away from bank financing.

Loss of good customers is not the only reason why Japanese banks may have difficulty in future in fulfilling their position as main banks. The financial deregulation of the 1980s may have damaged their ability to function in this role through another channel: by worsening their balance sheets. Figures 9.11 through 9.14 show some aspects of the changes that took place in the Japanese banking portfolio in the 1980s. Figure 9.11 plots the share of loans and discounts to manufacturing firms in banks' total loans and discounts. As manufacturing firms moved away from bank borrowings, the proportion of loans to this sector in the banks' portfolios declined. Considering that large firms were more likely to satisfy the bond issue criteria and reduce their reliance on bank borrowings, it can be expected that the share of loans to small and medium sized corporations will have increased in the banking portfolio. Figure 9.12 shows that this was indeed so — loans to corporations with capital of ¥1 million or less increased from 40 per cent in 1978 to 58 per cent in 1990.

As banks began to lose the business of large manufacturing firms, loans to real estate companies, many of them small, must have appeared increasingly attractive. The property market was booming, and investment in land was quite profitable. As Figure 9.13 shows, the proportion of real estate loans in total bank loans increased sharply during the 1980s, with most of the rise stemming from the expansion of loans to small and medium sized real estate companies. Loans to the industry were also made indirectly, through non-bank financial institutions. Noguchi (1992, pp. 129–31) has estimated that, in the late 1980s, about 40 per cent of non-bank loans were made to this sector. Figure 9.14 shows that the share of bank loans to financial companies other than banks, security firms and insurance companies increased from a negligible 0.9 per cent in 1974 to almost 10 per cent in 1990. If we assume, following Noguchi (1992),

THE IMPACT OF FINANCIAL DEREGULATION ON CORPORATE FINANCING

Figure 9.11   Proportion of bank loans to manufacturing firms, 1974–93

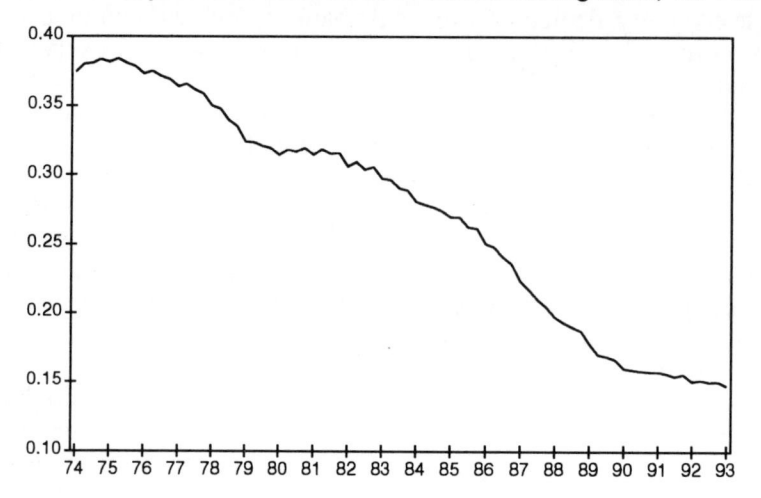

Source: Bank of Japan (monthly), 'Loans and Discounts Outstanding, and New Loans for Equipment Funds by Industry', *Economic Statistics Monthly*, Research and Statistics Department, Bank of Japan, Tokyo (various issues).

Figure 9.12   Proportion of bank loans to small and medium sized firms, 1978–93

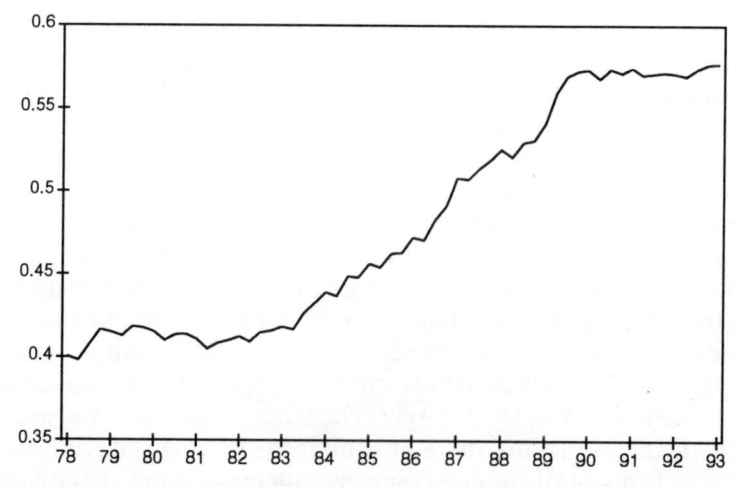

Source: Bank of Japan (monthly), 'Loans and Discounts Outstanding, and New Loans for Equipment Funds by Industry', *Economic Statistics Monthly*, Research and Statistics Department, Bank of Japan, Tokyo (various issues).

Figure 9.13   Proportion of bank loans to real estate industry, 1977–93

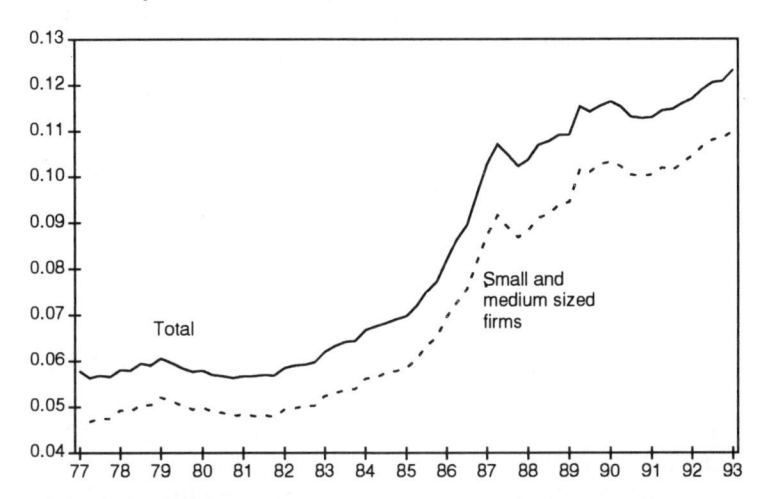

Source: Bank of Japan (monthly), 'Loans and Discounts Outstanding, and New Loans for Equipment Funds by Industry', *Economic Statistics Monthly*, Research and Statistics Department, Bank of Japan, Tokyo (various issues).

Figure 9.14   Proportion of bank loans to non-banks, 1974–93

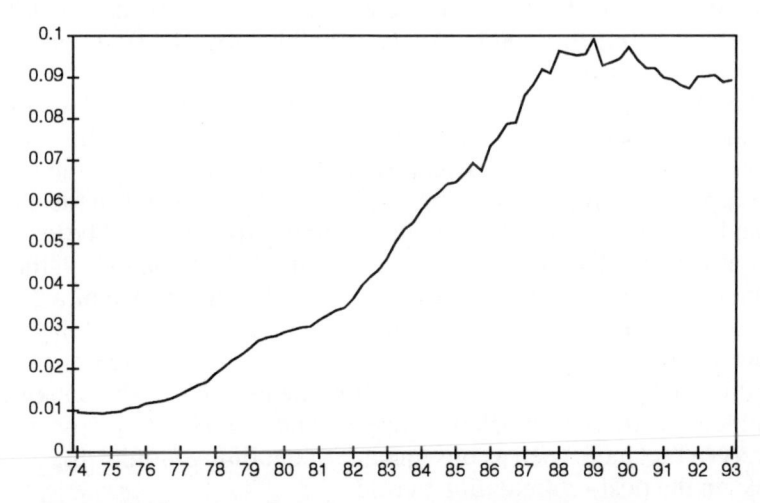

Source: Bank of Japan (monthly), 'Loans and Discounts Outstanding, and New Loans for Equipment Funds by Industry', *Economic Statistics Monthly*, Research and Statistics Department, Bank of Japan, Tokyo (various issues).

that about 40 per cent of such bank loans were then lent on to real estate industry, Figures 9.13 and 9.14 jointly imply that about 15 per cent of all bank loans were flowing — directly or indirectly — to the sector at the end of the 1980s.

Noguchi (1992) points out that the sudden decline in the budget deficit in the late 1980s was another important factor propelling the banks into real estate lending. He argues that the reduction in government debt forced banks to adjust their portfolios, with the result that many then chose to lend to the real estate industry. He estimates that the increase in bank loans to the industry was roughly equal to the reduction in government debt that occurred in the late 1980s (Noguchi 1992, pp. 136–7).

Deregulation of interest rates, which raised the cost of funds for banks, was yet another factor behind changes in the composition of banks' portfolios. In response to decreasing profit margins, Japanese banks introduced various measures to reduce their operating costs (computerisation, for example) while competing for deposits and loans more fiercely than ever. To lower costs and accelerate the loan approval process, many cut back on their loan examination departments, often delegating the task to the loan sales department (Oka 1992, pp. 7–8). The monitoring capability of Japanese banks seems to have suffered during this process of cost reduction. With their reduced monitoring capability, banks were attracted to loans to real estate business simply because the collateral was land, a seemingly safe commodity. Japanese banks thus seem to have chosen the easy path of collateralised loans rather than seek out worthy projects conducted by expanding firms.

The high proportion of real estate related lending became a burden for many banks when land prices began to fall in the early 1990s. The Ministry of Finance has estimated the amount of problem loans held by 21 major banks (including all city banks, long-term credit banks and trust banks) to be ¥12.5 trillion.[9] Including the bad loans of other financial institutions, the total amount of problem loans has been estimated at around ¥40 trillion. Some analysts believe that the figure may be even higher, exceeding ¥100 trillion.

The Japanese banking sector is now going through a slow process of restructuring. The future of the main bank system will depend on both the speed of this process and the health of the banks following restructuring. As discussed above, demand from high-growth corporations for the main bank system will continue. But the question is whether the banks will be ready and able to play their traditional role. The loss of better performing companies will make it increasingly difficult for them to bear the costs of rescuing financially distressed firms. More directly, the emergence of a diversified debt structure as a result of deregulation is likely to raise the extent of the collective action problem among creditors when a firm becomes financially distressed (see, for example, Hoshi, Kashyap and Scharfstein 1990; Sheard 1994). The banking sector also faces problems with its own balance sheet because of its heavy exposure to real estate. This may in fact have been a consequence of declining monitoring activity by Japanese banks in the post-deregulation period.

Conclusion

The chapter has surveyed important regulatory changes in Japanese finance in the 1980s and investigated their impact on patterns of corporate financing. Many large corporations took advantage of new opportunities in bond financing to move away from banks, traditionally the dominant source of funds. This suggests that regulation was important in shaping the bank-led financial system in Japan: given the opportunity to reduce their reliance on bank financing, many firms chose to do so.

But regulation was not the only reason for the development of a bank-led financial system, as my discussion of the increased heterogeneity of corporations' financing patterns shows. Even though deregulation made it possible for firms to issue bonds, many still chose to rely on bank loans. These firms clearly value the benefits of the main bank relationship and will continue to find close bank ties attractive in the near future.

Can banks continue to provide the benefits of a close bank–firm relationship? The loss of the more profitable firms may undermine the banks' ability to help their clients out of financial difficulty. Perhaps more importantly, financial deregulation has already contributed to the worsening of the banks' balance sheets. As large customers reduced their dependence on bank loans and financial deregulation narrowed bank profit margins, the banks rushed into property related lending in the late 1980s. When land prices fell in the early 1990s, many property related loans turned bad, leaving Japanese banks with a serious bad loan problem. The fate of the main bank system depends largely on whether Japanese banks can rebound from this current trouble.

Notes

1. See Packer (1994) for more on the role of long-term credit banks in the Japanese financial system.
2. Whereas the *gensaki* market is open to all corporations, only financial institutions can participate in the *tegata* market. In a *tegata* transaction, the vendor sells a bill before maturity at a discount. In a *gensaki* transaction, the vendor sells a security with an agreement to repurchase it at a fixed time and price.
3. Some corporations were not included in the survey even though they were capitalised at more than ¥1 billion. The Bank of Japan (1992) claims that it sampled just enough firms 'to more or less reflect the conditions in each industry'. The survey also included some small or unlisted firms that were nonetheless important for each industry.
4. In the survey, numbers in the source of funds table are obtained as the annual change in the level of the relevant items on the liability side of the balance sheet. For example, the change in the sum of paid-in capital, proceeds of new share issues, and capital reserves is recorded as new stock issues, and short-term borrowing in the source of funds table is the change in the short-term borrowing in the balance sheet. Thus the numbers can be negative.

5   The conclusion reached by Campbell and Hamao (1994) is not entirely inconsistent with those of Anderson (1995) and Hoshi, Kashyap and Scharfstein (1993). It is possible that main bank affiliation as defined by Campbell and Hamao is related to the extent of agency problems.

6   Sheard (1992) makes a similar attempt, presenting three possible scenarios for future corporate financing in Japan. These range from a conservative scenario, in which the main bank system survives as a substitute for the takeover mechanism, to a radical one incorporating transformation of every aspect of the Japanese financial system. Aoki, Patrick and Sheard (1994) also take up this issue.

7   For a survey and comparative study of the main bank system in Japan, see Aoki and Patrick (1994).

8   Aoki, Patrick and Sheard (1994, p. 48) reach a similar conclusion: '[T]he Japanese system seems unlikely to shift to the Anglo-American type arm's-length banking system in the near future. One reason is the peripheral nature of the equity market, which, partly due to stable shareholding practices, lacks effective monitoring functions to replace those performed by banks'.

9   This is the figure given in the 'Standard Policy for Management of Bad Loans at Financial Institutions' published by the Ministry of Finance on 8 June 1995 (*Nihon Keizai Shinbun*, 9 June 1995).

References

Anderson, Christopher W. (1995), Deregulation, Disintermediation, and Agency Costs of Debt: Evidence from Japan, Unpublished paper, University of Pittsburgh, Pittsburgh.

Aoki, Masahiko and Hugh Patrick (eds) (1994), *The Japanese Main Bank System: Its Relevancy for Developing and Transforming Economies*, Oxford: Oxford University Press.

Aoki, Masahiko, Hugh Patrick and Paul Sheard (1994), 'The Japanese Main Bank System: An Introductory Overview', in Masahiko Aoki and Hugh Patrick (eds), *The Japanese Main Bank System: Its Relevancy for Developing and Transforming Economies*, Oxford: Oxford University Press, pp.3–50.

Arai, Akira (1991), *Nichibei Kōshasai Shijō Hikaku* [Comparative Study of Bond Markets in the United States and Japan], Tokyo: Nihon Keizai Shinbunsha.

Bank of Japan (1992), *Shuyō Kigyō Keiei Bunseki: Heisei 3-Nendo* [Financial Statements of Principal Enterprises: Fiscal Year 1991], Tokyo: Bank of Japan.

Bank of Japan Institute of Monetary and Economic Studies (1995), *Shinban: Waga Kuni no Kin'yū Seido* [The Financial System of Our Country: New Edition], Tokyo: Nihon Shin'yō Chōsa Kabushiki Kaisha.

Campbell, John, and Yasushi Hamao (1994), 'Changing Patterns of Corporate Financing and the Main Bank System in Japan', in Masahiko Aoki and Hugh Patrick (eds), *The Japanese Main Bank System: Its Relevancy for Developing and Transforming Economies*, Oxford: Oxford University Press, pp. 325–49.

Gotō, Takeshi (1986), 'Minkan-Sai no Hakkō Shijō' [Issuance Market for Non-Government Bonds], in Kaichi Shimura (ed.), *Gendai Nihon no Kōshasai Shijō* [Government and Corporate Bond Markets in Contemporary Japan], Tokyo: Tōkyō Daigaku Shuppankai, pp. 99–158.

Hamada, Kōichi and Akiyoshi Horiuchi (1987), 'The Political Economy of the Financial Market', in Kōzō Yamamura and Yasukichi Yasuba (eds), *The Political Economy of Japan, Vol. I: The Domestic Transformation*, Stanford, CA: Stanford University Press, pp. 223–60.

Horiuchi, Akiyoshi (1989), 'Informational Properties of the Japanese Financial System', *Japan and the World Economy*, 1, pp. 255–78.

—— (1992), 'Financial Liberalization: The Case of Japan', in Dimitri Vittas (ed.), *Financial Regulation: Changing the Rules of the Game*, Washington DC: World Bank, pp. 85–119.

Hoshi, Takeo and Anil Kashyap (1990), 'Evidence on q and Investment for Japanese Firms', *Journal of Japanese and International Economies*, 3, pp. 371–400.

Hoshi, Takeo, Anil Kashyap and David Scharfstein (1990), 'The Role of Banks in Reducing the Cost of Financial Distress in Japan', *Journal of Financial Economics*, 27, pp. 67–88.

—— (1991), 'Corporate Structure, Liquidity, and Investment: Evidence from Japanese Industrial Groups', *Quarterly Journal of Economics*, 106, pp. 33–60.

—— (1993), 'The Choice Between Public and Private Debt: An Analysis of Post-Deregulation Corporate Financing in Japan', NBER Working Paper No. 4421, Cambridge, MA.

Hsieh, Psieh-Shun and Robin Wells (1992), 'The Japanese Financial Market: Evidence on Firm Financing Choice and Investment after Deregulation', Working paper, University of Southampton, Southampton.

Kōshasai Hikiuke Kyōkai [Public and Corporate Bonds Underwriters Association] (1980), *Nihon Kōshasai Shijōshi* [History of Public and Corporate Bonds Markets in Japan], Tokyo: Kōshasai Hikiuke Kyōkai.

Ministry of Finance (1992), *The 16th Annual Report of the International Finance Bureau, 1992*, Tokyo: Kin'yū Zaisei Jijō Kenkyūkai.

Nakatani, Iwao (1984), 'The Economic Role of Financial Corporate Grouping', in Masahiko Aoki (ed.), *The Economic Analysis of the Japanese Firm*, Amsterdam: North-Holland, pp. 227–58.

Noguchi, Yukio (1992), *Baburu no Keizaigaku: Nihon Keizai ni Nani ga Okotta ka* [Bubble Economics: What Has Happened to the Japanese Economy?], Tokyo: Nihon Keizai Shinbunsha.

Oka, Masao (1992), *Tenkan-ki no Ginkō Keiei* [Bank Management in Transition], Tokyo: Yūhikaku.

Okumura, Hiroshi (1990), *Kigyō Baishū* [Corporate Takeover], Tokyo: Iwanami Shinsho.

Packer, Frank (1994), 'The Role of Long-Term Credit Banks within the Main Bank System', in Masahiko Aoki and Hugh Patrick (eds), *The Japanese Main Bank System: Its*

Relevancy for Developing and Transforming Economies, Oxford: Oxford University Press, pp. 142–87.

Rosenbluth, Frances (1989), *Financial Politics in Contemporary Japan*, Ithaca, NY: Cornell University Press.

Schoenholtz, Kermit and Masahiko Takeda (1985), 'Jōhō Katsudō to Mein Banku Sei' [Informational Activities and the Main Bank System], *Kin'yū Kenkyū*, 4, pp. 1–24.

Sheard, Paul (1989), 'The Main Bank System and Corporate Monitoring and Control in Japan', *Journal of Economic Behavior and Organization*, 11, pp. 399–422.

—— (1992), 'Japanese Corporate Finance and Behavior: Recent Developments and the Impact of Deregulation', in Colin R. McKenzie and Michael Stutchbury (eds), *Japanese Financial Markets and the Role of the Yen*, New York, NY: Columbia University Press, pp. 55–72.

—— (1994), 'Main Banks and the Governance of Financial Distress', in Masahiko Aoki and Hugh Patrick (eds), *The Japanese Main Bank System: Its Relevancy for Developing and Transforming Economies*, Oxford: Oxford University Press, pp. 188–230.

Suzuki, Sadahiko and Richard Wright (1985), 'Financial Structure and Bankruptcy Risk in Japanese Companies', *Journal of International Business Studies*, pp. 97–110.

Taiyō Kōbe Mitsui Bank (1990), *Gaisai DR Hakkō Handobukku* [Handbook of Foreign Bond and DR Issuance], Tokyo: Taiyō Kōbe Mitsui Bank.

Teranishi, Jūrō (1982), *Nihon no Keizai Hatten to Kin'yū* [Japanese Economic Development and Financial System], Tokyo: Iwanami Shoten.

Tōyō Keizai Shinpōsha (1982), *Kigyō Keiretsu Sōran 1983 Nenban* [Directory of Corporate Affiliations, 1983 Edition], Tokyo: Tōyō Keizai Shinpōsha.

—— (1994), *Kigyō Keiretsu Sōran 1995 Nenban* [Directory of Corporate Affiliations, 1995 Edition], Tokyo: Tōyō Keizai Shinpōsha.

10 Financial liberalisation and the safety net

*Akiyoshi Horiuchi**

The fragility of Japan's financial system was revealed by the huge amount of non-performing loans in the banking sector after the 'bubble' burst in 1990. The bad loan problem has not only caused serious concern about the credibility of Japanese financial institutions, it has also paralysed the macroeconomy by forcing banks to restructure their equity capital positions. Specifically, the deterioration of banks' equity capital seems to have restrained the banks from actively supplying credit to industrial firms, and particularly small-scale businesses, in the early 1990s, exacerbating a macroeconomic recession triggered by tight money policy.

The Ministry of Finance and the Bank of Japan — the regulatory authorities in the Japanese financial system — have been criticised for their failure to prevent this sort of financial turmoil and for their management of the safety net for dealing with banks or other financial institutions in distress. Many believe that, to regain financial stability, the current safety net and related regulations need to be reorganised. Thus it is clear that, in spite of its tremendous development since the end of World War II, the Japanese financial system has not yet resolved the issue of how to maintain stability in the face of the dynamic evolution of Japan's financial markets. This chapter reviews the evolution and workings of the safety net in postwar Japan.

Relationship between financial regulation and stability

Governments provide a financial safety net in order to minimise the spillover effects of the managerial failures of banks and other financial institutions on the financial system as a whole. The safety net also has important implications for risk sharing in

---

* This chapter is based on a paper presented at a seminar held in 1994 at the Reserve Bank of Australia in Sydney. The author is grateful for valuable comments on the original manuscript from Gordon de Brouwer and Peter Drysdale, and particularly from Paul Sheard and John Stachurski.

the financial system. Appropriate incentive mechanisms are required to prevent moral hazard type behaviour that could endanger the stability of the safety net system. 'Moral hazard' refers to the distortion of behaviour that can result when economic agents are shielded from the full consequences of their actions. In this section, I will briefly describe the safety net mechanisms adopted by the regulatory authorities in postwar Japan before discussing how the system was maintained.

The safety net in the financial system

It has been a widely accepted view that the regulatory authorities will at times need to intervene in the process of dealing with financially distressed banks and other financial institutions in order to maintain stability within the financial system. The large number of people who would suffer in the event of a bank becoming bankrupt makes the system especially vulnerable to financial disturbances (Diamond and Dybvig 1983). When depositors develop an expectation that a bank may not be able to meet its deposit liabilities, a bank run may ensue; because of liquidity constraints and the nature of credit creation, such a run can result in this expectation becoming self-fulfilling. The failure of one institution may trigger that of others as depositors act on the narrow incentive to recover their money. Following the conventional view, monetary authorities in almost all industrial economies have intervened in cases of financial distress of individual banks and related financial institutions. This intervention to prevent the managerial failure of banks and financial institutions that are endangering the stability of the financial system is known as the safety net.

The regulatory authorities employ a number of methods to deal with distressed banks. One is to pay depositors of banks in default under the deposit insurance system. This protects depositors, but not managers, shareholders or other debtholders. In other cases, the central bank or regulatory authority may decide to step in to rescue the financially distressed bank. Such intervention quite often allows almost all bank debtholders to escape the losses associated with the failure. This has been an important function of the safety net in industrialised countries such as Japan.

The function of the safety net has an obvious *ex post* implication for risk bearing in that some part of the risk in bank management is transferred to regulatory authorities, not only from bank managers and equity holders, but also from holders of bank debt. Should the regulatory authorities be unable to control management under the safety net, bank managers and equity holders would have an incentive to engage in excessive risk taking. A bank may, for example, aim to increase its profits by making loans that are risky but which have a high upside potential — if the gamble pays off, the bank wins; if it doesn't, the taxpayers lose. This is a typical moral hazard problem, and shows the need for other regulatory mechanisms to prevent problems arising because of the existence of the safety net.[1] The wider the scope of the financial safety net operated by the government, the stronger the incentives for private banks to engage in moral hazard type behaviour, and the more energetically the regulatory authorities will be required to monitor to prevent such behaviour. Because monitoring is costly, however, it is impossible for regulators to prevent all moral hazard type behaviour engaged in by banks.

The safety net in postwar Japan

The Japanese financial system operates under an extensive safety net provided by the regulatory authorities. In tight collaboration with the Bank of Japan (BOJ) and private financial institutions, the Ministry of Finance (MOF) has executed programs to rescue financially distressed institutions, particularly major banks. The number of banks that has come close to failing has been small, with the largest rescue program involving, not a bank, but Yamaichi Securities Company in 1965. In the rescue coordinated by the MOF, the BOJ provided emergency loans of ¥28.2 billion to Fuji Bank and two other banks, all of which functioned as conduits supplying financial support to Yamaichi.[2]

In some cases the MOF has ordered private banks to rescue financially distressed peers. In 1965, for example, Kawachi Bank, a small regional bank in financial distress, was absorbed by Sumitomo Bank, while in 1978 Mitsui Bank absorbed Tōto Bank, which had experienced rather stagnant performance for a long time. In other cases, the MOF has placed its officers on the board of the distressed bank with a view to restructuring its management. For instance, it sent an officer to Taikō Sōgo Bank, a small regional bank in Niigata prefecture, in 1979 to reorganise its management.

Since the actions taken by the regulators in rescuing troubled banks have almost always been covert, it is difficult to estimate the social costs of the safety net and the distribution of the burden among the various agents. However, the costs of preserving financial stability seem to have fallen disproportionately on sound private banks, particularly major banks. The regulatory authorities, including the BOJ, have only rarely paid the costs of the bail-out procedure, tending to confine their role to coordinating the rescue program and providing information to the relevant parties. In some cases, the BOJ may have extended loans to financially distressed banks at the official discount rate — which was substantially lower than money market interest rates — but it is impossible to obtain precise information about these unofficial rescue programs.

The experience of the US financial system suggests that deposit insurance is an important potential element of the safety net. This has not been the case in postwar Japan, however, where deposit insurance was not introduced until 1971. According to the official MOF explanation, deposit insurance was introduced in anticipation of a rise in the number of bank failures occurring because of increased competition. In the second half of the 1960s, the MOF had embarked on a re-evaluation of the Japanese financial system as it had existed since the end of the war. The main theme concerned the efficacy of the MOF's traditional financial administration, which relied on competition restricting regulations. Anticipating a substantial increase in competitive pressures in Japanese financial markets, some analysts argued for reform of the administration so as to foster more efficient financial mechanisms. Others regarded competition restricting regulations as indispensable to the maintenance of financial stability and favoured continuation of the traditional approach. In 1970, the Financial System Research Council (Kin'yū Seido Chōsakai) published a report emphasising the importance of promoting efficiency in the management of private banks and other financial institutions in preparation for increased competition (Financial System Research Society 1970). The report also advocated the introduction of a deposit insurance system.[3]

However, in the early 1970s, the view favouring the traditional approach to financial administration was still dominant in the MOF (MOF 1991, pp. 376–8). Since this view won the day, regulations in the financial system have been dismantled only gradually since the mid 1970s. For a long time, the Deposit Insurance Corporation was a rather nominal institution. Until 1986, its functions were very limited compared with those of its US counterpart, being confined to paying off insured deposits in cases of bank failure. In fact, the deposit insurance system was utilised for the first time only in April 1992, when ¥8 billion was supplied to help Iyo Bank absorb Tōhō Sōgo Bank.

Role of competition restricting regulations

Under the Japanese safety net, the regulators could rely on private banks to collaborate in the process of rescuing troubled banks, and major or financially sound banks faithfully bore an uneven share of the costs involved. In spite of its reliance on ad hoc rescues, Japan's extensive safety net did not induce widespread moral hazard behaviour on the part of private banks. Why did the safety net mechanisms work so successfully in postwar Japan? The existence of rents in the banking sector provides one key. Without these rents, private banks could not have afforded to collaborate with the authorities' rescue programs.

Such traditional competition restricting regulations as interest rate controls and restrictions on new entry into banking and other financial business effectively contributed to the accumulation of rents in the financial sector. Figure 10.1 shows average profit rates (current profits divided by equity capital) in the banking industry since 1955. Japanese banks enjoyed relatively high profit rates during the high growth period from the late 1950s to the early 1970s, when extensive competition restricting regulations were in operation and domestic financial markets were segregated from foreign markets. Since the mid 1970s, bank profit rates have declined considerably. As will be seen later, this decline corresponded to structural changes in the financial system, and these changes were induced by the gradual introduction and enforcement of deregulation measures.

Small-scale financial intermediaries, such as credit associations, credit cooperatives and regional banks, were particular beneficiaries of competition restricting regulations. For example, the MOF principle of 'one bank to one prefecture' suppressed competition among banks and other financial institutions by preventing new entry into regional banking markets.[4]

The MOF's administration of branch offices (*tenpo gyōsei*) was another significant area of regulation. During the high growth period, when almost all interest rates were

Figure 10.1 Average profit rates in banking industry, 1955–93[a] (per cent)

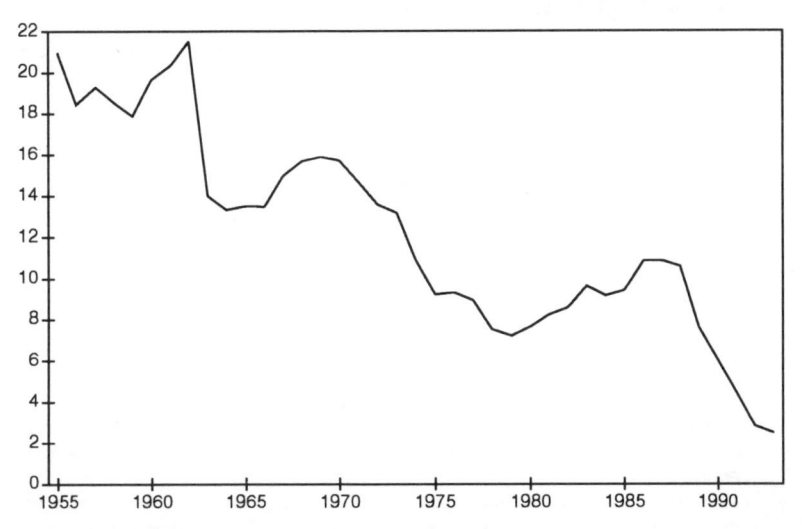

Note: a Current profits divided by equity.
Source: Federation of Bankers Associations of Japan (annual).

regulated, branch offices were an important means of 'non-price competition' for banks and essentially the vehicle by which they competed for deposit funds. Under the MOF's administration, banks were free neither to expand nor to change the location of their branch networks. In permitting new branches, the MOF gave preferential treatment to small banks. As Table 10.1 shows, the number of their branch offices increased more rapidly than did that of city banks, not only during the high growth period but also after the mid 1970s. This policy stance towards the financial industry has been called the 'escorted convoy method' *(gosōsendan gyōsei)*, in that the government restricted full-scale competition in order to stop the weakest banks from falling too far behind the leaders, and the leaders from getting too far ahead.

Competition restricting regulations were also utilised by the regulators to provide private banks with incentives to accept administrative guidance. The authorities manipulated these regulatory means to do favours for those who toed the line and to penalise those who failed to heed their guidance. In 1994, for example, Mitsubishi Bank obtained preferential treatment from the MOF in exchange for bailing out the Nippon Trust Bank (NTB), which had been seriously damaged by the accumulation of a huge amount of bad loans since the early 1990s. Mitsubishi Bank was 'rewarded' by being allowed to pursue a full complement of trust banking business through NTB, which is now its subsidiary. Other banks are prohibited by the MOF from engaging in full-line trust banking business through their trust bank subsidiaries.[5]

Table 10.1   Average annual change in number of branch offices and amount of deposits (per cent)

	City banks		Regional banks		Thrifts[a]	
	Branch	Deposits	Branch	Deposits	Branch	Deposits
1951–55	−0.1[b]	18.8[c]	4.4	14.5[c]	8.4[c]	19.4[c]
1956–60	−0.4	18.5	−0.1	20.0	4.0	24.3
1961–65	3.1	17.7	1.9	19.5	5.6	26.2
1966–70	1.1[d]	14.3	1.2[d]	15.4	3.1[d]	17.8
1971–75	0.9	17.2	2.7	18.3	3.3	20.3
1976–80	1.2	10.4	2.6	12.2	3.3	11.8

Notes: a   The thrifts are small-scale financial institutions catering to small and medium sized businesses. They comprise the mutual loan and savings banks, the credit associations and the credit co-operatives.
b   In 1955, Nihon Kangyō Bank and Hokkaidō Takushoku Bank were reclassified as city banks. This increased the number of city bank branch offices by 230. The influence of this reclassification is adjusted for in this table.
c   1954–55.
d   In 1968, Nihon Sōgo Bank, the largest of the mutual loan and savings banks, became a city bank. Saitama Bank was converted from a regional to a city bank in 1969. The influence of these conversions is adjusted for in this table.

Source: BOJ (annual).

Daiwa Bank (a city bank) incurred the MOF's disfavour when it resisted a MOF direction in 1954 requiring separation of commercial and trust banking business. Whereas other city banks separated these functions by establishing independent trust banks, Daiwa Bank refused to do this, and was reportedly treated unfavourably by the MOF for many years with respect to the distribution of branch offices.

The intricate procedures adopted by the MOF helped it to obtain detailed information about the management of individual banks. Similarly, the BOJ's daily transactions with commercial banks through interbank money markets enabled it to monitor individual banks' behaviour. Thus not only did the traditional competition restricting regulations give banks a handsome amount of rents, which could be utilised to support the regulators' operation of the safety net, but they also provided the monetary authorities with opportunities to monitor the banks. The close relationship between regulators and banks seems to have been effective in preventing banks' moral hazard, in spite of the existence of a far-reaching financial safety net.

Did the rents which had accumulated in the banking sector contribute to the rapid industrial development of postwar Japan? This is an important and interesting question. The conventional assessment of Japan's low interest rate policy gives an affirmative answer. It is claimed that the rents were effectively transferred from the banking industry to non-bank industrial sectors, thereby promoting industrial investment (Teranishi 1982, pp. 451–506). However, it is far from obvious that rents in the banking sector were actually transferred to key industries (Horiuchi 1993). Some authors show that a substantial portion was retained within the banking industry during the high growth period (Hamada and Iwata 1980, pp. 201–16).

More importantly, Aoki (1994) and Hellman, Murdock and Stiglitz (1994) hypothesise that the rents produced by competition restricting regulations are an effective instrument in motivating banks to engage in efficient monitoring and financial mediation under circumstances of imperfect information. Their hypothesis can be regarded as a 'new paradigm' on the relationship between industrial development and financial regulation, against the neoclassical paradigm proclaimed by Shaw (1973) and McKinnon (1973). I will not comment on the relevance of the new paradigm here, except to point out that the regulatory authorities were endeavouring not so much to promote industrial development as to maintain financial stability.[6]

Prudential regulations in the postwar period

Prudential regulations aim to ensure that banks have sufficient liquidity and equity to keep the risk of bankruptcy to a minimum. The purpose of the regulations is not to restrict competition in financial markets, but to restrain banks operating under the safety net from shifting managerial risk from their shareholders to debtholders (depositors), and particularly to taxpayers. In this respect they differ from competition restricting regulations. Capital adequacy requirements are a typical means of prudential regulation.

During the period of economic reconstruction immediately after World War II, the MOF was seriously concerned about the prudence of bank management: banks' equity capital per deposit had fallen sharply from 29.9 per cent in 1930 to only 5.6 per cent by 1953 (Tanimura 1955). With a view to strengthening their capital bases, the MOF instructed banks to reduce current expenses to 78 per cent or less of current revenues. This administrative guidance started in 1953 and continued until 1973. Table 10.2 presents a list of prudential regulations for commercial banks as of January 1962.

Table 10.2   Prudential regulations as of January 1962

1	Loans/deposits ratio should be lower than 80 per cent.
2	Liquid assets/deposits ratio should be higher than 30 per cent.
3	Ratio of current expenses (excluding tax) to current revenue should be lower than 78 per cent.
4	Annual dividend per share should be less than 12.5 per cent of the face value of the share.
5	Broadly defined capital/total deposits ratio should be higher than 10 per cent.

Source: MOF (1991), pp.185–6.

In 1954, the MOF introduced a capital adequacy regulation that required banks to raise their broadly defined capital ratios to more than 10 per cent of total deposits.[7] This could be regarded as a forerunner in Japan of the international capital adequacy regulation introduced by the Bank for International Settlements (BIS) in 1987 (although, unlike the BIS, the ministry did not include a formula for assessing the risk of a bank's assets). It was, however, obviously ineffective, not only during the high growth period but afterwards as well. As Figure 10.2 shows, from 1960 to the mid 1970s, the average of the broadly defined capital/deposits ratio of the banking sector remained at around 6 per cent, far below the MOF's requirement of 10 per cent.[8]

In the 1980s, the ratio dropped abruptly to less than 4 per cent (Figure 10.2). The MOF amended the capital adequacy regulation in 1986 by changing the accounting rules governing bank financial statements. Through this amendment, the MOF probably intended to make the capital adequacy regulation more practical and realistic, and it is unclear whether it was as yet aware of the increasing importance of prudential regulations to banking as of the mid 1980s. The new capital adequacy rule required banks' broadly defined capital to be equal to or higher than 4 per cent of total assets, hardly a stringent requirement. Moreover, the MOF itself mitigated the impact of this new rule by setting the date for banks to achieve this target at March 1990 (Federation of Bankers Associations of Japan 1987, p. 59).

Figure 10.2 Ratio of equity capital to total deposits, FY 1960–85

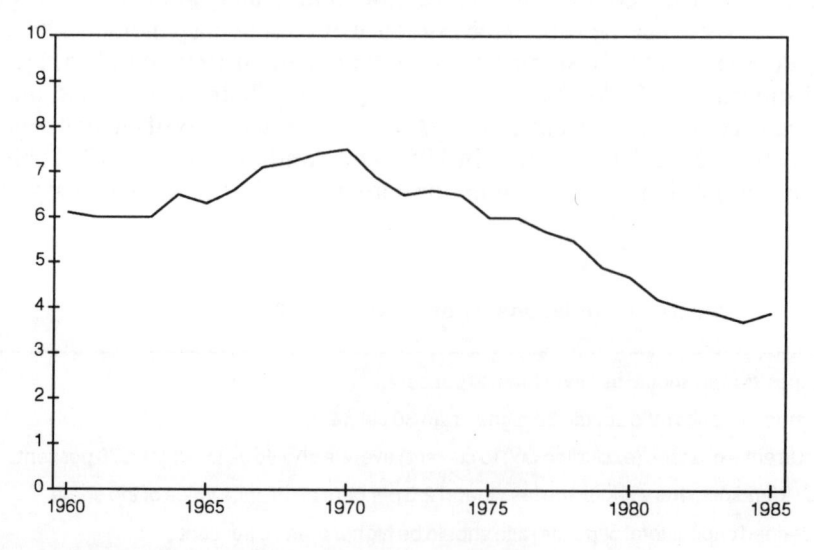

Source: Federation of Bankers Associations of Japan (annual).

It is no exaggeration to say that prudential regulations were not effective in Japan until the end of the 1980s. On the whole, bankers did not consider that the official targets were to be attained at any cost, and the MOF was generous enough to permit some divergences between the required figures and the actual figures achieved by individual banks. The regulatory authorities did not regard the regulations as essential for financial stability, even though the gradual but steady deregulation of the financial system was already undermining the effectiveness of the traditional safety net.

Impact of financial liberalisation on the safety net

I have argued that the Japanese monetary authorities adopted a full-scale safety net system during the high growth period, and that the safety net was supported by competition restricting regulations that helped private banks and other financial institutions to accumulate handsome amounts of rents. Prudential regulations did not play a significant role in the financial system until the late 1980s. The merits of competition restricting regulations should not, of course, be exaggerated. Although they fulfilled an important role in the traditional safety net, they also deprived the financial system of both flexibility and innovative dynamism.

Since the late 1970s, the financial system has experienced structural changes as the amount of government bonds outstanding has grown and major companies have reduced their reliance on bank loans. These changes have led to a decline in the relative importance of banking in the financial system, which in turn has undermined bank profitability. The decline in the relative importance of the banking sector has had two related consequences: it has become more difficult for the authorities to maintain the traditional safety net mechanisms; and imprudent risk taking on the part of banks led to the emergence of a serious bad loan problem in the early 1990s.

Structural changes in financial markets

There are various facets to the evolution of the Japanese financial structure after the end of high economic growth. Here it will suffice to focus on the impact of rapidly growing government debt and structural changes in corporate finance on bank profitability.

Rapidly growing government debt

The Japanese economy entered a period of low growth in the mid 1970s. Associated with this shift, the financial structure changed remarkably. With the relative decline in corporate sector investment, there was a fall in the amount of funds required to be raised externally by the corporate sector. The government took its place as the largest consumer of funds, issuing huge amounts of government bonds to finance budget deficits (Table 10.3). The proliferation of the bonds exerted great pressure on Japan's strictly regulated financial system. Individual investors regarded them as a safe and liquid asset that was highly substitutable for bank deposits.

Table 10.3   Japanese government debt, 1965–90[a] (¥ billion)

	Total national government debt	National government bonds outstanding (domestic)	Refinancing bonds	Foreign currency bonds	Liability to Trust Fund Bureau
1950	554	240	–	100	2
1955	1,057	425	–	88	19
1960	1,340	446	–	81	41
1965	1,766	688	–	57	198
1970	6,226	3,597	–	54	504
1973	13,154	8,267	606	39	948
1975	22,795	15,776	1,677	33	2,677
1980	95,011	71,905	3,299	15	10,894
1985	163,571	136,610	24,295	1	16,188
1990	223,793	168,547	77,136	0	31,155

Note: a   End of fiscal year.
Source: BOJ (annual).

The marketability of long-term government bonds soon made them a basic instrument for short-term financial transactions, with the market for repurchase agreements (repos or *gensaki*) based on long-term bonds developing rapidly since the latter half of the 1970s. The prevalence of government bonds forced the banking sector to introduce new instruments in order to preserve the status quo in the financial system. In 1979, negotiable certificates of deposit were introduced at the initiative of banks — the first step in the subsequent liberalisation of Japan's financial markets.

As the amount of government bond issues increased, their sale became an important activity in securities markets. The banks, which did not want to be excluded from this lucrative market, lobbied the MOF for permission to sell the bonds to individual investors. The Securities Exchange Act does not prohibit banks from engaging in the sale of government bonds, and since 1985 the MOF has allowed them to sell the bonds, despite encountering strong resistance from the securities industry. This can be regarded as the start of the dismantling of the separation between banking and securities business.[9]

Structural changes in corporate finance

The transition to the low growth period was accompanied not only by an expansion of government bond issues, but also by a reduction in the borrowing of major companies from banks. These can be regarded as two sides of the same coin: low economic growth implied a decrease in the amount of corporate sector investment expenditure needing to be financed. Major companies reduced their dependence on borrowing from banks, while increasing their reliance on internal funds (depreciation plus retained profits). At the same time, fundraising in the form of securities issues became relatively more important to Japan's major companies.[10] Table 10.4 depicts these changes.

The liberalisation of foreign exchange transactions and international capital movements, which began in 1980 with the revision of the longstanding Foreign Exchange and Foreign Trade Control Law, partly accounts for this change in corporate finance. Many Japanese firms, particularly large ones, were issuing corporate bonds in the Euromarket and other foreign markets. This exerted strong pressure on the notoriously restrictive domestic corporate bond market to relax the rules governing corporate bond issues. The number of Japanese firms recognised as eligible to issue bonds in the domestic market has increased rapidly since the mid 1980s (Horiuchi 1994). The firms did not necessarily sever their intimate relationship with banks when they issued corporate bonds; often their main banks supported bond issuance in foreign markets by providing issuing firms with a guarantee (Horiuchi 1989). However, the influence of banks on major firms' finance and management was substantially weakened by financial internationalisation.

Table 10.4 Structure of fundraising by big and small/medium sized business, 1970–89 (per cent)[a]

	1970–74	1975–79	1980–84	1985–89
Big business[b]				
Internal funds	28.0	38.3	42.9	43.5
Borrowing	35.5	30.0	21.4	15.2
Trade credit	17.1	11.2	8.1	0.0
Issue of securities	7.3	16.4	17.8	29.4
Bonds	3.0	6.8	5.0	12.8
Stocks	4.2	9.6	12.8	16.6
Other	12.1	4.1	9.8	11.9
Small/medium sized business				
Internal funds	31.2	38.3	42.3	37.4
Borrowing	37.2	30.0	40.1	54.4
Trade credit	20.0	23.2	11.6	8.0
Issue of securities	1.7	−0.5	−0.4	−11.1
Bonds	0.0	0.0	0.0	−5.4
Stocks	1.6	−0.5	−0.4	−5.6
Other	9.9	9.0	6.4	11.3

Note: a Estimated from total amounts outstanding.
       b Firms capitalised at more than ¥1 billion.
Source: MOF (monthly).

It should also be noted that small and medium sized businesses continued to rely on bank credit even after the mid 1970s (Table 10.4). Japanese securities markets were unable to accommodate small businesses, with stringent eligibility requirements for corporate bond issues in effect crowding them out of the corporate bond market (Horiuchi 1994). The loan market for small and medium sized business therefore continues to be important territory for banks, particularly small regional banks and credit cooperatives. In the early 1980s, large city banks started to invade this market. This has threatened the profitability of small banks, which had dominated this market throughout the high growth period.

The reduction in borrowing of large companies, although gradual, eroded the profitability of the banking sector. The drop in the banking sector's profitability shown in Figure 10.1 is thus closely related to the changes in corporate finance presented in Table 10.4. These changes may have been a major cause of the aggressive risk taking of the 1980s which led to the very serious problem of bad loans in the early 1990s.

Imprudent banking and the decline in bank profits

In spite of the policy of deliberate gradualism adopted by the monetary authorities during the 1970s and 1980s, Japan's financial system has not been immune to problems. This failure may seem surprising given that in the late 1980s the MOF adopted BIS capital adequacy regulations that had the explicit purpose of enforcing prudent bank management. I believe that the failure was related to the decline in bank profits, that is, the decreased franchise value of banking.

Table 10.5   Bank loans to small and medium sized firms, 1968–89[a]

	Total of loans (¥ trillion) (A)	Loans to small/medium sized firms (¥ trillion) (B)	(B/A) (%)
1968	28.8	9.6	33.4
1973	71.3	26.2	36.7
1978	118.1	49.2	41.6
1983	181.0	78.4	43.3
1988	288.2	153.0	53.1
1989	355.1	203.5	57.3

Note: a   End of year.
Source: BOJ (annual).

Table 10.6 Major city bank loans to small and medium sized firms, 1975–89 (per cent of total loans)

	March 1975	March 1985	March 1989
Daiichi Kangyō Bank	32.5	51.6	66.0
Fuji Bank	32.9	50.9	69.0
Sumitomo Bank	35.0	51.4	73.0
Mitsubishi Bank	33.4	54.1	68.7
Sanwa Bank	39.3	54.0	73.2

Source: Annual reports published by banks.

The increase in risk taking

The financial difficulties of the early 1990s can be traced directly to the expansion of risk taking by banks in the 1980s.

- During the late 1970s and early 1980s, Sumitomo Bank and other major banks downgraded their credit investigation sections. Other banks then followed suit. These organisational changes were a direct manifestation of the change in the risk attitudes of banks. After 1990, the majority of banks reportedly switched back to the old organisational form.

- Japanese banks increased long-term loans to the private sector. According to the BOJ, the proportion of short-term loans decreased from 55 per cent in 1985 to 31 per cent in 1990, while that of long-term loans (with maturities of more than one year) increased from 39 per cent to 56 per cent. In contrast, the maturity of the liability side of the banks fell substantially. For example, the proportion of deposits with the shortest maturities (from one month to less than six months) rose sharply from a few per cent of total time deposits in 1985, to 25 per cent in 1988, and then to 40 per cent in 1989 (BOJ, annual).

- Banks substantially increased their loans to small and medium sized businesses (Tables 10.5 and 10.6). Large city banks in particular aggressively increased loans to these businesses, which had not been preferred customers during the high growth period. This switch in direction of supply of loans reflects the securitisation of major companies' fundraising (Table 10.4). Although most loans to small and medium sized firms were secured by assets such as real estate, the firms were not well-known clients and therefore loans to them should have been regarded as being more risky than those to major companies. The market value of collateralised real estate became increasingly uncertain after the 'bubble' burst in the early 1990s.

- During the 1980s, and especially towards the end of the decade, Japanese banks directed an increasing amount of credit towards the real estate industry, as well as towards non-bank finance companies and housing finance companies specialising in loans for real estate development and housing. Much of this was invested in real estate development projects, effectively representing a dramatic escalation of exposure by major banks to land price risk (Table 10.7).

The problem of bad loans

Bad loans in the banking sector have emerged as a serious problem for the monetary authorities since 1990, when the financial 'bubble' burst. The non-performing loans of the 21 largest Japanese banks were officially estimated at ¥12.7 trillion in September 1993 and about ¥14 trillion, or 3 per cent of the banks' total loan portfolios, as of the end of March 1994. Thus the situation seems to be worsening.

To make matters worse, the official figures do not include restructured loans, loans by subsidiaries, loans for which a token amount has been paid every six months, and zero coupon loans. During the past few years, many loans to non-bank finance companies have been 'restructured' so as to carry low (often zero) interest — but these are not officially recognised as non-performing loans. A good proportion, amounting

Table 10.7 Bank credit to manufacturing, real estate industry and non-bank finance companies, 1951–91 (per cent)

	Manufacturing	Real estate industry	Non-bank finance companies
1951–60	49.0	0.6	na
1961–70	46.7	2.8	na
1971–80	35.7	5.9	na
1981	34.8	5.7	3.5
1982	33.8	6.0	4.4
1983	31.9	6.4	5.5
1984	30.6	6.9	6.5
1985	28.8	7.7	6.8
1986	25.9	9.6	7.9
1987	22.5	10.2	9.1
1988	20.1	10.9	9.6
1989	20.5	11.5	9.5
1990	16.7	11.3	9.2
1991	16.0	11.6	8.7

Note: na = not available.
Source: BOJ (annual).

to approximately ¥4.8 trillion for the 21 major banks, consists of loans to housing finance companies. Most observers estimate that total debt is twice the official figure, that is, approximately 6 per cent of total loans. This is Japan's first experience in the postwar period of such a widespread bad loan problem.

The MOF has been extremely reluctant to disclose the actual figures for individual banks' non-performing loans, making it very difficult to assess accurately the seriousness of the problem. The ministry recently estimated the total amount of bad loans for all categories of deposit taking institutions at about ¥37.4 trillion as of the end of September 1995, but this was disaggregated only to the level of banking subsectors. The MOF's secretiveness seems to be driven mainly by its concern for some of the smaller banks, whose capital bases, including hidden reserves, are weak. Needless to say, its reluctance to disclose relevant data prevents financial markets from efficiently evaluating the performance of individual banks, thereby distorting investment. The ministry seems to believe that, if it can keep the lid on damaging information for long enough, a potentially catastrophic situation may right itself and the costs of financial distress be minimised. However, this strategy of 'forbearance' could make the problem even worse (Kane 1993). There is no assurance that covering up information on bad loans really contributes to the stabilisation of financial markets; investors may still become pessimistic and attempt to withdraw their money en masse. Moreover, it surely hinders the efficiency with which financial markets allocate resources in Japan.

The increase in non-performing loans and the decrease in asset prices have led to a deterioration in the asset value of the banking sector, reducing banks' equity in terms of market prices. I tentatively estimate that the aggregate value of the equity capital of city banks — the group which discloses most openly the current value of non-performing loans — dropped by ¥20.9 trillion from March 1990 to March 1994. This was due to both a fall in the market prices of securities and an increase in bad loans. The fall in securities prices accounted for ¥12 trillion, or more than half of the total decrease in city banks' equity capital. This estimation suggests how important is the market risk of bank balance sheets, an aspect overlooked by the BIS capital adequacy regulations.

Responding to the decline in the value of their equity capital, the city banks increased their provision for bad loans by ¥2.1 trillion in 1990–94 and issued subordinated debt of ¥8.2 trillion. They also adopted the rather conservative strategy of restraining asset expansion in order to recover their equity capital: the total book value of their assets fell by 10 per cent, from ¥943.6 trillion in March 1990 to ¥849.8 trillion in March 1994. This conservative strategy may have worsened the stagnant macroeconomic situation in Japan since 1991 (Horiuchi 1995).

Under the MOF's guidance, the banks have formed a new corporation, the Cooperative Credit Purchasing Corporation (CCPC), to help them write off bad loans. The banks sell bad loans to the CCPC at discounted prices, as determined by an independent price appraisal committee made up of experts in the fields of law, accounting, taxation and particularly real estate. Banks are required to fund the purchase of the loans that they bring to the CCPC. The essential purpose of the scheme is to make losses on non-performing loans explicit so that banks can obtain tax relief. When banks transfer loans to the CCPC, they are allowed to deduct the difference between the appraised and face value of the loan. At the end of March 1994, the losses claimed by banks amounted to about ¥2.28 trillion, allowing them to obtain tax relief of around ¥1.1 trillion (Table 10.8). Apart from reducing the tax burden, the CCPC does not contribute directly to a recovery in the banks' equity position — something which is badly needed in the current situation. Writing off non-performing loans through the CCPC does reveal, however, the decrease in equity capital otherwise concealed in accounting terms.[11]

Table 10.8   Loans sold to Cooperative Credit Purchasing Corporation, FY 1992–93

	Number of loans sold	Face value (¥ billion) (A)	Appraised losses (¥ billion) (B)	Claimed losses (¥ billion) (A – B)	Claimed losses (% of face value)
2nd half of 1992	229	681.7	452.1	229.6	33.7
1st half of 1993	510	1,180.0	602.9	577.1	48.9
2nd half of 1993	1,381	2,654.2	1,176.0	1,478.2	55.7
Total	2,120	4,515.9	2,231.0	2,284.9	50.6

Source: Packer (1994).

Decreases in the franchise value of Japanese banking

Why did Japanese banks engage in excessive risk taking in the late 1980s? Was it related to moral hazard type behaviour under the safety net? As has been explained, the incentives for excessive risk taking under the safety net existed before 1980, and so this cannot constitute the whole story behind the expansion of risk taking after the mid 1980s. I believe that the change in the banks' behaviour is traceable to a decrease in their franchise value. 'Franchise value' refers to the present discounted value of the stream of rents that banks can capture in their unique role as deposit taking and credit creating institutions, backed by the safety net provided by the banking authorities.

As Figure 10.1 shows, there was a noteworthy decline in profit rates in the banking sector after the high growth period. This suggests that there was also a fall-off in the franchise value of Japanese banks from the mid 1970s. Bank profit rates recovered in the latter half of the 1980s, but behind this recovery lay an increase in risk taking, which was promoted by the banks' declining position in corporate finance.

Economic theory predicts that a decrease in franchise value will induce banks to extend risk taking. According to Weisbrod, Lee and Rojas-Suared (1992), two factors may account for the reduction in franchise value in banking both in the United States and Japan during the 1980s (see also Herring and Vankudre 1987). One is the decline in corporate demand for bank liquidity. The other is the decrease in the banks' informational advantage over other lenders in the process of financial mediation. As Weisbrod, Lee and Rojas-Suared point out, the amount of demand deposits held by the Japanese corporate sector has been decreasing steadily since the high growth period. The authors argue that the corporate sector's decreased demand for bank liquidity led to a decline in the franchise value of banks, not only in Japan but also in the United States.

It is difficult to counter this argument. Nevertheless, it should not be forgotten that Japanese banks have been losing their informational advantage in Japan's financial system since the late 1970s. Major companies in particular have reduced their reliance on borrowing from banks, while increasing the amount of funds raised through the issue of securities. This securitisation of corporate finance put strong pressure on banks to reconsider their traditional way of doing business. In terms of economic theory, the securitisation of corporate finance brought about a decrease in the franchise value of banks, which in turn induced banks to take on more risk under the safety net provided by the monetary authorities.

The detrimental effects of the BIS regulation

Many analysts have pointed out the defects of the BIS capital adequacy regulation introduced in 1988.[12] Under the regulation, banks engaging in international banking business were required to maintain equity capital at a minimum of 8 per cent of their risk assets, measured by a rather simple formula which took account only of 'credit risk'. The regulation did not take sufficient account of the risk caused by fluctuations in asset prices (market risk). As has already been pointed out, the decrease in securities prices, particularly stock prices, was of more significance than the increase in non-performing loans in explaining the substantial reduction in banks' equity capital during the early 1990s. More importantly, the regulation did not differentiate between loans to the private sector in terms of degree of risk, so that the shift of loans from well-established companies to small-scale and less creditworthy firms did not alter the assessment of risk assets for individual banks. This characteristic of the BIS regulation may have induced banks to expand their loan supply to riskier borrowers, such as small businesses and real estate developers. If so, its introduction was counterproductive to financial stability.

It is difficult to say definitively whether the BIS regulation motivated private banks to expand their risk taking. They had started to do so before it was introduced. But even if the regulation was not the primary cause of excessive risk taking in the 1980s, it may have exacerbated it. Equity capital in banking is, of course, important. The BIS has started to rationalise the rules determining banks' risk position by taking the market risks of securities and risks associated with banks' off-balance activities into consideration. This is a positive step.

Limitations of traditional rescue methods

Since the beginning of the 1990s, when the 'bubble' burst, it has become increasingly difficult for the MOF to maintain the traditional safety net mechanisms. This is reflected in the utilisation of the deposit insurance system since 1992 to cope with the financial distress of individual banks. The scale of the Deposit Insurance Corporation is as yet limited, but its increasing use marks a significant change in the operation of the safety net. One of the reasons for this shift is that, with structural changes in financial markets, there are fewer rents in banking that the MOF can use to influence banks.[13]

A few recent cases exemplify the difficulties the MOF faces in using its traditional bail-out policies. In the summer of 1992, Tōyō Shinkin Bank, located in Osaka, was broken up because of insolvency due to bad loans. The MOF reportedly wanted Sanwa Bank, a leading city bank, to absorb it in the traditional fashion, but it was unable to persuade it to do this. Instead, Tōyō Shinkin was broken up into a number of pieces, each of which was absorbed by a different financial institution. In the process, the Deposit Insurance Corporation paid ¥20 billion to Sanwa, which absorbed the largest part and which played a major role in the reorganisation.

Another event signalling that traditional methods are running into trouble occurred early in 1994. Three local banks in the Tōhoku area jointly announced a plan for a merger, another typical MOF bail-out method. One of the banks had a serious bad loan problem, and many parties, including the ministry, were pessimistic about its future viability. The merger plan, which undoubtedly was the result of MOF administrative guidance, had to be abandoned following fierce resistance from employees of the relatively sound banks involved. Some of the banks' managers also reportedly argued against the merger.

Table 10.9 presents a short chronology of the Deposit Insurance Corporation's assistance to troubled banks. Traditional safety net mechanisms have not yet disappeared from the Japanese financial system and, as the table suggests, many private banks are still playing an important role by collaborating with the regulators. However, the role of the corporation in the process appears to have become increasingly important, and it is likely that the deposit insurance system will be utilised substantially in the future.

The Japanese banking system is clearly suffering from excess capacity. Use of the deposit insurance system to facilitate reorganisation does not, however, imply that banks will undergo formal bankruptcy procedures. It seems likely that the MOF will continue to avoid explicit bank failures, but by using the deposit insurance system, rather than preferential regulatory treatment, to provide incentives to sound banks to merge with insolvent ones. This implies a slow reorganisation of the financial system

Table 10.9 Chronology of financial assistance provided by Deposit Insurance Corporation, 1992–96

Troubled bank (date)	Ex post disposal	Amount
Tōhō Sōgo Bank (April 1992)	Absorbed by Iyo Bank	¥8 billion loaned
Tōyō Shinkin Bank (October 1992)	Absorbed by multiple banks after being dissolved	¥20 billion given
Kamaishi Shinkin Bank (October 1993)	Dissolved, with deposits being taken over by Iwata Bank	¥26 billion given
Ōsaka Fumin Credit Cooperative (November 1993)	Absorbed by Ōsaka Kōyō Bank	¥19.9 billion given
Gifu Shōgin Credit Cooperative (March 1995)	Absorbed by Kansai Kōgin Bank	¥2.5 billion given
Tōkyō Kyōwa Credit Cooperative; Anzen Credit Cooperative (January 1995)	Both integrated into the new Tokyo Kyodou Bank sponsored by the BOJ	¥40 billion given
Yūai Credit Cooperative (July 1995)	Absorbed by a labour credit cooporative in Kanagawa	¥3 billion given
Hyōgo Bank (January 1996)	Dissolved, with remaining assets restructured into new bank	¥473 billion given
Cosmo Credit Cooperative	Dissolved, with remaining assets transferred to Tokyo Kyodou Bank for liquidation	¥125 billion given
Kizu Credit Cooperative (pending)	Dissolved, with remaining assets transferred to Tokyo Kyodou Bank for liquidation	Up to ¥500 billion likely to be given
Fukuiken Daiichi Credit Cooperative (pending)	Absorbed by Fukui Bank	Up to ¥0.6 billion likely to be given
Ōsaka Credit Cooperative (pending)	Absorbed by Tōkai Bank	Up to ¥70 billion likely to be given

Source: *Nihon Keizai Shinbun* (various issues); *Nikkei Kin'yū Shinbun* (various issues).

and a marked increase in the burden borne by the Deposit Insurance Corporation. To keep this burden manageable, the corporation will need to have its monitoring power strengthened. In particular, it should be able to order banks in distress to cease operating before the negative value of their net wealth becomes too great.

The explicit involvement of the Deposit Insurance Corporation in the operation of the safety net should be beneficial to the Japanese economy. The social costs of bailing out distressed banks will become more transparent, and this will facilitate assessment of the efficiency of the current financial safety net. It will also make the regulatory authorities' administration more accountable, as suggested by the recent experience involving two credit cooperatives in Tokyo.

The future role of the regulatory authorities

This chapter has reviewed the changing relationship between the safety net and financial regulations in postwar Japan. The safety net was so extensive that losses associated with de facto bank failures were confined to a few major banks and some related entities. Its effectiveness was dependent on the rents accumulated in the banking sector during the high growth period, and these seem to have been sustained by various competition restricting regulations. Sound banks could afford to collaborate with regulators in bailing out distressed banks and other financial institutions. Moreover, the existence of rents gave banks incentives not to engage in expanded risk taking and other moral hazard type behaviour.

The deregulation and internationalisation undertaken gradually but steadily in Japanese financial markets since the late 1970s substantially changed the environment in which the safety net operated. More competitive financial markets deprived banks of their monopoly status as financial intermediaries, and major companies reduced their reliance on borrowing from banks. The rapid decline in the profitability of banks in the decade after the mid 1970s shook the traditional safety net in two ways. First, the banks were no longer able to cooperate completely with the authorities in operating the safety net. Second, a decline in profitability increased the incentives for banks to take excessively risky positions under the safety net. Japanese banks extended their risk taking during the late 1980s, leading to the destructive bad loan problem of the early 1990s.

From this analysis of the recent malfunction of the Japanese financial system, we can derive the following lessons regarding public policy in financial markets. The monetary authorities should have paid much more attention to prudential regulations, such as the capital adequacy requirement. Although the regulations had been in place for a long time, the regulators did not attach sufficient importance to them. If the authorities are to maintain an extensive financial safety net, they will need to find effective ways to monitor and prevent moral hazard behaviour by banks. The Japanese authorities did, in fact, begin to strengthen prudential regulations in the late 1980s, taking advantage of the introduction of the BIS capital adequacy regulations. But there remains room for improvement in the monitoring power of the authorities. In particular, it should be noted that some small-scale institutions, such as the credit cooperatives (*shin'yō kumiai*) and the agricultural cooperative institutions (*nōkyō kumiai*), are only imperfectly monitored by the authorities, and that the monitoring authorities are independent of the MOF and the BOJ.[14]

Even if a more rational system for monitoring banks and financial institutions had been put in place, the authorities would not necessarily have been able to maintain perfect stability in financial markets under the traditional safety net. Deregulation has produced very sophisticated and complicated financial transactions in markets, making it costly for the authorities to monitor appropriately and prevent moral hazard behaviour. Many participants in financial markets, on the other hand, have accumulated expertise in obtaining relevant information about their counterparts, and so are better able than the authorities to assess and manage risk.

While it has reduced the ability of the regulatory authorities to monitor, financial deregulation has strengthened the market mechanisms which serve to stabilise the financial system. The Japanese authorities would be able to transfer some monitoring tasks to market participants if they were prepared to institute a more perfect system of disclosure regarding individual bank management. This would require a fundamental shift in the regulators' policy stance. At present they hesitate to allow full-scale disclosure of the non-performing loans and other activities of individual banks because they are afraid of the panic that this might cause, particularly in the case of small banks. However, it is not clear that restricting the disclosure of information enhances the stability of the financial system any more than does disclosing it. When information is suppressed, markets price in their own assessments of the bank's position. This can have a debilitating effect on the bank, particularly if the market becomes sceptical and pessimistic.

The policy of not disclosing relevant information about individual bank performance requires the regulators to monitor private banks intensively in place of markets and to keep the traditional safety net operating. This is becoming more and more costly in Japan, so that regulators are now confronted with the difficulty of maintaining the safety net. The authorities need to reduce their reliance on direct intervention in the process of dealing with distressed banks. Rather, they should specialise in collecting and disseminating relevant information on bank performance.

Notes

1   See, for example, Edwards and Scott (1979) and Benston (1986).
2   The banks in question were main banks of Yamaichi (MOF 1991, pp. 620–37).
3   The MOF had the introduction of deposit insurance on its policy agenda even before 1970. It was not realised earlier mainly because the large banks were unwilling to bear the costs associated with the anticipated failure of small banks (MOF 1991, p. 414). This resistance seems a little strange considering that the safety net, without

the deposit insurance system, forced large banks to bear uneven costs in the case of another bank's financial distress.

4 Under the principle of 'one bank to one prefecture', the MOF did not allow an increase in the number of banks locating their headquarters in a prefecture. It adopted this principle early in the postwar period with a view to stabilising the Japanese banking system (MOF 1991, pp. 95–8).

5 The Financial Reform Act of 1992 allows commercial banks to engage in trust banking business through their trust bank subsidiaries. However, the scope of trust banking business opened up for subsidiaries of commercial banks is restricted by administrative guidance, which the MOF maintains with a view to avoiding destructive shocks to the present framework of the financial system. The same administrative guidance is applied to the subsidiaries of securities companies set up by commercial banks. These subsidiaries are not allowed to engage in stock brokerage, a profitable business line for other securities companies.

6 See MOF (1991, pp. 76–9). Moreover, without public intervention, market mechanisms can provide the rents needed to induce banks to perform efficient monitoring even under imperfect information (Klein and Leffler 1981).

7 Broadly defined capital includes not only equity capital (book value), but also some reserve items.

8 See the statistics presented by the MOF to the Financial System Research Council (Gendai Burein 1977, p. 268).

9 See Cargill and Royama (1988, pp. 114–20) and Horiuchi (1993). It should be noted that the MOF has controlled the speed of liberalisation of domestic financial markets very carefully. It restricted the negotiability and minimum denomination of certificates of deposit, for example, so as to prevent a too rapid expansion of the new instrument. The MOF was concerned that the introduction of certificates of deposit could upset the status quo of the financial system.

10 Hoshi (Ch. 9, this volume) discusses the relationship between financial deregulation and structural changes in corporate finance from a slightly different perspective to that adopted in this chapter.

11 In February 1994, the MOF announced another method for dealing with non-performing loans, particularly those lying outside the purview of the CCPC; that is, bank loans to non-bank financial companies. Under this framework, banks are permitted to create Special Purpose Companies (SPCs), which receive transfers of restructured loans in return for a specified number of shares in the new entity. The difference between the face value of the loans and the appraised market value of the shares can be deducted by banks for tax purposes. Ironically, SPCs and organisations such as the CCPC originally became necessary because of the rigorous tax treatment of troubled loans by the Tax Bureau of the MOF. In Japan, tax-free write-offs of bad loans are not allowed until a bankruptcy procedure has begun, or until an excess of liabilities over assets has existed for at least two years.

12 Kapstein (1991) evaluates the current BIS rules.

13 With financial liberalisation, it has become difficult for the authorities to manipulate regulatory means to favour some financial institutions over others. With interest

rate deregulation, for example, the allocation of branch offices — formerly an important administrative tool — has lost its importance for bank profitability.

14. The MOF entrusts the monitoring of credit cooperatives to the prefectures in which they are located; the agricultural cooperatives are supervised by the Ministry of Agriculture, Forestry and Fisheries. The regulators responsible for monitoring these financial institutions tend to adopt a policy of 'forbearance' even when they know that an institution is in financial distress. In January 1995, for example, two credit cooperatives found to be in serious distress, Tōkyō Kyōwa and Anzen, were merged with Tokyo Kyodou Bank under a plan formulated by the BOJ. Before ceasing business they were allowed to continue to accept deposits at interest rates higher than the normal level. It has been reported that over 80 per cent of their deposits were large denominated time deposits from professional investors attracted by the higher interest rates (*Kin'yū Zaisei Jijō*, No. 2160, 30 January 1995, pp. 42–3). This is a typical example of moral hazard. Of the 13 troubled institutions listed in Table 8.9, nine are credit cooperatives. Furthermore, according to the National Federation of Credit Cooperatives, nearly 40 per cent of credit cooperatives had violated the regulation limiting lending to a single party (to 20 per cent of capital in the broad sense) as of September 1994. This suggests a serious defect in the regulators' monitoring system in Japan.

References

Aoki, Masahiko (1994), 'Monitoring Characteristics of the Main Bank System: An Analytical and Developmental View', in Masahiko Aoki and Hugh Patrick (eds), *The Japanese Main Bank System: Its Relevancy for Developing and Transforming Economies*, Oxford: Oxford University Press, pp. 109–41.

Benston, George J. (1986), 'Supervision and Examination', in G.J. Benston et al. (eds), *Perspectives on Safe and Sound Banking: Past, Present, and Future*, Washington DC: American Bankers Association, pp. 245–72.

BOJ (Bank of Japan) (annual), *Economic Statistics Annual*, Tokyo: Statistics Department, Bank of Japan.

Cargill, Thomas F. and Shoichi Royama (1988), *The Transition of Finance in Japan and the United States: A Comparative Perspective*, Stanford, CA: Hoover Institution Press.

Diamond, Douglas W. and Philip H. Dybvig (1983), 'Bank Runs, Deposit Insurance, and Liquidity', *Journal of Political Economy*, 9 (3), pp. 401–19.

Edwards, Franklin R. and John H. Scott (1979), 'Regulating the Solvency of Depository Institutions: A Perspective for Deregulation', in F.R. Edwards (ed.), *Issues in Financial Regulation*, New York, NY: McGraw Hill, pp. 65–105.

Federation of Bankers Associations of Japan (annual), *Zenkoku-Ginkō Zaimushohyō Bunseki* [Analysis of Financial Statements of All Banks], Tokyo: Federation of Bankers Associations of Japan.

—— (1987), *Kin'yū* [Finance], Tokyo: Federation of Bankers Associations of Japan.

Financial System Research Society [Kin'yū Seido Kenkyūkai] (1970), *Kin'yū Seido Chōsakai Shiryō* [Collection of Documents Submitted to the Financial System Research Council], Vol. 1, Tokyo: Kin'yū Zaisei Jijō Kenkyūkai.

Gendai Burein (1977), *Kin'yū Seido Chōsakai Shiryōshū* [Collection of Documents Submitted to the Financial System Research Council], Tokyo: Gendai Burein.

Hamada, Kōichi and Kazumasa Iwata (1980), *Kin'yū Seisaku to Ginkō Kōdo* [Monetary Policy and Banks' Behaviour], Tokyo: Tōyō Keizai Shinpōsha.

Hellmann, Thomas, Kevin Murdock and Joseph Stiglitz (1994), Financial Restraint: Towards a New Paradigm, Paper presented to the World Bank EDI Workshop on the Roles of Government in Economic Development: Analysis of East Asian Experiences, Kyoto, September.

Herring, Richard J. and Prachant Vankudre (1987), 'Growth Opportunities and Risk-Taking by Financial Intermediaries', *Journal of Finance*, 42 (3), pp. 583–99.

Horiuchi, Akiyoshi (1989), 'Informational Properties of the Japanese Financial System', *Japan and the World Economy*, 1, pp. 255–78.

—— (1993), 'Financial Liberalization: The Case of Japan', in Dimitri Vittas (ed.), *Financial Regulation: Changing the Rules of the Game*, Washington DC: World Bank, pp. 85–119.

—— (1994), An Evaluation of Japanese Financial Liberalization: A Case Study of Corporate Bond Markets, Paper presented to the 5th Annual East Asian Seminar on Economics, Singapore, June.

—— (1995), Nihon no Ginkō-Shisan no Rekka [Deterioration of Bank Assets in Japan], Paper presented to the Federation of Bankers Associations of Japan workshop, Tokyo, January.

Kane, Edward J. (1993), 'What Lessons Should Japan Learn from the US Deposit-Insurance Mess?', *Journal of the Japanese and International Economies*, 7 (4), pp. 329–55.

Kapstein, Ethan B. (1991), *Supervising International Banks: Origins and Implications of the Basel Accord*, Princeton, NJ: International Finance Section, Department of Economics, Princeton University.

Klein, Bejamin and Keith B. Leffler (1981), 'The Role of Market Forces in Assuring Contractual Performance', *Journal of Political Economy*, 89 (4), pp. 615–41.

McKinnon, Ronald I. (1973), *Money and Capital in Economic Development*, Washington DC: Brookings Institution.

MOF (Ministry of Finance) (monthly), *Zaisei Kinyū Tōkei Geppō* [Monthly Report on Fiscal and Monetary Statistics], Tokyo: Printing Office of the Ministry of Finance.

—— (1991), *Shōwa Zaisei-Shi 1952–1973* [Fiscal History of the Shōwa Period 1952–1973], Vol. 10, Tokyo: Tōyō Keizai Shinpōsha.

Packer, Frank (1994), The Disposal of Bad Loans in Japan: A Review of Recent Policy Initiatives', Paper presented to the conference on Current Developments in Japanese Financial Markets, Center for International Business Education and Research, University of Southern California, Los Angeles, 9–10 June.

Shaw, Edward S. (1973), *Financing Deepening in Economic Development*, New York, NY: Oxford University Press.

Tanimura, Hiroshi (1955), *Ginkō Gyōsei no Genjō to Tenbō* [The Current Situation and Prospects of Bank Administration], Tokyo: Federation of Regional Bankers Associations.

Teranishi, Jūrō (1982), *Nihon no Keizai-Hatten to Kin'yū* [Economic Development and Finance in Japan], Tokyo: Iwanami-Shoten.

Weisbrod, Steven R., Howard Lee and Lilian Rojas-Suared (1992), 'Bank Risk and the Declining Franchise Value of the Banking Systems in the United States and Japan', IMF Working Paper 92/45, Washington DC, June.

11 Deregulation and the structure of the money market

*Gordon de Brouwer**

Japan's money market underwent substantial reform and liberalisation in the late 1980s. This raises the important issue of how to now characterise the relationship between interest rates in this market. This chapter identifies the major changes in instruments, practices and management techniques that occurred in the late 1980s, and then formally assesses the relationship between key money market interest rates from 1988 to 1990 using Granger causality tests.

Major money market reform was initiated by the Bank of Japan in November 1988. Commentators have argued that this led to near perfect linkage between all sections of the Japanese money market, as well as between the Japanese and overseas money markets. In order to identify these linkages between the various rates in the Japanese money market, I apply multivariate Granger causality tests to the four key interest rates representing the main sections of the Japanese money market. If one interest rate is shown to Granger cause the others, then it can be said to be a predictor of the other interest rates and in a sense to 'drive' the system of money market rates. A multivariate framework is chosen, because of the greater insight it provides and because it reduces the risk of inferring spurious Granger causal relations.

---

* This chapter was written while I was employed by the University of Melbourne. The opinions expressed in it are personal and do not represent the views of either the University or my current employer, the Reserve Bank of Australia. I would like to express my appreciation to Dr G.C. Lim and Dr R.T. Dixon, who provided valuable advice and time. I am indebted to Professor Peter Drysdale of the Australia–Japan Research Centre at the Australian National University for allowing me to use the Centre's facilities. I would also like to thank the Centre's staff and students, especially Kuni Tanaka and Randall Watson for their generous help with Nikkei database services. My discussions with Professor Masahiro Kawai of the University of Tokyo, Professor Chon Pyo Lee of Seoul National University and Professor Betty Daniels of the State University of New York were helpful and encouraging. Two anonymous referees also made useful comments and suggestions. Responsibility for any errors remains mine.

The Japanese money market

The money market is the market in securities with a maturity of less than one year. In Japan, it consists of an interbank market and an open market. The interbank market, comprising call and discount bill markets, has been the principal source of short-term market funds for financial institutions in the postwar period, and hence has been the focus of monetary management by the Bank of Japan. The open market, comprising the *gensaki*, certificate of deposit, commercial paper, treasury bill, financial bill, yen banker's acceptance, non-negotiable deposit and Euroyen markets, started in the mid 1970s and expanded rapidly throughout the 1980s as funds moved between financial and non-financial institutions alike. The increasing importance of the open markets is shown in Table 11.1, which outlines the structure of the Japanese money market.[1]

The rapid expansion of the open markets, in both volume and instruments, was due to a number of factors. These included pressures arising from the bond issues that followed the huge fiscal deficits of the latter half of the 1970s; the continuing breakdown of Article 65 of the Securities Exchange Law, which separates banking and securities business; the sharp easing of shortages of corporate funds in the 1980s; the shift away from sole reliance on indirect finance; the internationalisation of domestic markets and growth of Euroyen markets; the development and integration of world financial markets; foreign (especially US) pressure; and progress in data storage, data processing and communications technology. Table 11.2 catalogues money market developments between 1985 and 1990. Similar summaries may be found in McKenzie (1993) and Okina (1993).

This chapter is a case study of events and markets from 1988 to 1990. With changes in markets and regulations, some of the material in the chapter has been superseded, though it is still relevant to understanding the nature and operation of Japan's markets at the time. To give a better insight into how markets *currently* operate, Table 11.1 includes details of the structure of the market at the end of 1994. These underscore the importance of open money markets in Japan. The commentary on the different segments of the money market which follows also refers to major changes that have occurred since 1990.

The main participants in the Japanese money market are the Bank of Japan (the central bank), the *tanshi* companies, the city banks, the securities companies, the regional and second-tier regional banks (former Sōgo banks), the trust banks and the foreign banks (more for their influence through foreign governments than for their market size). Non-financial institutions are also active in the open market.[2] The *tanshi* are short-term money market dealers and brokers, licensed and supervised by the Ministry of Finance. They play a key role in the implementation of monetary policy in that they act as intermediaries between borrowers and lenders, especially in the interbank and treasury bill markets. The Bank of Japan uses *tanshi* as its agents for market operations in the commercial paper, financial bill and, most importantly, discount bill markets. *Tanshi* have determined (notably in the posted rate regime) or otherwise influenced the interest rate outcome, as well as performing a brokerage role.

Table 11.1 Structure of Japanese money market, 1970–94[a] (¥ trillion)

	1970	1975	1980	1985	1986	1987	1988	1989	1990	1994
Interbank market										
Call	1.82	2.33	4.13	5.11	10.23	16.04	15.67	24.48	23.99	42.75
Unsecured call	(–)	(–)	(–)	(0.82)	(1.62)	(2.94)	(6.04)	(10.07)	(12.33)	(25.61)
Discount bill	–	4.40	5.74	14.66	13.54	13.11	18.04	20.76	17.06	8.26
Subtotal	1.82	6.73	9.87	19.77	23.77	29.15	33.71	45.24	41.05	51.01
Open market										
Certificate of deposit	–	–	2.36	9.67	9.93	10.83	15.97	21.86	18.86	19.07
Commercial paper	–	–	–	–	–	1.70	9.29	13.07	15.76	11.05
Gensaki	na	na	4.51	4.64	7.12	6.92	7.35	6.30	6.61	8.33
Financial bill[b]	–	–	–	5.71	9.98	8.34	4.60	10.43	8.63	1.50
Treasury bill	–	–	–	1.02	2.23	2.00	2.40	4.01	7.61	11.30
Subtotal	–	–	6.87	21.04	29.26	29.79	39.61	55.67	57.47	51.25
Total interbank & open markets	1.82	6.73	16.74	40.81	53.03	58.94	73.32	100.91	98.52	102.26
Free rate time deposits	–	–	–	4.60	16.27	43.52	73.65	152.62	192.31	274.07
Large money market certificates	–	–	–	5.96	8.03	15.13	22.76	11.23	2.47	–
Non-resident yen deposits	–	–	1.14	2.41	1.78	2.02	2.10	2.10	2.18	0.76
Foreign currency deposits	0.35[c]	2.59[c]	6.58	18.02	18.74	22.88	20.25	25.61	33.63	20.27
Subtotal	0.35	2.59	7.72	30.99	44.82	83.55	118.76	191.56	230.59	295.10
Total	2.17	9.32	24.46	71.80	97.85	142.49	192.08	292.47	329.11	397.36

Notes:
a The money market includes the interbank and open markets. Non-negotiable free rates are included here because they are close substitutes for open market instruments and are an important source of short-term funds for financial institutions. Figures are for end of year.
b Financial bills held by financial institutions excluding the Bank of Japan.
c Includes yen deposits held by non-residents.

Source: Bank of Japan (monthly), *Economic Statistics Monthly*; Bank of Japan (annual), *Economic Statistics Yearly*.

Their role as policy conduit is illustrated by the *tanshi*'s practice of hiring retired Bank of Japan executives: in the late 1980s around 30 per cent of directors were reported to be former bank staff (*Japan Economic Journal*, 23 December 1989). Liberalisation, however, has reduced this role, and the *tanshi* appear to be assuming more of a strictly brokerage type function.

The interbank market

In the call money market, financial institutions execute their transactions through the *tanshi*: the lender transfers funds to a *tanshi*, receiving a promissory note in return, while the borrower delivers a promissory note to the *tanshi*, receiving the lender's funds in return (Viner 1987). The monetary authorities have long regarded the principle of collateralisation as being of key importance to financial stability, and its application was eased to allow unsecured call transactions only in July 1985. This concession was made to promote arbitrage links to the growing Euroyen market and to satisfy demands for easier access to call money by foreign banks (which tend to lack appropriate collateral). At the end of 1990, the principal borrowers in the call market were the city banks (50 per cent); the principal lenders were the trust banks (70 per cent).

The discount bill market was carved from the call market in May 1971. It trades in blue chip industrial and commercial bills and in trade bills, either as original bills or in consolidated or bundled form as cover or accommodation bills (Suzuki 1987). Discount bill transactions are conducted through the *tanshi*. The largest sellers at the end of 1990 were the city banks (71 per cent), while the trust banks (31 per cent) and the Bank of Japan (around 41 per cent) were the largest buyers. Indeed, the Bank of Japan's main tool of liquidity management was bill operations conducted through the *tanshi*, and at times it bought up to half of the bills available. The bill market declined substantially in the late 1980s as the corporations issuing bills sought to avoid stamp duty by shifting to alternative sources of funds, thereby depleting the supply available for discounting by the banks. This was reported to have caused problems for the Bank of Japan's monetary management during 1990 (*Nihon Keizai Shinbun*, 29 June 1990). Accordingly, in January 1991, discount bill trade was extended to public corporation bonds and foreign currency denominated trade bills (*Nihon Keizai Shinbun*, 18 December 1990). The discount bill market has continued to decline during the 1990s, while the call market has expanded.

In the 1970s, interbank market rates were posted rates set by the Bank of Japan. This system was progressively abolished throughout 1978 and 1979, to be replaced by what the Bank of Japan called a 'free-rate' system (Suzuki 1987, p. 155). In fact, though, the new system was free in name only. Until November 1988, interbank rates were indicator rates, set by the Bank of Japan through the *tanshi* after taking cognisance of market conditions. The unsecured overnight call money rate is regarded by the market as a benchmark, and as such it is the key money rate (*Japan Economic Journal*, 16 February 1991; *Nihon Keizai Shinbun*, 19 July 1991; Bank of Japan 1990). Given the continuing operational importance of the interbank market to policy

Table 11.2   Summary of money market reform, 1985–90

1985	
March	Single market participants permitted to use interbank market as borrower and lender at same time.
April	Money market certificates introduced. Medium to long-term Euroyen loans to non-residents liberalised.
June	Yen denominated banker's acceptance market established.
October	Interest rates on large time deposits liberalised.
1986	
February	Issue of 6-month short-term government bonds (treasury bills) begins.
June	Foreign banks granted permission to issue Euroyen bonds.
December	Japan offshore market established.
1987	
February	Japanese banks granted permission to underwrite foreign commercial paper.
November	Domestic commercial paper market established. Foreign firms granted permission to issue Euroyen commercial paper.
1988	
January	Permission granted for issuance of Samurai commercial paper.
November	Range of maturities of instruments widened in the unsecured call and bill markets to overnight to 6 days and 1 week to 6 months respectively, and narrowed in the secured call market to overnight to 6 days. Bank of Japan bill market operations focus on short end of bill market. Bank of Japan abolishes indicator rate status of all interbank rates except secured call rate.
1989	
April	Minimum lot of large denomination deposits reduced from ¥30 million to ¥20 million.

and the rapid development of the open market (over which the Bank of Japan had little direct control), it has been essential to monitor, if not deepen, arbitrage links between the interbank and open markets. This imperative has driven the expansion of the range and conditions of call and bill funds available. In July 1988, for example, open rates rose in anticipation of higher domestic inflation and greater US growth (hence higher US interest rates) but the Bank of Japan sought to contain the rise by holding down interbank interest rates. Funds flowed offshore to the Euroyen market, causing the

Table 11.2 Summary of money market reform, 1985–90 (continued)

May	Ceiling for maturity of instruments in bill and call markets extended to 1 year. Regulations in the Tokyo offshore market relaxed on excess balances as well as on confirmation procedures for partners and how funds are used. Residents given permission to obtain medium to long-term Euroyen loans. Buying operations in commercial paper begin.
June	Small-lot money market certificates introduced, with 6-month and 1-year maturity. Limitations removed on maturity and standards for Euroyen loans to non-residents.
August	Bank of Japan begins release of forecasts and outcomes of daily interbank market supply and demand for funds.
September	Ministry of Finance introduces 3-month treasury bill.
October	Minimum lot of large denomination deposits reduced from ¥20 million to ¥10 million. Small-lot money market certificates with 3-month, 2-year and 3-year maturity introduced.
November	Bank of Japan extends collateralised loans to foreign banks and Shinkin banks.
December	Ban lifted on direct dealing between Japanese and foreign banks in bills, call money and other short-term instruments.
1990	
April	Ministry of Finance allows securities institutions to issue commercial paper. Minimum lots for small money market certificates reduced from ¥3 million to ¥1 million.
July	Flooring and capping rates on small-lot money market certificates abolished. Foreign currency denominated deposits liberalised. Participation in treasury bill operations extended to *tanshi*.
November	Bank of Japan abolishes indicator rate status for secured call rate.

Source: Shigehara (1990); OECD, *Japan Economic Survey 1989/90*, Paris; *Nihon Keizai Shinbun* (various issues).

interbank market to shrink substantially and the interbank–open market rate spread to widen dramatically. To regain influence and repatriate funds, in November of that year the Bank of Japan widened the maturity spectrum of bills, shifted bill operations to the new, shorter dated instruments and abolished the indicator rate status for all interbank rates except the secured call rate. The secured call rate had been set by the *tanshi* each morning at about 0.156 percentage points below the market-determined unsecured call rate, but in November 1990 the Bank of Japan abolished this system. The market was permitted to set the rate through an offer–bid system, leaving the *tanshi* with a brokerage function only (*Nihon Keizai Shinbun*, 15 November 1990).

The open market

Gensaki market

A *gensaki* transaction is one in which the buyer/seller of a security agrees by contract to resell/repurchase the same security on a fixed future date and at a fixed price. The term typically refers to government bond repurchase agreements ('bond repos') since the transaction originated in 1949 as a means for securities companies to finance their inventories of overpriced government bonds. This market grew substantially in the 1970s owing to the large fiscal deficits run by the government and the growth in the securities companies' inventories of bonds. However, *gensaki* transactions in certificates of deposit, commercial paper and treasury bills are also widespread, though they are termed 'certificates of deposit *gensaki*' and so on. While the underlying security is long term, *gensaki* is treated as a short-term instrument since it is essentially a short-term financing device. The *gensaki* market is free and open to financial and non-financial institutions but excludes individuals. The principal sellers as of December 1990 were bond dealers of securities companies (61 per cent). The principal buyers included trust banks, smaller financial institutions and foreign institutions (reflecting positions in interest arbitrage and swaps). *Gensaki* transactions have declined relatively because of the securities transaction tax (which increases the cost of turnover the shorter the holding period) and the development of other open markets.

Certificate of deposit market

Banks were permitted to issue negotiable certificates of deposit in May 1979 to counter competition from the securities companies' domination of the *gensaki* market. With the easing of the regulatory framework (Suzuki 1987) the market has grown substantially, aided by a well-developed secondary market, which is not subject to transaction tax, and a certificate of deposit *gensaki* market. The latter market effectively shortens the instrument's maturity. The major issuers at December 1990 were the city banks (63 per cent); the major buyers were private corporations. The three-month certificate of deposit rate is regarded by the market as the key rate at the long end of the money market (*Nihon Keizai Shinbun*, 13 June 1990; Bank of Japan 1990).

The market for certificates of deposit declined somewhat during 1990 as banks attempted to meet the Bank for International Settlements (BIS) capital adequacy requirement. Although the banks responded by issuing fewer of the certificates, which carried a 100 per cent risk weighting, the certificate of deposit market remained the largest domestic open market in Japan. In March 1986, the Bank of Japan initiated certificate of deposit operations through the *tanshi*. This process involved the bank making loans to the *tanshi*, who in turn bought the certificates from the market (Osugi 1990). These operations were limited, partly because the transactions were unsecured, but also because the Bank of Japan was sensitive to the claim that its purchases of certificates were tantamount to making a deposit (Fukui 1986) and thus effectively insuring the bank which issued them.

Commercial paper market

After much debate, the domestic commercial paper market was finally launched in November 1987. It has since become the second largest domestic open market. Commercial paper was introduced to prevent hollowing out of domestic markets as Euroyen markets expanded, as well as to satisfy the demands of domestic companies, securities companies and foreign governments (though it was initially opposed by the banks, which feared the loss of loan custom) (Schaede 1988). The range of authorised issuers expanded steadily in the late 1980s to encompass around 600 blue chip companies, banks and securities companies. The minimum denomination was ¥100 million, with maturity ranging from two weeks to nine months (Nihon Keizai Shinbunsha 1989).

The market grew rapidly, spurred initially by fierce dealer competition between banks and securities companies and buoyed subsequently by companies taking advantage of arbitrage opportunities — by, for example, investing funds raised through the issue of commercial paper in higher yielding, large lot time deposits and investment accounts.[3] The market was also stimulated by the existence of a relatively well-developed secondary market, which provided liquidity to commercial paper buyers. The Bank of Japan took advantage of the market to conduct very short-term (mainly overnight) buying operations through the *tanshi*. Under the bank's direction, the *tanshi* bought commercial paper, with repurchase conditions attached, from banks, securities companies and non-financial institutions. They endorsed the paper to ensure its creditworthiness and then sold it to the Bank of Japan (*Nihon Keizai Shinbun*, 16 May 1990). This allowed the Bank of Japan to increase its expertise in market operations while obtaining a high-quality and far-reaching instrument and exercising influence over the formation of overnight rates.[4] The problem with this type of operation was that it required a stable primary market, and in the early 1990s there was considerable doubt about whether this would be the case. In the late 1980s commercial paper was issued mainly for opportunistic reasons, embodied in the approach to finance known as *zaiteku*.[5] As the opportunities to exploit rate differentials dried up, it was feared that the market would contract substantially. In fact, the market did decline, but it remains one of the largest of the open money markets in Japan.

Yen banker's acceptance market

The yen denominated banker's acceptance market was inaugurated in June 1985 as a direct result of US pressure for financial liberalisation, for increased international use of the yen and for a reduction in Japan's trade surplus with the United States. It was believed this move would increase demand for the yen, causing the currency to appreciate and the bilateral trade balance to improve. The yen denominated banker's acceptance market was intended to operate as an open market in which banks could purchase bills of exchange at a discount from importers and exporters, attach a payment guarantee and then onsell the bills to investors through the *tanshi* (*Nihon Keizai Shinbun*, 14 December 1989; Viner 1987).

Given that the banker's acceptance rate was set by the market at a margin above the interbank rate, the Bank of Japan was keen to conduct banker's acceptance operations through the *tanshi* and strengthen the link between the interbank and open markets (Viner 1987). The market remained stunted, however, due to the imposition of a progressive stamp duty and the ability of the oil, general trading and steel production companies to obtain cheaper short-term funds elsewhere (*Nihon Keizai Shinbun*, 14 December 1989). It became defunct in November 1989 but is worthy of note for three reasons. First, its fate suggests that markets established for political rather than economic reasons are intrinsically weak (Schaede 1989). Second, it shows the inherent distortions and inefficiency of the mixed free-rate posted-rate system: banker's acceptance paper was bank guaranteed and issued by top corporations, yet its rates were above the short-term prime rate, which was posted at a margin above the official discount rate (officially until January 1989, unofficially thereafter). Naturally, companies preferred cheap bank loans. Third, it has been argued that the failure of the market to embody the low risk of banker's acceptance in its interest rate may suggest that the market in Japan does not readily discriminate between the quality of borrowers (*Nihon Keizai Shinbun*, 14 December 1989) — at least in the short run — during periods of strong economic growth.

Financial bill market

Financial bills are discounted short-term government bonds issued by the Ministry of Finance on subscription for short-term deficit financing. In the early 1990s they had a maturity of 60 days and a minimum denomination of ¥10 million, reduced from ¥50 million in April 1990. The Bank of Japan automatically subscribes to that portion not purchased by the public. Since the Ministry of Finance set rates below both the official discount rate and market rates, the Bank of Japan was forced to take up a large part of every issue and hold it to maturity (Suzuki 1987; Feldman 1986). In October 1990 it held 87 per cent of the total ¥25.35 trillion of financial bills on issue. The Bank of Japan reopened the sale of financial bills in May 1981 as a means of absorbing excess funds in the market. Only after 1989, however, did it use the sale of financial bills on short-term repurchase agreements (that is, as *gensaki*) as an effective and regular tool to absorb excess liquidity in the banking system. The *tanshi* acted as intermediaries for the sale of financial bills by the Bank of Japan and for trade in financial bills (*Nihon Keizai Shinbun*, 18 October 1989). The market has subsequently all but disappeared.

Treasury bill market

Faced with the need to refinance the 10-year government bonds issued on a massive scale in the mid 1970s, in February 1986 the Ministry of Finance began to issue treasury bills publicly. The bills had a minimum denomination of ¥50 million and maturity of six months. Since treasury bills are deficit re-funding bonds, the Bank of Japan is not allowed to purchase them directly (Suzuki 1987). It can and does buy them on resale agreements, however, as part of its new monetary management. The Ministry of Finance was initially reluctant to issue treasury bills, arguing that the sale of short-term debt at market prices would increase public debt interest, and hence the budget deficit, since long-term bonds were being sold at above market prices and long-term rates were at historically low levels. It eased its position progressively from early 1989 onwards, for a number of reasons.

First, the need to refinance deficit bonds was becoming pressing. The advantage of cheap long-term bond financing had been lost due to the shift in the government long-term bond market to market pricing and sale by auction (*Nihon Keizai Shinbun*, 28 August 1989). The inversion of long and short rates in late 1989 also made the sale of longer term securities relatively more difficult. Second, there was sustained pressure by the United States and the European Community for the development of a treasury bill market: to promote further liberalisation of domestic financial markets; to foster a shift from direct central bank lending to open market operations as the preferred method of regulating liquidity in the banking system; and to encourage the use of the yen as a reserve currency. Third, the Ministry of Finance seemed to have accepted the validity of the Bank of Japan's oft-stated claim that a well-developed treasury bill market was necessary for effective monetary management — that the bill was a homogeneous, widely accepted and low-risk instrument whose operations affected all market participants and not just banks. Finally, expanding the issue of treasury bills and allowing market operations constituted, it is said, a show of respect by the Ministry of Finance to Satoshi Sumita, a former ministry official who was about to retire as governor of the Bank of Japan (*Nihon Keizai Shinbun*, 16 December 1989), although this would have affected at most the timing of the decision.

Treasury bills are sold by the Ministry of Finance in the primary market by tender. In April 1990 the minimum denomination was ¥10 million. With the ministry's change of heart, the stock of treasury bills grew substantially, increasing from ¥5 trillion at the end of 1989 to ¥7.5 trillion at the end of 1990. Issues outstanding have grown steadily in the first half of the 1990s, initially boosted by bills issued to finance Japan's contribution to the Gulf War. The issue of three-month treasury bills commenced in September 1989. Since July 1990, treasury bills have been issued twice a month, with auction results being released on the same day through the Bank of Japan's financial network system. Bidding in the primary market by domestic institutions was heavy. Securities companies in particular sought keenly to establish market share, acquiring treasury bills for *gensaki* sales to small and medium sized firms with cash surpluses (*Nihon Keizai Shinbun*, 2 May 1990). Foreign interest in treasury bill issues was limited, however. Excessively high prices for treasury bills, caused by intense domestic demand in the primary market, poor circulation in the secondary market and the burden of the 18 per cent withholding tax (*Nihon Keizai Shinbun*, 13 February 1990) reportedly deterred foreign buyers from dealing in this instrument. The strong domestic interest in treasury bills kept the primary rates relatively low — below primary rates on commercial paper of comparable maturity — and this accorded with the risk structure of interest rates.

The initial development of *gensaki* and secondary markets for treasury bills was not as smooth. The treasury bill *gensaki* was popular, with over 90 per cent of treasury bill secondary transactions in the year to July 1990, for example, taking this form (*Nihon Keizai Shinbun*, 2 August 1990). However, treasury bill *gensaki* interest rate formation did not proceed as smoothly; the risk structure was on occasion not reflected in treasury bill and commercial paper *gensaki* rates, as in April–May 1990, when rates were almost identical in both markets. Commentators explained this as follows (*Nihon Keizai Shinbun*, 2 May 1990). While there was strong interest in treasury bills in the primary market, the sentiment in the *gensaki* market was rather that there was excess supply. This occurred at a time when the volume of commercial paper being issued in the market was easing, generating conditions of excess demand. Consequently, in a generally rising interest rate environment, treasury bill *gensaki* rates rose faster than commercial paper *gensaki* rates, to reach the same level by around May 1990. While issue rates were closely tied to secondary market rates in the more mature commercial paper market, this was not so with the less developed treasury bill market. Excess demand in the primary market suppressed the rise in primary rates while excess supply in the secondary market pushed up *gensaki* rates. Accordingly, the risk structure was seen to work in the primary but not in the secondary market. This was interpreted by some as an indication that the Japanese market did not readily differentiate between risks: in a normally low interest rate and stable economy like Japan, there was no substantive risk difference between the short-term debt of blue chip companies and that of the government (*Nihon Keizai Shinbun*, 2 May 1990). Though this may have sounded arrogant, it was not necessarily contrary to risk theory — at the time the market was confident and Japan's economic performance impressive. Nevertheless, it does not explain why participants in the primary market had a different perception from that of participants in the secondary market when both groups overlapped to a large extent. The episode is thus better taken as an example of a market still in development.

Other than as *gensaki*, treasury bills did not circulate well in the secondary market. Holders faced capital losses in selling the paper on the secondary market because primary rates set in overheated auctions were below market rates. Banks preferred to hold treasury bills to maturity because they were a riskless asset which did not require capital backing under BIS regulations (*Nihon Keizai Shinbun*, 24 March 1990, 10 June 1990). In October 1990, the treasury bill trading settlement period was reduced from 7–10 days to four days in order to reduce settlement risk.

In February 1990 the Bank of Japan began to buy treasury bills on repurchase agreements. This was an important step in realising its plan to make treasury bills the key money market and treasury bill operations the principal tool of monetary management. Market operations were hampered, however, by the relatively small size of the market, the unwillingness of treasury bill holders to participate, and long and cumbersome settlement procedures. The small market size could only be remedied by further issues. If the Bank of Japan's plan was to be realised, the size of the market would need to reach ¥30–40 trillion or even ¥50–60 trillion (*Nihon Keizai Shinbun*, 29 June 1990). With issues outstanding in the mid 1990s at about ¥12 billion, this is still a long way off. The Ministry of Finance initially excluded the *tanshi* from any role in the treasury bill market, reportedly against the wishes of the Bank of Japan (*Nihon Keizai Shinbun*, 15 December 1989). To promote the development of the secondary market and to smooth operations, the *tanshi* were permitted in July 1990 to act as intermediaries in interbank treasury bill deals and to participate in the treasury bill market — though they remained excluded from the primary market and from secondary market dealing other than between banks (*Nihon Keizai Shinbun*, 29 June 1990, 3 July 1990). This move encouraged regional banks and other financial institutions with surplus funds to enter the market. By late 1991 the Bank of Japan was conducting all market operations electronically on BOJ-Net —the bank's computerised settlement system — with same day rather than three-day settlement for both buying and selling (*Nihon Keizai Shinbun*, 3 July 1990).

Non-negotiable deposits

Non-negotiable deposits have long been regarded as part of the open market in Japan (see Schaede 1989, for instance) because they have been close substitutes for open market instruments and highly liquid. They consist of large-lot deposits, money market certificates and foreign currency deposits. Non-negotiable deposits were unusual in Japan in the 1980s in that they offered market rates of interest. Only by October 1994 did all bank deposits (apart from current deposits) offer market rates of interest. Non-negotiable deposits became an increasingly important source of funds for banks during the 1980s as restrictions on minimum denomination and term to maturity eased (Schaede 1989). These deposits have also been a major destination of surplus corporate funds.

The Euroyen market

The Euroyen market covers yen denominated financial assets traded outside Japan. Instruments include Euroyen certificates of deposit and Euroyen commercial paper, introduced in December 1984 and November 1987 respectively; short and long-term Euroyen lending, comprising yen lending to residents and non-residents by non-residents; external yen lending by banks in Japan to non-residents; and Euroyen bonds (Osugi 1990). Short-term Euroyen lending had been fully liberalised by June 1984, long-term lending by May 1989, and banks' external yen lending to non-residents by April 1984. The driving force behind the progressive liberalisation of the Euroyen market was US pressure, embodied in the Yen–Dollar Committee's May 1984 report. In it, the United States argued forcefully for the development of the Euroyen market on the grounds that it would stimulate demand for the yen, pushing the currency up and helping to correct the bilateral trade imbalance. Part of the attraction of the Euroyen market lay in its freedom from domestic controls and transaction rules, such as reserve requirements, interest rate regulations, collateral requirements and window guidance; in addition withholding tax was not applied on interest income, and firms could profit from interest rate arbitrage and swap transactions (Suzuki 1987). Its development was aided by the establishment in December 1986 of the Japan offshore market. The perceived advantage of the offshore market was that it would promote internationalisation of the yen and allow domestic institutions to participate in profitable Euroyen activity without the financial burden of establishing overseas branches (Suzuki 1987).

The Euroyen market, notably the offshore market, expanded rapidly. The total value of assets in the Japan offshore market at the end of 1988 was a substantial US$393.9 billion. While over half of these assets was denominated in foreign currencies, mostly US dollars, the value of those denominated in yen was ¥24.3 trillion (US$179.9 billion using an exchange rate of US$1 = ¥135) at the end of 1988 (Osugi 1990). Interoffice and interbank transactions respectively comprised 21.9 and 75.2 per cent of assets and 22.1 and 77.7 per cent of liabilities in the Japan offshore market. The extent of interbank transactions indicates that the Japan offshore market functioned 'virtually exclusively as an outright interbank market' (Osugi 1990, p. 26). Market commentators stated at the time that the November 1988 interbank market reforms made the Euroyen and unsecured call markets almost identical (*Nihon Keizai Shinbun*, 19 October 1989).

Interest rate linkages in the money market

The diversification and liberalisation of the interbank market, the liberalisation of existing open markets and creation of new ones, and the introduction of new market oriented intervention techniques by the central bank together imply that supply and demand for funds is the principal determinant of rates and that the linkages between money market rates have been strengthened through the creation of new arbitrage possibilities. Based on graphical and statistical analysis, Osugi (1990) concluded that the linkage between Euroyen and Eurodollar rates had been close to perfect since the abolition of swap limits in 1984, as had that between Euroyen and domestic open market rates. He found that the linkage between interbank and domestic open market rates was loose until November 1988, when the interbank market was reformed, but that it had been near perfect since then. Table 11.3 provides correlation coefficients for a variety of interbank and open market rates based on data collected daily from November 1988 to December 1990 (see page 293). The data support the claim of many commentators that the linkages between rates are very close. The form of these linkages is investigated further in the latter part of this chapter.

This study concentrates on money market developments and does not examine change in the loan or capital markets. The alterations that occurred in the way financial institutions procure short-term funds can be expected to have affected how they obtain long-term funds and the composition of their asset portfolios. They also have implications for the transmission of monetary policy. These issues are not addressed here, except to note that change in the formation of loan rates has occurred in the 1990s. As banks rely more on funds acquired at market rates of interest, they are less able to afford to price loans at non-market rates, especially given their obligation to meet BIS capital requirements and their declining capital position since the fall in share prices in 1990. While the introduction of the new short-term prime rate in January 1989 did not bring much flexibility into loan rate determination, the introduction in July 1990 of so-called treasury bill loans for big customers, and of Euroyen loans for small to medium-sized customers, can be seen as a step towards spread banking. These developments signal the degree to which the new open markets are influencing the overall financial structure. De Brouwer (1995a) gives a more detailed examination of the relationship between the money market rates and bank deposit and loan interest rates in Japan and elsewhere in East Asia.

Monetary management by the Bank of Japan

In broad terms, the transmission mechanism for monetary policy may be summarised using the conventional framework of instruments and objectives (Figure 11.1). By controlling the supply and cost of reserves to financial institutions, the Bank of Japan is able to influence interbank and open market rates, thereby determining the rate of growth of broadly defined money (M2 + certificates of deposit) and prices. In this section, I examine and assess the operating procedures of the Bank of Japan, but not the relationship between interest rates, money and prices.[6]

The Bank of Japan uses two policy instruments to influence short-term money market conditions. Changes in the official discount rate influence money market rates both through an announcement effect (by revealing changes in policy stance) and a cost effect (by raising the cost of direct loans made by the central bank). The bank has

Figure 11.1   Instruments and objectives of monetary policy in Japan

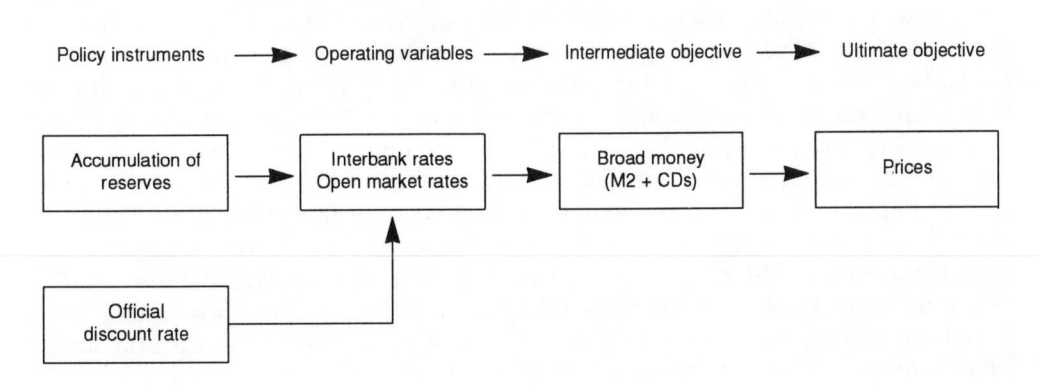

Policy instruments ⟶ Operating variables ⟶ Intermediate objective ⟶ Ultimate objective

Accumulation of reserves ⟶ Interbank rates / Open market rates ⟶ Broad money (M2 + CDs) ⟶ Prices

Official discount rate ⟶ (Interbank rates / Open market rates)

argued that because it has discretion over the balance of loans, the cost effect is insignificant. This reasoning is not persuasive given that these loans have been extensive (¥3.87 trillion in November 1990 and ¥6.3 trillion in December 1990) and in fact operate as a subsidy. In recent years the Bank of Japan's official discount rate policy has been seen as reflecting rather than leading movements in the market (*Nihon Keizai Shinbun*, 23 August 1990).

The second key policy instrument is the bank's control of the accumulation of reserves by financial institutions. This became more important with the decision by the Bank of Japan to publish daily on BOJ-Net the level of reserve deposits and the average reserve deposit shortfall or surplus.[7] Movements in the reserve deposits of financial institutions as a whole occur due to the flow of currency to and between financial institutions and individuals and corporations, the transfer of funds between the government and non-government sectors, and changes in credit provided by the central bank to financial institutions. The Bank of Japan acts to neutralise movements in the shortfall or surplus of funds to ensure that the reserve requirement is always satisfied. However, by influencing the rate of accumulation of reserves over the maintenance period, it alters the supply and demand for funds and their cost in the short-term markets. Longer term, projected trend rises in the monetary base are satisfied by neutral, outright purchases of long-term government bonds. The Bank of Japan's active instruments to influence the accumulation of reserves included direct, collateralised lending at the official discount rate, sales of discount bills and financing bills, and purchases of treasury bills, certificates of deposit, commercial paper and long-term government bonds on short-term repurchase agreements. Figure 11.2 provides a visual summary of how the Bank of Japan used these instruments to carry out policy.

Unlike the central banks of other countries, the Bank of Japan has relied heavily on direct loans to banks and securities companies in its management of markets. This is principally because direct loans are flexible, reliable and effective and because the money markets have still not been sufficiently developed. Direct loans provide further operational flexibility in that they are the only tool which the Bank of Japan could use to both provide and absorb funds. In response to repeated foreign criticism that direct lending was a subsidy to Japanese institutions at the expense of foreign banks, the Bank of Japan began providing direct collateralised loans to foreign banks in December 1989 and raised loan limits in December 1990. The difficulty for the foreign banks, however, lay in acquiring the appropriate collateral. The idea of raising the cost of direct loans to a margin above the official discount rate in order to remove the subsidy element of loans has been mooted (*Nihon Keizai Shinbun*, 11 October 1990) but not implemented. *Gensaki* operations in long-term bonds began in December 1987. These were not successful owing to the burden of the securities transaction tax (which impeded short-term trading), the use of a tender system (with bidding at prices that were unacceptable to the Bank of Japan) and the market view that *gensaki* operations in long-term bonds were an unnatural way to influence short-term market conditions (Nihon Keizai Shinbunsha 1989).

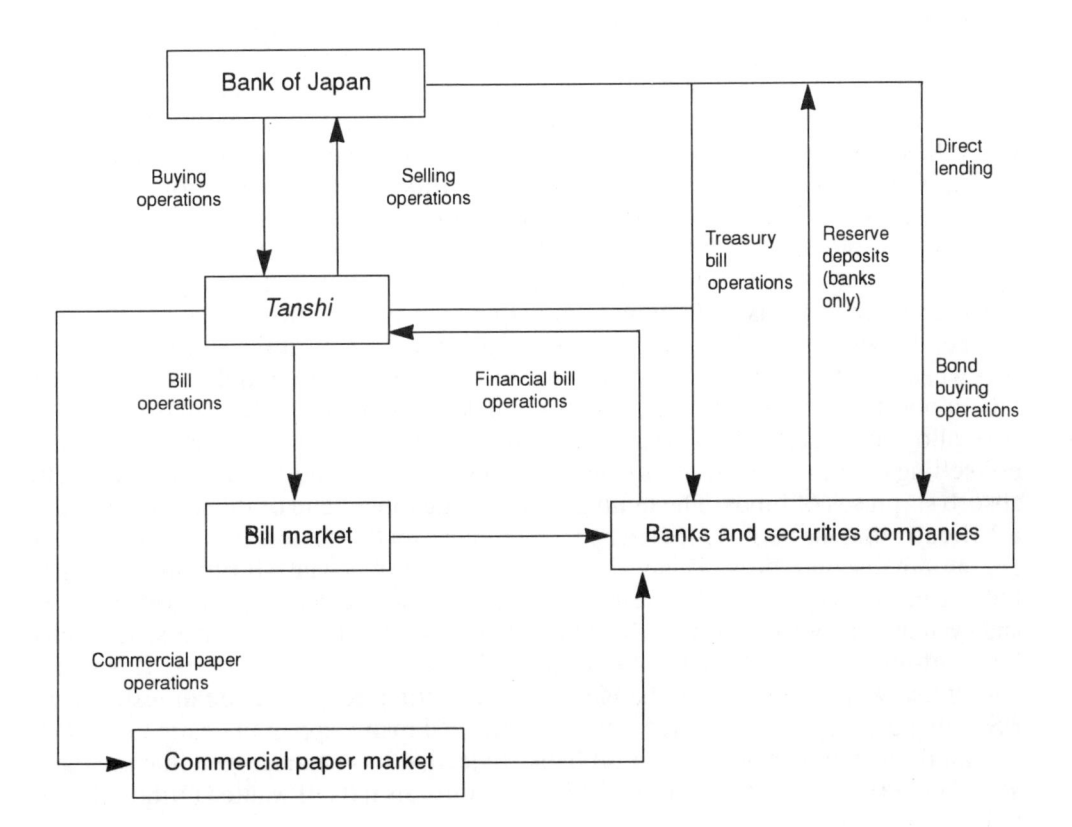

Figure 11.2   Principal money market operations of Bank of Japan

Note: Arrows indicate direction of flow.

Source: *Nihon Keizai Shinbun*, 11 October 1990 and other issues.

Maintaining control over the financial system, specifically influencing the formation of interest rates, has been a constant challenge for the Bank of Japan since the mid 1980s. It is a truism to state that once the process of liberalisation and internationalisation begins, it is impossible to stop or reverse. In this context, developments in the money market in the late 1980s may be seen as an attempt by the Bank of Japan to regain and expand control. The bank had direct control over the interbank market through the *tanshi*, but much of the growth in money markets was occurring in the more elusive open market. To maintain their influence, the monetary authorities had to progressively liberalise and expand the interbank market, promote arbitrage with the open market, and establish new markets and introduce market operations in the domestic open market. In this sense, the Bank of Japan was reactive rather than proactive.

It appears that the Bank of Japan has no intention of returning to the days of direct control even if it could. Rather, it envisions a developed, Western style money market based on market intervention techniques (*Nihon Keizai Shinbun*, 11 October 1990). It has long sought to introduce market oriented intervention techniques. Only from the late 1980s, however, did it take steps to increase the transparency of its operations and intentions (by, for example, releasing reserve positions) or to actively promote a more ordered, market-oriented and market-consistent process of interest rate determination (by, for example, freeing the secured call rate). The bank also attempted to structure its operations so as to influence the term structure in an even manner. Specifically, it introduced direct loans and commercial paper buying operations aimed at the very short end (overnight), discount bill buying operations aimed at the short end (one to two weeks) and treasury bill buying operations aimed at the middle of the market (about one month). The introduction of same day settlement for treasury bill operations allowed treasury bills to be used to cover the very short to middle range. Financial bill selling operations were conducted at the very short to short end of the market to absorb surpluses of funds. The main gap was at the longer end of the money market, a difficulty that the bank remedied by introducing a tender system for the purchase of 2–3 month discount bills. This was important not only because it promoted greater linkage between rates with different maturities but also because it reduced the interest and system risk faced by banks who had to rely on the sale of one-week discount bills for short-term supply of funds (*Nihon Keizai Shinbun*, 11 October 1990). It is worth noting that while many of the changes to market structure were made in response to US demands, they also accorded with the Bank of Japan's apparent desire to be seen as a modern, market oriented central bank. Indeed, it has been alleged that the bank used foreign pressure as a means to achieve the reforms it itself wanted (Nihon Keizai Shinbunsha 1989).

A major reason why the Bank of Japan was left behind by market developments was that it was powerless to effect change. The bank repeatedly called for the development of a short-term government paper market — described by one commentator as the Bank of Japan's *higan*, or Buddhist prayer for the salvation of humanity (*Nihon Keizai Shinbun*, 25 August 1990) — but was for a long time held back by the Ministry of Finance. The ever budget conscious Ministry of Finance also refused to review taxes on financial instruments, despite requests for it to do so by, for example, academics and the government's Short-Term Money Market Research Group in July 1990.

While in Japan decisions are made and enforced in a framework of consensus, there is very real conflict and friction between the institutions which regulate and supervise the financial system.[8] The Bank of Japan's conduct of monetary policy is closely monitored by the Ministry of Finance, whose wide powers of control over the central bank reflect the enactment of the current Bank of Japan Law under wartime conditions in 1942. Two episodes of operational conflict are instructive. The first concerns the increase in the official discount rate by the Bank of Japan in 1990 (*Japan Economic*

Journal, 21 April 1990). Formally, the official discount rate is determined at the sole discretion of the Policy Board of the Bank of Japan, which includes a non-voting official from the Ministry of Finance (Suzuki 1987). In practice, however, ministry approval has been required for any change in the official discount rate, because of the nature of Japanese decision-making and because the ministry has had the right to propose changes to the regulated structure of deposit interest rates, which have in turn been based on the official discount rate. When the previous Governor of the Bank of Japan, Yasushi Mieno, sought to contain inflationary expectations by raising the official discount rate, Finance Minister Ryūtarō Hashimoto opposed the move on the basis that inflationary pressures were already contained. He claimed that a further increase in rates would destabilise the jittery domestic stock market, force rates up in the United States and elsewhere, and stymie international growth and stability. The Bank of Japan won, but only after considerable public brawling. An important factor in this falling out may have been the origins of the bank's governor: Mieno had risen up through the ranks of the Bank of Japan rather than being a Ministry of Finance appointee.

The second episode concerns the organisational structure of the bank (*The Economist*, 26 May 1990). Given its operational constraints, the Bank of Japan sought to enhance its policy effectiveness by introducing a computerised settlement system (BOJ-Net) under Governor Sumita in 1989 and by carrying out a sweeping internal reorganisation under Governor Mieno in May 1990. BOJ–Net provides facilities for interbank funds settlement, transfer of Bank of Japan funds to all financial institutions, and the processing of foreign exchange payments and government bond transactions. More controversially, as part of its reorganisation the bank set up a Financial and Payments System Department, which for the first time gave it the means to study long-term monetary issues. By improving the bank's information collection, funds processing and long-term policy formulation, these reforms allowed the Bank of Japan to consolidate and expand its position vis-à-vis the Ministry of Finance. The ministry accepted the challenge. It pushed for a ministry official to be made chair of a government–industry committee on BOJ-Net, thereby gaining veto power over future developments. It used its veto to halt the bank's plans to use data processing to confirm unsecured call money dealings, and to stop it from setting a minimum amount on transfers of funds through BOJ-Net. It also set up a money market monitoring section in its Banking Bureau. This was reportedly viewed by the bank as an attempt to monitor it.

Granger causality

This section investigates the relationship between the key interest rates in Japan in terms of Granger causality (Granger 1969). Granger causality is not causality as this word is commonly understood but refers, in a statistical sense, to precedence in time and hence whether the past values of one variable (z) help predict the current value of another variable (*y*). In general terms, the variable *z* is said to Granger cause the variable *y* if taking account of past *z* improves the accuracy of the prediction of *y* (Harvey 1990). The aim here is to determine whether any of the key interest rates are predicted by other rates, and if so which rate or set of rates 'drives' the system of interest rates in Japan. The analysis is conducted in a four-variable framework. This provides a realistic representation of the Japanese money market and offers potentially greater insight than is afforded by a two-variable framework by allowing identification of direct, indirect and spurious Granger causality (Hsiao 1982).

De Brouwer (1992) provides a detailed technical explanation derived from Hsiao (1982) of direct causality, feedback, indirect causality and spurious causality in a four-variable framework. These are best illustrated by examples. The variable *z* directly causes *y* when using past values of *z* reduces the prediction error of *y*. There is direct feedback between *y* and *z* when *z* directly causes *y* and *y* directly causes *z*. Indirect causality from *z* to *y* is typified by the situation in which a variable *x* appears to cause *y* but in fact it is the variable *z* which drives *x* and hence causes *y*. This may be tested as follows: if including past *z* does not reduce the prediction error for *y* when past values of *x* are included but does so when past *x* are excluded and when *z* directly causes *x*, then indirect causality from *z* to *y* through *x* is said to occur. No causality occurs if *z* neither directly nor indirectly causes *y*. There are two types of spurious causality, but only one is empirically important. It occurs when *z* appears to cause *y* but does so only because it acts as proxy for the missing *x* (*x* causes both *z* and *y* but, if *x* is not included, *z* appears to cause *y*).

Data

The Japanese money market rates used in the four-variable Granger causality tests are the unsecured overnight call money rate; the two-week discount bill rate; the average new issue, three-month certificate of deposit rate quoted by banks; and the average three-month Euroyen deposit rate quoted by banks in the Japan offshore market. These rates represent respectively the call market, discount bill market, domestic open market and offshore open market, and so reflect the structure of the Japanese money market. As discussed in the first part of this chapter, these are the key money market rates. Restricting the analysis to these four rates provides a clearer picture of market structure and reduces both the computational burden and risk of multicollinearity (which is high given the high degree of correlation between interest rates). The data were taken from the Nikkei Telecom Japan News and Retrieval service, and covered 520 weekday observations from 5 November 1988 to 13 December 1990. The post-reform period — in which money market rates showed the strongest linkage — was chosen because structural change can affect Granger causality results (McMillin 1986). The correlation coefficients and the mean for each rate for the period are presented in Table 11.3.

A time series may be regarded as the realisation of a stochastic process with a given probability distribution. In order to draw inferences about that process — specifically,

Table 11.3 Correlation coefficients for interbank and open market rates

	R1	R2	R3	R4	Mean
R1	1.0000				6.0657
R2	0.9822	1.0000			6.1572
R3	0.9862	0.9841	1.0000		6.3754
R4	0.9848	0.9825	0.9988	1.0000	6.4140

Notes: R1 = unsecured overnight call rate.
R2 = two-week bill rate.
R3 = three-month average certificate of deposit rate.
R4 = three-month Euroyen rate.

to apply Granger causality — the moments of the probability density function must exist. That is, the stochastic process must be stationary. The formal test of stationarity used in this chapter is the adjusted Dickey–Fuller (ADF) test for the existence of a unit root (Dickey and Fuller 1981). This is the test most commonly applied in the empirical literature. The test results are summarised in Table 11.4. Interest rates are not uniformly non-stationary series over the short interval studied in this chapter. The call and bill rates are stationary in levels, while the certificate of deposit and Euroyen rates are only stationary in first differences. Accordingly, the latter set of rates enters the estimation in first differences.[9]

Given that two of the variables are integrated of order one, it may seem appropriate to test for cointegration, as is done by McKenzie (1993). This is not pursued here. In

Table 11.4 Augmented Dickey–Fuller test statistics

	Levels (t-test)	Levels (F test)	First differences (t-test)
Unsecured call rate (4)	−4.23*	8.99*	−
Bill rate (5)	−5.02*	12.65*	−
Certificate of deposit rate (5)	−1.89	1.82	−8.16*
Euroyen rate (5)	−2.24	2.52	−10.05*

Note: Number of lags in the augmented Dickey–Fuller (1981) test is in brackets.
* indicates significant at the 1 per cent level. The critical value for the t-test is from Table 8.5.2 in Fuller (1976, p. 373). The critical value for the F test is from Table VI in Dickey and Fuller (1981, p.1,063) and tests the joint null hypothesis that there is a unit root and no time trend.

Figure 11.3   Multivariate Granger causality

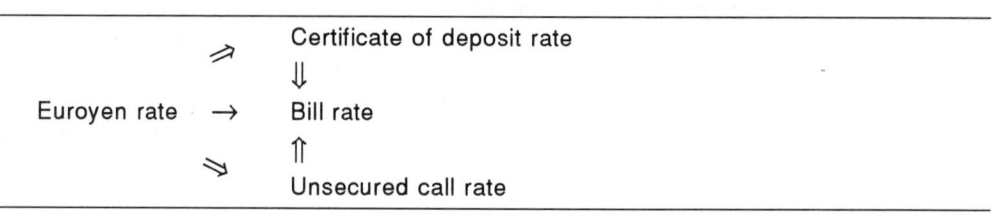

```
                    ⇗   Certificate of deposit rate
                        ⇓
   Euroyen rate  →   Bill rate
                        ⇑
                    ⇘   Unsecured call rate
```

Note: Single arrow indicates indirect Granger causality; double arrow indicates direct Granger causality.

the first place, some rates are integrated processes and others are stationary, so it does not make sense to look for cointegration over the full set. Furthermore, while the sample set is itself large, the sample period is only a relatively short two-year period, and so cointegration is less likely to be an important factor in determining the interaction between rates. McKenzie (1993) looks at the relationship between various rates over a much longer time period.

Akaike's final prediction error criterion and the Hannon–Quinn information criterion are both used to select the lag lengths for the multivariate test equations. De Brouwer (1992) discusses these methods and sets out the results in detail.

Results

Figure 11.3 provides a visual summary of the Granger causality results, while Tables 11.5 and 11.6 provide summaries of Granger causality using the final prediction error criterion and Hannon–Quinn information criterion respectively. The results do not change qualitatively with the alternative lag specification procedures.

The results provide a clear view of the relationship between the four key interest rates. First the Euroyen rate appears to be the key predictor of the system, directly Granger causing the unsecured call and the certificate of deposit rates and indirectly Granger causing the bill rate through the unsecured call rate. None of the other key rates directly cause the Euroyen rate. The null hypothesis that other rates do not cause the Euroyen rate is rejected at the 5 per cent level, though barely so. The result that the Euroyen rate drives the domestic system of rates is not unexpected since the Euroyen market is substantial and free. Its rates reflect market conditions, and the Euroyen rate is properly called a 'market rate'. More unexpected is the absence of feedback from domestic rates to the Euroyen rate. The implication is that it is essentially the market — the forum in which the demand and supply of loanable funds are equated — rather than the monetary authorities which determines interest rates over time.

However, it is incorrect to conclude that the Euroyen rate is exogenous: the model is in reduced form and the rate itself could be endogenous in a wider system. Indeed,

Table 11.5 Summary of multivariate Granger causality: final prediction error criterion

---

Direct Granger causality
Euroyen rate   ⇒   Unsecured call rate
Euroyen rate   ⇒   CD rate
CD rate   ⇒   Bill rate

Bidirectional direct Granger causality (feedback)
Unsecured call rate   ⇔   Bill rate

Indirect Granger causality
Euroyen rate   →   Bill rate (through unsecured call rate)

Type 2 spurious causality
Unsecured call rate   to   CD rate
Bill rate   to   CD rate

Notes: CD = certificate of deposit.
Single arrow indicates indirect Granger causality; double arrow indicates direct Granger causality.

Table 11.6 Summary of multivariate Granger causality: Hannon–Quinn information criterion

---

Direct Granger causality
Euroyen rate   ⇒   Unsecured call rate
Euroyen rate   ⇒   CD rate
CD rate   ⇒   Bill rate

Bidirectional direct Granger causality (feedback)
Unsecured call rate   ⇔   Bill rate

Indirect Granger causality
Euroyen rate   →   Bill rate (through CD rate)

No causality
Euroyen rate is not caused by the other rates

Type 2 spurious causality
Bill rate   to   CD rate

Notes: CD = certificate of deposit.
Single arrow indicates indirect Granger causality; double arrow indicates direct Granger causality.

the Granger causality tests are not based on any economic model, and to describe the Euroyen rate as exogenous only begs the question of what determines it. The Euroyen market is very closely tied to other Euro markets, the Eurodollar market in particular, and hence the implication is that Japanese interest rates are determined by world (and especially US) monetary conditions. Indeed, de Brouwer (1995b) presents evidence that the Eurodollar rate affects the Euroyen rate more than the Euroyen rate affects the Eurodollar rate. The result that the previous day's offshore rate helps predict the current day's domestic rate suggests that past values of the Euroyen rate carry valuable information and that there is some lag in information acquisition and/or processing. This lag may reflect barriers to capital flows between the offshore and onshore yen markets, or inefficiencies in or the poor development of domestic markets.

Second, there is direct feedback between the unsecured call and two-week bill rates, indicating that interbank rates are jointly determined. This is a sensible result. Open market rates, on the other hand, predict interbank market rates, with the Euroyen rate directly causing the unsecured call rate and indirectly causing the bill rate, and the certificate of deposit rate directly causing the bill rate. Bivariate tests were also applied to the data, though these are not reported. The results showed feedback between interbank and open markets. On the more powerful multivariate tests these results proved incorrect, indicating that the causality from bill rate to certificate of deposit rate and from unsecured call rate to certificate of deposit rate is spurious.

Third, given that the Bank of Japan conducts its operations in the domestic money market and concentrates on the interbank market, two results — that the Euroyen rate unidirectionally predicts domestic money market rates, and that open market rates unidirectionally predict interbank market rates — lead to the inference that the Bank of Japan was either unable or unwilling to influence the formation of open money market interest rates between November 1988 and December 1990. This result is surprising in that the bank's reforms, up to and including those of November 1988, were designed to promote arbitrage and strengthen its position. Even if linkage between rates has improved substantially, it has not resulted in a process of interest rate formation which favours the control methods used by the monetary authorities.[10]

The results indicate that it is fundamentally the market which determines interest rates. The key role of the Euroyen market underscores the need for the Bank of Japan to continue to promote interest rate arbitrage between the interbank and open markets and to develop effective open market operations. On a more cautious note, it would be premature to state that policy formulation by the Bank of Japan has necessarily been ineffective. First, the results are consistent with an accommodatory policy stance, and so the proposition of policy effectiveness may not have been tested. Second, the results cover a broad two-year period, and restricting analysis to periods of perceived policy activity may yield different results. Third, viewed from a short-term perspective, as long as the banking system needs settlement funds the central bank is able to influence interbank interest rates. However, although it may be able to affect these rates in the short term, it will not necessarily be able to affect open market interest rates on a sustained basis. Also, the reduced form equations do not explicitly test instantaneous

Granger causality and so do not directly identify intra-day arbitrage effects. This can only be considered explicitly in the full model. Fourth, from a wider perspective, through its influence over bank liquidity the central bank may affect the supply of funds and economic conditions and thereby influence domestic and offshore Japanese interest rates (which in turn has economic effects). Fifth, the results may alter with the inclusion of quantity policy variables, such as a surplus or shortfall of funds or reserves. Such information is not available for the full period.

Conclusions

The Japanese money markets underwent significant and substantial change in the late 1980s in terms both of market depth and the availability of instruments. The Bank of Japan adopted a policy of making its intentions and operations more transparent to the market. The catalyst for this was the pressing need to find effective, market oriented ways of influencing money market developments. There is, however, considerable scope for further change. Indeed, it appears that the process of liberalisation and internationalisation, once begun, is impossible to stop.

The principal conclusions from the analysis are as follows. First, while correlation coefficients provide information about linkages between variables, Granger causality tests can offer valuable information about the form or structure of such linkages. Multivariate as opposed to bivariate tests of Granger causality are preferred since the former provide additional information about indirect causality and reduce the risk of spurious causality.

Second, it is generally argued that there was an improvement in the linkage between money market interest rates in Japan after the reforms of November 1988. Tests of the nature of that linkage show that open market rates unidirectionally predict interbank market rates and that offshore Japanese open money market rates (that is, the Euroyen rate) unidirectionally predict domestic open market and interbank market rates with a lead of one day. This does not imply that Euroyen rates are exogenous. The popular view is that Euroyen interest rates are intimately linked to Eurodollar rates, with the result thus implying that domestic conditions are determined by international, especially US, monetary conditions.

Third, since the Bank of Japan conducts its operations principally in the interbank market, this result is consistent with the proposition that monetary policy was either ineffective or accommodatory from November 1988 to December 1990.

Fourth, the results are robust in the sense that they do not vary substantially as the lag specification technique changes (from Akaike's final prediction error to the Hannon–Quinn information criterion). Provisos include the criticisms that the estimation precludes intradaily arbitrage effects (or instantaneous Granger causality) and excludes possibly relevant variables, and so may be misspecified.

Finally, if the results are correct, they underscore the need for the further development of the domestic money market, and particularly of the treasury bill market, which is the preferred location of central bank market operations.

Notes

1. Suzuki (1987), Viner (1987), Schaede (1989) and Shimamura (1989) provide further details of these developments.
2. Suzuki (1987) gives a detailed explanation, but a brief comment here on the *tanshi* is warranted.
3. In early September 1990, for example, rates for commercial paper were 8.3 per cent and those for large lot deposits 8.45 per cent (*Nihon Keizai Shinbun*, 5 September 1990).
4. The Bank of Japan did not accept commercial paper issued on the day of operations. This was because it did not want paper issued only for use in the bank's market operations (letter from the Institute of Foreign Bankers, 17 May 1989).
5. Viner (1987, p. 268) explains *zaiteku* as: a 'slang neologism coined from part of the Japanese word for finance (*zaimu*) and part of the English word "technology" (by analogy with "high-tech"). A vague term referring to domestic and international finance arbitrage conducted by treasurers of Japanese corporations'. It is often translated as 'financial engineering'.
6. The Bank of Japan's techniques of monetary management are detailed in Fukui (1986), Suzuki, Kuroda and Shirakawa (1988), Nihon Keizai Shinbunsha (1989), Kneeshaw and van den Bergh (1989), Shigehara (1990) and Okina (1993).
7. While the Bank of Japan is still able to vary minimum reserve requirements, it has not actively used this tool since 1981 (Shigehara 1990).
8. See Horne (1985) for details of episodes similar to those recounted here.
9. See de Brouwer (1992) for a more detailed discussion.
10. This result underscores the limitation of relying on simple graphical and statistical analysis for conclusions about policy effectiveness: Granger causality analysis is a more powerful tool.

References

Bank of Japan (1994), 'Characteristics of Interest Rate Indicators', *Bank of Japan Quarterly Bulletin*, November, pp. 35–61.

de Brouwer, G.J. (1992), 'An Analysis of Recent Developments in the Japanese Money Market', *Pacific Economic Papers*, 211, Australia–Japan Research Centre, Australian National University, Canberra, September.

—— (1995a), 'The Liberalisation and Integration of Domestic Financial Markets in Western Pacific Economies', Research Discussion Paper, RDP 9506, Reserve Bank of Australia, Sydney.

—— (1995b), Interest Parity Conditions as Indicators of Financial Integration in East Asia, Australia–Japan Research Centre, Australian National University, Canberra, November (mimeo).

Dickey, D.A. and W.A. Fuller (1981), 'Likelihood Ratio Statistics for Autoregressive Time Series with a Unit Root', *Econometrica*, 49, pp. 1,057–72.

Feldman, R.A.(1986), *Japanese Financial Markets*, Cambridge, MA: MIT Press.

Fukui, T. (1986), 'Recent Developments of the Short Term Money Market in Japan and Changes in Monetary Control Techniques and Procedures by the Bank of Japan', Bank of Japan Research and Statistics Department Special Paper No 130, January.

Fuller, W.A. (1976), *Introduction to Statistical Time Series*, New York: John Wiley & Sons.

Granger, C.W.J. (1969), 'Investigating Causal Relations by Econometric Models and Cross-Spectral Methods', *Econometrica*, 37 (3), pp. 424–38.

Harvey, A.C. (1990), *The Econometric Analysis of Time Series*, London: Philip Allan.

Horne, J. (1985), *Japan's Financial Markets*, Sydney: Allen and Unwin.

Hsiao, C. (1982), 'Autoregressive Modeling and Causal Ordering of Economic Variables', *Journal of Economic Dynamics and Control*, 4, pp. 243–59.

Kneeshaw, J.T. and P. van den Bergh (1989), 'Changes in Central Bank Money Market Operating Procedures in the 1980s', Bank for International Settlements Economic Paper No 23, Bank for International Settlements, Basel, January.

McKenzie, C. (1993), 'The Money Markets in Japan', in S. Takagi (ed.), *Japanese Capital Markets*, Oxford: Blackwell, pp. 426–51.

McMillin, W.D. (1986), 'Federal Deficits, Macrostabilisation Goals and Federal Reserve Behaviour', *Economic Inquiry*, 24, pp. 257–69.

Nihon Keizai Shinbunsha (1989), *Nihon Ginkō no Kenkyū* [Research on the Bank of Japan], Tokyo: Nihon Keizai Shinbunsha.

Okina, K. (1993), 'Market Operation in Japan: Theory and Practice', in K.J. Singleton (ed.), *Japanese Monetary Policy*, Chicago, IL: University of Chicago Press, pp. 31–62.

Osugi, K. (1990), 'Japan's Experience of Financial Deregulation since 1984 in an International Perspective', Bank for International Settlements Economic Paper No 26, Bank for International Settlements, Basel, January.

Schaede, U. (1988), The Introduction of Commercial Paper, Hitotsubashi University, Tokyo (mimeo).

—— (1989), 'Liberalization of Money Markets: A Comparison of Japan and West Germany', *Journal of International Economic Studies*, 3, pp. 25–43.

Shigehara, K. (1990), Japan's Experience with Monetary Policy and Financial Liberalization, Paper presented to the Pacific Region Central Bank Conference on Monetary Policy and Market Operations, Sydney, October.

Shimamura, T. (1989), 'Japan's Financial System: Creation and Changes', *Japanese Economic Studies*, Spring, pp. 43–88.

Suzuki, Y. (1987), *The Japanese Financial System*, Oxford: Clarendon Press.

Suzuki, Y., A. Kuroda and H. Shirakawa (1988). 'Monetary Control Mechanism in Japan', *Bank of Japan Monetary and Economic Studies*, 6 (2).

Viner, A. (1987), *Inside Japan's Financial Markets*, Tokyo: Japan Times/Economist.

Index

administration of branch offices, 252–3
ageing society, 216–17
agency
   agency costs, 4, 5, 26, 61
   agency problems, 12, 57
Anglo-American model, 8, 9, 10, 114, 246
anticompetitive behaviour, 22, 25, 26–7, 32, 33, 34–5, 36, 37, 38, 46n
   see also market, market access; market, market closure; trade barriers
antitrust policy, 30, 32, 33, 35, 36, 37, 39, 40, 41, 42, 43
Anzen Credit Cooperative, 267, 271n
arm's-length trading, 28–30, 32, 37, 172, 223, 238, 246n
artificial barriers, 25
asset quality, 7, 14
asymmetric information
   see informational asymmetries
Ataka & Co., 185n
auditor, 170
automobile industry, 58, 59, 62, 65

bad debts
   see non-performing loans
bad loans
   see non-performing loans
bank (profit) margins, 146–7
   see also profitability
bank borrowings, 231, 234, 235, 236, 238, 241
bank debenture market, 14
bank debt ratio, 233, 234

Bank for International Settlements (BIS), 157, 163n, 216, 218, 256, 260, 263, 265–6, 270n, 280
Bank for International Settlements capital adequacy regulations
   see Bank for International Settlements
Bank of Japan Law, 290
Bank of Japan, 16, 136, 149, 153, 158, 224–5, 230, 232, 238, 245n, 249, 251, 254, 261, 269, 271n, 275, 277, 278, 279, 280, 281, 282, 283, 284, 285, 287–91
bank shareholding, 145, 162, 168
bank–firm relations
   see bank–firm ties
bank–firm ties, 1, 6, 11, 12, 24, 127–8, 245
banker's acceptance market, 281–2
banks
   city banks, 150, 153, 244, 254, 261, 263, 275, 277
   commercial, 161n, 199, 270n
   long-term credit banks, 244, 245n
   regional banks, 251, 252, 254, 260
   second-tier regional banks, 275
   trust banks, 140, 225, 244, 253, 270n, 275, 277, 280
   see also bank–firm ties
blockholders, 8, 168, 170, 171
board of directors
   see directors
Bond Issuance Committee, 224, 225, 226, 228, 231, 260
Bond Issuance Round Table, 224

bondholders, 92, 98, 99, 197
bonds, 222–46, 257–8, 280
   bond covenants, 92
   bond financing, 223–38
   bond issue criteria, 225, 228, 229–30, 241
   bond markets, 12, 96, 224
   convertible bonds, 228, 229, 230, 231, 234, 237, 238, 239
   corporate bond ownership, 239, 259
   junk bonds, 96, 111, 196
   warrant bonds, 221, 227, 231
bubble (economy), 6, 7, 8, 11, 12, 13, 15, 143, 146, 158, 214–15, 261, 266
business groups
   see keiretsu
business relationships
   see keiretsu

call market, 226, 277
capital
   capital investment, 11
   cost of, 11, 33, 193, 194, 197, 198, 206–12, 217–18, 224
   international comparison of cost of capital, 204–6
   opportunity cost of capital, 200, 201
capital investment, 11
cartels, 3, 14, 22, 43
certificate of deposit market, 15, 16, 258, 270n, 280–1, 295
chief executive officer (CEO), 9, 95, 99, 106, 111, 112, 113, 180, 181
   see also executives; management, top management; presidents
class action suits, 96
closed markets
   see market, market access; market, market closure
collective bargaining, 99
commercial paper market, 278, 279, 281, 284, 289, 298
compensating balances, 147, 148, 224

competition restricting regulations, 13, 252–3, 257
computerisation, 60, 291
consumer price index (CPI), 67, 68, 69–76, 77, 79–81, 82
consumption, 58, 63
convertible bonds
   see bonds, convertible bonds
convoy system, 13, 15, 53, 253
Cooperative Credit Purchasing Corporation (CCPC), 263–4, 270n
Corporate Bonds Act 1993, 221
corporate finance, 221–46
corporate governance, 1, 2, 4–9, 14, 15, 91–114, 158, 166–84
   definition of, 5, 91
   insider based system, 107–11, 166–70
   open bidding system, 111–12, 166–7
corporate groups
   see keiretsu
corporate organisation, 104–6
Cosmo Credit Cooperative, 267
costs
   agency costs, 4, 5, 198
   cost characteristics of distribution channels, 63
   minimising costs, 38
   monitoring costs, 134, 136, 144
   retail costs, 60
   trade costs, 25
   see also capital, costs of
credit cooperatives, 252, 267, 269, 271n
credit rating, 14
credit rationing, 225, 226
credit unions
   see credit cooperatives
credit worthiness, 6
cross-holdings
   see interlocking shareholdings
cross-shareholdings
   see interlocking shareholdings

Daiichi Kangyo Bank (DKB) group, 23,

138n, 174, 177, 261
Daishowa Paper, 185n
Daiten-Hō (Daikibo Kouri Tenpo Hō) 59, 60, 78
Daiwa Bank, 21fn, 254
debt levels, 111, 112
Deposit Insurance Corporation, 13, 252, 266, 267, 268
deposit insurance system, 13, 15, 250, 251, 252, 266, 269–70n
deregulation
  see financial deregulation
directors
  board of directors, 8, 110, 112–13, 169, 170, 181, 277
  outside directors, 9, 170–84
  shareholder suits against, 10
discount bill market, 277, 289
distribution
  distribution channels, 3, 4, 55–9
    exclusive, 62–3
    length of, 61–2
    model of, 81–2
  price formation models, 66–9
  price responsiveness of different distribution channels, 69–76, 79
  types of, 63–6
distribution networks, 22, 24, 56
distribution systems, 3, 4, 22, 54–87
  cost structure, 66
  decentralisation of distribution systems, 54–5, 55–61, 77
diversifying risks
  see risk sharing
dividends, 99, 103, 110, 111, 112, 199, 201, 205, 228
downstream firms, 2, 3, 28, 29, 36, 37–43, 61, 62, 81

econometric theory, 33–5
Economic Development Institute of the World Bank, 161
Economic Planning Agency, 217, 224

economics of organisation, 5, 21–44
efficiency theories, 103–6
employee share ownership plans (ESOPs), 97
employment system, 45
enterprise groups
  see keiretsu
entrepreneurs, 94, 114n
equitable subordination, 137
escorted convoy system
  see convoy system
Euromarket, 221, 259
Europe, 91, 166, 283
Euroyen market, 15, 16, 275, 277, 278, 285–6, 292, 293, 294–7
exclusion, 41
  exclusive distribution channels, 62–3
  exclusive lending, 127–8
exclusionary behaviour, 43
executives, 92, 97, 98
external appointees
  see directors, outside directors

family control, 173, 179, 195
final market
  see product markets, final product markets
financial bill market, 276, 282
financial deregulation, 6, 8, 11–12, 15, 144, 146, 147, 153, 158, 159, 161n, 215, 221–46, 269, 274–99
financial distress, 99, 100, 110, 125, 132, 137, 137n, 144, 145, 146, 150, 151, 152, 154, 157, 162n, 163n, 171, 200, 238, 241, 249, 250, 251, 252, 266, 268, 270n, 271n
financial intermediaries, 153–5, 193, 252, 268
financial liberalisation
  see financial deregulation
financial organisation, 1, 4
Financial Reform Act 1992, 270
financial regulation, 2, 3, 7, 13, 76, 155,

225, 249–71, 266
financial safety net
    see safety net
Financial System Research Council (Kin'yū Seido Chōsakai), 252, 270n
financial system, 2, 10–16, 191–4, 221, 238, 245, 249, 250–2, 260, 270n
firm
    definition of, 27
    firm organisation, 2, 24, 28, 38, 291
firm-specific investments, 42, 108
Foreign Exchange and Foreign Trade Control Law, 221, 227, 259
France, 86n, 198
free-riding, 62, 21, 102, 110, 115n, 128, 129, 134, 135, 139, 149
    see also monitoring: non-monitoring banks; monitoring: shirking monitoring activities
Fuji Bank Group
    see Fuyō group
Fukui Bank, 267
Fukuiken Daiichi Credit Cooperative, 267
Fuyō group, 23, 174, 177, 251, 261

GATT, 21, 24
gensaki market, 226, 245n, 258, 275, 276, 280, 284, 288
Germany, 86n, 96, 107–11, 198, 206, 217
Gifu Shōgin Credit Cooperative, 267
globalisation
    see internationalisation
government debt, 257–8
Granger causality, 15, 16, 274, 291–2, 298n
Great Britain, 206
    see also United Kingdom

Herfindahl index, 72
Hokkaidō Takushoku Bank, 254
Home Affairs Agency, 224
horizontal ties, 35–7
Hyōgo Bank, 267

incentives
    employee incentives, 104, 105, 109, 113
        see also labour, wages
    managerial incentives, 105
        see also management, management compensation
Industrial Bank of Japan, 224
industrial organisation theory
    see industrial organisation
industrial organisation, 27, 34, 35, 44n
informational asymmetries, 67, 69, 72, 75, 76, 92, 129–36, 138n, 145, 219
Institute of Fiscal and Monetary Policy, 146
interbank market, 15, 16, 275, 276, 277–80, 287, 296
intercorporate shareholdings
    see interlocking shareholdings
interdependence, 61
interfirm relationships
    see *keiretsu*
interest rate regulation, 13, 15, 16, 244, 286–97
interlocking shareholdings, 1, 2, 4, 11, 12, 14, 23, 24, 34, 102, 168, 169, 194, 196, 197, 198, 206, 215, 218
internal labour markets, 28, 108, 110, 114
internal organisation, 28, 115n
internationalisation, 6, 11, 12, 216, 221–2, 259
intervention, 166–81, 185n, 269, 270n
    see also financial distress
investors
    arm's-length investors, 5, 167, 169, 185
    institutional investors, 12, 103, 195
    owner investors, 199
    peripheral investors, 185
    relationship investors, 11, 194, 195, 197, 199, 219, 219n
    responsibility of, 15
Iwata Bank, 267
Iyo Bank, 252

Japan Development Bank, 224
Japanese firms, 9, 10, 11, 14, 22, 25, 27, 35
Japanese-German model, 107–11
junk bonds
   see bonds, junk
jūsen, 7

kakaku hakai
   see price destruction
Kamaishi Shinkin Bank, 267
Kansai Kōgin Bank, 267
Kawachi Bank, 251
keiretsu, 1–4, 11, 21–47, 107, 216, 237, 241
   definition of, 1, 22, 23
   distribution *keiretsu*, 1, 24, 58, 59, 65, 69, 78
   financial *keiretsu*, 23
   horizontal *keiretsu*, 34, 35
   market closure and *keiretsu*, 24–44
   supplier keiretsu, 1, 24
   vertical *keiretsu*, 34, 35
kigyō shūdan
   see keiretsu
Kizu Credit Cooperative, 267

labour
   influence of labour, 99–100
labour force, 216
   wages, 99, 108, 109–10, 112
Large-Scale Retail Stores Law
   see *Daiten-Hō*
lifetime employment, 9, 42, 104, 108, 114, 127–8, 169, 180, 211
liquidity, 7, 167
long-term
   long-term contracts, 24, 41, 42–3, 47n
   long-term relations
     see long-term ties
   long-term ties, 24, 28, 29, 34, 37–43, 57, 198

main bank
   main bank system, 6, 7, 11, 12, 23, 34, 107, 108, 124–40, 143–61, 194, 197, 198, 200, 202, 223, 238–45
   main bank contract, 131–4, 136, 138n, 139n
main banks
   see main bank, main bank system
management
   management compensation, 95, 101, 102–3, 103, 110, 112, 113
   management entrenchment, 5, 112
   top management, 8, 9, 15, 93, 95, 110, 169
   see also chief executive officer; directors; executives; presidents
managerial autonomy, 9, 15
managerial firms, 94, 104–5, 114n
manufacturing firms, 241, 242
market
   arm's-length markets, 32, 92
   market access, 2, 3, 12, 13, 30, 38, 45n
   market closure, 2, 6, 24–44
   market organisation, 2
   market power, 35, 40, 45
markets, product
   see product markets
Matsushita, 13, 23, 86n, 226
Mazda, 23, 185n
Ministry of Agriculture, Forestry and Fisheries, 271n
Ministry of Finance, 7, 14, 15, 136, 202, 218, 223, 224, 232, 249, 251, 252, 253, 254, 255, 256, 260, 263, 266, 269, 269n, 270n, 275, 279, 282, 283, 290, 291
Mitsubishi Bank, 138n, 174, 253, 261
Mitsubishi group, 23, 196
Mitsui Bank, 174, 177, 251
Mitsui group, 23, 196
monetary policy, 7, 15, 287–92
   instruments of monetary policy, 287–8
money market, 15, 16, 275–8, 292
   structure of money market, 276
   summary of reform of money market, 278–9

monitoring, 107, 108, 143–63
  costs of monitoring, 134, 136, 144, 162, 250
  delegated monitoring, 2, 5, 6, 156, 168, 172, 200, 218
  ex ante monitoring, 111, 126, 134, 137, 146, 149, 150, 156, 158
  ex post monitoring, 126, 134–6, 137, 145, 150, 151, 152, 154, 162, 250
  integrated monitoring, 149, 158, 162n
  interim monitoring, 145, 150, 152, 156, 157, 158
  model of bank monitoring, 125–9, 149–54
  non-monitoring banks, 133–4
  reciprocal delegated monitoring, 7, 108, 124–40, 151, 156
  shirking monitoring activities, 126, 132–3, 139n, 144, 151, 152–3, 158, 162
  see also free-riding
monopoly power, 3, 22, 25, 26, 35, 36, 39–40, 46n, 49, 268
monopsony power, 22, 39
moral hazard, 7, 115n, 129, 143–61, 180, 250, 252, 268, 269, 271n
  definition of moral hazard, 250

National Federation of Credit Cooperatives, 271n
Nihon Kangyō Bank, 224
Nihon Sōgo Bank, 254
Nippon Densō, 43
Nippon Steel, 23
Nippon Telegraph and Telephone Corporation (NTT), 231
Nippon Trust Bank, 253
non-negotiable deposits, 285
non-performing loans, 7, 8, 13, 143, 146, 151, 157, 158, 260, 262–3
non-tariff trade barriers, 3, 21, 25, 43
Nōrin Chūkin Bank, 224

official discount rate, 287–8

oil industry (US), 111
open market, 275, 276, 278, 280–6, 287, 296
organisation of firm
  see firm organisation
Ōsaka Credit Cooperative, 267
Ōsaka Fumin Credit Cooperative, 267

parent firm, 23, 24, 38, 171, 175
pension funds, 96, 97, 101
Plaza Accord, 157
Poisson process, 150
predatory pricing, 11, 21, 25, 26, 35, 44n, 45n
presidents' clubs, 23, 24, 44n, 173, 175, 183
presidents, 176–80
price/earnings ratios, 204, 205
prices
  monopoly pricing, 46n
  price changes, 61, 66–76, 77, 79, 81, 87n
  price destruction, 61
  price fixing, 35
  price formation, 3, 54–87
  price responses, 4, 69–79
  price rigidities, 69, 76, 77, 87n
principal–agent theory (model), 130–1, 139n
product markets
  intermediate product markets, 3, 28, 30, 31, 32, 38, 41, 43, 45n
  final product markets, 3, 28, 30, 32, 36, 38, 40, 45n, 46n
profit margins
  see profitability
profit maximisation
  see profitability
profitability, 13, 35, 36, 42, 81–2, 108–9, 146, 156, 157, 162n, 181, 204–5, 206, 207–12, 214, 218–19, 228, 236–7, 252, 260, 264, 268, 271
prudential regulations, 14, 255–7, 268

real estate lending, 7, 140, 241, 243–4,

262, 265
recession, 60
Reconstruction Bank
   see Japan Development Bank
regulation
   see financial regulation
regulatory authorities
   see Bank of Japan; Ministry of Finance
relationship investment
   see investors, relationship
relative performance evaluation, 109
rents, 13, 100–2, 106, 149, 156, 162n, 252, 254–5, 264, 266
reorganisation, 136, 140n, 146, 170, 217, 244, 257, 258–60, 266, 291
reputation, 95–6, 108–9
resale price maintenance, 76
restructuring
   see reorganisation
retail markets, 4, 58, 59–61
retailers, 59–65
   large-scale retailers, 58, 59, 60, 65, 76, 79, 87n
   small-scale retailers, 4, 54, 60, 76, 77, 78, 86n
risk
   risk aversion, 111, 115n, 127, 138n, 159
   risk sharing, 42, 57, 125, 127, 159, 249–50
   risk shifting
      see risk sharing
   risk taking, 261–2, 264–5

safety net, 13, 14, 249–71
Saitama Bank, 254
Sakura Bank, 12, 13
Sanwa Bank, 12, 13
Sanwa group, 23
Securities Exchange Act, 258, 275
self-regulation, 228
shachōkai
   see presidents' clubs
share price, 103, 104, 110, 112, 113, 199–203, 201, 204, 206
shareholder wealth, 12–13, 14, 36, 92, 94, 95, 97, 99, 100, 104, 105, 111, 114
shareholders, 5, 92, 94, 95–100, 101, 102, 103, 104, 105, 106, 110, 111, 114, 115n, 137, 138, 162, 167, 169, 171, 179, 181, 185
   US–Japan shareholder comparisons, 198
   see also investors
Shinkin banks, 279
Short-Term Money Market Research Group, 290
short term
   short-term contracts, 47n
   short-term relations, 30
small-scale retailers, 4
Sony Corporation, 218
Special Purpose Companies (SPCs), 270n
spot market contracts, 30, 37, 38, 41, 42
stable shareholding, 169, 180, 181, 195, 200, 219, 246
staff monitoring, 42
stock exchanges, 169, 202, 219n
stock market, 2, 9, 197, 200, 201, 204, 207, 215, 217, 218
   historical patterns of stock market changes, 203
stock ownership structure, 10
stock price
   see share price
straight bonds
   see bonds
strategic behaviour, 11
structural change
   see reorganisation
Structural Impediments Initiative (SII) talks, 216
subcontracting, 24, 57, 61
subcontractors
   see subcontracting
Sumitomo Bank, 13, 23, 174, 177, 251, 261
Sumitomo group, 23, 36, 196, 206
supply networks, 2, 24, 40, 41, 45n

INDEX

Taikō Sōgo Bank, 251
takeovers, 96, 97, 100, 101, 103, 114n, 167, 181, 238, 240
   anti-takeover legislation, 102
   hostile takeovers, 96, 104, 107, 115n, 240
tanshi money market brokers, 275, 277–81, 282, 289, 298n
tegata market, 226, 245
tenpo gyōsei
   see administration of branch offices
textile industry 56–7
theory of the firm, 44n, 91–2
ties
   bank–firm ties, 1, 6, 11, 12, 24
   business ties, 1
   horizontal ties, 35–7
   long-term ties, 24, 28, 29, 34, 37–43, 57
   ownership ties, 1
   supply ties, 2
   transactional ties, 28–9, 40
   vertical ties, 29, 35–7
   see also keiretsu
Tobin's q, 236, 237, 241
Tōhō Sōgo Bank, 252, 267
Tōkai Bank, 12, 267
Tokyo Kyodou Bank, 267, 271n
Tōkyō Kyōwa Credit Cooperative, 267, 271n
Toshiba, 23
Tōto Bank, 251
tournament system, 109–10
Tōyō Kōgyō
   see Mazda
Tōyō Shinkin Bank, 266, 267
Toyota, 12, 13, 23, 43, 226
trade barriers, 3, 24–5
   see also anticompetitive behaviour
transaction costs, 42, 61, 76, 94
transaction governance mechanisms
   see transaction governance structures
transaction governance structures, 94

transactional ties, 28–9, 40
transparency, 10, 15
treasury bill market, 276, 282–5, 289

United Kingdom, 86n, 166, 219n
   see also Great Britain
United States, 11, 25, 30, 32, 37, 44, 60, 86n, 91, 94, 96, 97, 98–9, 102, 104, 114, 137, 166, 191, 194, 196, 197, 207, 219, 219n, 240, 265, 275, 278, 283, 286, 297
   US–Japan comparisons, 30, 32, 45n, 60, 108, 191, 195–6, 197, 198, 199, 202, 203, 206, 207–12, 213, 217, 252
   US–Japan trade, 25, 33, 40
upstream firms, 2, 3, 28, 29, 37, 39, 41, 43, 81

vertical
   vertical contract, 38, 40, 41,
   vertical foreclosure, 40
   vertical integration, 3, 28, 30, 43
   vertical organisation, 2–3, 36
   vertical ties, 29, 35–7, 38, 39, 43, 46n, 63, 64, 65

warrant bonds
   see bonds, warrant
wealth redistribution, 100–3, 104
Western comparisons, 5, 9, 23, 30, 32, 86n
wholesale price index (WPI) 67, 68, 69–76, 77, 79–80, 82
wholesaler network, 60, 64
wholesalers, 4, 55–6, 57, 58, 62, 63, 86n

Yamaichi Securities Company, 251, 269n
yen, appreciation of, 4, 55, 60, 61, 77, 78, 281
Yen–Dollar Committee report, 221, 285
Yūai Credit Cooperative, 267

zaibatsu, 23
zaiteku, 281, 298n